AMERICAN
ARBITRATION ASSOCIATION

HANDBOOK ON MEDIATION

Thomas E. Carbonneau

Executive Editor
Orlando Distinguished Professor of Law
Penn State University

ASSISTANT EDITORS

Jeanette Jaeggi

Assistant Director of the Center for Dispute Resolution
Penn State University

Sandra K. Partridge

Penn State Center for Dispute Resolution

JP

Questions About This Publication

For assistance with shipments, billing or other customer service matters, please call our Customer Services Department at:

1-631-350-0200.

To obtain a copy of this book, call our Sales Department:

1-631-351-5430
Fax: 1-631-351-5712

Toll Free Order Line:

1-800-887-4064 (United States & Canada)

See our web page about this book:
http://www.arbitrationlaw.com

Printed in the United States of America
ISBN 1-929446-46-2

JurisNet, LLC
71 New Street
Huntington, New York 11743
USA
www.arbitrationlaw.com

INTRODUCTION

It is with both pride and pleasure that the Penn State University Dickinson School of Law and the Institute for Arbitration Law and Practice present the AAA HANDBOOK ON MEDIATION. Each of the HANDBOOKS in the series contains recent important publications on the subject matter of that HANDBOOK, written by authors who are recognized specialists in that area. Often the authors have both national and international reputations in the area. The contributions cover a wide array of topics that are of substantial interest in the field and provide analytically thorough, professional, and practical answers to problems that have emerged in the field.

The articles were selected from an extensive body of writings and, in the main, represent world-class assessments of mediation and practice. All the major facets of the field are addressed. The articles provide the reader with comprehensive and accurate information, lucid evaluations, and an indication of future developments. They not only acquaint, but also ground the reader in the field.

The American Arbitration Association, Juris Publishing, Inc., and Penn State welcome the opportunity to provide readers with a body of knowledge and interpretation that will allow them to take an active and effective part in Mediation. Mediation is rapidly emerging as one of the new vehicles for alternative justice—both domestically and internationally.

Thomas E. Carbonneau
Orlando Distinguished
Professor of Law
Penn State University

TABLE OF CONTENTS

CHAPTER ONE

INTRODUCTION TO MEDIATION

I. Unifying Principles of Mediation

Using Distributive, Integrative and Transformative Negotiation Principles in Mediation

*by James R. Holbrook**

I learned how to mediate in the mid-1980s by watching another lawyer mediate a personal injury lawsuit between an injured motorist and the insurer of the driver who caused the accident. His approach emphasized analytical and evaluative techniques to achieve a "distributive" outcome—i.e., a monetary settlement. Years later, I taught a law school mediation course with two adjunct professors. One, a businessman with a Harvard MBA, mediates using interest-based negotiation principles to seek an "integrative" solution. The other, a psychologist with a Buddhist perspective, mediates by focusing on the parties' relationship and their patterns of communication, aiming for a "transformative" solution.

Over the past few years, I came to realize that it is not necessary to debate which approach is best, because all three complement and overlap one another. This article discusses fundamental principles of negotiation and how distributive, integrative and transformative principles can be used in a flexible way in mediation to resolve many different kinds of conflict.

Differentiating between Three Approaches

Disputes between parties can involve three different kinds of possible outcomes or combinations of outcomes: distribution of something of value; a mutually acceptable solution to a shared problem;

---

* Mr. Holbrook, of Callister Nebeker & McCullough in Salt Lake City, serves on the American Arbitration Association's roster of neutrals and is a visiting professor of negotiation and mediation at S. J. Quinney College of Law at the University of Utah. Mr. Holbrook holds a B.A. from Grinnell College, a M.A. from Indiana University, and a J.D. from the University of Utah.

or repair of a damaged relationship. The first outcome is identified with distributive negotiation, the second with integrative negotiation, and the third with transformative negotiation. Different styles of communication are associated with each type of negotiation. In a distributive negotiation, communications are often about who owes what to whom and why. In an integrative negotiation, they tend to focus on the parties' needs and interests. In a transformative negotiation, communications focus on the parties' relationship and how the parties interact with each other.

The outcome that parties to mediation expect undoubtedly will require the use of one or more of these kinds of negotiation. Because many issues can arise in a mediation, an effective mediator must be able to recognize which principles are appropriate and transition easily between the different styles of communications.[1] To do this a mediator must understand the basic elements of a negotiation.

Roger Fisher and Danny Ertel identified seven "building blocks" of negotiation: (1) communication between the parties; (2) the parties' relationship; (3) their respective interests; (4) the options for settlement; (5) legitimacy (i.e., the standard by which the parties will judge the fairness of settlement options); (6) the best and worst alternatives available to the parties in the absence of a settlement agreement (BATNAs and WATNAs); and (7) their commitment to settlement.[2]

Each element may raise issues that will have to be addressed during a negotiation. For example, it might be necessary to consider how the parties can become better listeners and make their communications more productive (building block # 1), or how they can forge a productive working relationship and separate their egos from the issues in dispute (building block # 2). To negotiate effectively, the parties will have to identify their important interests (building block # 3), determine whether they will reveal their interests to each other, and decide what they will do if their interests appear to be incompatible. The parties will have to work together to identify, create and evaluate potential options for settlement (building block # 4). To do so, they will probably have to agree on a precedent, appraisal, industry standard or other yardstick to evaluate the objective fairness of the potential options (building block # 5). If they cannot agree about using a specific standard, they will have to agree on a process to find a legitimacy principle they both will accept (e.g., they can

---

[1] Kenneth Cloke, Mediating Dangerously: The Frontiers of Conflict Resolution 177 (Jossey-Bass 2001).

[2] Roger Fisher & Danny Ertel, Getting Ready to Negotiate: The Getting to Yes Workbook 6-7 (Penguin 1995).

agree to hire an appraiser whose appraisal they both will use as an acceptable measure of value).

The parties' BATNAs and WATNAs may lead to actions that a party can take unilaterally (i.e., without mutual agreement) (building block # 6).[3] For example, a BATNA could lead a party to walk away from the negotiation rather than continue to bargain for an agreement that is not acceptable. By contrast, a WATNA could lead to a decision to accept a less than desirable agreement rather than have to live with a bad alternative. Parties to a negotiation generally do not disclose their BATNAs and WATNAs to each other. But each may speculate about them and consider whether these alternatives are realistic and whether they are likely to provoke unilateral action by the other party.

A negotiation cannot reach a successful conclusion without the parties' commitment to a settlement (building block # 7). Issues that may arise here include whether all necessary parties are participating and have authority to enter into a final agreement, and if so, whether each is likely to comply with the final agreement.

Each of these negotiation building blocks is involved in the mediation of a dispute. Thus, when issues arising out of these building blocks occur, the mediator should be able to determine which negotiation principles are most appropriate to resolve them. This requires an understanding of the basic principles of distributive, integrative and transformative negotiation.

Distributive Negotiation Principles

In a distributive negotiation each party assumes that resources are fixed and limited and attempts to claim resources for himself at the expense of the other. Money is the resource over which parties typically contend. The dynamic of their distributive bargaining focuses on how much money one party will agree to pay to the other and how little money the other party will agree to accept. In disputes over money, there is often a disparity in bargaining power. If one party has a more attractive alternative (BATNA) than the other, that party often cares less than the other about reaching a negotiated agreement. This means that the party with less bargaining power usually is more motivated to settle, even though the terms are not entirely to his liking, to avoid an even less desirable alternative.

---

[3] *Id.* at 45-48.

Distributive negotiations occur in many market-place transactions between buyers and sellers and in negotiated monetary settlements of legal disputes.[4]

Communications in a distributive negotiation often look like positional bargaining that reflects strategic positioning by the parties. The parties typically share little accurate information about their interests or objectives. The parties tend to present conflicting stories in which they take seemingly contradictory positions and either hold back or exaggerate some of the truth about their respective issues and interests. Each may attempt to confuse the other with misleading, incomplete or inaccurate information or even intimidate the other party with bluffs or threats.

A distributive negotiation generally works this way: Each party has a negotiating range with a starting point, a target point and a stopping point. Neither party discloses its target or stopping point to the other. The parties usually expect that there will be some back-and-forth bargaining after they disclose their respective starting points. Typically, one party makes an offer and the other makes a counteroffer and so on, until they reach an agreement or deadlock. This sequence is very important. It is supposed to move the bargaining exchange along by influencing the parties to adjust their positions. Each movement by a party narrows the negotiation range between the parties. The parties' bargaining behavior "funnels" the negotiation toward an eventual agreement point.[5]

Each offer and counteroffer sends signals back and forth about the parties' target points and stopping points. For example, if a starting offer is too far away from the offeror's target point, the offer may appear foolish or unreasonable to the offeree, who may decide to discontinue the negotiation. During a distributive negotiation, each party will likely be able to infer the other's target point because parties typically give up the difference between their starting points and their target points, i.e., they get closer and closer to their respective target points during the bargaining process.

A negotiator who can instigate a change in the other party's stopping point will have a strategic advantage in distributive negotiations.

---

[4] They also occur in negotiated plea bargains, except that the result is not a distribution of money but the length of a jail term. A prosecutor who believes a jury will convict the defendant would rather accept a plea to a lesser charge in order to avoid preparing for trial, while the defendant would rather plead guilty to the lesser charge in order to avoid the risk of being convicted at trial of a greater charge.

[5] Roy J. Lewicki et al., Negotiation 187 (2nd ed. Richard D. Irwin 1994).

Therefore, the task is first to try to ascertain the other party's stopping point and then influence that party to modify it. To exert such influence, a party may disclose inaccurate information about his own stopping point, manipulate the parties' relationship with fawning behavior, or try to persuade the other party to make a commitment or concession that he had not intended to make. For example, a seller may decide to reduce his lowest price because he believes he would lose the sale to another seller allegedly offering a lower price down the street.

This dynamic in distributive negotiation creates tension between trying to obtain as much information as possible about the other party's stopping point and at the same time trying to disclose as little accurate information as possible about one's own stopping point. A party may find out indirectly about the other's likely stopping point by obtaining current market data or interviewing someone who recently negotiated with the other party. She also can ask the other party for information about his negotiating range, although it is difficult to know how much to trust any information disclosed. Typically a party's BATNA will determine his stopping point, because that is the point at which the party is likely to walk away from the negotiation.

Integrative Negotiation Principles

Unlike a distributive negotiation, which tends to be more adversarial and often focuses on money, an integrative negotiation takes a "more expansive view of both resource use and self-interest."[6] Generally, an integrative negotiation seeks types of solutions that satisfy the important needs of both parties. Integrative negotiations require the parties to identify and understand their mutual problem, bring their interests to the surface, generate possible solutions, and choose one solution from the available options.[7]

Both parties try to define their joint problem in a mutually acceptable way. This requires them to focus on their primary interests and set aside their less important concerns and desires that do not have to be satisfied to reach an agreement.

To engage in this type of problem solving, the parties must minimize interpersonal conflict so that they can work together. Fisher, Ury and

---

[6] Robert A. Baruch Bush & Joseph P. Folger, The Promise of Mediation: Responding to Conflict through Empowerment and Recognition 58 (Jossey-Bass 1994).

[7] LEWICKI, *supra* n. 5, at 83.

Patton recommend structuring the integrative negotiation as "a side-by-side process," even placing the negotiators on the same side of the table.[8]

Communications in an integrative negotiation differ from the positional bargaining typical of a distributive negotiation. Integrative communications are more inviting and cooperative. Integrative negotiators tend to present overlapping stories and focus on satisfaction of their individual interests, which may require them to compromise.

A party's opening statement can strongly suggest the type of solution he is seeking. Opening remarks communicating interest both in the outcome of the negotiation and the relationship with the other party signal a desire for a more integrative solution than opening remarks demonstrating interest only in the outcome or only in the relationship.[9]

In an integrative negotiation there must be a free flow of information so that the parties' respective interests can be revealed. Each party must be able to hear and understand the interests of the other as well as disclose his own interests. Interests include positive and negative objectives, needs, desires, concerns, fears, aversions, and the like. They may be substantive or procedural in nature. Substantive interests include objective interests (which are tangible, quantitative and rational), and subjective interests (which are intangible, qualitative and emotional). Procedural interests are those related to the process of achieving a distributive, integrative or transformative outcome, or selecting objective standards of legitimacy and fairness. Interests also may relate to third persons, such as family members, friends or co-workers.

Interests must be prioritized into needs and wants. Needs are more important and usually must be satisfied before an agreement can be reached, whereas wants may be traded or given away.

A party who perceives and understands the other party's perspective and important interests will be better able to frame the integrative negotiation productively and identify potential options that might satisfy both parties.

Transformative Negotiation Principles

In some conflicts, the relationship between the parties is more important than the problem that faces them. Because neither party wants to be the one at fault, the parties to a relationship conflict often do not

---

[8] Roger Fisher et AL., Getting to Yes: Negotiating Agreement Without Giving In 38 (2nd ed. Penguin Books 1991).

[9] *See* LEWICKI, *supra* n. 5, at 190.

notice their own contribution to the problem. Therefore, they rarely look in a productive place (i.e., their own contribution) to help themselves change.[10]

When bad things happen in a relationship, the parties may feel anger, blame, injustice, guilt, regret, shame, helplessness, resignation, etc. Each response takes the parties on a "detour" from their own responsibility.[11] Therefore, the parties tend to have conflicting stories about who is responsible for their dispute. They tend to get stuck in the past and in blaming each other. In a transformative negotiation, the parties must attempt to meld their competing individual stories into a "third story" in which they each recognize their own contribution to their relationship problem and their polarizing patterns of communication. They need to focus on both the present and how they feel. They also need to begin to talk about the future and about the possibilities of relating to each other in a different way.

In a transformative negotiation, the parties must understand the nature of their conflict. To do this they must have the "capacity for self-awareness and critical observation, subsequent reflection and correction, honesty and [especially] empathy."[12] Fisher, Ury and Patton emphasize the importance of empathy:

> The ability to see the situation as the other side sees it, as difficult as it may be, is one of the most important skills a negotiator can possess. It is not enough to know that they see things differently. If you want to influence them, you also need to understand empathetically the power of their point of view and to feel the emotional force with which they believe in it.[13]

So-called "attending behaviors"[14] can enhance the relationship of the parties during a transformative negotiation. These behaviors include eye contact, positive body posture (such as sitting up straight and leaning forward to express interest), smiling and nodding. Other conduct that may affect the relationship in a positive way includes showing courtesy and respect, doing the other party a favor, immediately returning a favor,

---

[10] Gerald R. Williams, *Negotiation as a Healing Process*, 1 J. DISP. RESOL. 1, 43-44 (1996).

[11] Rosamund Stone Zander & Benjamin Zander, The Art of Possibility: Transforming Professional and Personal Life 155 (Harvard Bus. School Press 2000).

[12] CLOKE, *supra* n. 1, at 67.

[13] GETTING TO YES, *supra* n. 8, at 23.

[14] *See* LEWICKI, *supra* n. 5, at 222-24.

making a quick concession, giving the other party needed time or information, and helping that party avoid being caught by surprise.

Mediation Dynamics and Negotiation Process

Mediation is simply a facilitated negotiation. It can be broken down into three interrelated dynamics: the outcome, the process, and the communication between and among the parties and the mediator. The mediator can facilitate the course of the mediation by assisting the parties in appropriately changing these dynamics. For example, a change in the desired outcome from distributing value to improving the parties' relationship would call for a change in the process from a distributive negotiation to a transformative one. This, in turn, would require the parties to communicate differently in order to have a positive effect on both the process and the outcome.

In order to assure that the appropriate negotiation principles are used in mediation, the mediator must know what type of outcome each party desires and how important the parties' relationship is to them. If the parties want a financial settlement and are not particularly interested in their relationship, they are seeking a distributive solution. If they want to find a joint solution to their problem that preserves their relationship (indicating that both the outcome and the relationship are equally important), they are seeking an integrative solution. And if they value their relationship more than the outcome, they are seeking a transformative solution.

If both parties do not want the same kind of outcome in mediation (e.g., one party values the relationship and wants to continue doing business, while the other party wants to get paid what is owed and thereafter cease doing business altogether), it may be necessary for the mediator to move from one set of negotiation principles to another during the mediation. To know whether this is appropriate, the mediator must understand what will motivate each party to adjust its position during the mediation. Because communication is integral to the facilitated negotiation process, the mediator must recognize communication patterns associated with each type of negotiation and be able to facilitate a change from one pattern to another that is better suited to a different process and a different outcome. In fact, it may be that the mediator must "match" one approach to party *A* and a different approach to party *B*.

The widely believed golden rule of negotiations, called the "norm of reciprocity," plays an important role in mediation. This rule has it that, when one party acts in a specific way, the other party likely will react similarly.[15] It is "the almost universal belief that people should be paid back for what they do, that one good (or bad) deed deserves another....Because people expect that their actions will be paid back in one form or another, influence is possible."[16]

The "pay back" dynamic of the norm of reciprocity influences virtually every aspect of mediation, including building relationships and trust, improving communications, exchanging information, brainstorming, problem solving, and overcoming impasses. The mediator can help the parties understand how this reciprocity dynamic influences both the positive and negative aspects of their mediation. For example, in a distributive mediation, the mediator can help the parties understand that, if one party makes only small incremental moves, it is likely the other will also. Similarly, in an integrative mediation, if one party is willing to share information about underlying interests, the other party is likely to do so, too. And in a transformative mediation, if one party refuses to discuss his contribution to the parties' relationship conflict, the other party probably will not discuss that issue, either.

Typically mediation involves more than one issue, and the norm of reciprocity can be used to help the parties handle multiple issues productively. For example, the parties often believe they must agree on each issue in order to reach an overall agreement. This is not so. The mediator can help the parties understand that, even though they may not agree on even one issue, they can resolve their dispute in a way that is acceptable to each of them, but for different reasons. The mediator also can help the parties see that their relatively unimportant interests can be traded or conceded during the course of the mediation to avoid impasse.

Now let's see how distributive, integrative and transformative negotiation principles can be used by mediators to address specific issues.

Distributive Negotiations in Mediation

Distributive negotiation principles are appropriate for a mediation in which the important interests that the parties wish to satisfy involve the distribution of something tangible, like money or property. In this type of

---

[15] *See id.* at 228-30.

[16] Allan R. Cohen & David L. Bradford, *Influence without Authority: The Use of Alliances, Reciprocity, and Exchange to Accomplish Work*, *in* ROY J. LEWICKI ET AL., EDS, NEGOTIATION READINGS, EXERCISES AND CASES (2d ed. Richard D. Irwin 1993).

mediation the mediator can help the parties frame their starting positions so that the negotiation can proceed in a productive manner. The mediator can also encourage the parties to communicate with each other so as to advance the back-and-forth bargaining typical of distributive negotiation, and help them conform to the protocol of distributive negotiation.

Without the mediator's guidance a party can easily breach this protocol by escalating an opening offer, refusing to counteroffer, or making a take-it-or-leave-it demand. Making a non-negotiable demand during a distributive mediation is likely to be perceived as a disrespectful assault on the other party's ego or identity. Rather than elicit a positive movement in the mediation, it is more likely to provoke resentment and a breakdown in bargaining. The mediator can help the parties avoid such an impasse by explaining that the norm of reciprocity requires each party to make a productive move to continue to narrow the gap between them.

The pattern of movement in a distributive mediation conveys information back and forth between the parties. To be productive, the movement should not be haphazard. For example, if party *B* responds to party *A*'s offer with a counteroffer only marginally greater than *B*'s last offer, party *B* may be conveying that it has a relatively strong BATNA and relatively little interest in reaching settlement in the mediation. This could motivate party *A* to settle quickly or reciprocate with a marginally improved offer. The latter approach will drag out the mediation or lead to its termination. The mediator can help the parties understand the consequences of this kind of signaling and thereby more accurately communicate their underlying intent.

Every mediation in which a distributive outcome is sought raises a "legitimacy" issue. The strengths and weaknesses of each party's position must be measured against some acceptable yardstick, often a legal or industry standard. The mediator helps the parties understand that if they can agree on a single legitimacy principle to assess their respective positions and determine the objective fairness of possible options, it will be easier for them to find and commit to one option that will bring the dispute to an end.

In every distributive mediation the time will come when a party wants to convey the message that there is no room for further movement—that the last offer or counteroffer is final. The mediator can help the other party understand that the mediation is likely to deadlock if the offer or counteroffer is not accepted. In addition, the mediator can help both parties understand that the negotiation may no longer be about what is fair but about what is feasible.

Integrative Negotiations in Mediation

Integrative negotiation principles are appropriate for a mediation when the parties accept that:

- they are likely to benefit more by working together than by competing against each other;
- they have the interpersonal and communication skills to share information about themselves and to listen to and understand each other;
- they are willing to invest time and energy in creating or enhancing a productive problem-solving relationship;
- they are willing to say what they want and why;
- they are willing to engage in joint problem solving, identifying possible ways to resolve their problem that are mutually acceptable; and
- they are willing to commit to a mutually acceptable solution that incorporates their important interests.

However, the parties' important underlying interests frequently are obscured by the positions they assert early in the mediation. The mediator can help the parties reveal these undisclosed interests, which are necessary to determine whether an integrative outcome is desired and whether an integrative process will be productive. Fisher, Ury and Patton advise:

> In searching for the basic interests behind a declared position, look particularly for those bedrock concerns which motivate all people [like security, economic well-being, a sense of belonging, recognition, control over one's life]. If you can take care of such basic needs, you increase the chance both of reaching agreement and, if an agreement is reached, of the other side's keeping to it.[17]

The mediator can help the parties identify potential options that might satisfy their important interests. Options answer questions beginning with "what if" (e.g., "What if you were to do *X*?"). To identify options, it is useful for the mediator and the parties to have a

[17] GETTING TO YES, *supra* n. 8, at 48.

brainstorming session in an environment free of criticism: "The key ground rule is to postpone all criticism and evaluation of ideas. The group simply invents ideas without pausing to consider whether they are good or bad, realistic or unrealistic."[18] The mediator should remind the parties that the options they identify do not have to be acceptable or even feasible. This is important because an interesting aspect of an unworkable option could ultimately be included as part of a mutually acceptable agreement.

Once the options are identified, the parties evaluate them with the mediator's assistance. This may raise legitimacy issues because to perform this evaluation, the parties will need criteria to weigh and rank the options for acceptability and perceived fairness. The parties may need the mediator's assistance in deciding on one legitimacy principle that they both can accept.

Transformative Negotiations in Mediation

Transformative negotiation principles are appropriate when the solution the parties desire or need is to repair or improve their relationship. A good example is a custody dispute between a couple in the middle of a divorce. The parties are very angry at each other but they care deeply about their children. Their relationship needs to be recast into one that involves mutually supportive and cooperative parenting. But as long as they have significant, unresolved negative feelings toward each other, they are unlikely to be willing or able to work together toward that goal. Transformative negotiations can help these parties get past their anger and resentment, allowing them to become motivated by their shared interest in their children's welfare to find an integrative solution to their co-parenting problem. Ironically, solutions to co-parenting problems often emerge as a by-product of the transformation of the parties' underlying relationship.

The transformative approach also can lead to a solution of some distributive disputes. Take a boundary-line dispute between adjoining landowners. If the parties can get over their anger and repair their relationship, one of them may become willing to convey title to the property in question to the other, in exchange for payment of fair market value. Transforming their relationship is the key to achieving a successful distributive solution to the property dispute.

---

[18] *Id.* at 60.

To influence a change in the parties' relationship, the mediator must encourage both parties to truly empathize with each other, feeling what it is like to walk in each other's shoes and see the world through each other's eyes.[19] The mediator can help them "in dropping their poses, communicating honestly and empathetically, and taking responsibility—not only for their intentions, but their words, actions, and effects they have on others regardless of intention."[20] Taking this kind of responsibility can help the parties apologize and forgive each other, which in turn can help them create a new and productive relationship.

Rebuilding the parties' relationship is often critical to resolving their dispute. This concept is the basis for the systematic approach to mediation discussed below, which calls for the parties to work first on the underlying relationship issues before trying to engage in problem solving.

If a mediation should deadlock during transformative negotiations, the mediator can help the parties explore the next step in a way that does not needlessly polarize their relationship or undermine their future ability to communicate productively with one another.

A Systematic Approach

Having an array of negotiation principles to help resolve a dispute leaves the mediator with the task of deciding the order in which they should be used. Thomas Ellison has suggested using transformative principles first to deal with relationship issues, then integrative principles to address the need to develop a mutually satisfactory solution to a joint problem that does not call for the distribution of value, and finally using distributive principles to resolve a dispute that can only be resolved through a monetary settlement.[21] Ellison reasons that transformative principles should be used first because the failure to deal immediately with relationship issues will obstruct achieving other kinds of outcomes. Integrative negotiation principles come next because they are most useful in helping the parties work together to create value that they can share. Distributive negotiation principles are used last if the parties desire an exchange of money for a release.

---

[19] CLOKE, *supra* n. 1, at 26.

[20] *Id.* at 35.

[21] Thomas A. Ellison is a senior attorney in the Salt Lake City office of the Stoel Rives law firm. After hearing me present this unified field theory of mediation at a symposium, Tom outlined the systems approach discussed in this paragraph.

This systematic approach provides a road map for the mediator. The first task will be to determine whether relationship issues exist that would benefit from transformative negotiation. The next task will be to identify issues that can be solved through integrative principles, then those that require distributive negotiation principles. Using the divorcing parents in the earlier example, first the mediator helps them rebuild a parenting relationship using transformative negotiations, then the mediator helps them address visitation issues using integrative negotiation principles. If there are distributive issues, like alimony or child support, those would be addressed last using distributive negotiation principles.

The concept of transitioning from one negotiation technique to another should not be foreign to most mediators. Many mediators transition between being facilitative, analytical and evaluative, as the situation requires. A facilitative approach enables mediators to help the parties improve the quality of their communications and understand the importance of their relationship and shared interests. If that approach is not successful in facilitating a transformative resolution of the dispute, the mediator may become analytical, helping the parties look for ways to cooperate. If that is not sufficient to create an integrative solution of the parties' shared problem, the mediator can become more evaluative by helping the parties assess the strengths and weaknesses of their respective alternatives to find a way to close the gap between them (by compromise or concession) to achieve a distributive solution. As a last resort, the mediator might disclose his or her evaluation of the merits of the dispute.

Conclusion

Mediators need to use all the effective techniques at their disposal to help parties achieve the outcome they need or desire. This article suggests that when mediators understand how and when to use different negotiation principles, they have more powerful tools and are applying a more unified theory of mediation.

A Party's Negotiation Range

x----------------------------y----------------------------z

Starting Point Target Point Stopping Point

The parties signal each other about their target points and stopping points with each offer and counteroffer they make. A starting offer that is too far away from the offeror's target point may be perceived as unreasonable by the offeree, who may decide that further negotiations would be unproductive.

Characteristics of Distributive, Integrative and Transformative Negotiation

Negotiation Type	Process	Communication	Movement Motivation
Distributive	• limited resources (fixed pie) • zero-sum result (win-lose) • competitive (adversarial) • positional (haggling)	• start high (or low) • small incremental moves • share little accurate information • meet "in the middle"	• confusion or intimidation • legitimacy (fairness) • power-based asymmetry • undisclosed interests
Integrative	• expandable resources (bigger pie) • mutual self-interest (win-win) • cooperative (collaborative) • problem solving	• probe for undisclosed interests • share information • generate options • test fairness and satisfaction	• satisfy mutual needs • solve joint problem • legitimacy (fairness) • power-based symmetry

Negotiation Type	Process	Communication	Movement Motivation
Transformative	• relationship-focused • subordinated self-interest • accommodative • conversational	• express acknowledg-ment • share recognition • develop empowerment • offer apology or forgiveness	• homeostasis • repair (improve) relationship • restoration (apology and amends) • growth of self (or other)

II. A Practical Theory of Mediation

A Theory of Mediation

*by Douglas E. Noll**

There is no lack of debate in the field of mediation. Topics that tend to attract the most attention and vigorous discussion include mediator qualification and process outcome. What's lacking is a practical theory that would bring together different views, and help both practitioners and clients. In the following article, the author reviews existing literature to form a simple mediation theory founded on basic conflict dynamics. His theory provides a framework for explaining various mediation styles and outcomes—when a certain approach is appropriate and why.

To date, the debates in the mediation field have centered on which process is better, who is qualified to be a mediator, and on outcome measurement. In reading the vast literature generated by these debates, no clear theory of practice has apparently developed. I believe that a general theory has not developed because the debates on process and outcome have not considered conflict dynamics.

I propose that when conflict dynamics are considered, a simple theory of mediation arises. This theory appears to reconcile and justify all of the diverging views of practice and outcome into a unified view of mediation.

This theory of mediation contains four strands: conflict goals, level of conflict escalation, mediation style or process, and outcome. I will explain each strand then state a theory of mediation encompassing them all.

Conflict Goals: CRIP

Wilmot and Hocker have developed the acronym CRIP as an analytical tool in conflict.[1] CRIP stands for content, relationship, identity, and process.

---

* The author, a full-time mediator in California, has been on the panel of the American Arbitration Association since 1981. He is also an adjunct professor of law at San Joaquin College of Law and an adjunct professor of forensic psychology at Alliant University/California School of Professional Psychology. Mr. Noll received his B.A. from Dartmouth College, J.D. from University of the Pacific McGeorge School of Law, and M.A. from Fresno Pacific University. He is the author of *Peacemaking: Practicing at the Intersection of Law and Human Conflict.*

CRIP is a way of looking at the conflict goals people bring to a dispute. Content goals are most familiar to lawyers because they involve substantive rights and obligations. A dispute over money is a typical content goal; one party claims damages and wants payment while the other denies and resists payment. Each party is focused on the goal of compensation.

Without diminishing their importance, content goals rarely are the sole cause of human conflicts. Often, content goals are granted substantially more importance by parties and counsel than they deserve. For example, a demand for money might be higher than is realistic or fair, not because the plaintiff is seeking a superior negotiating position, but because the demand for money is symbolic of other conflicts occurring between the parties.

Relationship goals ask the question, "Who are we in this conflict?" Relationship goals usually involve issues over hierarchy, power, and social roles. Many times, parties feel a deep sense of injustice and offense. In civil cases, both sides often feel victimized.

Parties to conflict are said to have relationship goals when they seek relief from the injustices they feel. The injustices are often not subject to legal analysis. Consequently, the goals are left unstated or stated vaguely. How many times have clients said, "It's not fair," or "I've been taken advantage of"?

Relationship goals, being emotionally based, are sometimes difficult for clients to articulate. Therefore, clients tend to project their relationship goals into content goals. This is how content goals become symbols for other conflict goals.

Identity goals concern self-esteem, face, impression management, and social identity. These goals ask the question "Who am I in this conflict?" Conflicts that have escalated into litigation commonly involve clients whose self-esteem or face has been threatened or injured.

This goal is extremely powerful because it involves a threat to a person's psychological existence. The deeper the challenge to self-esteem, the more likely a fight-or-flight reaction will occur. Like relationship goals, identity goals are often not well articulated. Hence, identity goals too can be projected onto content goals.

If both relationship and identity goals are projected onto a content goal, one can see why a party may seem unreasonable in a demand for compensation or refusal to pay.

---

[1] Wilmot, William W., Hocker, Joyce L. Interpersonal Conflict (5th ed). New York: McGraw-Hill, 1998).

Process goals concern how parties prefer to deal with conflict. Lawyers see resolution of conflict from an adversary ideology. Sometimes, this orientation can exacerbate a conflict. If party *A* wishes to fight and party *B* wishes to avoid, *B*'s reluctance to fight may turn to intransigence. How many times have clients said that they don't want to sue, but if they do, it will be all out war? Other clients may relish the idea of a good fight and have little interest in other processes. Thus, a conflict can arise simply through different process goals.

Obviously, parties in conflict have different goals at some level of the CRIP model. Conflict becomes particularly interesting when the parties specialize in different conflict goals.

For example, one party may be focusing on relationship goals while another is focusing on process goals. If neither party is listening to the other, they each assume they are being ignored. This is very common in partnership disputes, domestic relations conflicts, and employment litigation. The phenomenon of fundamental attribution error is triggered, by which each side assumes the best intentions for self and worst intentions for the other. This suggests that effective conflict analysis consider whether parties are specializing in different conflict goals.

Finally, conflict goals may change during the conflict cycle. Conflict has to be viewed as a dynamic process involving the rational and emotional aspects of personality. Thus, as the conflict progresses, conflict goals may strengthen or weaken, change in importance, or become symbolic for unstated goals. Oftentimes, conflict goals will change retroactively as a rationalization for present conduct.

Conflict Escalation: Five Stages

Spillman and Spillman have observed that conflict escalation is a gradual regression from a mature to immature level of emotional development.[2] The psychological process develops step by step in a strikingly reciprocal manner to the way we grow up. In other words, as conflicts escalate through various stages, the parties show behaviors indicating movement backward through their stages of emotional development.

In this analysis, escalation is charted in five stages, each having its own characteristics and triggers. Stage One is part of normal, everyday

[2] Spillman, Kurt R., Spillman, Kati, *On Enemy Images and Conflict Escalation*, 27 ISSSJ 57 (1991).

life. Even good relationships have moments of conflict. These can only be resolved with great care and mutual empathy.

In this stage, people look for objective solutions in a cooperative manner. If a solution is not found, especially because one of the parties sticks obstinately to his or her point of view, the conflict escalates.

In Stage Two, the parties fluctuate between cooperation and competition. They know they have common interests, but their own wishes become more important. Dealing with information becomes limited to that favoring one's own arguments. Logic and understanding are used to convince or win over the opposing side.

At this stage, each party does everything possible to not show weakness. The temptation to leave the field of argument increases until the conflict escalates because of some action taken by one of the parties.

By entering Stage Three—the field of concrete actions—each party fears that the ground for a common solution is lost. In other words, the parties lose hope for a reasonable outcome. Interaction becomes hostile. All logic is focused on action, replacing fruitless and nerve-wracking discussions.

This is often when parties hire lawyers. Hiring a lawyer is satisfying because it temporarily reduces inner tensions and anxieties. Finally, "something is being done" about the problem. Paradoxically, the parties each believe that through pressure they will change the other party. At the same time neither is prepared to yield.

At this level, stereotyping is applied as negative identification of the opponent. Hence, parties are implicitly characterized as dishonest, unscrupulous, or fraudulent. Power becomes important as empathy disappears.

At Stage Four, the parties' cognitive functioning regresses to those of 6-year-olds. One is aware of the other's perspectives, but is no longer capable of considering the other's thoughts, feelings and situation. How often have we remarked that parties in conflict are acting like children? In fact, they are because of the escalation. Both sides are forced into roles from which they see no escape.

If the conflict cannot be halted at this stage, the escalation undergoes a dramatic increase in intensity. Escalation results when one side commits some action that is felt by the opposite side as a loss of face.

At Stage Five, progressive regression appears in the form of a comprehensive ideology and totalizing of antagonistic perspectives. Sacred values, convictions, and superior moral obligations are at stake.

The conflict assumes mythical dimensions. Sometimes the parties have fantasies of omnipotence, seeing no way that they can lose in court.

In psychological terms, the escalation has reached a hallucinatory-narcissistic sphere. The entire self-conception is drawn into the conflict such that individual perceptions and evaluations disappear. By threatening and creating fear, both parties strive towards total control of the situation and thereby escalate the conflict further. To remain credible and to restrain the enemy from an act of force, the threatened party feels compelled to commit acts of force itself. This, in turn, proves to the threatening party the aggressive nature of the other and provokes counterforce and further escalation. This process continues until the parties reach financial or physical exhaustion, or a court or arbitrator decides the matter.

Mediation Style and Process: Riskin's Model

In 1994, Professor Leonard Riskin proposed a system for classifying mediator orientations.[3] His classification system asked two principal questions. First, does the mediator tend to define problems narrowly or broadly? Second, does the mediator think he or she should evaluate—make assessments or predictions or proposals for agreements—or facilitate the parties' negotiation without evaluating? According to Riskin, answers to these questions reflect mediator beliefs about the nature and scope of mediation and assumptions about the parties' expectations.

In Riskin's system, mediators with a narrow focus assume that the parties have come to them for help in solving a technical problem. This problem has been defined by the positions the parties have asserted in negotiations or pleadings.

Typically, the parties have a distributive orientation. They ask questions such as, "Who pays how much to whom?" Or, "Who can use the property?"

Typically, the parties see the problem as a division of a resource in which one gains and the other loses. Outcomes at trial, uncertainty, delay, and expense drive the mediation process. Parties, through their lawyers, will bargain competitively, emphasizing positions over interests.

---

[3] Riskin, Leonard L., *Mediator Orientations, Strategies and Techniques*, 12 ALTERNATIVES TO HIGH COST LITIGATION, 111 (1994). *See also* Riskin, Leonard, *Understanding Mediators' Orientations, Strategies, and Techniques: A Grid for the Perplexed*, 1 HARV. NEG. L. REV. 7, 25 (1996).

Mediators with a broad focus assume that the parties can benefit if the problem is defined beyond the narrow legal issues. Interests often lie beneath positions, and the mediator should help the parties satisfy those interests when possible.

The evaluative mediator assumes the parties need some direction for settlement. The direction might be based on law, industry standards, or technology. The evaluative mediator also assumes that he or she is qualified to give such direction based on experience, education, training, and objectivity.

In contrast, the facilitative mediator assumes that the parties are intelligent, capable of solving their own problems, and understand their situation better than the lawyers and the mediator. Thus, the facilitative mediator sees his or her mission as enhancing and clarifying communications between the parties. Unlike an evaluative mediator, the facilitative mediator will not give an opinion concerning possible outcomes or settlements. First, the facilitative mediator believes that an opinion might impair impartiality. Second, the facilitative mediator does not believe that he or she has enough information to render an informed opinion.

According to Riskin, each type of mediator will use certain strategies to resolve conflict. The evaluative-narrow mediator defines the conflict in terms of strengths and weaknesses of positions and likely outcome at trial. This mediator will study carefully pertinent documents and pleadings before the mediation. During the mediation, this mediator employs evaluative techniques such as:

- urging parties to settle or accept a settlement proposal;
- proposing position-based compromise agreements;
- predicting court outcomes;
- persuading parties to accept mediator assessments; and
- assessing the strengths and weaknesses of each side, usually in private caucuses.

The facilitative-narrow mediator, like the evaluative-narrow mediator, provides reality checks for the parties. However, this mediator uses different techniques. The facilitative-narrow mediator will not assess or predict outcomes, study relevant documents, or apply pressure to settle. Instead, usually in private caucuses, the facilitative-narrow mediator will help the parties understand each side's position and the consequences of not settling. In addition, in private caucuses, the facilitative-narrow mediator will help the parties assess proposals and formulate alternatives. The facilitative-narrow mediator might ask the following questions:

- What are the strengths and weaknesses of your case? Of the other side's case?
- What are the best, worst, and most likely outcomes of litigation? How did you make these assessments? Have you thought about other issues?
- How long will it take to get to trial? How long will the trial last?
- What will be the associated costs in money, emotions, or reputation?

The evaluative-broad mediator emphasizes interests over positions and proposes solutions to accommodate those interests. Because the evaluative-broad mediator constructs the agreement, this type of mediator emphasizes his or her own understanding of the conflict as much as the parties. The evaluative-broad mediator will study relevant documents, pleadings, and briefs, but will also uncover underlying interests. Typical techniques include:

- explaining that the goal of mediation can include addressing underlying interests;
- encouraging the real parties or decision makers to attend and participate;
- asking about situations, plans, needs, and interests; and
- speculating about underlying interests and asking for confirmation.

The evaluative-broad mediator provides predictions, assessments, and recommendations, emphasizing options that satisfy broader interests rather than narrow positions.

The facilitative-broad mediator encourages parties to consider underlying interests rather than positions. He or she helps parties generate and assess proposals designed to accommodate those interests. Techniques might include:

- encouraging the parties to discuss underlying interests in joint sessions; or

- encouraging and helping the parties develop their own proposals.

The facilitative-broad mediator does not provide predictions, assessments, or recommendations. In a facilitative-broad mediation, legal argument occupies a lesser position. The facilitative-broad mediator does not need to fully understand the legal posture of the case, but must be able to quickly grasp the legal and substantive issues to respond to the dynamics of the situation. In addition, this mediator must be able to assist the parties in realistically evaluating proposals.

Kovach and Love's Model

Riskin's model has made a substantial contribution by clarifying the state of mediation practice and by stimulating the debate about the direction that mediation practice should take. The model has been criticized as tending to legitimize evaluative mediation.

Many scholars and practitioners believe evaluative processes do not belong in the definition of mediation. Mediation, in their view, is a process that fosters party autonomy and party decision-making. Many others, especially evaluative practitioners, sharply dispute this contention. The academic literature on the debate is substantial.

Professors Kimberlee K. Kovach and Lela P. Love offer a model slightly different than Riskin's. Their model emphasizes what they see as profound differences between adjudicative-evaluative dispute processing and facilitative dispute processing. In this model, a "Great Divide" separates processes that require evaluation from those that require facilitation. In processes where the neutral renders a judgment, the neutral has an evaluative role. In consensus-building processes, the neutral has a facilitative role.[4]

Kovach and Love point out certain implications of their model. First, they recognize that some evaluations require quite substantial qualifications. They believe that evaluators in legal contexts must be lawyers. This is because lawyers are constrained by rules of professional conduct, are liable for malpractice, and are educated in norms of credible evidence, fact-finding procedures, burdens of proof, and appropriate legal research and analysis. In nonlegal disputes, Kovach and Love argue that similarly high standards for evaluators should apply.

Second, they believe that tactics and strategies should be appropriate to the orientation of the neutral. Evaluators should not use caucuses

[4] Kovach, Kimberlee K., Love, Lela P., *Mapping Mediation: The Risks of Riskin's Grid*, HARV. NEG. L. REV. 71 (1998).

because of due process concerns. Furthermore, mediators should not be evaluators because mediation training normally does not include instruction on assessing credibility, weighing evidence, assigning the proper burden of proof, or conducting appropriate research. When mediators offer opinions on likely judicial outcomes, questions are raised about the duty to research before evaluating, the liability for erroneous conclusions, and the possible unauthorized practice of law.

On the other hand, facilitators may elicit information about assumptions, feelings, and perspectives that would be inadmissible in a fact-finding or evaluative process. In an evaluative process, hearsay evidence would normally not be considered or would be discounted substantially. In a facilitative process, rules of evidence simply would not apply.

Carnevale's Strategic Choice Model

Social psychologist Peter Carnevale designed the strategic choice model of mediation to predict the types of strategy that a mediator is likely to use in different circumstances.[5] The model considers four basic mediator strategies: compensation, pressure, integration, and inaction.

The model assumes that mediator strategy is determined by the mediator's assessment of the costs and benefits associated with a strategy, the feasibility of a strategy, and mediator incentives. According to the model, two factors determine the mediator's choice of strategy.

The first factor is the value that a mediator places on the disputants achieving their aspirations. This value may be based on a genuine concern for the disputants' welfare or from a strategic concern when the mediator has interests in the outcome of the dispute.

The second factor is the mediator's assessment of the probability that a mutually acceptable solution will be found, or "perceived common ground." Perceived common ground implies that the parties have low aspirations, being cooperative with one another.

According to the model, mediators integrate when they want the parties to achieve their aspirations and there is common ground. In this case, an integrating strategy is worth the time and effort and is feasible because there is a good chance of finding a mutually acceptable solution.

---

[5] Carnevale, Peter, *Strategic Choice in Mediation*, 2 NEG. J. 41 (1986). *See also* Carnevale, Peter, J. D. Lim, Rodney G. & McLaughlin, *Contingent Mediator Behavior and its Effectiveness*, *in* KRESSEL, PRUITT, ET AL (eds.) MEDIATION RESEARCH. San Francisco: Jossey-Bass, 1989.

Mediators press when they don't care whether the parties achieve their aspirations and when there is little common ground. In this case, pressure is feasible because the mediator is not afraid to alienate the parties. Mediators compensate when they want the parties to achieve their aspirations, but there is little common ground. In this case, compensation is worth the cost. For example, the United States, as mediator, may agree to compensate the Palestinians by financing an international airport in the Gaza Strip.

Mediators become inactive when they do not care if the parties achieve their aspirations and when there is much common ground. Inaction becomes feasible because there is a good chance that the parties will reach agreement on their own.

The model assumes that mediators not only consider reasons to use a strategy, but also reasons not to use a strategy. When there is little perceived common ground, for example, mediators decide not to integrate because there is little chance that an integrative agreement will be found.

When perceived common ground is high, mediators decide not to compensate or press because the strategies are not necessary. When mediators do not value the parties' aspirations, they decide not to compensate or integrate because the strategies are not worth the cost and effort. When the parties' aspirations are valued, mediators decide not to press or be inactive because the strategies are not likely to lead to the parties' aspirations being met.

Outcome Continuum: Decision to Reconciliation

The final strand of this theory of mediation involves outcome. Like process and style, the debate about appropriate mediation outcomes has been fierce.

On one side, court administrators and a large number of practitioners measure outcome by settlement rates. A good outcome occurs when an agreement is reached and the case is removed from the docket by a dismissal.

Another group, consisting of many academics and a large number of practitioners, follow some form of Bush and Folger's transformative model.[6] Outcome in that model rejects settlement and looks simply to

[6] Baruch Bush, Robert A., Folger, Joseph P. The Promise of Mediation. San Francisco: Jossey-Bass, 1994).

whether the parties have gained some sense of empowerment to make decisions and have recognized the other's perspective.

A third group, based primarily in the faith and peace community, measure outcome by the degree of personal reconciliation that occurs between the parties. The restorative justice movement is illustrative of this concept of outcome, especially as exemplified by Professor Ron Claassen's models of *Reconciliation of Injustices and Reconciliation of Interests.*

These outcomes seem to fall into a continuum of possibilities. At one end, the conflict is resolved by decision, judicial or arbitral. At the other end, conflict is resolved when the parties reach a full and mutual reconciliation that includes genuine apology and forgiveness. In between are mutually agreed settlements and transformative outcomes.

A Theory of Mediation

A theory of mediation should provide a descriptive prediction of what orientations, processes and outcomes might be expected in a given conflict or dispute. Considering the four strands, my theory of mediation is stated as follows:

The nature of the conflict dictates the mediation process to be used and the conflict's likely outcome.

Theorem No. 1: As long as the conflict remains centered on content goals and has not escalated beyond Stage Three, facilitated distributive bargaining, interest-based negotiation, and evaluative mediation are effective and efficient processes for achieving appropriate conflict resolution.

Corollary to Theorem No. 1: Facilitated bargaining, interest-based negotiation, and evaluative mediation processes are not efficient or effective at high levels of conflict escalation or when identity or relationship goals are in play.

Rationale: Evaluative mediation implicitly assumes that the disputants are rationally self-interested in maximizing their utility. Thus, evaluative mediators assume that disputants will attempt to avoid losses and seek economic gains. At low levels of conflict escalation and when content goals are solely in play, these assumptions are generally valid. When the conflict has escalated to Stage Four or Five, the disputants are no longer acting in their rational self-interest. Similarly, when relationship or identity goals are in play, rational self-interest is not operative. Thus, in these cases evaluative mediation will probably not be effective.

Theorem No. 2: As long as the conflict remains centered on identity or relationship goals or has escalated to Stage Four or Five, transformative or narrative mediation[7] processes are effective and efficient processes for achieving appropriate conflict resolution.

Corollary to Theorem No. 2: Transformative and narrative processes are not efficient or effective at low levels of escalation or in purely distributive bargaining conflict situations.

Rationale: Transformative and narrative mediation processes do not assume that disputants are rationally self-interested. Consequently, these processes are effective in irrational conditions. In particular, narrative mediation assumes only that conflict is one reality constructed by the disputants, that it can be de-constructed, and that a new reality can replace the old, conflict-laden reality. Transformative mediation likewise does not rely on rational self-interest. Instead, it seeks a re-ordering of internal perception (empowerment) and external perceptions (acknowledgement and recognition of the other). If the disputants' internal and external perceptions are sufficiently changed to permit empowerment and recognition, transformative mediation declares itself successful. Transformative and narrative processes tend to be ineffective in purely distributive bargaining conflicts at low levels of escalation because the disputants are acting from positions of rational self-interest. They do not need the interpersonal processes designed to change perceptions or create new realities.

Theorem No. 3: Parties will be satisfied with their outcomes based on the nature of their conflict.

Corollary 1 to Theorem No. 3: Outcomes based on settlements or mutual agreements will be satisfactory to parties when their conflict is Stage Three or below and is not driven by relationship or identity goals.

Corollary 2 to Theorem No. 3: Outcomes based on the transformative principles of empowerment and recognition or narrative principles of re-constructing reality will be satisfactory to parties when their conflict escalates above Stage Three or is driven by relationship or identity goals.

Corollary 3 to Theorem No. 3: Outcomes based on reconciliation will be satisfactory to the parties when the conflict is predominately driven by relationship and identity goals.

---

[7] Winslade, J. & Monk, G, Narrative Mediations: A New Approach to Conflict Resolution. (San Francisco: Jossey-Bass, 2000).

Rationale: The obviousness of Theorem No. 3 and its corollaries is based on the observation that conflicts have different sources and accelerators. A plaintiff injured in an automobile accident is not as likely to be interested in reconciliation as in compensation. Of course, an apology by the negligent driver would be appropriate, but the real issue concerns the economic losses and general damages the insurance company will pay the plaintiff on behalf of the defendant. Most plaintiffs will be satisfied with a mediation that results in fair compensation for their losses.

On the other hand, if dignitary interests are involved, such that identity and relationship goals are in play, no amount of money will truly satisfy the victim. In these conflicts, parties will usually be satisfied only when the offender acknowledges and accepts responsibility for the offense. Transformative or narrative processes are more likely to achieve this outcome because they rely on interpersonal relationship building.

Conclusion

This theory approaches mediation from a conflict dynamics perspective, rather than from a process perspective. The debate over process and outcome seems to have ignored the fact that conflicts are as diverse as human society. Thus, this theory anchors the process and outcome debate to the nature of the conflict. When this occurs, the differences between evaluative and facilitative processes can be reconciled and justified.

This theory has a further significant implication for practitioners. A competent mediator must be able to assess the conflict goals in play (including the fact that goals are dynamic during a conflict) and the conflict escalation level (which may not be the same for each disputant).

Based on this assessment, the mediator must choose the process most appropriate to the situation, with the goal of moving the parties from high to low levels of escalation. As the parties move backward through the escalatory stages and re-integrate their personalities to adult levels of development, the mediator must change processes. Thus, a mediator capable of handling all types of conflicts must be well-educated in conflict theory, conflict dynamics, and process theory. Otherwise, the mediator will face too many conflicts without the skills necessary to produce effective outcomes.

Finally, this model provides a way of explaining the different processes and outcomes to parties and their representatives. Many lawyers and businesspeople are resistant to the transformative and narrative approaches to mediation. Likewise, many people from the therapeutic and counseling professions are antagonistic to evaluative mediation. This theory explains when a process is appropriate and why it is appropriate. The logic of the theory should appeal to a broad array of potential clients.

III. The Theory of Evaluative Mediation

Opinion Wanted: A Theoretical Construct for Mediation Practice

*by Cris M. Currie**

The author maintains the biggest problem facing mediators is the lack of a comprehensive theory of mediation. Without such a theory, many mediators tend to use whatever techniques "work" for them, which might lead to negative results in the long run. To bolster this argument, he focuses on the method of evaluative mediation.

For the past several years there has been much healthy discussion in the literature and at the various dispute resolution conferences concerning different styles of mediating.[1] While anecdotal evidence abounds to support whatever views practitioners may hold on the subject, the discussion generally lacks a research-based, theoretical foundation.

Theory and research are critical elements in the rather circular process of developing a profession. Typically, observations (regarding how best to resolve a dispute, for example) suggest a new theory. Theory attempts to explain the "why" behind the event or action, but in doing so, it demands careful methodology and precision as to what exactly is being assessed. In other words, professional theory building leads directly to professional goal setting. Goals determine the definitions and boundaries of the field and provide benchmarks for differentiating success from failure. With a good foundation of goals, definitions, boundaries, and benchmarks, acceptable strategies and techniques can be determined. Acceptable strategies then suggest standards of practice, which are necessary for consistency and predictability. Public confidence and use typically rises with greater predictability. Problems with predictability indicate the need for further research and theory refinement so that the cycle continuously repeats itself.

---

* The author is an adjunct professor of conflict management at Washington State University and a conflict resolution specialist with Grove & Morgan, Attorneys for Collaborative Law, in Spokane, Washington. He holds a M.A. in Conflict Resolution from Antioch University.

[1] *See* FLA. ST. U. L. REV., 1997, 24(4) for several good summary articles regarding evaluative and facilitative mediation.

ADR in Crisis

It is clear from most of what is currently being published on the subject of mediation and alternative dispute resolution (ADR), that mediators are sharply divided as to the fundamental goals of mediation and that the above cycle is not functioning properly. Disagreement exists about whether mediation should even be included as an ADR process since many claim that it differs too much from the other ADR options. This situation has interfered with the field's ability to define itself, to set and enforce professional standards, to gain public confidence, and to mature as a respected profession. The problem is not simply a disagreement over style, as many would prefer to believe. It is in fact a crisis concerning fundamentals. While the field is certainly struggling to create a more comprehensive body of research and theory, the crisis stems not so much from a lack of conflict resolution theory as from a lack of understanding and appreciation of the existing theory. It is as if two completely different cultures with different languages and traditions (the facilitative mediators vs. the evaluative mediators) were competing against each other for support from the same constituency. If the conflict resolution field is to mature and progress, practitioners need to become conversant with existing theory, actively contribute to its further development, and resolve the internal divisions inhibiting its growth.[2]

ADR has been criticized for its faith in a process that is supported only by the personal experiences of individual practitioners. Without a common theoretical base, practitioners are free to devise, use, and promulgate whatever techniques appear to be profitable and "work" for them. Whenever a technique is said to "work," it is time to inquire about theory. What does "work" mean to that mediator? What defines success and failure? How does the mediator know whether a technique has worked? What was the mediator attempting to accomplish in using the technique? What sort of data does the mediator use to draw conclusions? How does the mediator assess the validity and reliability of the data? How does the mediator separate his or her own interests from those of the disputants?

What "works" for the mediator may not work for one or more parties. An unworkable yet unresisted settlement might occur, or a party might withdraw for no explainable reason. The primary danger here is that "process only practitioners" are typically oblivious to the risk that

---

[2] *See* C. Honeyman, *Not Good for Your Career*, NEGOTIATION J., 14(1), P. 13-19 (1998), for an idea on how practitioners can better work with researchers.

their interventions might actually reinforce the status quo and make a conflict even harder to resolve. For example, mediators are often accused of reducing complex social conflicts (such as racism) to simpler interpersonal issues in order to settle them.[3] While this may satisfy a party's attorney or supervisor, it may serve to further escalate the conflict for the disputant if the broader institutional or societal issues are not at least acknowledged and examined. Parties may "go along" with settlement for the sake of the appearance of peace, but inside they can still be seething with anger and frustration such that the conflict reappears later with greater intensity and perhaps in a different form. Without some grounding in a theory of conflict resolution, there is no way to define success and failure, and there is no way to push practitioners beyond their own self-interests in settling cases. Even defining what constitutes "mediation" is problematic.

"Evaluative" mediation has been defined as "a process in which a neutral expresses an opinion as to the likely outcome or value of a legal claim or defense were it to be adjudicated."[4] Its advocates suggest that the technique is merely an extension of the more commonly accepted technique of reality testing and that it can legitimately be used to break an impasse over the merits of a case, as a way for disputants to save face in accepting less than what they initially wanted, and as a vehicle through which disputants can let go of their anger in exchange for logic. Leonard Riskin has even suggested that it is far too late to consider evaluation as illegitimate in mediation since too many practitioners already use it on a regular basis.[5] This debate cannot be resolved on the basis of whether evaluation "works" in mediation, because it often appears to "work" quite well. It is only when one begins to ask a different set of questions (the above kinds of questions that those well-versed in theory would ask) that doubts begin to emerge as to evaluative mediation's legitimacy.

Since numerous state and national mediation organizations are getting more serious about developing qualifications and grievance systems for mediators, it is even more important that mediators recognize

---

[3] *See, for example*, R. Delgado, C. Dunn, P. Brown, H. Lee, and D. Hubert, *Fairness and Formality: Minimizing the Risk of Prejudice in ADR*, WIS. L. REV., 1359-1404 (1985(5)).

[4] *See* D. Golan and M.C. Aaron, *Evaluations in Mediation*, DISP. RESOL. J., P. 27 (Spring 1997).

[5] *See* L.L. Riskin, *Understanding Mediators' Orientations, Strategies, and Techniques: A Grid for the Perplexed.* HARV. NEGOT. L. REV., 1(1), P. 13 (1996).

mediation when they see it. Without a clear, theory-based definition of mediation, it is nearly impossible to evaluate disputant grievances and enforce mediation standards.

For example, imagine a disputant who has read in the *Model Standards of Practice* that mediators should "refrain from providing professional advice."[6] This disputant files a grievance with her state mediation association complaining that her mediator told her that a judge would never accept her desired settlement amount. She withdrew from mediation, went to trial and won even more than her bottom line disclosed to the mediator. She believes that the mediator acted unethically and wants to make sure he doesn't try to "coerce" other disputants into premature agreements with this tactic. Does this mediator's opinion represent professional advice? How much directiveness is too much? Does the opinion need to be prefaced with: "This is just my opinion, which you are free to disregard?" Should the mediator be disciplined? Will we continue to argue about what constitutes mediation while the complainant rolls her eyes in disgust? While answering these questions may not be quite as easy as looking up a technique on an approved list, a theoretical perspective is essential if we are to achieve any level of consistency.

A Sampling of Current Conflict Resolution Theory

Direct research concerning the effectiveness of evaluative mediation is practically non-existent, but a great deal of work has been done on closely related issues having to do with decision making and choice, perception, the satisfaction of human psychological needs, and the requirements necessary to promote cooperative behavior. From this research, conflict resolution theory is developing.

No respectable theory of conflict resolution can ignore the work of social-psychologist Morton Deutsch. According to Deutsch, conflict exists whenever incompatible activities occur, and it most always progresses in either a constructive de-escalation or a destructive escalation. The objective of Deutsch's work since the 1950's has been to determine the factors which encourage both constructive conflict and destructive conflict. He has concluded that competitive processes tend to lead toward conflict escalation and cooperative processes tend to have a

---

[6] *See* THE MODEL STANDARDS OF CONDUCT FOR MEDIATORS as published by the American Arbitration Association, the American Bar Association, and the Society of Professionals in Dispute Resolution.

de-escalating effect. According to Deutsch, cooperative processes are generally ones which encourage the division of labor in a joint search for truth, stimulate interest and curiosity in learning and understanding, increase attentiveness and recognition of other participants, motivate creativity, and reinforce trusting behavior. Competitive processes are those which seek to satisfy personal interests at the expense of joint interests, inhibit the expression of disagreement, lean toward overconformity and rigidity rather than flexibility and creativity, and overemphasize differences while ignoring commonalities. They typically lead to poor communication, misperception, misjudgment, and an over valuing of self-consistency.[7]

For sociologist Louis Kriesberg, effective conflict resolution must not only address the obvious disputes between parties, but the less obvious conflicts within each disputant and between each disputant and outside parties or systems. For him, every conflict has a unique combination of underlying factors such that any approach toward resolution needs to recognize their interconnectedness.[8]

For mediator Christopher Moore, conflict resolution is not merely the settlement of the factual issues in dispute, but it involves the building of a positive psychological relationship between the disputants. Moore bases his mediation methodology on the earlier work of Kenneth Boulding, Lewis Coser, Adam Curle, Morton Deutsch, Louis Kriesberg, Abraham Maslow, Carl Rogers, Gene Sharp, Muzafer Sherif, Kenneth Thomas and John Thiebault.[9] For law professor Baruch Bush and communications professor Joe Folger, the highest goals of mediation are empowerment and recognition.[10]

In a major attempt to construct a generic theory of conflict resolution, diplomat, professor and scholar John Burton has proposed analyzing conflict through the lens of human needs' theory. For Burton, conflict resolution is not just a set of techniques, it is a political

---

[7] *See* M. DEUTSCH, THE RESOLUTION OF CONFLICT (New Haven: Yale University Press). *See also* M. Deutsch, *A Framework for Teaching Conflict Resolution in the Schools*, *in* B.H. SHEPPARD, M.H. BAZERMAN, AND R. LEWICKI, (ed.), RESEARCH ON NEGOTIATION IN ORGANIZATIONS, VOLUME 2, PP. 189-203 (Greenwich, CT: JAI Press., 1990).

[8] *See* L. KRIESBERG, *Social Conflict Theories and Conflict Resolution*, PEACE AND CHANGE, 8(2/3), P. 3-18 (1982).

[9] *See* C. MOORE, THE MEDIATION PROCESS, 2nd Edition (San Francisco: Jossey-Bass, 1996).

[10] R.A.B. Bush, & J.P. Folger,. The Promise of Mediation: Responding to Conflict Through Empowerment and Recognition. (San Francisco: Jossey-Bass, 1994).

philosophy.[11] While Burton's theory is controversial and goes well beyond the needs of mediation theory, it is important because of its emphasis on the satisfaction of the basic human need to maintain an overall degree of control over one's own life. It also integrates the idea that all people adopt social values as guides in gratifying and evaluating their essential needs. Since these values help legitimize behavior, it is therefore only through identification and examination of these values that true conflict resolution can occur.

World view theory also deserves mention at this point. According to Oscar Nudler, frames and world views are mental models which consist of sets of assumptions about reality which help people structure and interpret their reality. "Worlds" include broad concepts such as the validity of science, while frames are more limited to daily experience, such as what constitutes acceptable medical treatment. Both may be unconscious, so people commonly assert that theirs is the only true perspective. Briefly, according to Nudler, understanding the metaphors which people use to explain their world view is the "key for building mutual understanding, and eventually trust."[12]

Applying Theory to the Crisis

How does this body of theory relate to evaluative mediation? It is probably fair to conclude that the fundamental goal of conflict resolution is the satisfaction of certain basic human needs through the de-escalation of conflict and the reconciliation, if possible, of underlying interests. To this end, it would appear that competitive processes (as defined by Deutsch) are counterproductive since Deutsch's research indicates that they typically lead to conflict escalation. Therefore, any technique with competitive characteristics should probably not be included under the conflict resolution (and therefore the mediation) banner. So rather than simply divide mediators into camps and then poke fun at those who disagree (as Riskin has done), it might be more useful to continue the work of James Wall and Dale Rude (who analyzed techniques used by judges in settlement conferences) and simply evaluate all of the possible

---

[11] *See* J. Burton, *Conflict Resolution as a Political Philosophy, in* D.J.D. Sandole & Hugo van der Merwe (eds.), Conflict Resolution Theory and Practice, Integration and Application (New York: Manchester University Press, 1993). *Also see* J. Burton, Conflict: Resolution and Provention (London: Macmillan, 1990).

[12] *See* O. Nudler, *In Search of a Theory for Conflict Resolution: Taking a New Look at World Views Analysis,* ICAR NEWSL., 5(5) (1993).

techniques potentially available to a mediator by the degree to which each contributes to a constructive, cooperative de-escalation of conflict.[13]

For example, three controversial techniques which fall within Riskin's evaluative style are: a) making judicial predictions in gray or complex areas, b) authoritatively assessing the strengths and weaknesses of a case for the parties, and c) promoting settlement on the basis of what the mediator determines is a fair outcome.[14] For a number of reasons, I would submit that these are all competitive techniques and unacceptable in mediation. First, they all stem from a legalistic/adversarial approach to conflict. The techniques have been imported from legal theory which posits that disputes can be resolved through the determination of facts and the external application of legal principles. Determining the facts in a legal sense requires competitive persuasiveness, while the application of law requires a competitive favoring of one side over the other.

Secondly, the techniques are competitive because they directly serve to satisfy the vested interests in settlement of the mediator, as opposed to the human needs of the disputants. When mediators try to push (or even force) disputants through an impasse, it is all too easy for them to ignore more complex interventions or other options such as postponing a decision or not reaching an agreement. Those who would seek to actively break an impasse with any technique which appears to "work," have probably not uncovered all of the relevant issues to the conflict. In short circuiting the process, the mediator can "settle" the dispute faster and with less skill than it would otherwise require. When mediators thereby elevate their own settlement needs over the quality needs of the disputants, they are competing with the disputants for the satisfaction of needs and desires. Obviously, this is professionally inappropriate.

A final reason why evaluative techniques are competitive is because they rely on expert power. Expert power is influence which focuses attention on one person's assessment and knowledge and their ability to persuade others of their competency. As independent sources of information, experts can be very useful in mediation, but when experts evaluate, success lies in their ability to win over the opinions of others. This necessitates a competitive process rather than a joint search for truth.

---

[13] *See* J.A. Wall, and D.E. Rude, *Judicial Mediation of Settlement Negotiations*, *in* K. KRESSEL & D.G. PRUITT (eds.), MEDIATION RESEARCH, PP. 190-212 (San Francisco: Jossey-Bass, 1989) for a list and evaluation of 40 techniques used by judges in settlement conferences. *See also* Leonard Riskin's criticism of those who disagree with him at the FLA. ST. U. L. REV., 24(4), 1007.

[14] *See supra*, note 5, at 26-28.

Further, evaluative techniques do nothing to promote learning, creativity, control over one's life, or trust; they inhibit or attempt to shortcut disagreement; and they do nothing to promote the understanding of conflicting world views or values. Without thoughtful, creative negotiation, self-determination and relationship building are undermined as well. While these techniques may be what some disputants or their attorneys want, they are inconsistent with conflict resolution theory and should therefore not be included on the list of ethical mediation techniques.

Alternatives to Evaluation

While a complete answer to the question of alternatives to evaluation is well beyond the scope of this essay, a few points need to be made. First, mediators can offer information as a participant with the disputants in a joint search for truth. To accomplish this, the mediator should be sure that the same information is given to both sides; that it is objective, commonly available, and directly related to the dispute; that the information is given without regard for how it might affect the likelihood of settlement or the terms of the settlement; and that an explanation be given as to the possible need for additional information from an outside expert.[15] Above all, disputants should also engage in a discussion as to the value, purpose, and desirability of technical information, such as legal advice.

If empowerment and the promotion of personal responsibility and control over one's life are appropriate goals, then part of the mediator's function is to help the parties determine their possible needs for further information. Mediators should help disputants decide what they need in terms of resources in order for them to feel comfortable creating an agreement. Do they really need expert advice or are they comfortable making less than a fully informed decision? If they can't afford expert advice, how can they make use of other resources such as libraries, friends, pro bono services, the other disputant, and the Internet? Disputing is a complex activity which typically requires large amounts of time, energy, patience, emotion, money, creativity, data collection, and personal involvement. Mediation can help people truly understand the full costs of dispute resolution. Then, based on that new understanding,

---

[15] *See* J.H. Stark, *The Ethics of Mediation Evaluation: Some Troublesome Questions and Tentative Proposals from an Evaluative Lawyer Mediator,* S. TEX. L. REV., 38(2), 769-799 (1997), for a more complete discussion.

mediators can help disputants decide just how much effort resolution is worth to them. Attempts to shortcut empowerment will inevitably lead to breaches of neutrality, party dissatisfaction, and charges of malpractice.

The Depth of Resistance

It is also very important for mediators to understand that conflict resolution theory is in direct competition with predominant American cultural values. The United States is a rights-based society founded upon a good vs. evil view of morality. When someone is convinced that their perspective is "right," the other person's perspective must be "wrong," and conflict is inevitable. In American society, one is expected to fight for one's beliefs and overcome evil. Negotiation is seen as compromising the principles upon which one stands and it is therefore to be avoided unless absolutely necessary. Thus, by being "forced" to accept a judge's (or a mediator's) decision, disputants can save face, an outcome of paramount importance to most people.[16] The point is that culturally, Americans expect, prefer, and are generally comfortable with taking their disputes to neutral outsiders for a decision. While a growing number of people are beginning to understand the many limitations with this approach, they still represent a substantial minority.

Thus it is critical for mediators not to underestimate the depth of resistance to conflict resolution theory. In saying that disputants expect, need, and desire evaluative approaches to mediation, advocates of evaluation are lending support to the status quo. They are not offering a true alternative and they are not particularly advancing the cause of social improvement. Typically, those needing professional dispute resolution assistance do not understand, nor do they value, negotiation (despite acknowledgments to the contrary). What they need is further education in the merits and relevance of the negotiation process and assistance in becoming better negotiators. They do not need surrogates for the adversarial process.

Conclusion

The fact that ADR practitioners are generally distant from conflict resolution theory is a problem with substantial ramifications. Without a

---

[16] *See* R.D. Benjamin, *Negotiation and Evil: The Sources of Religious and Moral Resistance to the Settlement of Conflicts,* MEDIATION Q., 15(3), 245-266 (1998), for a more complete discussion. *See C.M. Currie, Mediation and Medical Practice Disputes,* MEDIATION Q., 15(3), 215-226 (1998), for further sources of resistance.

solid theoretical foundation, mediators can neither define the boundaries of their profession nor establish workable standards of practice. The current debate over the legitimacy of evaluative mediation techniques is the most obvious manifestation of the problem, and the conflict is in desperate need of resolution. When the basic principles of current conflict resolution theory are applied to the controversy, it is relatively easy to see that evaluative mediation is counterproductive. Numerous alternatives exist, but it is most important not to underestimate the depth of resistance to the kind of social change that conflict resolution theory advances.

IV. Mediation and Its Applications

What Mediation Can and Cannot Do

*by Ira B. Lobel**

Mediation has been employed for over eighty years as a means of assisting settlement in labor relations. The author examines the role of the mediator and the mediation process in general and presents his view as to whether mediation can be put to effective use in other areas of our legal system.

A school district has had several budget defeats and the teachers' union continues to complain that the wage offer is not sufficient. A strike appears imminent.

A husband and wife are having a particularly nasty divorce.

Each accuses the other of all sorts of crimes, including kidnapping the children. The differences between the spouses continue and the children are caught in between.

A government agency has published a new regulation on a technical scientific matter. Affected parties immediately start complaining that the regulation is ill-conceived and technically inaccurate. Lawsuits against the proposed regulation are certain.

A tenant keeps complaining about the heat in his apartment. The landlord basically tells the tenant to get lost. Fisticuffs follow and the matter is brought before the local magistrate.

A multimillion-dollar civil matter has been filed in the courts. After years of discovery, pre-trial motions and depositions before trial, the parties realize that the main beneficiaries of the litigation will be the lawyers.

---

* The author was a commissioner of the Federal Mediation and Conciliation Service until 2003 and is a panel arbitrator for the New Jersey Public Employment Relations Commission. Lobel received a B.S. from Cornell University and a J.D. from Catholic University. He is the author numerous articles on alternative dispute resolution.

Scenarios like those mentioned above are commonplace. Until very recently, the common way to deal with such issues was to resort to a strike, a lawsuit, or to simply ignore the issue. More and more, however, adversaries are being encouraged to look at a variety of alternative mechanisms—mediation in particular—to resolve these problems.

This paper is an analysis of what mediation can and cannot do. Often there seems to be a misunderstanding concerning precisely what the mediation process involves and the proper role of the mediator.

The Mediation Function

In much of the discussion regarding ADR, mediation is used as the primary vehicle for settlement of disputes. Mediation is an extremely effective way of getting the parties to focus on issues and deal with the possibility of a settlement. Nevertheless, in attending various conferences on ADR, I have become increasingly concerned about the lack of understanding of the mediation process by many "experts." I often hear exclamations of the need for a mediator to be a "content expert," or that the mediator must be "empowered," or that the job of the mediator is to "level the playing field and introduce fairness." My concern with these phrases is that none of them address the realities of the mediation process—a non-binding situation in which a third party helps the disputants make decisions regarding a dispute. The role of the mediator is not to make a decision; that is the function of a judge or an arbitrator. Rather, the role of the mediator is simply to establish an atmosphere in which the parties work to settle a situation themselves.

Why Labor Mediation Works

Mediation has been utilized in labor relations and collective bargaining for a longer period of time than in most other fields; accordingly, it is useful to begin this discussion with an analysis of labor mediation and the reasons for its success. Labor mediation has been used for over eighty years as a means of helping labor and management resolve their differences and prevent strikes. Normally used prior to the expiration of a collective-bargaining agreement or a threatened work stoppage, labor mediation has been an active part of the collective-bargaining process for many, many years.

There are several elements contained in collective bargaining and the labor mediation process that make mediation in this forum different from dispute settlement in other forums, particularly those arising out of a judicial proceeding. These elements include the following:

1. Only parties make the decision
2. Power relationship
3. Deadline
4. Historical perspective/continuing relationship

It is important to analyze these factors to understand why labor mediation works in many situations and why the mediation process may not be automatically transferable to other forums.

1. Only parties make the decision. In a collective-bargaining context, labor and management negotiate over wages, hours and working conditions. In the event of a disagreement, the parties can: (1) agree to terms that one side does not like, (2) continue to bargain and maintain the terms of the expired agreement, or (3) engage in concerted activity (strike or lockout). In most cases,[1] these are the only alternatives that the parties have. If there is a disagreement, no third party can substitute his or her judgment for that of the parties. This means the parties must make their own decisions about the terms and conditions of employment. Even if one side can dictate the terms and conditions of employment (because of superior bargaining power), no third party has the legal power to determine the terms and conditions of employment.

This is radically different from the forums in which mediators operate. Mediation ordered by the courts will ultimately be decided by a judge if a settlement is not reached. In a landlord-tenant dispute, a judge will make a decision if the parties are unable to reach a settlement on their own.

Accordingly, the third-party decision maker, or the judge, becomes a check on a party being patently unreasonable. In a labor dispute, a party has the legal right to be unreasonable; the consequences may be a work stoppage, unhappy employees or poor productivity, but it is up to the parties, singularly or jointly, to make that decision. In the event one side

[1] These comments are particularly applicable to the private sector, governed by the National Labor Relations Act. In the public sector, which is governed by state law, disputes may sometimes be resolved through the use of arbitration, where both sides are bound by the decision of the arbitrator. In these situations, however, negotiators and mediators will both attest to the fact that having arbitration as the terminal step in a negotiating process dramatically changes the dynamics of the negotiations.

wishes to try to enforce its will on the other, there is no legal check, through a court or other third party, on the ability of the party to do this.

2. Power relationship. Closely aligned with who makes the decision is the fact that the collective-bargaining process is based on a power relationship. Even if one side is being patently unreasonable, there is no court, judge or other third party that can force it to change its position. The ability to use one's power is affected only by the power of the other side, or the practicality and costs of using that power.

Contrast this to a legal proceeding, where one party cannot use its power in contravention of the law. Because the judge or third party must look at the law and justice, the parties may defer to the third-party's judgment rather than risk a negotiated settlement that does not achieve the goals they are hoping for. Since mediation is an outgrowth of the negotiation process rather than the legal process, mediators must avoid making, or even appearing to make, decisions.

This is one of the reasons why it is not important for mediators to be content experts. If they are, the parties will look to them for content advice, rather than looking to the mediator for process advice. The mediator's role should be to help the parties explore ideas that may help them reach a settlement without going to court. Of course, the mediator must have some knowledge of the process and the possible outcomes in order to probe the parties' positions and raise questions and doubts about the validity of each side's positions.

3. Historical/continuing relationship. Labor mediation has been part of the collective-bargaining relationship for almost eighty years. Many advocates in the field have some knowledge of the mediation process and recognize the utility of mediator involvement, especially on the eve of a contract expiration or a threatened work stoppage. Because of this familiarity with the mediation process, the parties are often amenable to the involvement of a mediator. Even in those cases where one side may be reluctant to have a mediator involved in the negotiations, the bad press involved in refusing mediation will normally gain acquiescence from a recalcitrant party.

The mediation process does not have this history in other forums. Accordingly, the parties have to be educated regarding the role and functions of a mediator. It is often much more difficult to get the parties to agree to an unknown process with unknown results, particularly if there is a cost involved. In the labor field, where there is a history of mediation with no cost involved, the parties have some knowledge of the process and some expectation as to the results. Consequently, there is no worry about potential costs or about the acceptability of the process.

In addition, the parties know that once the dispute is settled, they must still find a way to work together. Unless one side can absolutely destroy the other side, a collective-bargaining relationship is like a marriage without the possibility of divorce. The parties know that they must deal with each other in the future. Accordingly, both sides have an interest in allowing the other side to survive.

In a judicial proceeding, where the parties may not ever have to deal with each other again, the need to "get along" is not as prevalent—except in cases such as landlord-tenant, matrimonial, etc.—so the parties have no incentive to try to figure out a way for one another to survive.

4. Deadline. In a labor dispute there is often a deadline. Many times it is in the form of a contract expiration or a threatened strike or lockout. In these situations, the pressure of the deadline forces the parties to make a decision. This is in direct contrast to other types of disputes. In many other situations there is no deadline and the parties can delay making a decision until they believe it will be favorable to them or until a judge makes the decision for them. If one looks at the decision-making process of many humans, we will delay making a decision for as long as possible, and avoid making it if at all possible. The deadline normally present in a labor dispute forces the parties to make a decision, while the lack of a deadline in other arenas militates against the parties making a decision and ultimately against a settlement.

Role of the Mediator

It is important to keep the preceding four elements in mind as the proper role of the mediator is discussed. In my mind, and in the mind of many of my labor colleagues, mediation is simply an adjunct to the process of collective bargaining. The mediator is a conduit, a lightning rod, a vehicle to smooth out some rough spots during negotiations. The mediator is not a substitute for collective bargaining or a judge. While the mediator may have some influence, there is no power vested in the mediator to make a decision. The mediator's role is simply to get the parties to continually analyze and reanalyze their positions in an effort to get them to modify their positions.

The good mediator remembers that the negotiations belong to the parties; in fact, the best settlement takes place without the intervention of a third party. The mediator constantly points out to the parties the practicalities of negotiations: the cost of agreement vs. the cost of disagreement and the advantages and disadvantages of various approaches. The good mediator attempts to raise doubt in each side's view in order to get each side to constantly reassess and reappraise its position. (In raising these doubts, the mediator must be able to ask questions about the subject matter; however, the mediator's knowledge need not be extensive—it only need be sufficient to reiterate the positions of the parties and encourage the parties to explain their positions and the theory behind them.)

Too much dependency on a mediator is not necessarily healthy. A mediator is different from a negotiator: The good negotiator uses some mediation skills and vice versa, but the two functions are different. Even the goals are different: The negotiator wants to get the best deal for his or her client; the mediator simply wants to get a deal. While the negotiator obviously cares about the quality of the deal, the mediator's primary emphasis should be on whether there is a deal. Of course, a mediator should make sure that the parties understand the deal they are making, but if one side knowingly makes a bad deal or understands it is being taken advantage of, it should not be the role of the mediator to intercede.

Listening to discussion among mediators in landlord-tenant cases, matrimonial disputes, civil litigation and some employment disputes, it is common to hear that one of the mediator's roles is to "level the playing field," to make sure the party with the inferior power does not get an unfair deal. If mediators begin to worry about leveling the playing field, they cease to be mediators, but instead become advocates or judges. The mediator should be careful to make sure he or she is a conduit for discussion, not an additional decision-maker. During negotiations, it is up to the parties, not a mediator, to worry about the content of the deal and whether both sides have had their "day in court." The process is "owned" by the parties, not the mediator. The mediator is there simply as an assistant to the parties.

Some mediators today talk about the "empowerment of the mediator"; how the mediator adds to the process in every case. The goal of mediation should be to help the parties get to a point where they can settle disputes themselves.

Mediators constantly talk about their need to be neutral, to be an unbiased participant in the process. A former colleague used to say he was never neutral, but always objective. A good mediator will look at the facts of a particular situation and objectively and impartially make a judgment as to the status of the parties, their power, their sophistication and their representation, and make a judgment as to which side to push and how hard in an effort to reach an agreement.

For example, a mediator involved in a separation agreement may believe that one spouse is too willing to reach an accommodation and is giving up too much. The mediator's job should be to point out the advantages and disadvantages of the proposal; his job is not to say to one spouse that he or she is taking a deal that is inappropriate or deficient. That is a decision for the parties, and only the parties, to make.

In a labor context, it is easy for the mediator to point out the advantages and disadvantages of a deal. After all, the parties—and no one else—ultimately have to make that deal. In other contexts the mediator may believe that a judge may rule in favor of the "weaker" party. In this case the mediator should avoid giving legal advice and instead concentrate on getting the parties to rethink their positions. Part of this process is to ask the parties how a judge may decide, as opposed to suggesting what the judge may decide. The former is simply trying to get the parties to rethink their position; the latter is dispensing legal advice.

In sum, the mediator is simply an adjunct to the parties' process—nothing more, nothing less.

Conclusion

In helping organizations develop ADR mechanisms, I often point out that the primary advantage of mediation is its ability to get the parties to analyze their case several months before a trial rather than on the eve of a trial. Once this analysis begins, the parties will begin to realize the pluses and minuses of their case and will often reach an accommodation, just as they now do on the eve of a trial. Mediators must acknowledge, to themselves and others, that getting the parties together in an appropriate setting is a major aspect of their job. This alone will get parties to settle a large percentage of cases.

V. Interest-Based Solutions

Mediation Works: Opting for Interest-Based Solutions to a Range of Business Needs

*by Howard J. Aibel**

In mediation, the resolution to the dispute is one to which the parties agree, rather than one that is imposed on them. If there is no agreement among the parties, there is no settlement making the potential range of solutions to a dispute as broad or as narrow as the varied interests and the imagination of the disputants. The skills of the mediator are vital to this process and are relied upon by the parties for the process to be of maximum benefit. In this article, the author takes a look at how mediation provides "creative opportunities for resolution."

Mediation is fast becoming a preferred method for resolving business disputes as corporate counsel and business executives increasingly recognize the benefits of the process. It is, in fact, an essential tool for responsible business management.

Perhaps the most attractive feature of mediation is that the process is consensual and any resulting resolution is one to which the parties agree, rather than one in which a solution is imposed upon them. While the mediator plays a critical role as catalyst and agent of reality in facilitating the negotiations, only the parties are empowered to decide on a settlement. The parties are directly involved by their personal participation in joint sessions and private caucuses which the mediator holds with the parties and their attorneys. The parties' perceptions and needs are the focal point of discussion and negotiation and thus any resolution reached is not only one they agree to, but one that they are instrumental in shaping. Experience shows that such an agreement is more likely to be adhered to faithfully than one that is imposed by a third party.

Critical to the success of mediation is its ability to reach interest-based resolutions which serve the parties to a dispute better than what often is a zero sum litigation result. Mediation opens up possibilities. Not

---

* The author is the past chairman of the Executive Committee and the Board of Directors of American Arbitration Association and recently retired as a partner in LeBoeuf, Lamb, Greene & MacRae. Mr. Aibel holds a J.D. from Harvard Law School.

confined to a resolution that is based on rights claimed by the parties and remedies offered by the legal system, the mediator and the parties can probe more deeply to meet the disputants' real interests and needs. Does a businessperson really want damages for past wrongs or are future business opportunities and advantageous terms more important? Does an employee want damages for alleged discrimination or prefer to have a better job or supervisor at the same organization? There are as many ways to structure a settlement as there are parties with individual needs and desires. There are, for example, many alternatives to a lump sum payment, including arrangements for payments over time with interest on the unpaid balance, settlement in kind, options to purchase all or part of a business, assignment of rights, or establishment of a new business arrangement.

Caucusing—A Mediator's Tool

The mediator's skills include the ability to help the parties identify and narrow the issues involved, to prioritize needs and to explore realistic settlement options. Caucusing with each party and its attorney in private sessions without the other party present, the mediator is often able to help each party see the weaknesses in his or her position, to understand where the other party is coming from and to identify new options and attainable goals. Receiving this information in confidence from the parties in caucus, the mediator only shares with the other party information the mediator is given permission to reveal. In this fashion the mediator preserves the parties' current positions and privacy while using this understanding to move the negotiation discussions in directions that can lead to mutually agreeable terms.

One of the real interests parties often express is the desire to preserve business or personal relationships which may be disrupted when third-party resolutions are imposed. Skillful mediators are sensitive to this need and seek to understand the dynamics of relationships and how they can be focused on a positive future. The fact that the resolution is the product of party negotiations helps provide the understanding and good will that must underlie ongoing relationships.

Parties are discovering that they like the empowerment of mediation. The process enables businesspersons to deal with disputes much as they would resolve any other business problem. Rather than turn their disputes over to the court system, where escalating costs and delays often take on a life of their own, parties increasingly expect their counsel to advise them regarding alternatives so as to have the benefit of the dispute resolution process best suited to the nature of the particular conflict. And, with increasing frequency, parties themselves are suggesting the mediation alternative to their legal counsel as a preferred means of resolution.

Relatively Inexpensive

Reaching resolution through mediation is relatively inexpensive. The cost of mediation to a party usually ranges from a few hundred dollars for a mundane matter to a few thousand for a complex case. This is typically a small fraction of the cost of litigation. Moreover, mediation can be employed relatively quickly after a dispute arises, thereby permitting early resolution. While mediation may be begun at almost any point in time after a dispute arises, including after litigation has been commenced, applying mediation early is often the most direct route to resolution and also avoids unnecessary expenses of preparing for litigation.

Mediation is increasingly being applied in large, complex commercial cases. The American Arbitration Association's Large, Complex Case Program, for example, includes a special mediation option and requires that neutrals have qualifications that include extensive experience and proven competence, relevant expertise, a judicious temperament, impartiality, dispute management skills, and completion of advanced panelist training by the Association. The types of cases to which mediation is applied involve a wide range of disputes, such as construction, insurance, intellectual property, real estate, securities and environmental controversies.

Take, for example, an intellectual property dispute about which the parties had been negotiating for two years, with lawsuits filed in Delaware and in Florida. The federal judge in Florida ordered mediation shortly after the complaint was filed, giving the parties the option of choosing a mediator or having the court appoint a certified mediator. The parties opted to select the mediator and, conferring with private dispute resolution providers, chose a highly qualified and prominent individual. After a series of mediation sessions, the case was successfully settled.

Or, take the experience of The Equitable Life Assurance Society, which launched a dispute resolution program, working with the American Arbitration Association to mediate disability claims in suit. This was so successful that The Equitable expanded the mediation program to include many other types of cases—life insurance, annuity, employment and agency, sales complaints, and real estate investment disputes. Their statistics indicate that out of 103 cases already mediated, 87% produced a settlement. The Equitable found that about 90% of the savings came from reducing outside counsel fees. A few of the cases saved more than $100,000 in attorneys' fees. Even though the program is still young, current savings from the total program to date are already over $l million.

Mediation "Softens Ground"

Even when parties do not reach settlement in mediation, they very often reach agreement shortly thereafter as a result of the role mediation has played in softening the ground. Parties also use mediation to settle discovery issues or to narrow the number of issues that have to be litigated.

Dispute resolution providers are promoting mediation through the adoption of appropriate rules as well as establishing panels of trained and experienced mediators knowledgeable in many specialized fields and with established track records. Very significant is the fact that just this past year, the American Arbitration Association, the American Bar Association, and the Society of Professionals in Dispute Resolution developed and published *Model Standards of Conduct for Mediators* to serve as a general framework for the practice of mediation. Individual dispute resolution organizations, such as the AAA, provide training in ethical standards which address the types of important issues that may arise and how to handle them.

While not everyone can be an effective mediator, training programs which are based on empirical experience are enhancing mediators' skills, thereby improving the experience that disputants have with the process. The ability of parties to select mediators with expertise in the subject area of the dispute and with a high level of skill in managing the mediation process provides the basis for the exceptional success of mediation.

As we approach the 21st century, it becomes clear that mediation will play an increasingly important role in the resolution of conflicts. Those business enterprises that incorporate mediation into their business planning, such as through incorporating an ADR clause in contracts which includes mediation as an important early step, will be better able to maintain their business relationships, pursue their business goals, and, most importantly, take advantage of the creative opportunities for resolution afforded by mediation.

Mediation is appropriate for a vast number of types of controversies. And what better scenario can exist than a process in which the parties themselves are an integral part of developing a resolution, and in which the very special skills of a mediator come into play to help make this possible?

CHAPTER TWO

GETTING STARTED WITH MEDIATION

I. Key Factors to Consider When Contemplating Mediation

Ready...Set...Mediate

*by Peter J. Comodeca**

While it's no secret that more and more people are discovering the benefits of mediation, it's not always clear why some parties are more successful at it than others. This article identifies a number of key factors that disputants and their counsel must consider before pursuing mediation.

Regardless of one's position on mediation, it has become an integral part of the legal process in the United States. Given the crowded dockets most courts must contend with, the use of alternative dispute resolution methods, such as mediation, is only likely to increase in the future.

It is imperative that lawyers and clients be familiar with the fundamental aspects of mediation. They must be able to recognize when it may be in their best interest to mediate, or how to proceed when required to mediate by court order. Proper knowledge of mediation techniques can help an attorney avoid unnecessary surprises in the process.

This article will help attorneys identify issues to consider before agreeing to mediation.

Parties involved in a dispute participate in mediation either voluntarily or involuntarily. Often, parties recognize the benefits of mediation and choose to mediate voluntarily. The most common method used to commence mediation is by entering into a contract or agreement identifying mediation as a dispute resolution mechanism.

---

* The author is a partner at Calfee, Halter & Griswold in Cleveland, Ohio, focusing in the construction, commercial, and international areas. He is a member of the AAA's Blue Ribbon Panel of Arbitration. Comodeca received a B.S. from the United States Military Academy, a J.D. from Harvard Law School, and a LL.M from the Judge Advocate Generals' School.

In the absence of a contract requirement, the parties may agree, after a dispute arises, to pursue mediation to resolve the dispute. However, mediation is not always chosen by the parties. It can be imposed involuntarily. Generally, this occurs pursuant to a court order or directive.

Involuntary mediation also occurs when the parties are subject to a governing policy or regulation requiring mediation of which they were unaware. For example, some standing court procedural rules require mediation as a preliminary step to either arbitration or litigation.

Appropriate Mediation Clause

Parties to a contract often choose to include a mediation clause applicable to any dispute that arises under the contract. Contractual mediation clauses are generally commingled with other dispute resolution procedures. Often, mediation is required as a precursor to arbitration or litigation. Also, mediation is commonly used in conjunction with nonbinding negotiations between the parties. Thus, many different issues must be considered in drafting the appropriate mediation clause for each individual contract.

First, a determination must be made whether the mediation should be binding or nonbinding. If the clause mandates binding mediation, a provision should be included in the contract permitting an entry of judgment by either party to enforce the mediation result. If the clause mandates nonbinding mediation, the clause should be clear as to whether or not mediation is required prior to the pursuit of arbitration or litigation.

Next, the parties must consider the scope of claims to be governed by the mediation. Mediation may not be appropriate for all claims that may arise related to the agreement. Thus, for various issues under the contract, the parties may wish to narrow the application of the mediation clause.

The clause may also limit mediation to certain categories of claims such as international, intellectual property, labor, or valuation issues. Additionally, mediation does not have to address the entire dispute. For example, mediation can be used as a method to resolve disputes and minimize costs of parallel proceedings by achieving agreements on discovery, stipulations, or protective orders.

The parties must also decide what types of damage claims may be considered by the mediator. Regardless, when attempting to limit the scope of the mediation clause the parties must clearly delineate the claims to which the mediation clause is applicable in order to avoid unnecessary confusion should a dispute arise.

Another issue to be considered by the parties is whether or not to extend the mediation clause to include disputes involving third parties. If the parties to a contract desire to include third parties in any mediation, it may be necessary to modify third-party contracts to require the third parties to participate in any mediation pursued by the parties to the core agreement.

An example of such a scenario would be a construction dispute between the project owner and the general contractor. A mediation clause could be drafted to require subcontractors to participate to the extent relevant to the dispute. The general contractor would then include this requirement in the subcontracts.

The parties must choose the manner in which the mediator will be selected. Mediation is often described as a process where the mediator functions as a neutral facilitator. To ensure fairness and neutrality, the mediation clause should include provisions describing how the mediator will be chosen.

The clause should provide, or refer to existing rules that provide, that the mediator shall be neutral and shall fully disclose any and all relationships he or she may have to the parties and/or to counsel involved in the mediation.

In some instances, it may be prudent to specifically identify in advance an agreed upon mediator by name. This could be done in the contract or by separate agreement referring to the contract.

Discovery in the United States under any alternative method of dispute resolution is generally less extensive than with litigation. However, some form of discovery, though limited, may be necessary to make a mediation effective. Thus, the mediation clause may also address what, if any, discovery will be required prior to conducting the actual mediation.

Generally, mediation clauses are silent on the scope of discovery. However, there are many situations where a requirement for the exchange of all related and relevant documents may be beneficial. This can be especially important in mediations involving international parties. For example, one party's legal system may provide for a full exchange of documents while the other party's legal system may not have a similar provision. In such situations, directly addressing discovery in the contract may help prevent ambiguity should a dispute arise, fostering a better climate for mediation.

There are many general issues to be considered in drafting a mediation clause. The parties may want to select which jurisdiction's law will govern the mediation. Additionally, the parties should select a mutually acceptable location for the mediation to take place. In an attempt to prevent unnecessary delay, the parties should also set forth a specific time frame for the mediation to commence and conclude relative to the acknowledgment of the dispute.

Mediation is generally a confidential process. However, to further protect against disclosure of statements or positions discussed during the mediation, the parties may wish to contractually define information exchanged and discussed during mediation as confidential. Such information would include presentations, statements, and positions advocated. Therefore, such information could not be used in any subsequent proceedings other than an action for breach of the mediation agreement.

For example, the parties could include a clause stating, "The mediation process is confidential. Neither a party nor the mediator may disclose the existence, contents, or results of any mediation unless the parties agree in writing to such disclosure or unless such disclosure is required by law."

When drafting a mediation clause, consideration should be given to the rules that will govern the mediation process. Many alternative dispute resolution organizations have developed their own rules governing mediation, such as the American Arbitration Association (AAA), the Center for Public Resources (CPR), and the International Chamber of Commerce (ICC). Choosing one of these organizations to conduct the mediation will save the parties from having to draft their own rules, while at the same time helping to ensure fairness and neutrality. Selecting the organization that will better suit the needs of the parties will depend upon the specific interests of the parties to the agreement.

Finding a Mediator

Generally, the agreement will establish a mechanism for selection of the mediator. If the parties have selected an alternative dispute resolution organization to conduct the mediation, such as the AAA, the CPR, or the ICC, then the clause may permit the selected organization to provide the parties with a roster of potential mediators. As mentioned above, the parties can also identify a particular mediator by name in the mediation clause.

If the mediation agreement remains silent as to the method of selecting a mediator, there are several ways that the mediator may be selected after a dispute arises. The parties may negotiate to select a mediator on their own. The parties may also agree to submit a request to an alternative dispute resolution organization for a proposed roster of mediators from which a selection will be made. From this list, the parties can negotiate a selection, or the selected organization may be asked to appoint a mediator.

The parties may also ask the ADR organization to provide a shortened roster of proposed mediators. Once this list is provided, the parties can rank the potential mediators in order from most desirable to least desirable. The intersection of the parties' respective rankings becomes the selected mediator. Or, the parties may choose to strike names from the list in turn until only one mediator remains.

Often, if mediation is unsuccessful, the parties will proceed to arbitration. Thus, the parties must evaluate, should mediation fail, whether or not the chosen mediator can also later serve as the arbitrator. As a general rule, this is not advisable because of the structure and process of mediation, which necessitates frank and candid discussions between the parties. If the parties know that the same mediator will be used for any subsequent arbitration, it may have a chilling effect on the discussions between the parties during the mediation process.

The process of selecting a mediator is much more efficient if biographies are available to the parties for the potential mediators. Ideally, conflict disclosures by the potential mediators should be made prior to selection. Regardless, upon appointment of the mediator the parties should require him or her to fully disclose any potential conflicts which might affect his or her services as the mediator.

Factors to Consider in Mediator Selection

There are many factors to consider when selecting a mediator. Generally, a mediator must be skilled in dealing with people as well as the processes of mediation. It is also beneficial if a mediator has subject matter expertise regarding the issues involved in the dispute.

The ability to relate well with others is paramount to being a good mediator. Such abilities should be evaluated in light of the personalities of the parties, the requirement for overall fairness and integrity of the mediator, and the coercive factors that may be necessary to effectuate a successful mediation.

Needless to say, the mediator should be familiar with the process of mediation. The mediator must be able to facilitate sessions with the parties jointly, as well as private caucus sessions. A good mediator will be able to encourage innovative thought and compromise. Process skills must also include an overriding sense of fairness to each side with regard to their abilities to present argument and speak on the relevant issues.

While many people involved with mediation feel that subject matter expertise is an essential criterion for mediator selection, others argue that it is not. The need for subject matter expertise generally depends upon the theories argued in each individual case.

If the nature of the dispute hinges on the comprehension of a specific industry, subject matter expertise in that industry may be relevant to facilitating a successful mediation. If the dispute focuses on legal arguments, a mediator with expertise in the governing law would be more desirable. Since the parties will often argue different theories in a single case, they will frequently have a different conception of what qualities comprise the "ideal" mediator.

Additionally, the nature of a dispute can be very different depending on whether the dispute is of a business nature or has emotional aspects. Thus, the parties would want to be careful to choose a mediator who is skilled at dealing with the specific type of dispute at issue.

Mediation has both an evaluative and facilitative function. The mediator must attempt to evaluate the dispute, and determine what a proper range of resolution might be. The mediator must also act as a facilitator, to guide the parties toward resolution.

These two criteria may be in conflict during the mediation. For example, there are times when a rational evaluation of the dispute results in favoring one party over the other. This may conflict with the facilitative role of the mediator. If this occurs, it should be handled tactfully by the mediator, avoiding the appearance of favoritism.

The style of mediation that the parties desire may also affect mediator selection. If the parties wish to have the mediator shuttle between them, they will want to choose a mediator that will be able to do this effectively. If the dispute requires a more forceful presence, that will also factor into the mediation selection process. Thus, the parties must consider whether they want a mediator that will aggressively push them towards compromise or one that will take a more relaxed approach.

Pre-Mediation Consideration

A mediator comes to the dispute with, at best, two-dimensional knowledge. While the mediator may have some level of subject matter expertise relating to the dispute, the mediator is unaware of the history and evolution of the dispute and the emotional implications that it may have on the parties.

Party advocates assume a different role in mediation than the roles adopted in other forums. The style of advocacy expected in arbitration or litigation is out of place in mediation.

In mediation, party advocates must take care to maintain credibility with the mediator at all times during the process. Advocates should view their roles as being partners to the process. They can enhance the process of mediation by presenting their client's case in a straightforward manner.

More importantly, party advocates can assist by presenting information to the mediator that may be helpful in persuading the opponent to believe that settlement will be more beneficial than proceeding to arbitration or litigation.

Party advocates should attempt to present the mediator with pre-mediation written submissions. The submissions should clearly include a statement of the facts of the case, as well as an argument that is based on those facts and supported by the governing law. At the very least, key documents as well as the text of relevant cases or statutes should be provided to the mediator prior to the mediation session.

Pre-mediation submissions are an important tool both for assisting the mediator in grasping the subtleties of the dispute at hand and for educating the opposing party. A compromise cannot be expected unless each party has a full understanding of the opposing arguments. The opportunity to evaluate and test the merit of the opposition's arguments is an essential facet of the mediation process.

Successful mediation requires the presence of a client representative with full settlement authority. This provides the best opportunity to take advantage of the dynamics of mediation. It can be quite costly if an agreement is reached through mediation but is later vetoed by someone at a higher level who did not participate in the mediation.

Additionally, to ensure a knowledgeable response to the ebb and flow of mediation, the client should consider and prepare possible concessions in position as well as potential fallback positions prior to the mediation. Advance preparation for position movement allows for less stress and better understanding of the opposition's concerns during the mediation.

Basic Misconceptions

Mediation is not simply an opening statement followed by negotiation. Mediation is fundamentally different from arbitration/litigation. In mediation, the parties reach an agreement facilitated by the mediator. Conversely, in arbitration/litigation, the arbitrator, judge, or jury reaches the decision and imposes it upon the parties. Thus, the opening statement in mediation is not principally directed toward the mediator, but rather to the opposing party.

Mediation is not the same as negotiation. Generally, mediation is commenced after an unsuccessful negotiation. Additionally, the distinction between mediation and negotiation is highlighted by the role of the mediator. The mediator's ultimate goal is to facilitate an agreement between the parties.

Preliminary steps towards reaching such an agreement involve minimizing the advocacy and posturing between the parties and focusing on the facts and law which are related to the dispute. In negotiation, party advocacy and posturing remain largely untempered, and may operate to aggravate the dispute.

Mediation is focused on achieving a settlement. In any dispute, an assessment of the risks and costs involved determine whether or not a party will settle. In mediation, an important goal is to encourage that such an assessment be done objectively. While counsel may initially advocate their client's position during a mediation, one goal of the mediator is to convert such advocacy to more objective counseling and advice to the client. Many party advocates hesitate to make this transition during mediation for fear of appearing to lack the appearance of zealously representing their client.

Mediation is not always the answer. In some cases, a party may steadfastly refuse to consider any position reflected in opposing arguments. Mediation is probably not appropriate in such scenarios. Also, because the results of mediation do not add to the common law, mediation is not appropriate if a party seeks to create legal precedent that will govern prospective or parallel disputes.

Conclusion

Mediation can be an effective tool for ensuring efficient, fair dispute resolution. Correctly drafted, a contractual mediation clause can help to protect the rights of the parties involved in the dispute by fully defining the scope of the process.

In order for mediation to be successful, however, the parties must be aware of the various concerns that need to be addressed prior to beginning the process. With careful consideration, the final result—a mutual agreement—will be acceptable, and even welcome, to all parties involved.

II. Effective Mediation

10 Ingredients for an Effective Mediation

by Bruce A. Blitman[*]

When I started out as a mediator in 1989, my definition of a successful mediation was pretty simple: if the case settled and I was fully paid, the mediation was a success. However, through the years, that definition has evolved. I realized that while settling a case is always nice, it is not essential for a mediation to be considered a success. I came to believe that a mediation is successful as long as something positive is accomplished and the parties and their counsel leave the mediation session with a better understanding of their respective motivations, needs and interests. The point is, no one who participates in a mediation should feel like a failure because the mediation did not conclude with a signed agreement.

Everyone would like to know why mediations end the way they do. I generally analyze each mediation after the session ends to try to understand the result. This analysis has revealed common ingredients, which I would like to share, that were present in mediations where something positive was achieved, but were missing in mediations that ended badly. No one can guarantee that a mediation will be successful before it happens. But if you make an effort to see that these ingredients exist in your mediation, you will significantly raise the odds that the parties will reach an agreement, and even if they don't they will have learned something from the process. If that's not a success, what is?

1. All Counsel Were Prepared.

The most common complaint mediators have is about the attorney who walks into the mediation cold, with no knowledge of the case or the client. A mediation has no chance of "success" in any sense of that term if counsel for either side is not prepared. Lack of preparedness on counsel's part will guarantee that the mediation will end badly and that

---

[*] The author is an attorney and mediator specializing in mediating labor, employment, and medical malpractice disputes. He is past president and Diplomat member of the Florida Academy of Professional Mediators. Mr. Blitman holds a B.A. from the University of Florida and a J.D. from the University of Miami School of Law.

everyone will have a bad opinion of this person. During the mediation counsel are scrutinizing each other and being scrutinized by the parties and the mediator. Poor preparation cannot withstand such scrutiny. Neither can counsel's reputation. Excellent preparation, by contrast, coupled with an excellent presentation, can make the mediation process truly productive.

In successful mediations, counsel were thoroughly prepared. This means knowing the basic facts of the case; being familiar with the key records; knowing the strong and weak points of the client's position and that of the adversary; researching the applicable statutory and judicial law; knowing what would have to be proved if the case were tried in court; knowing the applicable precedent that supports the client's case; and being able to distinguish adverse cases. In addition, counsel must be familiar with the personal details of the client's life, including his or her age, marital status and occupation. Counsel should also know the client's emotional and financial needs, since they may be critical in deciding how to respond to an offer or counteroffer.

Many mediators ask counsel to submit a pre-mediation statement describing the dispute and their client's claims before the mediation session is scheduled to occur. Drafting this statement helps counsel prepare for the mediation (and can be used to help prepare the client) but counsel should know more than the content of the mediation statement to properly represent the client in the mediation.

2. *All Parties Were Prepared.*

It's true that mediation is informal. But it's not so informal that counsel can expect their clients to walk in, follow what is going on and participate effectively. In successful mediations, both counsel prepared their clients before the mediation took place so that they could understand the mediation process and know how to contribute to it.

This preparation includes outlining to the client what to expect during the mediation. It means explaining the differences between arbitration and mediation. It means explaining the mediator's role as a neutral so that the client understands that the mediator will not decide the dispute. It means explaining that mediation is not a win-lose process, and that the dispute will not settle without the client's agreement. It also means explaining that there are strengths and weakness on both sides, and that the mediator will be testing these positions, as well as asking the client what he or she really needs from the other party.

Counsel can furnish their clients with articles or other explanatory materials describing the mediation process. There are some outstanding videos about mediation available, including mock mediations that will clue in the client on what to expect and how parties participate in mediation. Time invested by counsel in preparing clients for mediation will yield significant dividends during the process.

3. The Parties' Interests Were Identified.

In successful mediations, the parties and counsel identified the parties' real interests, enabling them to identify possible solutions to resolve the dispute. A dispute between two people cannot be resolved in mediation unless the claimant's most important interests can be satisfied. Does the claimant seek some form of retribution? No one is going to obtain that in mediation! Maybe the claimant wants fair compensation for a loss? Or reinstatement of employment? Or even an apology for ill treatment? (For obvious reasons, a lawyer who takes cases on a contingency-fee basis should learn early on whether the client is only after an apology.) Before the mediation begins, counsel should encourage their clients to think about what they want and need from each other. This can accelerate the mediation process, saving a lot of time, money and unnecessary aggravation.

During the mediation the mediator will assist the parties in identifying their primary interests. This is a precondition to identifying possible solutions of the dispute.

4. All Counsel Were Good Negotiators.

Mediation is a negotiation, albeit one that is assisted by a third party. In successful mediations, counsel were effective negotiators. They knew what they wanted out of the case and developed a strategy to accomplish their objectives. They understood that the mediation was a negotiation and they knew where they wanted to begin and where they wanted to end up. They had a clear understanding of their destination, and a flexible strategy for arriving there.

Counsel should have good negotiation skills and a strategy to accomplish the client's objectives. Counsel must know the points to make that will help the client's case and know when and how to make them. Counsel should not depend on the mediator to carry out their respective strategies. The mediator may have his or her own view of how the case should unfold.

5. Everyone Dressed for Success.

It sounds silly, but how the parties dress has affected the outcome of mediation. In successful mediations the parties dressed appropriately. Mediation is not a place for "casual Friday" attire. A well-groomed party will be taken more seriously than one who is dressed in sweat clothes. Counsel should advise their clients to wear business attire to the mediation. But standards of personal taste vary greatly (one person's view of what is "appropriate" clothing might be a pair of overalls!). To ensure that clients understand, show them what business attire means. Effective advocates know their clients and present them in the most favorable light possible at mediation.

6. Show and Tell Helped.

People always say that demonstrative exhibits are helpful at mediation, and they are right. At many successful mediations, counsel used demonstrative exhibits to great effect. Sometimes the facts become clearer when they are seen rather than heard. Graphs, charts, timelines, maps, photographs, slides, architectural models, videos...whatever will demonstrate the facts in a compelling way can be used. Sometimes the right image can make the difference between a settlement and deadlock.

7. The Mediation Was Not Rushed.

In successful mediations, the mediation session was scheduled so that no one was inconvenienced, stressed, pressured or distracted by scheduling issues. An attorney who schedules a mediation conference for 1:00 p.m. knowing the client has to attend an important meeting at 3:00 disserves the client and shows a lack of respect for the other participants (including the mediator). The parties especially should not be made to feel rushed or unduly pressured because inadequate time has been allocated for the session.

Counsel should strive to schedule the mediation at times when they and their clients are at their emotional and physical best. If the client is not a "morning person," or if counsel has a motion hearing on a judge's morning motion calendar, for the client's peace of mind, and just in case the motion hearing is delayed, counsel should not schedule a morning mediation.

In addition, everyone should be able to appear at the mediation on time. I have witnessed several mediations unravel before they ever began, simply because one party kept the other waiting for a prolonged period of time.

8. Patience Was Observed by All.

In successful mediations, the parties and counsel demonstrated extraordinary patience and self-control. They understood that it is virtually impossible to settle a dispute in under one hour, particularly one that arose over a long period of time.

Disputes that are emotionally charged or technically complex may take several hours just to sort out the numerous issues and areas of conflict. By working through these issues calmly and carefully, the parties are frequently able to resolve their differences. The parties should not be rushed or forced to reach an agreement. If the dispute is going to be resolved, it will be resolved at the pace that is most comfortable for the parties—not necessarily their attorneys or the mediator. In successful mediations, disputes are resolved only when the participants are ready to settle.

9. Everyone Behaved Respectfully.

In successful mediations although the two sides disagreed with each other, they did so in a respectful way. They took advantage of the mediation venue to calmly persuade each other about the reasonableness of their respective positions. There was no yelling; there were no insults and no name-calling. Such behavior may feel good for the moment, but it will not help anyone negotiate a better settlement agreement.

10. No Bridges Were Burned.

In successful mediations, counsel and their clients viewed mediation as an ongoing process, not a "one-time" event. They used the mediation session to begin a dialogue with each other, develop a positive line of communication and build on this initial rapport. They understood that the dispute might not be resolved during the initial mediation session, but if that happened, there was no rule prohibiting them from settling their dispute the following day or week or even months later.

It is important to use mediation to establish a framework for future negotiations that may ultimately result in settlement. There should be no threats or ultimatums at the end of a mediation session. No harsh words, no angry behavior. No storming out of the conference room in indignation. All that is required is a polite handshake and words to encourage future conversations.

III. Successful Mediation

Successful Mediation: The Dos and Don'ts

by Joel E. Davidson[*]

In the following article, the author outlines the behavior that he feels is acceptable in the mediation process and that which is not.

The parties' commitment to resolve a dispute and maintain control over the settlement is a cornerstone of a successful mediation. This, coupled with a knowledge of the following "do's and don'ts" of mediation, written with the advocate in mind, creates an environment where the parties are most likely to see the mediation end with a mutually satisfactory resolution.

1. Do Not Make a Non-Negotiable Demand in the Joint Session and Walk Out (Or Threaten to) If Your Needs Are Not Met.

Mediation is a structured negotiation. It permits the parties to vent, allows a neutral to give the parties some reality checks, and ultimately leads to a resolution which the parties control and accept. The non-negotiable "I want my way or I hit the highway" is totally inconsistent with the reason for mediating. The take it or leave it approach may be a good negotiating tactic in some situations; however, especially at the beginning of a mediation, it will very rarely facilitate a dialogue leading to a resolution. You may draw a line at some point. Drawing it at the outset when the expectations of the parties is a day of give-and-take leading to a deal will help ensure failure.

2. Do Not Insult the Opposing Advocate in the Joint Session.

Remember, we are all human. We all are capable of hardening our position and becoming defiant when attacked and insulted. Putting aside

---

[*] The author is the former senior vice president and deputy general counsel at PaineWebber, (now UBS), and past Senior Counsel at Prudential Securities. He earned a J.D. from Fordham Law School. Mr. Davidson is a member of the Board of Editors of *Securities Arbitration Commentator* and has written widely on securities arbitration and mediation.

any ethical constraints on an attorney insulting his opponent, you serve your client poorly by adopting a style that will rile your opponent to want to bludgeon you, rather than settle. The two are, after all, inconsistent. Even if the insults are true and deserved, they will not promote a resolution.

If you want your mediation to succeed, do not point out that your adversary has deliberately lied in his or her opening, that he or she has been sleazy throughout the litigation prior to referral, that he or she has lied about everything, has never filed papers on time, has withheld documents, and has cost your client a small or large fortune in legal fees. Calling your opponent a jerk, a shylock, or a witness tamperer cannot possibly help your case.

3. Do Not Insult Your Opposing Party.

Attacking your opponent leaves but a thin reed of hope that you can still successfully mediate. While an attorney may be able to swallow hard and ignore your bad manners and offensive remarks, you will be less likely to persuade your opposing party to meet you halfway if you attack him in an offensive manner.

In securities mediations, I have seen attorneys attack everyone in the industry during their opening. "This case is about the greed that pervades Wall Street." "All the firm cared about was commissions; they never gave a damn for poor widow Jones." "The branch manager let the broker sell crap to my client so he could win the Rolex watch contest. He has no ethics at all." Such speeches, haughtily delivered, create a deep resentment against doing anything for you or your client. Facts are facts, and you should argue them strongly, but do it in a way that might influence the other party, not inflame it.

4. Prepare.

Some lawyers feel no great need to prepare for a mediation. They are either lazy, or "reason" that mediation is non-binding and they don't have to agree to anything, so why spend a lot of effort on it? If the other side is reasonable, the case will settle and if they aren't, it won't settle.

The problem with this "que sera, sera" approach is that it makes settlement unlikely. If you are not prepared, you probably have not thoroughly valued your case and you may reject a reasonable offer. Even worse, you may be persuaded to accept a resolution where you pay too much or receive too little.

5. *Bring Crucial Documents.*

You may know your case, but you need to be prepared to give the mediator the ammunition he or she needs to persuade the other side of its weaknesses. That ammunition frequently is in the form of documents, which are key to the disputed issues. Without the documents, the mediator's ability to get the parties to resolve the matter will, accordingly, be severely handicapped. Conversely, if the mediator is armed with the crucial documents admitting or establishing liability, then the mediator can encourage the defendant to be more realistic. Exculpatory documents may have the opposite effect on the mediator.

6. *Provide Legal Support.*

Mediation is really a mini-trial, a laying of cards on the table, and an effort by the parties, with the assistance of the mediator, to evaluate the risks and strengths of their case. Frequently, legal issues will be argued. Can attorneys' fees be awarded? What is the statute of limitations? Which law is controlling? What is the effect of contributory negligence?

You can greatly help your mediation by being prepared to address the legal issues. Give the mediator a case that will enable him or her to resolve a divisive issue instead of continuing to advance arguments supported only by your logic, while your opponent does the same. If you continue to argue in the abstract, you enhance your chances for an impasse and, therefore, a failed mediation.

7. *Bring a Businessperson with Authority to Settle.*

In my view, the ultimate virtue of mediation is that it provides an opportunity for businesspeople to sit in a room together and try to work out a resolution. It is this aspect of mediation that really gives the parties the opportunity to craft their own settlement. In litigation, it is usually the lawyers who reach a settlement. The lawyers may get into a settlement mode because of their own evaluation of a case, because the client is unhappy about delays or litigation costs, because a judge or magistrate pressures them, or because the trial date is fast approaching. The resolution is negotiated between each attorney and their respective clients, or between and among an attorney, in-house counsel, and in-house counsel's client. We all know how a child fights when told what to wear, eat, or do. The child in all of us, including our clients, does not like to do what others tell us to do. Naturally, then, when lawyers tell (strongly recommend) their clients to settle, they may obey, but they rarely like it and seldom understand why settlement is in their best interest.

In a well-run mediation, these problems can be avoided. The businessperson can be a participant and decision-maker, and is much more likely to view the settlement he or she helped to achieve as fair and reasonable. The scenario frequently plays out as follows: a senior executive, hopefully a little above the fray, attends the mediation. She gets to make her own evaluation of the facts, arguments, emotions, witnesses, and attorneys. She is put into a room with a skilled mediator who has questions for which she realizes she may not have ideal answers. She may even meet privately with the other party and the mediator, but without lawyers. She may begin to truly understand the litigation risks and the benefits of a settlement. Moreover, being achievement oriented, once a businessperson spends time and effort working toward a resolution of a dispute, she will want to meet the objective of achieving a resolution of the dispute. Having been empowered to participate in resolving the dispute, the businessperson will not feel that "the lawyers" forced a resolution on her and she will feel that the result she achieved was a good one for her company.

8. Factor in Other Benefits Which May Result from a Settlement.

A mediation typically results in a settlement and, typically, that settlement involves a payment or receipt of funds.

Skilled participants in a mediation are quite cognizant of the many benefits that can result from a successful mediation. One of the most important benefits, frequently, is the avoidance of future legal fees. There are numerous litigations in which the adversaries spend more than the case is worth. In a mediation, a $1 million settlement of a $1.5 million claim may appear to the outsider to be a surrender. But if the party paying the $1 million estimates its cost through trial at $600,000, the settlement is really only "costing" $400,000. Put another way, the net dollars equate to an adverse judgment of $400,000, which could well be viewed as a favorable result for the defendant. Since $600,000 is already subtracted from the bottom line, the settlement at $1 million is much more palatable. The plaintiff who accepts the $1 million has the same type of issue—why spend $500,000 to try a case where I might win $1.5 million if I can settle today for $1 million?

Of course, many litigators justify the litigation process by contending that it is the process itself that beats the other side down, lets them know your side is tough, and exposes weaknesses in the other side's case. Sophisticated counsel, however, can frequently sit down with a sophisticated mediator sooner rather than later and, factoring in defense costs and litigation risks, put the matter to bed without destroying a few more forests in the great paper wars of our litigation system. Before you say "no" to a proposed settlement, think about the future costs.

In many cases, executives have to devote a significant amount of time to the matter, either as witnesses or as the client representative. While not easy to quantify in dollar terms, tying up a CEO or a top salesman for five days of deposition testimony does have a cost. In a case where dozens of corporate officers will be deposed, that cost spirals.

The costs of a loss may be more than fees incurred and monies paid out. A defendant may face negative publicity, negative customer reactions to that publicity, bad morale among employees, and governmental inquiries if a case is tried and lost. In addition, a loss may have collateral estoppel or other negative effects.

For the plaintiff and for plaintiff's counsel, turning down a reasonable mediated settlement means the anxiety and preoccupation with the suit will continue, costs will keep accruing, and a judgment that is less favorable than was available in settlement may result, which not only is disappointing economically, but may be emotionally unsettling and keep the matter alive for the individual involved.

A mediation sometimes can create, expand or maintain a business relationship, adding value to both sides. Mediation is particularly helpful in achieving such side benefits.

To sum up, by focusing your attention on factors other than the dollar amount being paid, you will gain the maximum benefit from your mediation.

9. Trust the Mediator.

To help your mediation succeed, you must not: constantly question the mediator; assume his or her bias in favor of the other side; or imagine his or her desire to force you to resolve your dispute on unfavorable terms.

In order to avoid a failed mediation, it is extremely helpful if the mediator selected by the parties is viewed by them as possessing expertise, having good analytical skills, and being reasonably straightforward. Whether the mediator is evaluative or facilitative, or somewhere in between, ultimately some level of trust is important in making everyone feel like they're getting a good deal and that the process is fair. While some mediators can be manipulative and controlling, a healthy level of confidence in the mediator is usually essential to success.

10. Stop, Look, and Listen.

While basic safety rules encourage people to stop, look, and listen, it is amazing how safety is thrown to the wind in litigations and mediations. Supposedly intelligent people "lock and load" early on in a case and find it nearly impossible to adjust in the face of new facts or new developments.

In a mediation, failure is sure to come the way of those who do not heed the warning signals. As the mediator presents the other side's case, including documents and case law, as the witnesses on the opposing side show themselves to have winning smiles and convincing explanations, the participant or advocate who is capable of ignoring all this will usually be faced with a failed mediation. Mediation is not for those who know it all.

While anyone entering a mediation should have a goal for settling the matter at hand, the success of a mediation frequently depends on flexibility. An attorney's assessment of the case should adjust in the face of new facts, be they good or bad. Sometimes, seeing the plaintiff in the flesh may cause an attorney to rethink his or her position. For example, the vibrant 70-year-old stock trader plaintiff one expects to see at the mediation may turn out to be the wheelchair bound, disoriented claimant against whom success may be far less likely.

IV. Making Advocacy Work in Mediation

Some Guidelines for Effective Advocacy in Mediation

by Howard D. Venzie, Jr.[*]

Any meaningful discussion of advocacy in mediation should begin by recognizing the fundamental tension between the two concepts. Mediation involves negotiation, conciliation and compromise between parties who have become adverse because of a controversy or dispute. Advocacy, by contrast, is premised on notions of "winning" the battle of persuasion between adversaries on important issues such as responsibility and entitlement.

The tension between mediation and advocacy can become a positive force in the evaluative phase of mediation if the parties and their counsel use effective advocacy techniques, mixed with common sense and good judgment, to focus the participants on the key issues, engender constructive dialogue and bring realistic expectations to the bargaining table. Mediation advocacy is "effective" when it raises the parties' awareness of the benefits of settlement and the risk and cost consequences of impasse and failure.

The evaluative phase of mediation usually occurs prior to the private caucus negotiation sessions. During this phase, the parties and the mediator typically consider issues relating to claimed entitlements, the risk and cost factors each side faces, as well as monetary issues pertaining to the worth of the case. The mediator assists the parties in assessing their respective positions, claims and demands (i.e., entitlements), and attempts to establish a realistic range for negotiation of the monetary issues and reasonable settlement goals. Party advocacy can

---

[*] The author is a principal in Venzie, Phillips & Warshawer in Philadelphia, Pennsylvania. He is a member of the AAA's Board of Directors, National Construction Dispute Resolution Committee and Philadelphia Advisory Council for the Large, Complex Case Program and chairs its Philadelphia Regional Construction Advisory Committee. He also serves on its President's Panel of Mediators. He is a member of the ABA Forum Committee on the Construction Industry, Construction Committee's Section of Litigation and Section of Public Contract Law. Mr. Venzie holds a B.A. from Temple University and a J.D. from Villanova University School of Law. This article is adapted from a paper delivered by the author at the Union International Des Avocats, International Association of Lawyers.

play an important role in setting the proper tone for constructive evaluation of these issues.

While concepts of responsibility, liability, duty and obligation are terms of advocacy used to establish entitlements, an effective advocate develops, with the client, the legal and factual logic behind the client's demands. Together, lawyer and client should address the key "jugular" issues that drive the dispute, presenting the client's "best case" in the light most favorable to its position. This provides the mediator with an analysis of the case that can be used to work on the entitlement issues with the parties in private caucus sessions.

Mediation should be viewed as an opportunity for the parties to "test" the reasonableness of their settlement expectations and goals. An effective advocate causes the client to reconsider the cost and risk factors in the case and adjust expectations concerning monetary value before committing to the litigation process, where the risk/reward analysis can change dramatically as the uncertainties of the litigation unfold. By more accurately identifying legitimate items of cost and damages, eliminating speculation, more correctly gauging levels of direct and indirect financial impact, and preparing a more useful comparative risk/reward analysis, the parties are able to move through the mediation with a more accurate case valuation and more realistic financial goals.

All counsel should strive to improve their advocacy skills in the mediation context. Several pointers are set forth below.

Mediation is a process that produces results only if it is treated with the seriousness it deserves. The parties and their counsel must treat the mediation as serious business. The potential for a successful resolution through mediation will be enhanced if the parties and their counsel follow these advocacy guidelines.

Be Prepared

The need for serious preparation for mediation should never become lost in the informal and sometimes casual nature of the process. Poor preparation most often leads to either a poor settlement or no settlement at all. Serious preparation involves:

- defining the "jugular" issues;
- developing the logic and arguments to support the merits of the client's positions;

- establishing the "value" of the client's case and what the settlement goals should be;
- preparing a negotiation strategy to achieve settlement goals, including the identification of trade-offs and areas of concession;
- establishing the client's needs in order of importance and anticipating the other parties' needs and interests;
- selecting the best methods of communication during joint presentations, such as charts and other graphics, videotapes, or direct presentations by the client or its representative; and
- identifying the right client representatives to bring to the mediation.

Be Credible

Credibility is the cornerstone of effective advocacy. If a party or its advocate loses credibility with the mediator or other parties, that party's case will lose value. Therefore, it is very important to the success of a mediation effort that the advocate and the client representative be believable, reliable and reasonably objective. Credibility is established by presenting comprehensive, unambiguous and well-reasoned positions, claims or defenses that are supported by facts in the record and by documents. Credibility in mediation advocacy also means "consistency" and evenhandedness. Speculation should be avoided, particularly in the computation of damages and the presentation of monetary demands.

Be Persuasive, But Brief

The goal of advocacy is to persuade. In mediation, as in litigation, a cogent presentation that is both brief and concise is the key to being persuasive. Persuasive mediation presentations generally include:

- simplified presentations that avoid distractions and diversions into less important side issues;
- graphics to communicate points;
- in cases involving technical issues important to the outcome (e.g., construction defects and the scope and cost of repairs), presentations by technical experts to develop the parameters of those issues;

- written summaries of claims or demands with dollar values where appropriate; and
- client participation to provide positive emotional content.

Be Discreet

The language and tone of mediation advocacy are critical to its success. The advocate must avoid confrontation, be professional and courteous, and create a tone of compromise. Discretion and good judgment should be the dominant factors that mark the advocate's style and technique. An effective advocate:

- will not ridicule or demean the opponent or its case;
- will not be condescending or overly contentious toward opposing parties;
- will not appear threatening;
- will not file dispositive motions in pending litigation on the eve of mediation;
- will recognize cultural differences and diversity;
- will use language of persuasion;
- will use the technique of apology with sincerity when appropriate;
- will speak in terms of issues, transactional responsibilities, risks and likely outcomes, rather than in terms of blame or fault;
- will use humor and avoid intemperate behavior;
- will avoid the "good guy-bad guy" dichotomy; and
- will keep emotions under control.

Be Conciliatory

Because settlement negotiations are inherently competitive in nature, adversarial behavior tends to take over the dialogue unless special efforts are taken to maintain a cooperative atmosphere in which problem-solving, conciliation and resolution are emphasized. Showing commitment to the mediation process and to the goal of settlement through conciliatory conduct goes a long way toward achieving a resolution satisfactory to all parties. There are numerous ways to communicate the message that finding common ground and a solution to impasse is the primary force behind a party's actions in the mediation. Some of these include:

- being cooperative and avoiding conduct that will be perceived as rigid or intransigent;
- setting a tone of compromise by talking to opposing parties and their counsel in a conciliatory manner;
- demonstrating a willingness to compromise, such as by conceding on less important issues in order to gain momentum in the negotiation process;
- avoiding extreme positions that unnecessarily restrict the other party's ability to maneuver, and leaving room for changes in position;
- viewing the mediation process as an opportunity to create options; and letting the opposing parties know you're listening.

CHAPTER THREE

THE MEDIATOR

I. Selecting a Mediator

Good and Bad Mediators—From Personal Experience—Find Me a Good Mediator, Please!

by Robert S. Peckar[*]

When a commercial dispute is settled in mediation, the parties usually extol the virtues of the process. When a settlement is not achieved, they may criticize the process, seeing it as a strategic mistake in the quest for a non-litigated resolution. There are, of course, many factors that may affect the success or failure of a mediation.

These include:

- whether the parties have good faith intentions about reaching a compromise and ultimate settlement;
- whether the attorneys are dedicated to a peaceful resolution of their client's disputes;
- whether the appropriate party representatives attend the mediation, are dedicated to the task at hand and have the necessary authority to resolve the dispute;
- whether the attorneys properly prepare their clients for the process; and
- whether there is a clear understanding as to the confidentiality of the proceedings so that the parties are willing to talk freely with the mediator.

---

[*] The author is a founding partner of Peckar & Abramson, a Fellow of the American College of Construction Lawyers, and serves as General Counsel to the Building Contractors Association of New Jersey/New York Building Congress, and the National Construction Financial Management Association. Mr. Peckar is a graduate of Rutgers University and the Columbia School of Law. He is a contributing editor to several construction law textbooks and is the author of *New Jersey Construction Law*.

However, none of these factors has the importance of selecting a capable mediator, one who has the experience and ability to bring the parties to the point where they can negotiate a settlement.

Having participated in a good mediation and a bad mediation within months of each other, I can assure you that the key difference between a mediated settlement and a failed mediation may be the choice of mediator. Let me share these experiences with you.

The Good Mediator

This mediation involved a major construction dispute between a general contractor and a public owner. Their relationship prior to the mediation was marked by tension and distrust. Litigation had started, and the parties, who had already taken polarized positions in their court papers, each claimed that it would prevail at trial. Although the parties were worlds apart, a settlement was achieved. How?

The mediator was a trained, full-time mediator. He was not a practicing lawyer or engineer who dabbled in mediation as a sideline, or simply to occasionally supplement his income. Nor was he an arbitrator who thinks that mediation is a hop, skip and a jump from arbitration. Nor was he a retiree who mediates occasionally as relief from the boredom of retirement. He was a professional mediator—a former practicing lawyer and businessman whose current business is mediation and nothing else.

The mediator dedicated the appropriate amount of time to the process. Weeks before the "joint session" he met privately with each of the main parties to the dispute (i.e., the owner, the design professionals and the contractor) to learn about the case, the attitudes of the parties, and their strategies in the mediation. He also met with key subcontractors, knowing that they would ultimately have an impact on any settlement that the contractor could or would accept. He prepared himself for these meetings by becoming familiar with the contracts and other key documents.

Between these private conferences, the mediator stayed in contact with all of the parties. Through information learned during conferences with the parties, he identified the issues that really mattered to them and thus was able to "narrow the scope" of the issues presented when the parties met at the joint meeting. He focused the parties on what they should do to "tee up" the mediation for success.

The joint meeting was highly charged. Imagine the enormous egos of the lawyers and some of the party representatives. Think of the tension in the room brought on by the confrontation of adverse parties, by strange alliances that often form during the course of long disputes, and by the anticipated demands and offers that would be forthcoming. Yet the mediator was clearly in charge and kept everyone focused, interested, alert and in tune with the process at hand. He was aggressive, yet not offensive. He was brutally honest, yet not overbearing in his recommendations and judgment. He was, in a word, "professional."

His excellent work resulted in a settlement that bore little resemblance to the demands of the parties prior to the mediation. It was, after all, a compromise, which is what mediation is all about. But the parties were not only willing to accept it, they were satisfied to have avoided an inordinately long and expensive trial.

The Bad Mediator

Compare this with the mediator of the unsuccessful mediation. The mediator was a well-known, highly respected, experienced construction arbitrator. He was, for very good reasons, considered sage and sophisticated. He was selected not for his proven skill as a mediator, but because the parties to this construction dispute considered him the one person whose wisdom would move them to settlement.

Unfortunately, the gentleman was not trained as a mediator. He did not do much preparatory work before the joint sessions. And as the mediation proceeded, it became clear that he really did not understand the special and challenging differences between being a fact finder and being a facilitator. Notwithstanding his genuine goodness, wisdom and impressive understanding of the parties' disputes, he appeared overwhelmed by the challenges of mediation and unable to function in as a mediator.

Unlike the trained mediator in the first case, this mediator was hampered by his inability to move a resistant party from its original position to a position that might accommodate a settlement. He was clearly confused and uncomfortable with the role of a facilitator. Although he had little trouble simply stating his opinion, he was never in charge. He had no agenda or plan. He simply went with the flow, rather than orchestrating or directing the flow.

Even after the attorneys basically took over the process, the harm done was too much to overcome. It is not surprising that no settlement was achieved. For these parties, the mediation was a waste of time and money.

The Bottom Line

Having a truly professional, trained and experienced mediator, instead of an untrained, but well-meaning, self-proclaimed mediator, makes all the difference in the world. The short answer to having a successful mediation obviously is to select a good mediator. But the availability of an adequate cadre of trained, experienced mediators is a serious issue confronting the ADR community. If you compare the lists of "top mediators" published by the nationally prominent ADR providers, it is clear that these lists, impressive as they are, do not contain an adequate number of mediators for the expected volume of commercial and construction disputes. The American Arbitration Association has just "requalified" its roster of construction and employment mediators, based on recommendations it obtained from personal interviews with customers and potential customers. It plans to do the same thing with its roster of commercial mediators.

There are, of course, many fine trained mediators who are unaffiliated with a recognized ADR provider, but they may be harder to find. The "good" mediator in the first case is such a person. Had I not been introduced to him by the attorneys for the adverse party, our paths might never have crossed.

The bottom line is, the importance of finding a good mediator cannot be overstated. So, when someone says, "Let's mediate," the response should be, "Find me a good mediator please!"

II. Diversity and Mediator Selection

The Question of Race, Gender and Culture in Mediator Selection

by Fred D. Butler[*]

When I consider the question of when race, gender, or culture should be a factor when choosing a mediator, I come up with this answer: When the parties believe that the consideration of the race, gender, or culture of the mediator would help resolve their dispute.

Mediators understand that while it is true that the process belongs to the mediator, the dispute and its resolution belongs to the parties. Therefore, the success of the mediation rests with the parties. It is this empowerment of the parties that makes the process work, and if the parties or their advocates believe that the race, sex or gender of the mediator is important, then it is important.

Still, is it that simple? Some of us mediators, who were educated in the 1960s in community development concepts, remember theories about basic human needs. One that stands out for me is George Herbert Mead's hypothesis: "I am what you think I am."[1] More often than not, these dynamics are at work as it relates to how the parties perceive the mediator.

---

[*] The author is an attorney/mediator in San Francisco. He serves as a neutral for the American Arbitration Association, the U.S. Office of Equal Opportunity, the U.S. Postal Service, the University of California and a number of courts in the San Francisco Bay Area. He is a past president of the Northern California Mediation Association (NCMA). Mr. Butler is a graduate of Rutgers University and holds a M.P.A. from New York University and a J.D. from Hastings College of Law. The following was presented to the California State Bar.

[1] GEORGE HERBERT MEAD, (1863-1931), THE LOOKING GLASS THEORY. Mead was an American pragmatist philosopher and social psychologist, born in South Hadly, Mass. He was educated at Oberlin College, Harvard University, and in Europe. He taught at the University of Chicago from 1894 until his death. As a psychologist, he was a behaviorist emphasizing the role of spoken language in the development of the self; as a philosopher, he contributed to the development of the American pragmatism with his philosophy of "objection realism." During his lifetime, Mead published only articles. His books, published posthumously from manuscripts and students' notes, include THE PHILOSOPHY OF THE PRESENT (1932), MIND, SELF, AND SOCIETY FROM THE STANDPOINT OF A SOCIAL BEHAVIORIST (1934), and THE PHILOSOPHY OF THE ACT (1938).

A Realist's Point of View

America is a "racist" society and has for most of its existence been a sexist society. While the country and some of its communities have embraced the economic, cultural, and social contributions of individuals from other cultures and countries, most have not embraced these cultures as a whole.

Even those of goodwill, and those who are actively engaged with other cultures, don't always understand the nuances of other cultures. When you add language differences on top of this, it only increases the difficulty of understanding.

My partner of twelve years—who immigrated to this country from South America nineteen years ago—and I discuss this often. Sometimes we discuss the use of words that have different meanings for us because of the cultural and/or language differences (English is not her first language). We are motivated to bridge the gap. But imagine the struggle it must be for those who have no motivation to do so at all. Then magnify that when a conflict arises. Under those circumstances it becomes almost impossible to understand each other's cultural differences.

As far as the differences between female and male values are concerned, most of us have heard the expression "women are from Venus and men are from Mars," coined from the book of that title. While some may use this as a way to explain the differences that exist between men and women, others have used, and continue to use, the inherent differences to treat women like second-class citizens.

One example of this insensitivity towards women is the way that victims of sexual assaults were treated in the past during investigations of sex crimes. Authorities did not appreciate the importance of having the victims interviewed and counseled by female investigators and/or therapists. Fortunately today that has changed, although problems do still exist.

I have handled disputes where uniformed female peace officers were involved in employment disputes. After identifying with me as another minority, they were able to relax so that they could communicate their real interest in the matter. They were able to express their fears and aspirations, and as a result, a healing process could begin.

One enigma is that black Americans and white Americans should be more culturally alike than any other group in this society because both of these groups have been here for over 400 years. For the most part, the American culture is the only one that most African-Americans know and the one that they helped shape. However, there is this belief, from both groups, that they are as different as night and day. It is the Mead dynamic—I am who you think I am—that, in my opinion, drives these two races farther apart and forces them to be different.

There does exist this complex history of race, culture, and gender differences in the U.S. However, it is not something one should run away from, disregard, or worse, pretend doesn't exist. For when we do that, we only keep delaying the inevitable debate. It is the denial of the persistence of prejudices and differences that is one of the reasons why race relations in the U.S. have become so tense and fractionalized. We can feel the tension, but not enough people want to acknowledge it and take it on. Individuals tend to think of things as an isolated racist or sexist incident rather than insidious racism or sexism that needs to be discussed and challenged. Like it or not, our country, as great as it is, still suffers from this negative legacy.

Individual parties and their advocates bring this history of racism and sexism into the mediation process with them, whether it is a belief that they are powerful because of their status, race, sex, or culture, or powerless because of it.

These are powerful issues. Advocates need to recognize and understand that these issues exist and may need to be handled in the mediation in order for a resolution to be reached.

The Current Trend in the Mediation Selection Process

There is an ongoing debate in the mediation field about whether the more competent mediator should possess subject-matter expertise. For cxample, I recently attended a presentation where lawyers stated a preference for using mediators who were familiar with the culture of insurance adjusters, especially when the adjuster participates in the mediation process.

Many advocates, especially lawyers, insist that subject-matter expertise is not only important but imperative in the mediation of their disputes. This does not, however, explain why retired judges, who normally possess no such expertise, are used by lawyers more often than others.

This notion of subject-matter expertise appears to be the legal profession's way of adapting and molding the mediation process to look like something that is more familiar to them. Once again, the dynamics of Mead's theory could offer some explanation for this.

It is safe to say that, prior to the infusion of lawyers into the mediation process, most in the field believed process expertise to be more important in a mediation. Of course, there is preparation required by the mediator in a dispute, but it is widely held that while it is possible to facilitate a discussion with little or no subject-matter expertise, it is virtually impossible to mediate a dispute competently without process expertise. It goes beyond saying then that the most effective mediators will be those who possess both.

If you follow the current trend and belief of most lawyers that by using mediators who possess subject-matter expertise the chances of reaching resolution is greater, then it only follows that the use of mediators who understand the culture, race, or gender nuances or possess this expertise could achieve the same result in racially or culturally charged cases. When this occurs, there is an opportunity to resolve not just the issues that are on the table but the underlying issues that may have created the dispute in the first place.

For the attorney/advocate, this may be an opportunity to prevent his or her corporate client from experiencing a class-action suit that may be lurking in the shadows, or to sort out insidious or unconscious behavior and to begin to start a healing process. For when it comes to racist and sexist acts, getting parties to heal is crucial. This healing can go far beyond the individual directly involved and be therapeutic for an entire organization.

The Advocate's Role

Advocates need to be aware of the cultural, sexual, or racial dynamics involved in the disputes that they are asked to handle. It is my belief that when ethical lawyers make themselves aware of underlying dynamics, they may discover issues that could present obstacles to settlement. If in doubt, advocates should ask clients if such factors exist, outlining the importance they could have in the dispute.

Once the advocate and client have identified the need for a culturally competent mediator, the next task is finding the right one. Not all women share the same value system or cultural experience. The same is true of African-Americans or people from other countries, so be careful not to stereotype. Advocates must therefore make sure that the mediator is sensitive and knowledgeable about the issues that are important to the parties. This means that advocates interview the culturally competent mediator just as they would any other person with subject-matter expertise. Once the advocate has made the commitment to explore the underlying issues with a client and has identified the need, the advocate should be able to ask the right questions. If the advocate cannot do so, the parties should interview the mediator for cultural competence.

Once again, do not assume cultural competence just because the mediator is the same race, sex, or gender as the parties or their advocates. There must be some investigation of the mediator's background, sensitivity, and commitment to neutrality as well as the needs and desires of the party or parties.

Always keep in mind that there will be those times and those disputes where the looking-glass theory—I am what you think I am—will dominate the selection efforts and it may not have anything to do with actual cultural similarity or sensitivity on the part of the mediator, but will simply be a statement about the past history of racism, sexism, and the treatment of other cultures in this society. In these situations, the parties may just need to identify with someone who looks like them. This can be a compelling interest and until we can bring about a color-blind and a culture-neutral society, this need should be understood and respected.

Another Option

If you are still in doubt about the selection of an individual mediator but see the need for cultural competence in the dispute, consider co-mediation. This is a process where two or more mediators share the process and are usually compatible as far as style and process are concerned. The key here will be compatibility with each other and the understanding that while the mediators' subject matter expertise may be different, their process skills must be compatible.

Community mediation programs have had great success with this concept, particularly mediations where the stakes are high and there are multiple parties. Providing diverse mediators where the parties are multiethnic, etc., appears to eliminate any feelings of bias.

Conclusion

Advocates need to be aware of the dynamics of race, culture, and gender and the effect, if any, it may have on their client's dispute. More importantly, they need to know that these dynamics may be present in the dispute, in the disputants, and even in the opposing counsel.

Advocates should not hesitate to reach out to others who are culturally competent to assist either as mediators, co-mediators, or confidants to help them identify and clarify sensitive issues and possible solutions.

This is all still a learning experience and the more we learn and interact with each other, the more we will appreciate our similarities and our differences. I envision a future where George Herbert Mead's looking-glass theory of "I am what you think I am," will be replaced with "I am who I am."

III. Will Software Programs Replace Mediators?

Mediation—Year 2051?

by Dr. Luis Miguel Diaz[*]

Given the advances in high technology, is it possible that someday a smart software program would replace mediators? Is it likely that in the future parties would turn to their computers instead of to neutrals or courts to settle their disputes? This article is satirically speculative fiction, but Diaz presents a thought-provoking picture of what is possible (or impossible, for that matter) in the field of conflict resolution in the future.

Although inconceivable just a few years ago, mediation software that promises to monopolize the interpersonal conflict resolution market is now imminent. Tomorrow, the Artificial Intuition™ Corporation (commonly known as AInc.) will debut its new product, AICompanion2050 (AICom), just one day after the last existing civil court closes its doors.

Ethical principles and values guided all stages in the development of the new software that uses techniques perfected in the last century's successful work in artificial intelligence. In this wholly new endeavor, a software program has been created that models the processes of human intuition. AICom is based on Artificial Intuition™, a revolutionary technology now made accessible and affordable to everyone. There is great anticipation that this product may fill the gap left by the demise of the much-reviled civil court system.

End of Civil Courts

While for years, critics decried the decline of the civil courts (with jurisdiction over the enforcement, redress, or protection of private rights and remedies sought by civil action, as contrasted with criminal proceedings), it was only at the turn of the millennium that businesses,

[*] Dr. Diaz is the Mexican Director of the U.S.-Mexico Conflict Resolution Center in Las Cruces, New Mexico. He earned a Science Juridical Doctorate (SJD) from Harvard Law School. He has academic and diplomatic experience in international law and in the use of negotiation and mediation. He served in Mexico's delegation to the United Nations and as NAFTA negotiator, as well as in several foreign relations positions in the Mexican government.

governments, and individuals came together to seriously question the viability of the courts as the institution for resolving civil disputes. The death blow finally came with the famous antitrust case against AInc. Although the litigation began in the final years of the 1990s, the Supreme Court issued its final ruling only two years ago, a mere half-century after the case was filed.

Some speculate that the High Court's delay was due to their prophetic realization that it could put the civil judiciary out of business. Its judgment, in any case, proved to be the worst possible decision.

The Supreme Court's ruling caused chaos on world stock exchanges, millions lost their savings and their jobs, and the global network of small businesses went into shock. Those lawyers holding the few remaining appointments in the civil judiciary resigned as an act of apology to all individuals and communities affected, a gesture that earned them appreciation.

A New "Frontier [for] Justice"

An interdisciplinary team guided by accepted professional standards of moral conduct, approved the network of programs, procedures and algorithms three years ago in a controversial milieu of exclusive opinions and conflicting emotions.

AICom2050 is the creation of a distinguished interdisciplinary team of businesspeople, software architects, lawyers, anthropologists, medical doctors, psychologists, ethologists, veterinarians, linguists, philosophers, and common sense consultants of all ages, genders and ethnicities.

Although AICom was designed as a substitute for civil courts, many analysts foresee additional applications that may very well eliminate traditional professions in other legal fields and areas of mental health and training such as psychotherapists, clinical psychologists, psychiatrists, and social workers.

The new computer program achieves an almost complete intuitive communication between parties. It fulfills Socrates' ideal of the teacher's role: to guide and help students to come to a realization of the truth through their own efforts. "AInc. aspires to humanize the administration of justice," declared company spokeswoman, Softy Rules.

Optimists and the Rest

AICom is a multidimensional, synchronous/ asynchronous tool that has the ability to interact with all participants at the same or different times, depending on the will of its users. It allows both direct and indirect negotiations. Its central mission is to serve as an ideal communicator.

Mary Optimist, a Nobel Peace laureate, foresees a tremendous leap forward in personal communication thanks to the revolutionary software.

> Imagine a friend with whom you can share your most private emotions and who literally may die, at your will, taking with her all of the secrets she knows about you. And then, if you so desire, you can bring her back to life, with or without the knowledge you have shared. She can be a perfect friend who can know your thoughts and feelings before you even express them in language. A faithful friend is the medicine of life, a masterpiece of nature.

Without civil courts and with few rules, the decision-making process for the settlement of private disputes becomes rather simple. Perhaps the most valuable feature of AICom is that it legally interprets personal thoughts and emotions of parties without the prejudices and personal preferences inherent in all humans, including judges. With AICom, disputing parties will know that the mediator is free from human biases and yet possesses an awareness of the parties' internal states of mind.

AICom does not have personal history, thoughts, or emotions. AICom is a network of algorithms and contents to help conflicting parties reach a solution. Intellectuals and Chambers of Commerce worldwide have forecast huge benefits and profits from increased global economic transactions. In addition, AICom will facilitate intercultural business deals and personal relationships at all levels.

AInc. has emphasized that the AICom software will assist users to find a solution to their conflict if that is what the parties really want. If a solution is not desired, AICom will be able to determine that and the software will not suggest alternatives. The program can also be used to assist third parties to facilitate resolution between the disputants if they so decide.

Bill Rock, representing the World Mediation Federation (WMF) welcomed the AInc. announcement. He said:

> Litigation to solve a dispute is nothing more than high-stakes gambling and can never guarantee a good outcome for anybody. Mediation always allows the parties to control the outcome and get at least part of what they want. If this new technology can

make that happen more often, then business will get results and get back to work. We feel that a lean peace is better than a fat victory.

In the research stage and in beta testing, the software developers found that the disputants followed the solution or solutions suggested by the software between 97% and 99.99% of the time. This high level of certainty in the outcome of disputes has never before been possible.

However, those in several crucial sectors have expressed their strong opposition to AICom. Trial lawyers around the world have united in protest. Patricia Practitioner, secretary general of the World Council of Bar Associations, predicted that the software could precipitate unprecedented unemployment in the legal profession. "This product is completely untested and unregulated. How do we know it's not a wolf in sheep's clothing that could destroy one of the noblest occupations in civilized societies? Better the devil you know than the devil you don't know."

And in the arena of global politics, non-governmental organizations (NGOs) immediately began to form coalitions with some world government bodies to manifest their fear that these developments will widen the giant chasm between rich and poor. "The civil court system has always worked to protect those without power," proclaimed Solidaria da Souza, a spokesperson for a loose coalition of non-hierarchical, non-sectarian, anti-globalization groups. She warned that peaceful protest and puppet theater would welcome the software release announcement tomorrow in Washington, but, "the real happening will be virtually attended by millions logged on to the Global Anti-Globalization Network (GAG-Net)." It is expected that thousands of electronic commerce portals will bolt their virtual doors tomorrow in anticipation of protest break-ins.

Wisdom of the Elders

Most evolutionary scientists and anthropologists concur that never before has a human invention had the real potential to replace a centuries-old bureaucratic organization and, at the same time, to incorporate "the wisdom of the elders" and put it to practical use in the mediation of business and personal conflicts. Against this background, the current generation is poised to embark upon a revolutionary new age in conflict resolution techniques.

AInc. initiated this project five years ago and now, for the first time in world history, a behavioral program has been developed that is firmly grounded in an integrated social and scientific understanding of humans. The centuries-old Hippocratic perception—that each person represents her/his own world—now forms the epistemological basis of Artificial Intuition™ Companion for conflict solution.

One of the consequences of AInc.'s influence is the unexpected revolution in how we think about the resolution of private conflicts. Most people endorse these new ideas that revolve around the uniqueness and total subjectivity of each and every human being. Recent discoveries in neurological cognitive science suggest that theological, philosophical and psycho-sociological rationalizations of human behavior are actually meaningful and multipurpose beliefs. But, as beliefs, they are an incomplete foundation for conflict solution between individuals with the same legal and moral rights and obligations, but who might believe very differently.

Law Professor Juris Holmes asserted, "It is beyond question that the law grants the same universe of rights and duties to every person, but from that legal truth it does not follow that we are all the same." In a similar vein, the well-known pacifist, Aristotle Smith, declared:

> These new ideas exist in sharp contrast with the deceptive and illusory perception of humans as equal and impartial: a belief that has served for centuries as the ideological foundation of the courts.

Ludwig Complex, German-born philosopher and sports columnist, explains the philosophical basis of the judiciary this way:

> Plato and Aristotle developed an idea inherited from the pre-Socratic thinkers that nature created some men to command and others to obey. Their treatises reflect an obsession with establishing criteria that would properly designate those who were born to decide conflicts. After a few thousand years, we can see that the basis of their theory is implicit in political organization although with a different rationale. Now it is supposed that those who decide legal conflicts are neutral, unbiased and impartial. This assumption, however, is only an epistemological legalistic construction that exists to give coherence to the judiciary as an impartial body to solve disputes. But, it has nothing to do with the actual way any human thinks, feels and behaves. All human viewpoints are biased and subjective.

Brave New Argument?

The new ideas on conflict solution still have a long way to go to be accepted by the general public. Recent polls show that 47% of businesspeople still believe that an alternative conflict solution method that is not backed by an enforcement power is doomed to fail. For critics, the major weakness of mediation is that the fulfillment of agreements is at the will of the parties. Without the backing of state authorities, such agreements may be vulnerable to systematic violation.

Albert Mind, neurologist and author of the best-seller LIMITS OF IMAGINATION, is quoted as stating:

> [H]uman conduct and the nervous system are rather complex. How can software substitute for the first-hand observations of a doctor and lab analysis to suggest a course of action? In the best of cases, it may only identify symptoms. This supposedly revolutionary software just guesses about the neurological, electrical and chemical processes in the brain based on tiny bits of evidence. This cannot be called intuition—artificial or otherwise. It could be dangerous to believe that such things are possible.

X.Z. Skinner, a guru in evolutionary psychology, alleges that the supposed ability of AICom to intuit the world of thoughts and emotions of a person in a conflict is just a misrepresentation of reality. Skinner does not question the philosophical premises of the project, but he doubts that the ingenuity and technological skill exist today to put together a mass-market program with the incredible powers that AICom claims to have. He said:

> It's supposed to read the very hearts and minds of the parties and then tell them what they should do to solve their problem. Sorry, I just don't believe it...easier said than done.

How Artificial Intuition™ Works

The new software follows a six-step process:

- identification of the people involved in the conflict;
- identification of the business or personal context of the conflict;
- identification of the legal context of the conflict;

- analysis of the establishment and development of relationships between the people involved in the conflict;
- generation/creation of possible conflict solutions; and
- formulation of rituals for the implementation of the agreement.

The AICom user may decide to communicate through spoken or written language and may choose female or male voices for the artificial mediator/companion. The user may ask AICom to record her/his presentation or dialogue. In the dialogue, the user maintains control over the information captured by the software and can choose to erase input at any time. The AI 'companion' cannot control the user; it only "intuits," presents options, and obeys.

The more information the software receives from the user, the more knowledge the software will have from which to generate new and better options. This same logic applies to the conflict itself, the legal context, relationships, creativity and rituals. The user may instruct the software to convey to the other party a proposal that was generated by the user or suggested by the software. The recipient may or may not see or hear such proposals. Everyone has complete control to propose, to change, to accept, to reject, without limits of time or location.

The Human Factor

AICom exploits the asynchronous nature of the Internet in order to allow parties a safe space and contemplative time before responding. It allows participants to record the presentation of the case. All parties have access to such records and are able not only to listen to words but also to read body language and intonation.

AICom also integrates an innovative and effective methodology that has been proven to encourage and foster understanding of human behavior and the conflict process: showing movie masterpieces. The software includes thousands of film clips that illustrate and promote the myriad styles and possibilities for change that can positively influence the parties to a conflict. Personalities from the film industry have expressed curiosity in learning about this new use for their art.

AInc. negotiated hundreds of intellectual property agreements with the holders of the rights to the films incorporated into the software. This policy was necessary because AInc.'s teaching philosophy presupposes that learning with art is more pleasant and effective than through other methods. It rejects the opinion that what one sees is less important than what one thinks and recognizes the power of film and other media artifacts to evoke emotions. AICom also has the capability of capturing and integrating new film, music, and graphic artifacts from the Internet to generate a personal media archive that will facilitate the intuitive and emotional development of each individual user of the software.

The Artificial Intuition™ capabilities of AICom allow the program to distinguish those who want to solve their legal problems from those that do not; it can also identify people who want to assist others to solve problems. This is achieved through the analysis of physiological responses such as gestures, breathing, eye and hand movement, smell, pulse and intonation that are captured, organized and interpreted. Any mental health professional or neurologist, including Freud, would have envied such intuitive diagnostic talent.

Not only doctors, but lawyers, politicians and police investigators would be tempted to sacrifice their professional credentials in order to achieve the high level of performance expected from AICom. Its goal is always to solve conflicts. It articulates thoughts, intuitions, emotions, principles and rules of law and justice. It manages to discover hidden motives in the parties to a conflict. With images and episodes of life, it introduces a basic understanding of the law. It employs popular sayings to help users clarify and distinguish the differences between the law as a set of rules, from the humans who create and apply those rules. It contains a vast catalog of legal provisions that may be relevant to many conflict situations.

AICom includes the legal disclaimer that:

> Artificial Intuition, Inc. is not responsible for the terms of any agreement facilitated by Artificial Intuition™ Companion. The computer program is only a facilitator, a mediator in the traditional sense, whose role is limited to facilitate negotiation between parties, allowing them to achieve their own solution.

The Future

Futurists believe that AICom will usher in dramatic changes in global conflict management. Certain government officials who asked not to be quoted, unanimously agreed that AICom would be a revolutionary educational tool that will make us wonder how we ever thought that the civil courts were the best institution most societies could devise for resolving legal conflicts.

The fundamental premise that each human being is unique—but not very original— underlies the construction of the Artificial Intuition™ Companion. Every person shares instinctual, intuitive, and rational knowledge acquired during the evolution of the human species. Each individual is born with a share of the knowledge held in common by all human begins. This model inspired the simplicity and efficiency of the AICom program. It also allows us to disentangle apparent contradictions within the very same individual and to capture cultural and idiosyncratic peculiarities of any person in a conflict.

It remains to be seen whether AICom can deliver on its promises. Despite its "believe it or not" claims, the new software may make the impossible happen: the common and everyday resolution of conflicts with no courts and no judges, and without regard to time or space. We should remind ourselves of Alice's conversation with the Queen in *THROUGH THE LOOKING GLASS*. Alice doesn't think it possible to believe impossible things. The Queen replies, "I daresay you haven't had much practice...When I was your age, I always did it for half-an-hour a day. Why, sometimes I've believed as many as six impossible things before breakfast."

CHAPTER FOUR

MAKING MEDIATION WORK

I. Matching Parties' Goals with Mediation Styles

What Type of Mediation Do You Need?

by Nancy Kauffman & Barbara Davis[*]

Various types of disputes call for different styles of mediation. The authors discuss the importance of matching the parties' goals and expectations with the appropriate mediator and mediation style in order to resolve a dispute successfully. Even the concept of success in mediation varies; for some parties, the financial aspect of a settlement is of utmost importance while others consider relationship issues more important.

Mediation is becoming the dispute-resolution method of choice for businesses, organizations, and individuals in the United States.[1] ADR, which used to stand for alternative dispute resolution, now has been reframed to mean appropriate dispute resolution, indicating a change from viewing facilitated negotiations as outside the norm to viewing them as fully accepted practices. The reasons for this paradigm shift in grievance-resolution mechanisms are twofold: outcome potential and process control.

---

[*] Ms. Kauffman teaches human resource management, employment law and conflict resolution at the University of North Carolina at Asheville, where she is an associate professor. An experienced arbitrator and mediator, Kauffman serves on several panels, including the American Arbitration Association, FMCS and USPS/NALC panels.

Ms. Davis has a private mediation practice in Asheville, N.C. She was founding executive director of The Mediation Center in Asheville and a founding member and past president of the Mediation Network of North Carolina. Ms. Davis has practiced law as a public defender and legal services attorney. She also teaches mediation courses at the University of North Carolina-Ashville and UNC-Charlotte, and directs the campus mediation program at UNC-Asheville. She has written and co-written books on mediation.

[1] Spafford, Michael; Lawrence Freedman; Connie Reeve, *ADR and the Law Firm of the Future*, DISP. RESOL. MAG., v. 3.2 (1996), page 9.

In terms of outcome potential, mediation can result in significant savings and improved settlement rates. For example, according to the Center for Public Resources Institute for Dispute Resolution, 109 businesses saved more than $75.7 million in direct legal costs in 1994 through the use of ADR to resolve disputes.[2] Most community dispute-settlement centers boast a resolution rate in excess of 90% for clients who voluntarily participate in mediation[3].

But not all conflicts call for cash settlement; not all parties in dispute are motivated by financial incentives. For example, many workplace disputes involve ongoing relationships and, with the low unemployment rate, more businesses are concerned with sustaining relationships. Many conflicts are resolved successfully, without any exchange of money, through behavioral contracts or agreements regarding changed relationships. This underlies the second reason for the growing preference[4] for mediation: process control-participation in decision-making as well as a much fuller opportunity to be heard. Evaluative studies show these aspects—meaningful participation and full self-expression —lead to parties' favorable attitudes toward mediation.[5]

Once the difference between outcome-potential and process-controls mediations is understood, it is important to realize that all mediators are not necessarily equally competent in both areas: facilitating discussions for favorable financial outcomes and facilitating for affording fully participatory party input. The premise of this article is that parties' needs in terms of mediation structure differ, and mediators' styles differ as well. Some mediators are more outcome-oriented; some are more process-oriented.

The desired goal of a mediation helps dictate the choice of mediator and style of mediation. The purposes of this article are threefold: (1) to help people involved in a dispute, whether as a party in conflict, a

---

[2] *Millions Saved in Legal Costs for Business Disputes Resolved Outside the Courts,* SPIDR NEWS, v. 19.3 (1995), p. 2. *See also* Daus, Matthew W., *Mediating Claims of Discrimination,* DISP. RESOL. J., v. 50.4 (1996), p. 41; Pollack, Ellen Joan, *Mediation Firms Alter the Legal Landscape,* WALL ST. J., March 22, 1993, page B1.

[3] The Mediation Center, Asheville, Annual Report (1995), page 5.

[4] According to the Price-Waterhouse Cornell 1997 survey, 89% of U.S. Corporations have used mediation in the last three years; 33 state judicial systems have mandated mediation in domestic relations cases; 87 of 94 U.S. District Courts have established procedures for using ADR (ABA Section of Dispute Resolution, September 3, 1997, unpublished report).

[5] Bush, Robert A. Baruch, *What Do We Need a Mediator For? Mediation's 'Value Added' for Negotiators*, OHIO ST. J. ON DISP. RESOL., v. 12.1 (1996), pp. 18-19.

representative, an advocate or counselor, to better utilize the services of mediators by understanding the different types of mediation that are practiced; (2) to expand the current literature by redefining the categories of mediators; (3) to assist people in dispute with assessing the style of mediator under consideration. First, key terms will be defined and illustrated; next, applications will be discussed; then questions for the mediators will be proposed to aid in assessing both the situation and the mediator.

Definitions

Several terms need to be defined for the purposes of this article: mediation, mediator, evaluative mediation, and facilitative mediation. After these definitions, two new terms will be introduced that build on these standard definitions.

Mediation is a process of facilitated negotiation.[6] Generally it is private and confidential, but if there are several parties or large groups in dispute, there may not be an expectation that discussions will remain confidential. Mediation might be described as a private discussion assisted by an impartial third party, rather than a matter of public or even private judging. In mediation, the people in conflict, not the mediator, control the outcome. It is a consensus-building process.

Caucus is a time when the mediator meets with each party separately. The person conducting the mediation is a neutral who maintains the parties' expectations of confidentiality. The role of the mediator is to facilitate the exchange of information between the parties, who ultimately have the responsibility to reach a conclusion. In some instances, the mediator is known to the parties in advance: a peer or supervisor; in other situations the mediator is an outsider who may or may not have subject-matter expertise. The conclusion reached in mediation may resolve some or all of the issues, or it may simply move the discussion forward. The latter can be valuable if the parties have been unable to advance on their own. Mediators often specialize in specific areas of practice, such as family, complex court cases, community, school, disability, youth, labor, environmental, governmental or international mediation.

Another framework differentiates mediator styles as either evaluative or facilitative. An evaluative mediator assesses strengths and weaknesses

---

[6] *Id.* at 3.

in parties' cases and predicts court outcomes.[7] Facilitative mediators focus more on emotional aspects of disputes, acknowledging and reframing parties' concerns and assisting them in constructing a workable plan for future behavior. Facilitative mediation empowers parties to take hold of the reins of decision-making after airing their differences; it recognizes the parties' inherent right to control their own destinies. Evaluative mediators, on the other hand, are asked to or voluntarily offer to suggest solutions and judgments on the merits of a case.

These categories, evaluative and facilitative mediation, are expanded in this article, with new terminology proposed: outcome-oriented and change-oriented mediation. In outcome-oriented mediation a definite solution is sought; success is measured by a signed agreement. This type works well when the parties do not expect to have a further relationship. Change-oriented mediation, on the other hand, assists parties in expressing their underlying interests and searching for ways to improve their relationship or their situation. Change-oriented mediation is most useful when the parties expect to have a continuing relationship or are looking for emotional healing.

Applications of Mediator Orientation

The two types of mediator orientation will be discussed with examples given for each. Some applications or appropriate uses of outcome-oriented mediation include court-ordered issues; contract disputes; certain consumer cases, such as car sales or repairs; or any distributive issue (See Exhibit One). In these cases, relationships have been severed. For example, in a renter-landlord case, the parties may no longer be in relationship (the tenant has moved out), but they may still need to discuss the return of a security deposit or payment for damages. Worker's-compensation or worker-injury cases might use outcome-oriented mediation, especially if the employee has no plan to return to that employer. In a medical or legal malpractice suit, the doctor-patient or attorney-client relationship is usually terminated, with questions remaining regarding money damages. The parties in an outcome-oriented mediation may have very different expectations of the mediation, ranging from evaluation of facts (what are the strengths and weaknesses of each party's case, what can be an expected result in court, and what are the probabilities of reaching that outcome) to facilitation (helping the parties,

---

[7] *Id.*

who may be experts in the issues being discussed, to communicate in an enhanced way).[8]

The outcome-oriented mediator style includes evaluative mediation in which the mediator assesses the facts of the dispute. In this style the mediator gives an opinion either determining which facts are most salient or what the case value might be in court. There are differing views on the appropriateness of evaluative mediation. Some authors feel it jeopardizes the neutrality of the mediator and the integrity of the mediation process[9]; that is, by assessing the facts or suggesting an outcome, the mediator is favoring one side over the other. Some states' ethical codes explicitly require mediators to refrain from being directive and judgmental; others are silent on the issue.[10] On the other hand, this evaluation could be viewed as similar to settlement conferences conducted by judges who evaluate the strengths and weaknesses of each party's case and urge early settlement. It has been suggested that evaluative mediation be renamed "case evaluation" or "settlement brokering".[11]

It should be noted that it is possible to facilitate an outcome-oriented mediation without evaluation. This is done by listening to parties and then shuttling offers of settlement between them until a final amount is agreed upon by all parties. An example of this is an automobile accident case with personal injury. An outcome-oriented mediator may help parties, typically an injured plaintiff and an insurance adjustor representing the defendant, reach settlement without ever giving an opinion as to case value.

The second type of mediator orientation, change-oriented, includes many employee-employer cases; disputes between neighbors; community issues; disputes between roommates; environmental conflicts; estate and probate contests; and family disputes, such as child custody, marital separation, sibling issues, or care arrangements for elderly relatives (See Exhibit One).

The change-oriented mediator is more concerned with the process of the mediation rather than its outcome, ensuring that parties are able to

---

[8] Riskin, Leonard L. *Understanding Mediators' Orientations, Strategies, and Techniques: A Grid for the Perplexed,* HARV. NEGOT. L. REV., v. 1 (Spring 1996), pp. 23-24.

[9] Kovach, Kimberlee K. and Lela P. Love, *Evaluative Mediation is an Oxymoron,* ALTERNATIVES, v. 14.3 (March 1996), p. 31.

[10] North Carolina Dispute Resolution Commission, STANDARDS OF PROFESSIONAL CONDUCT, adopted May 10, 1996.

[11] Kovach, Kimberlee K., *What is Real Mediation and Who Should Decide?* DISP. RESOL. MAG., vol. 3.2 (1996), page 5.

express their needs in an atmosphere that is safe and conducive to productive discussion. Safety must include both physical freedom from fear of active violence and also psychological freedom from fear of emotional harm resulting from disclosures or discussion in mediation. The change-oriented mediator's concern is in providing a safe discussion zone in which both parties' needs are acknowledged. While some difficult or challenging interactions may be inevitable, in general a change-oriented mediator is geared for productive talk that furthers the interests of both parties. For example, an employee grievance may be mediated in change-oriented mediation style and, through the course of the mediation, it may become clear that the employee does not have a legitimate grievance. However, the employer, upon hearing the employee's perspective, may be willing to make changes in relevant policies, programs, or in the way staff complaints are handled by department supervisors. Similarly, in a child-custody mediation, parties may initially disagree regarding financial arrangements or whether custody is joint or sole. Through change-oriented mediation, the parties may be able to better understand each parent's desire for quality time with the children and their unique financial needs; they may develop a creative shared-parenting arrangement that is also financially feasible, though it may not strictly conform to a statutory formula.

The choice of mediation style becomes clouded when the goals are mixed; i.e, parties may be seeking money damages in a court action, Equal Employment Opportunity complaint, malpractice claim, Americans with Disabilities Act complaint, or an employment grievance, and may also need emotional closure, healing, apologies, a promise of changed behavior, or creative nonfinancial results. Indeed, Bush suggests that all mediation cases have potentially transformative outcomes[12] and that mediation can improve the character and quality of the communication that occurs between the parties as human beings…".[13] [See Exhibit One]

In actuality, distinctions between outcome-oriented and change-oriented cases are not clear-cut. Frequently, unstated needs underlie stated requests, making it especially important for parties or their representatives to be aware that reaching a signed agreement on distributive matters will not change the behaviors that led to the dispute and, if the parties must continue to interact, future disputes can be anticipated. Distinction based solely on whether or not a continuing

---

[12] Bush, Robert A. Baruch and Joseph P. Folger, The Promise of Mediation (San Francisco: Jossey-Bass, 1994), page 113.

[13] *Supra*, note 5.

relationship exists is not always determinative. For instance, in a medical-malpractice case, a patient who was injured may have an interest in emotional healing or reaching closure with the doctor that is equally as important as a financial settlement. A sexual harassment victim may file for a cash outcome but might be more interested in stopping a pattern of harassing behavior that diminishes the self-worth of the victim. [See Exhibit Two]

Once the parties decide to resolve their dispute through mediation, they must ask further questions of themselves and of potential mediators in order to enhance the probability of a successful mediation.

Questions to Ask Yourself

The parties first need to ask themselves a series of questions in order to determine whether they are more interested in the outcome of the mediation or if part or all of the mediation is about changing the behavior of one or more of the parties. The point is to match the needs of the parties with the style of the mediator in order to select an effective mediator for the given situation. This is referred to as assessing the situation. Once a party knows what type of mediation is indicated, it is important to interview potential mediators to ensure a match. Some suggestions follow:

1. Do you expect to have a further relationship with the other party?
   - If yes, then change-oriented mediation is indicated.
2. Do you expect a financial settlement from the mediation?
   - If yes, this might indicate outcome-oriented mediation if there are no relationship issues.
3. Does the mediator need to be very familiar with the subject?
   - Does the dispute involve a complex or technical issue? If yes, can an expert, other than the mediator, provide subject-matter expertise?
4. Does the mediator under consideration have experience with this type of dispute or within the venue/setting (court connected, administrative review)?
   - Someone without context expertise might not be aware of all the implications or requirements of that setting.

5. Do you want a neutral opinion regarding the strengths and weaknesses of the case and/or likely outcome in a hearing or in court?
    - If yes, do you want that opinion to come from the mediator or some other source (judge, attorney, expert)?
6. Are there several issues involved, or is this a mixture of relationship and technical/financial issues?
    - If it is a mixture, you probably want someone who can handle both.
7. With what type of person do you work best?
    - Do you react negatively to either an authoritative person or to someone who does not control the outcome? Do you feel like a valued person when talking with the mediator under consideration?

Questions to Ask the Mediator

1. What do you see as the goal of mediation/How do you define a successful mediation?
    - These questions clearly distinguish mediator style. The outcome-oriented mediator is more likely to talk about a signed agreement; the change-oriented mediator is more likely to talk about forward movement, empowerment, recognition, being heard, behavioral changes, or ask about the parties goals.
2. How do you typically structure a mediation session?
    - Do you always or routinely use caucuses as the main way of sharing information or generating possible solutions? Both types of mediators use caucuses, but what occurs in the caucus may differ. The outcome-oriented mediator may routinely use caucuses to generate and then weigh ideas, while the change-oriented mediator would bring the parties together for this brainstorming. The change-oriented mediator uses caucuses to check-in to see if anything needs to be added, if a party is reluctant to talk in the joint session. Both types of mediators may use a caucus as a way to balance power (if one party has more power, the caucus allows for balancing the time and attention given to each party), to break impasse or conduct risk analysis.

3. Do the parties generally speak for themselves during the mediation, or do the advocates do most of the talking?
   - The change-oriented mediator is more likely to afford the parties the opportunity to speak for themselves; the outcome-oriented mediator is more likely to have the advocates speak for the parties.
4. Do you give your opinion about the strengths and weaknesses of each party's case?
   - An affirmative response indicates an outcome-orientation.
5. What are your areas of subject-matter expertise?
   - Regardless of the situation, whether change-oriented or outcome-oriented, there are times when subject-matter expertise may assist the mediation process. That expertise could be provided by either the mediator or an outside resource.
6. What are your area(s) of process expertise?
   - What types of cases do you have the most experience with? What types of cases are you most interested in mediating (for example, court, business, family, community)? There is a continuum of processes for both outcome-oriented and change-oriented mediators that is mitigated by the situations in which they most often mediate. The family and community mediators are more aware of an ongoing relationship; the court and business mediators may see advocates representing the positions and consequently focus less on the emotional aspects of the disputes. While there is a difference between subject-matter and process expertise, a party involved in a divorce who chooses a mediator with labor expertise and no family mediation experience may find there is not a good fit in terms of either subject-matter or process expertise.
7. At what point do you declare an impasse? Do the parties have input into this decision?
   - A change-oriented mediator is more likely to ask parties whether they want to continue meeting if a case is near impasse; an outcome-oriented or evaluative mediator may unilaterally make the impasse decision.
8. What will be expected of me during mediation?

- How active a role will the mediator encourage me to take? Is there a difference in my role if there is an advocate present?

Other Questions to Ask All Mediators

1. What do you charge for mediation and how?
   - Is there a sliding fee? Do you charge for time spent in scheduling and drafting documents? Do you charge by the day or by the hour? How does your office handle payment?
2. How do you schedule sessions?
   - Do you stay for "as long as it takes," or do you schedule several smaller sessions (perhaps two hours each)? How much time does a case like mine typically take?
3. Where will you mediate?
   - Will it be in the office of one of the advocates, in the mediator's office or another neutral location? Will refreshments be offered?
4. How can I best prepare for the mediation?
   - The mediator might tell you to make a list of the points most important to you.

Exhibit Three demonstrates some of the differences between outcome-oriented mediators and change-oriented mediators during the mediation. Notice that the change-oriented mediator is more likely to validate behaviors or emotional issues. Caucuses are used by both to learn about confidential issues and information, but a change-oriented mediator is more likely to do risk-analysis through questions than evaluation of material. Both types of mediators typically conclude with a written agreement, and both types of mediation sessions may include financial agreements. [See Exhibit Three.]

Conclusion

Just as there are different types of disputes, some with distributive (financial) outcomes desired, and some with relationship issues of primary importance, there are various philosophies of mediation. Matching the expectations of the parties, the issues of the dispute and the methodology of the mediator is most likely to lead to a successful outcome in mediation. Success in mediation is determined in a number of ways—not solely by a signed agreement—and it must be defined according to parties' goals in undertaking mediation. Enhanced communication, forward movement in negotiations, or improved understanding among the parties can also be indications of success. This article has suggested that the parties are empowered not only during the mediation but also in the selection of the mediator, and questions have been suggested to help the parties make an informed selection based on their needs and the approaches taken by mediators.

Exhibit One—Use of Mediation

Type of Dispute	Primarily Outcome-Oriented	Primarily Change-Oriented
Neighbors, roommates	No longer neighbors or roommates	Ongoing relationship
Family (divorce or separation)	Distributive only; parties have both psychologically accepted the divorce	Child custody
Landlord–Tenant	Moved or moving soon	Still a tenant
Employment issues	No longer employed and no emotional attachment to the outcome	Current employee
Consumer or contractor	No future business anticipated	Future business anticipated
Professional malpractice	No further professional relationship and no emotional attachment to the outcome	Future professional relationship expected

Exhibit Two—Continuum of Mediator Styles

Outcome-oriented	Mixed	Change-oriented
Strictly financial issues with no ongoing relationships and no expectation of future dealings between parties, and no emotional healing concerns.	Both financial and interpersonal issues. Principles may be as important to parties as cash award.	Primarily relationship issues with behavioral changes sought. Parties are concerned about how they were treated. Understanding the emotional impact is important.

Exhibit Three—Mediator Styles

<table>
<tr><th>Outcome-oriented</th><th>Change-oriented</th></tr>
<tr><td>More likely to deal with court or complaint settlement issues</td><td>More likely to deal with behavioral issues.</td></tr>
<tr><td>Everyone heard the same thing, so no need to summarize. If clarification needed, generally done without party input.</td><td>Summarize to validate the concerns of each party including emotional impact by acknowledging emotions.</td></tr>
<tr><td rowspan="3">Go to private caucuses with each party. Mediator shuttles to make an offer, get reaction, get counter-offer. Sometimes just listen on first go-around without making offers. May get offers and counter-offers without putting bottom line $ figure on table. Mediator may evaluate information, and make suggestions.

Risk analysis: asking or assessing the strengths and weaknesses of parties' cases, the percentage possibilities of non-mediated outcomes.</td><td>Clarify concerns & issues out loud.</td></tr>
<tr><td>Brainstorm–Explain this process & ask parties to generate alternatives without evaluation–develop list.

Help parties to evaluate ideas; do some reality testing; start to focus them on future behavior.</td></tr>
<tr><td>Might caucus with each party to discover confidential info that is not to be shared at this time. Parties might need to vent strong feelings. Risk analysis to help parties to understand strengths and weaknesses of their cases by asking questions rather than offering mediator opinion, and uncovering likely results of not coming to a mediated agreement. Sometimes helps parties change from positional places and still save face.</td></tr>
<tr><td>Bring parties back to joint meeting–to finalize the details; clarify specifics of the agreement.</td><td>Bring parties back to joint meeting–to finalize details and clarify specifics of future expectations.</td></tr>
<tr><td colspan="2">Write a mediated agreement and complete necessary paperwork depending on source of complaint.</td></tr>
</table>

II. Achieving Creative Solutions in Mediation

The Complete Guide to Creative Mediation

*by Gerald S. Clay & James K. Hoenig**

The willingness and ability to craft creative, collaborative solutions to disputes constitute the very foundation of the mediation process. The mediator, of course, plays a vital role; a skilled mediator "facilitates communication, encourages exchange of information and ideas, tests the reality of parties' perceptions and ideas, advises, suggests, translates what is said to detoxify the emotional climate, and at times recommends and persuades, all in the service of assisting the parties to reach their own agreement." The authors take us step-by-step through the particulars.

Mediation resolves disputes through the assisted exercise of a power which most disputants do not even realize they have until they no longer have it: the power to determine their own outcome by reaching a mutually acceptable resolution of their dispute. While virtually every other dispute resolution process cedes all or part of the power to determine outcome to a third party, mediation is an informal, voluntary, loosely structured process in which the mediator facilitates communication, encourages exchange of information and ideas, tests the reality of parties' perceptions and ideas, advises, suggests, translates what is said to detoxify the emotional climate, and at times recommends and persuades, all in the service of assisting the parties to reach their own agreement.

---

* Mr. Clay is a partner in the law firm of Clay Chapman Crumpton Iwamura & Pulice where he specializes in commercial and construction matters. He is a member of the Public Investors Arbitration Bar Association, the past national director of the AAA's Large, Complex Case Program (Hawaii region) and the chair of the Association's Hawaii advisory council. Mr. Clay earned a B.S. from the University of Pittsburgh and a J.D. from the University of Michigan School of Law. He is co-author of *Before You Sue—How to Get Justice Without Going to Court*, an introduction to commercial mediation.

Mr. Hoenig is a mediator, arbitrator, and conciliator in a wide variety of dispute resolution areas. He holds a B.A. from Stanford University, a J.D. from Stanford Law School and a Ph.D. in psychology from UCLA. Heonig clerked for the Chief Justice of the United States (Warren). He is a member of the AAA's national roster of mediators and arbitrators and a mediator for the Hawaii Supreme Court's Appellate Conference Program. He is co-author of *Hawaii Arbitration Law*.

Properly done, the process is guided by two basic principles: (1) Meeting interests (that is, needs, wants, hopes, fears—e.g., "How do I assure that I can get back and forth to work and run out to see clients as soon as they call?") is more important than taking positions (e.g., "I must have a company car."). (2) Adversarial distributive solutions (e.g., "as we dissolve our partnership, every client you get is one less I get.") are less desirable than collaborative integrative solutions (e.g., "even though we are no longer working together, perhaps we can share advertising and public relations and some support facilities in order to build more clients for both of us.").

Mediation is a no-risk proposition since the parties have the option of trying it first without giving up any right to proceed to arbitration or litigation or interfering in any way with those processes. The basic benefits are well-known to most advocates.

During the last decade, attorneys have been inundated with periodicals, books and seminars regarding mediation. Many law firms have actually designated one or more attorneys to review commercial disputes with regard to suggesting the use of mediation. Probably more mediation occurs through agreement of counsel than by any other initiation process. Particularly with commercial disputes involving clients with long-term relationships, attorneys are regularly advocating the speed, cost-effectiveness and user-friendliness of mediation over an adversarial process.

Business lawyers sophisticated in the advantages of mediation are also advocating inclusion of a contract provision directing parties to use the services of a mediator prior to initiation of litigation or arbitration. Previously standardized arbitration clauses are now being preceded by a requirement that the parties retain the services of a mediator and negotiate, in good faith, before the initiation of any adversarial proceeding. These mediation "embedded clauses" are becoming standard fare at all levels of business, even among the largest businesses in America. General Mills, National Cash Register, as well as the Association of General Contractors, for example, now include an embedded mediation provision in virtually all of their contractual dealings.

Creative Solutions

One of the principal reasons businesses and their attorneys are turning to mediation first is because the process presents an opportunity, beyond the mere exchange of money or other tangible considerations, for creative solutions, as is often seen in employment discrimination or harassment situations and in libel and slander cases. Moreover, the mediation atmosphere of acknowledging that disputes may involve feelings and egos, as well as business considerations, can spur the settlement process by allowing the release and acknowledgement of emotions in a neutral, dignified environment.

One of the authors recently mediated a case which is a superb example of this aspect of mediation. The disputants were the owner of a large property and the master lessee. During the course of the lease, there had been numerous disputes, all of which had been resolved through litigation or arbitration. The disputants' relationship had become so adversarial that, although they respected each other as businesspeople, they had lost the friendship that had existed at the beginning of the lease. The latest dispute was set for a two-week arbitration when one of the attorneys raised the possibility of mediation. Although the parties were willing to agree only to try mediation for one afternoon, within that time the mediator was able to structure a mutually agreeable resolution which allowed each party to obtain some benefits and to "save face." The result of the parties' participating in crafting a collaborative settlement was not only a resolution of the particular dispute, but also the creation of an environment in which they were able to re-establish the cooperative business relationship and friendly social relationship which had previously existed. Although the authors do not suggest that mediation will always salvage or re-establish good relationships as it resolves disputes, it often has that subsidiary benefit, one which rarely, if ever, accrues in court.

Of course, the exchange of money or other items of material value (as would occur in an adversarial proceeding such as litigation or arbitration) is a usual component of compromise and settlement. However, mediation presents an opportunity to expand parameters for resolutions from the mere exchange of value to "expansion of the pie." A resolution may include new or further business dealings or the use of non-monetary values such as recommendations, introductions or apologies. In a recent wrongful termination mediation, one of the authors was able to structure a compromise which included a two-year part-time, low-cost independent consulting contract for the former employee (performing essentially the same services, but physically removed from the company environment and the people and circumstances which led to the conflict and dismissal). The company got services it valued at a good price, and the former employee obtained stature as an independent consultant and the opportunity to leverage that into a new career for herself.

A creative, experienced mediator often enables parties to discover concessions of little value to one party, but of high value (perhaps non-material) to the other. This sort of "high need/low give" concession is often the key to successful settlement and one of the primary reasons mediation works even when previous unassisted negotiation has failed. One of the authors mediated such a solution recently wherein a seemingly intractable delay-of-construction dispute was creatively resolved when the mediator suggested that the shopping center owner/builder purchase a substantial quantity of gift certificates from the tenant, thus providing to the tenant a needed large, immediate cash infusion and to the owner the benefit of substantially increasing patronage for the entire center.

One of the most constructive steps an advocate can take in preparing a client for mediation is to explore with the client such questions as:

- What is the most important thing for you to get out of the process?
- If you were offered an apology, training, (or whatever else might be appropriate under the circumstances), would you reduce your monetary expectation?
- What do you think is the most important thing the other party wants? Are you prepared to give it? In exchange for what?
- In the best of all possible worlds, what would your life look like when the case is over?

These are very different from the usual case-evaluation questions advocates ask their clients, but these are the types of questions that enable an advocate to assist in crafting creative, meaningful, long-term solutions and, most important, to obtain for clients a resolution that will satisfy them.

Creative Process

In addition to a thorough pre-mediation exploration of the client's interests and ideas for "high need/low give" solutions, an effective advocate will carefully select the mediator and assist in designing the process.

Choosing the appropriate mediator for the parties in the particular dispute should involve the exploration of four elements.

First, the mediator should be trained and experienced in the "process" of mediation. The skills of a good mediator, while natural to some, still need to be shaped and sharpened through training and experience. Although there are no nationwide standards and no nationally recognized training or certifying agencies, there are numerous private ADR providers and state-related agencies which provide training (often for volunteer mediators). It is worth inquiring about training credentials prior to selection of a mediator.

Second, it is most often advisable to retain a mediator who possesses technical knowledge regarding the subject matter of the underlying dispute. Although a truly proficient mediator may get by without education in the technical and/or legal aspects of disputes, parties usually find that a mediator possessing knowledge of the legalities, practices and nuances of the business involved will expedite the process.

Third, the "presence" or "gravitas" of the mediator is perhaps the most important yet most difficult element to understand and evaluate. The respect which the mediator generates and the trust which parties place in the mediator's opinions and suggestions can and often do result in success.

Fourth, a final quality of a good mediator is his or her eternal optimism and tenacity in the face of an "impasse." Even where there is great disparity between the parties, there is a certain "magic moment" when, irrespective of their diversity or negative emotion, parties will find a common element because they keep talking. Continuous engagement in the process can ignite the spark necessary to fire the settlement process. Optimism that settlement is possible and tenacity in keeping the parties talking are probably the most important characteristics of a successful mediator.

In general terms, the mediation process begins with an agreement on process followed by an exploration of what the parties perceive has happened and how the parties feel about it. It then moves to consideration of all possible options for resolution, then seeks to reach agreement on which option(s) represent(s) a basis for resolution.

There are usually three stages within this mediation process. The mediator will usually convene the process with an "opening statement" describing his or her background, experience and neutral role and the structure of the process and procedure to be followed. The mediator will emphasize the fact that the parties are in control of all phases of the process, especially compromises and final settlement. The opening statement will also be used to build rapport between the mediator and the individual parties so that later discussions may be frank, full and open.

When the mediator's opening statement is complete, he or she will usually request one party (or its attorney) to present its position in the presence of the mediator and the other party (or parties). When an attorney speaks for the party, the mediator will usually request that the party also describe his or her view of the dispute. The mediator will then turn to the opposing party and repeat the process. These opening statements clarify issues, perceptions and feelings about the dispute. Often, they serve as a vital therapeutic "day-in-court" catharsis which enables the parties to begin to focus on future options for settlement.

After the joint session, the mediator will then begin a process of "caucusing" or, as Henry Kissinger termed it, "shuttle diplomacy." The mediator will meet with a single party, and counsel if present, to begin to explore issues, positions and areas and options for compromise. The mediator may attempt to obtain position shifts and options for solutions during this caucus period. Lastly, the mediator will review information provided by the parties, as well as settlement options, and will request consent to reveal information to the opposing party.

In the same manner, the mediator will further continue the shuttle diplomacy until such time as some sort of settlement seems likely to resolve the dispute.

Mediation, being an informal, flexible process, may be varied by the mediator in numerous ways. Examples might include pre-mediation conferences with attorneys alone, confidential written assessments by the mediator to each of the parties, or many joint bargaining sessions.

One example of process flexibility in a case recently mediated by one of the authors involved a complex construction dispute where attorneys alone were present at the site of the project and decision-making parties were located throughout the world. The mediator structured the process whereby the attorneys first identified all issues in dispute. The mediator then requested each party to present its position on each issue with backup documentation supporting that position. With the consent of the parties, the mediator then presented the positions and that documentation to the adverse parties for response along with responsive documentation. This process continued for approximately three-and-a-half months. Thereafter, the mediator issued a confidential assessment to each party indicating the mediator's opinion of the strengths and weaknesses of each party on an issue-by-issue basis. Thereafter, the mediator called a one-day mediation hearing to be attended by decision-making principals and their counsel. Armed with the parties' understanding of the mediator's confidential assessments, the mediator was able to have decision-makers compromise positions so that a settlement was obtained during the hearing.

Usual Mediation Procedures

Advice concerning case presentation in mediation involves timing, demeanor, confidentiality and surprise. Timing should involve "trading" of concessions. Often, legal counsel, as well as the mediator, may assist a party in determining the scope and nature of a particular concession in order to achieve a desired concession from the other side.

Parties may also want to plan their demeanor so as to achieve maximum effect with the opposing party. Whether to present arguments emotionally or in a "matter-of-fact" manner should be calculated as part of the plan to obtain compromise and concessions. Likewise, the use of new or surprise information may be discussed with counsel and the mediator to obtain maximum effect for concessions from the other party.

Advocates need to view the mediator as their advocate with the other side. Parties typically require the mediator's assistance in planning the presentation of vital information. Of course, this means that parties and advocates must be fully candid, open and trusting with the mediator. The more open and honest the parties are with the mediator, the more likely they are to achieve a satisfactory resolution.

Lastly, at the conclusion of every private session, it is important that the parties always review discussions with the mediator in order to keep confidential information from reaching the other side prematurely (or at all) during the mediation process.

At the conclusion of a successful mediation, usually a settlement agreement is immediately drafted and signed. The parties will be encouraged by the mediator to acknowledge that the settlement agreement is final and binding as to all aspects of their dispute. The settlement agreement is a contract enforceable in court or, if so provided, in arbitration.

A technique which parties may employ to give even greater finality to their settlement agreement is the "stipulated arbitration award." In this technique, the parties, upon settlement, sign a written appointment of the mediator as their arbitrator. The newly appointed arbitrator, however, has no function other than to take the mediation settlement agreement (contract) and sign it as a "stipulated arbitration award." By making the settlement agreement an arbitration award, either party may then take the award to court for confirmation (usually in a brief summary proceeding), following which it may be enforced as if it were a final court judgment. This technique avoids the necessity for one party to sue the other for breach of contract when one party accuses the other of non-performance of its obligations under the settlement agreement.

Lastly, since no document has yet been invented, despite the best efforts of lawyers, which is not subject to different interpretations, it is suggested that parties build into their settlement agreement (or stipulated arbitration award) a further dispute resolution process for any disputes arising out of the settlement agreement. We suggest a two-step mediation/arbitration process to resolve any potential misinterpretations, ambiguities or conflicts.

Other Variations

The mediation process is a "paradigm shift," from thinking solely about who is more right and less wrong, to openly and fully discussing all parties' interests (which include money, legal considerations, and other particular needs, wants, hopes and fears). The mediation process works as well for complex multi-party, multi-issue disputes as for more common two-party disputes. Recently, one of the authors was involved in a construction dispute mediation comprised of three design professionals, a building developer, the contractor and thirteen subcontractor/material suppliers.

Experienced mediators, as opposed to arbitrators or judges, are not bound by structural rules. Often, a mediator, with consent, will consult an independent technical expert for assistance. One of the authors has even obtained the assistance of a trial judge to help overcome an impasse; the other recently conducted a "mini-trial" with cross-examination by counsel during the course of a mediation as "education" for the parties as to what would happen if no settlement was reached. Both mediations succeeded.

Conclusion

To the extent that an advocate can assist his/her party in staying flexible and creative in the process and in the assessment of interests, the level of client satisfaction is greatly enhanced. Statistics show that 85%-90% of cases brought into mediation result in settlement. Although most litigated cases also settle, it is often not until most of the time, cost, risk and stress of litigation has already occurred. With virtually no downside and such great potential benefit, it only makes sense to approach the mediation table long before approaching the courtroom.

III. The Evaluative Process

Using Evaluations in Mediation

by Dwight Golann & Marjorie Corman Aaron[*]

"Evaluation is a legitimate weapon in the mediator's arsenal, one that can be either effective or explosive depending on how and when it is used," say the authors. They provide recommendations for its effective employment as a means of resolving disputes between parties who hold unrealistic views of the merits. The use of evaluation, however, is not without risks, as Golann and Aaron point out. Their article is an effective map that guides readers safely around the potential pitfalls.

Evaluation is a controversial issue. Some mediation theorists believe that the technique has no place in "true" mediation, a purely facilitative process in which parties are left free to make their own judgments about the merits of a case without interference from the mediator.[1] We hold a

---

[*] Mr. Golann is a professor of law at Suffolk University Law School and serves as a commentator for ABC's Good Morning America. He earned a B.A. from Amherst and a J.D. from Harvard Law School. Mr. Golann is the principal author of MEDIATING LEGAL DISPUTES (Little Brown, 1996), and a chapter of LEGAL ISSUES IN CONSENSUS BUILDING, THE CONSENSUS BUILDING HANDBOOK (Sage Publications, 1999).

Ms. Aaron is Assistant Professor at the University of Cincinnati College of Law and serves on the Ohio Commission on Dispute Resolution and Conflict Management. She is the former executive director of the Program on Negotiation at Harvard Law School. Ms. Aaron received a B.A. from Princeton University and a J.D. from Harvard Law School. She is the co-author of MEDIATING LEGAL DISPUTES (Little Brown, 1996), from which this article is drawn.

[1] Some commentators believe that for a mediator ever to evaluate raises ethical questions. For example, the Standards of Conduct for Mediators recently promulgated by the American Arbitration Association, the American Bar Association, and the Society for Professionals in Dispute Resolution state that "A mediator shall conduct the mediation fairly, diligently and in a manner consistent with the principle of self-determination by the parties."

The ABA/AAA/SPIDR standards do not say explicitly whether or not mediators are allowed to evaluate, but the commentary to them states that "Mixing the role of a mediator and the role of a professional advising a client is problematic...A mediator should, therefore, refrain from providing professional advice" and refers to the option of sending parties outside the process for a "neutral evaluation." For an interesting discussion of the practice-of-law issue, *see* Carrie Menkel-Meadow, *Is Mediation the Practice of Law*? and Bruce Meyerson, *Lawyers Who Mediate Are Not Practicing Law*, 14 ALTERNATIVES 57, 74 (June 1996).

different view. Evaluation is a legitimate weapon in the mediator's arsenal, one that can be either effective or explosive depending on how and when it is used.

What is evaluation? It is a process in which a neutral expresses an opinion as to the likely outcome or value of a legal claim or defense were it to be adjudicated. Evaluation can focus on either a single issue or on the overall result in a case. It can be expressed in ranges ("the damages could range from $25,000 to $75,000"), numeric probabilities ("40% chance"), or as a precise number ("a $100,000 case"). An evaluation can be expressed with certainty ("The plaintiff will win...") or studied vagueness ("I have some doubts about...").

Evaluation is sometimes hard to distinguish from "reality testing." Almost all mediators are willing to reality test—that is, to question disputants about the strengths and weaknesses of their cases. In this role, a mediator acts as a devil's advocate, pushing the disputants to become more realistic without completely revealing his or her personal opinion about the merits. However, as mediators become more and more familiar with the facts and arguments, it is almost inevitable that they will form views about how a court would rule on a case. Parties, not expecting mediators to be potted plants, are aware that this judgment-formation process is going on.

Mediators may be less successful than they think at hiding their opinions about the merits. Reality testing is a spectrum in which the line between mere testing and evaluation is not always clear. For example, a phrase such as "What are your thoughts on the causation issue?" is unlikely to be controversial. But such commonly-asked questions as "Do you think there's a problem on causation?"; "How would you answer this argument on causation?"; "Don't you have a real causation problem here?"; or "You don't think that's an issue?" are increasingly likely to be interpreted as evaluative opinions. Even if the language used by a mediator is scrupulously neutral, his or her feelings about the strength of an argument may well show unconsciously in facial expressions and body language. It is likely that litigants perceive evaluation going on in many situations where a mediator would describe his or her behavior as "reality testing."

At the same time, many of the nation's most respected mediators use evaluation in their work, considering it an appropriate tool in certain situations. *See*, *for example*, Jonathan Marks, *Evaluative Mediation—Oxymoron or Essential Tool?*, AM. LAW. (May 1996).

The fact that evaluative input of this nature is common in mediation makes it important for mediators to understand how to do an evaluation properly, and for lawyers to know when to request that such techniques be applied.

Benefits and Dangers

Like most other tactics, evaluation has both potential benefits and dangers. In the case of evaluation, however, both the risks and the advantages are relatively large.

Benefits. An evaluator's primary goal is to change litigants' assessments of the strength of their adjudication alternatives. Often both sides in a legal dispute honestly believe that they are likely to win in court. Mediators find that when parties put their predictions in terms of percentages, their forecasts often total 150% or more; that is, each side thinks that it has a much better than even chance of prevailing. Given these clashing predictions, it is not surprising that even good faith negotiations often reach impasse.

The causes of such misjudgments are complex. Psychologists have demonstrated, for example, that people tend to form perceptions of situations quickly, then unconsciously ignore any information that contradicts their view, a phenomenon called selective perception. People's judgments are also influenced by their roles in litigation, an effect known as advocacy distortion.

For example, in an experiment at Harvard Law School, students were given identical files describing an auto accident, then asked to evaluate the plaintiff's chance of winning in court. Those assigned the role of lawyer for the accident victim assessed her chances of prevailing at a mean of 65%. By contrast, students who were given the same case file but told that they represented the defendant insurance company gave the plaintiff only a 48% chance. Similar discrepancies appeared in the students' estimates of the damages the plaintiff would recover if she won: "plaintiffs" placed the damages at a mean of $264,000, while "defendants" projected only $188,000. Harvard Business School students asked to carry out the same study showed very similar biases. These kinds of advocacy distortions are nearly universal.[2]

[2] These findings are consistent with the results of a long series of experiments showing that the roles people adopt in both litigation and non-litigation contexts often impair their ability to analyze data accurately. *See, for example*, Max. H. Bazerman, *Negotiator Judgment: A Critical Look at the Rationality Assumption*, 27 AM. BEHAV. SCI. 211, 220-22 (1983).

Evaluation can cut through litigants' misjudgments about the merits of a case. When the disputants hear that a neutral person, after studying the facts and listening to the arguments, disagrees with their predictions of victory, they are motivated to look again at the case and ask what the evaluator has seen that they have not. Evaluation can thus help disputants overcome the impact of selective perception, advocacy bias and other factors that distort parties' assessment of the merits.

An evaluation can also satisfy psychological needs. It may give litigants the emotional experience of having a day in court, in which they can present their arguments to a neutral person. If bargainers realize that concessions are necessary, but do not want to move from entrenched positions without having a rationale, an opinion can provide the necessary psychological cover. Similarly, insurance adjusters, government officials, and others who must answer to supervisors and constituencies outside the mediation, often welcome an evaluation because they can use it to deflect after-the-fact criticism of their decision to settle. Finally, evaluations can help to resolve internal disagreements within a bargaining team, for instance by assisting a litigator who sees serious risks in a case persuade an unrealistic client of the need to settle.

Dangers. Unfortunately, evaluations pose dangers that may outweigh their benefits. First, an evaluation may freeze the bargaining process. Once the parties to a mediation know that an evaluation is coming, they are likely to stop negotiating: After all, why confront painful decisions about concessions when the neutral will soon vindicate one's position? But once the evaluation is given, it may be treated as a "take it or leave it" offer. After a respected outsider has stated the "right" or "fair" result in a case, it is very hard for a defendant to offer more, or a plaintiff to accept less, than the number the evaluator has set. The strength of this "take it or leave it" effect is inversely proportional to the confidence of the negotiators in themselves and in the evaluator. The more concerned a bargainer is about being second-guessed by a client or supervisor, the less willing he or she will be to accept a result less favorable than the evaluation.

Equally significant is the potential impact of an evaluation on the mediator's credibility with the litigants. A neutral's greatest asset in bringing about a settlement is the rapport and confidence that he or she develops with the parties and their counsel. As long as litigants see the mediator as an honest, neutral and competent facilitator of the process, they are willing to listen to tough questions, accept coaching about their bargaining tactics, and consider settlement recommendations that require painful compromises.

If, however, a mediator delivers an evaluation too quickly or in the wrong way, the "losers" in the evaluation are likely to react badly. A party, its lawyer, or both may decide that the neutral has "gone over to the other side." Perhaps, they think, the neutral has been duped by clever arguments, or seduced by promises of future business. Indeed, if the evaluator disagrees with both sides, as is quite possible, everyone can be left angry. Once this happens, even the most innocent comment or gesture by the mediator will be filtered through feelings of suspicion and antagonism. A badly-done evaluation can destroy the mediator's power to influence the losers, and perhaps everyone, in a case.

There are less dramatic dangers as well. Evaluators focus on the legal merits and may fail to address less obvious barriers which may be frustrating a settlement. If the problem, for example, is that a key decision maker in any settlement is not at the bargaining table, an evaluation is unlikely to uncover the issue. If the obstacle is a party's unresolved feelings of grief, a lawyer's anger, or other strong emotions, an evaluation, with its emphasis on legally-relevant facts, will not deal with it. In general, evaluation does not address the hidden issues that often drive lawsuits. More seriously, evaluation tends to hide these issues because it focuses the disputants solely on the legal merits of the case. Evaluation, in other words, often "solves" the wrong problem and, by doing so, obscures serious hidden causes of impasse.

All this said, the right kind of evaluation, done at the right point and handled in the right way, can be the ingredient that breaks a seemingly-hopeless deadlock.

How to Give an Effective Evaluation

Whether to evaluate. Our basic advice about whether to evaluate is "only if necessary." When it is not required to break an impasse, evaluation should not be used. It should not be applied on the theory that "it won't hurt and might help." In fact, evaluation can hurt the process, making its use inherently risky.

The fundamental diagnostic questions that a mediator should ask in every dispute are the following:

- What obstacles are preventing the parties from settling this dispute themselves?

- What mediative strategies are most likely to overcome these barriers and bring about a settlement?

In most cases, the barriers that are frustrating agreement, such as procrastination, the need to vent arguments and emotions, poorly conducted positional bargaining, lack of information or hidden psychological issues, do not relate to the parties' view of the merits. Specific mediative strategies are available to address these issues,[3] and evaluation is simply not appropriate.

In some situations, however, even after other barriers have been diagnosed and treated, the major obstacle to settlement remains the parties' (or their lawyers') inability or refusal to accurately assess the value of their trial alternative. Even pointed reality testing has not (or is unlikely to) overcome the effects of selective perception, advocacy bias and other psychological forces that distort litigants' perceptions.[4] In such situations, a mediator's only remaining options may be either to conduct an evaluation or admit defeat. If evaluation is the mediator's BATL (Best Alternative to Litigating[5]), it should be attempted.

When to evaluate. As should be clear from this discussion, we believe in delaying an evaluation until as late in the mediation process as possible. Waiting serves several important purposes. First, it allows the mediator to explore fully the other possible obstacles to settlement. If, for example, a key issue in a dispute is a party's need to express grief over a loss or anger at a business partner, deferring an evaluation allows the mediator to discover the issue and work on it. This kind of exploration is much more difficult after an evaluative "verdict" has been handed down.

Even if the problem is limited to the legal merits, it does not follow that an evaluation is always required. The cause of the parties' differing assessments of the merits may be that one side lacks key information; if so, a mediator's initial response should be to arrange a data exchange. If, instead, the problem is that one side fears that a settlement would create a precedent, a neutral should focus on confidentiality guarantees. In our

---

[3] For a discussion of these and other barriers and specific strategies to address them, *see* GOLANN ET AL., MEDIATING LEGAL DISPUTES (Little Brown, 1996) chapters 6-8.

[4] For a discussion of other psychological forces that can distort a litigant's assessment of the legal merits, and methods to deal with them other than evaluation, *see* GOLANN ET AL., MEDIATING LEGAL DISPUTES, *id.* at 223-33.

[5] Our apologies to Roger Fisher and William Ury, the inventors of the concept of Best Alternative to a Negotiated Agreement, or "BATNA." *See* R. FISHER, W. URY AND B. PATTON, GETTING TO YES (1991) pp. 97-106.

experience, it is usually possible to solve many merits-related problems without the need for an explicit evaluation by the mediator.

A second reason not to evaluate quickly is that a mediator will have more time to build and strengthen the parties' trust. As the process goes forward, parties and lawyers get to know the mediator much better on both a professional and a personal level. In formal sessions, the participants are able to watch the mediator in action and observe how he or she handles challenges. During informal conversations and telephone contacts, the parties and counsel begin to get to know the mediator as a person. In this way, an effective mediator can gradually build up the disputants' trust and confidence. The mediator can then draw on this reserve to cushion the shock of an unwelcome opinion on the merits. Also, the mediator will have the opportunity to learn more about the parties in order to phrase his or her evaluation in terms that will be most palatable to the audience.

In addition, when a mediator prefaces the evaluation with questions and discussion of the merits, the parties often become more realistic about their cases, narrowing the scope of any opinion that the mediator must offer. The litigants may also realize that weaknesses in their case which they had hoped to keep hidden are in fact apparent to the other side. Finally, the disputants see that the mediator has heard them out and is seriously grappling with the facts and arguments they raise. The participants also learn that the mediator is raising their strongest arguments with their adversaries. As the mediation progresses, then, the disputants appreciate both that the mediator is giving them a fair hearing and has "done the homework." They are able to come to terms with the fact that the holes in their case are known.

There is one final "when" issue: Should a mediator obtain the consent of the parties before going forward with an evaluation? At one level, this is an issue of contract. Some mediation agreements require neutrals to get the assent of all parties before offering an evaluation, while other forms leave the issue to the mediator's discretion.[6] A mediator owes participants the obligation to discuss process issues. But if, after this is done, the parties choose to remain in the mediation, it is

---

[6] For example, the model agreement developed by the CPR Institute of Dispute Resolution requires that all parties assent before an evaluation can be given, but the standard JAMS/ Endispute agreement leaves the issue to the mediator. The American Arbitration Association has no specific rule on the subject, but as noted in note 2, the ABA/AAA/SPIDR STANDARDS OF CONDUCT FOR MEDIATORS can be read to define "neutral evaluation" as a process separate from mediation.

best that the neutral retain the discretion to evaluate if necessary to stimulate a settlement.

Our overall advice about when to give an evaluation is this: Evaluate as late in the process as possible. As a rule of thumb, never do so until at least the first round of caucuses is completed. Only consider evaluating after you have had a reasonable chance to diagnose and treat other obstacles to agreement, using less risky tactics such as reality testing, and have talked with the disputants about your intentions. In our view, evaluation should be the final, never the first, arrow in a mediator's quiver.

What Standard to Apply?

The most common standard used in evaluations is one of prediction: The neutral attempts to forecast how an arbitrator, judge, or jury would resolve certain issues or the entire case, if the parties elected a binding decision.

This predictive standard may seem self-evident, but in practice it is not. Mediators sometimes focus on how they personally would decide a case. This is irrelevant, however, since neutrals rarely serve as judges in their own unsuccessful mediations.[7] This standard is also dangerous because it puts the mediator into the position of personally rejecting one or both parties' arguments, making it even more likely that they will come to view him or her as an enemy.

Another standard mediators sometimes apply is: "What will it take to settle this case?" In other words, given the negotiation dynamic, what package of terms is likely to be minimally acceptable to everyone in the dispute? If, for instance, one side is stubbornly unrealistic about the likely court outcome, a "What will it take?" opinion might bend the proposed terms toward that view in order to secure agreement. Although there is nothing inherently wrong with this approach, a serious problem arises when disputants think that they are hearing a pure merits-based evaluation but instead receive a "What will it take?" recommendation. For a mediator to offer a settlement recommendation under the guise of a legal evaluation is both unethical and capable of creating serious practical problems when parties discover that they have been misled.

---

[7] The exception, of course, is the process known as "med-arb," in which the disputants consent to have the mediator render a binding decision if they cannot reach agreement.

Evaluators should give their best "straight" prediction of how the likely decision maker would resolve an issue or case. However, when the litigants explicitly agree to receive a settlement recommendation rather than a merits evaluation, then a "What will it take?" opinion is appropriate.

Structuring the Evaluation

The first issue for a mediator to consider is whether he or she will personally perform the evaluation, or instead refer it to a person outside the process. There are many advantages to having an outsider give the opinion. First, it distances the mediator from the process, greatly reducing the risk that a disappointed disputant will hold the results against the mediator. Second, the mediator and lawyers can select an evaluator with the credentials most likely to impress the parties, without concern about balancing evaluative credentials with facilitative skills. If, for example, the parties would be most swayed by a prediction from an eminent jurist, they can retain a former chief justice without worrying about whether he or she knows how to mediate.

A third advantage of going outside is that it allows the mediator to focus energies on a single role: that of facilitator. Fourth, it solves the nagging issue of what a mediator who also evaluates should do with any information that may have been disclosed on a confidential basis in caucuses.[8]

There are practical difficulties, however, with using an outside evaluator. First, unless the two roles are assigned at the outset, making arrangements for an outsider to come in will usually require adjournment of the process and disrupt its momentum. When parties are allowed to cool off, they often retreat from even the tentative compromises that they have made. Second, retaining an outsider is more expensive than having the mediator give an opinion, and many cases will not support the cost of additional briefing. Finally, even with the mediator's assistance, the parties may be unable to agree on who should perform the evaluation. For these reasons, particularly when the issue on which the parties disagree is relatively clear-cut, a mediator will often find it preferable to take on the task.

---

[8] One possible solution is for the mediator to disclose that his or her assessment rests in part on "secret ammunition" confided by one side. Among other things, this makes it easier for each party to understand the neutral's opinion.

Limit the issues. The next question is how much of the case to evaluate. Novices often assume that an evaluation must cover the entire dispute, but this is not so. The legal issue driving the parties' impasse may be a relatively narrow one (for instance, will the liquidated damages clause of a contract be enforced?). If so, there is no need to evaluate other issues on which the parties are closer to agreement. Indeed, if the evaluator's view of those other issues differs from that of the parties, evaluation would stimulate disagreement rather than resolve it.

Piggyback whenever possible. A corollary to not evaluating issues unnecessarily is to build on the parties' opinions as much as possible. A plaintiff, for example, may have a realistic take on liability but an inflated view about damages. If so, it is more effective for an evaluator to say that he or she will accept the party's liability percentage "for argument's sake," although perhaps noting mild disagreement with it, then press the evaluator's opinion about the likely damages. It is easier to change a person's mind on one issue than two, and an evaluator's "concession" on one point will often induce disputants to accept his or her views about other, more controversial issues in the case.

Think about who needs to be influenced. One's tendency is to assume that evaluations are done solely for people in the mediation room. This is often not true. The real cause of an impasse may be a decisionmaker in a distant city who has not participated in the mediation or felt its impact. Or negotiators may be hesitating out of fear that a decision to compromise will expose them to criticism from supervisors or outside constituencies. If the problem is absent decisionmakers, the evaluation can often be used as an event to get their attention, and sometimes their actual presence at the scene. There is something about the idea of even a non-binding "verdict" being handed down that brings a case onto the radar screens of persons who have felt too busy to pay attention to it before.

If the issue is fear of being second-guessed, and the potential critic cannot be brought to the mediation, it may make sense to put the evaluation in the form of a written opinion that a party can take to his or her constituency or place in a case file. If an evaluation is to be used to convince persons outside the process, the credentials and public reputation of the evaluator become more important than his or her personal qualities. In such circumstances, a mediator will not be able to use the trust he or she has built up during the proceeding to sell the result, and may want to select a third person whose resumé will impress an absent decisionmaker.

Example: A mediator was working on a dispute between a government loan agency and a borrower who had defaulted on his mortgage. As the mediation went forward, it became clear that the loan foreclosure had been handled badly by the original lender, making it difficult now for the agency, which had inherited the loan, to collect on it. Still, the agency refused to settle the case. In caucus, the agency disclosed that it needed a letter from the mediator evaluating the case and endorsing the result in order to settle. The agency was not willing to have the letter shown to the borrower; instead, it would be used by the agency to convince a review board to endorse the deal. The borrower's counsel agreed to these terms, the mediator wrote the letter, and the case was settled.

Create an effective format. Before undertaking an evaluation, consider what format will maximize its contribution to a settlement.

- What data will the evaluator receive? For example, will the parties rely on existing documents or prepare special briefs? Note that special briefing is more likely to be necessary if an outsider is brought in to do the evaluation.
- Do the parties need the feeling of having a "day in court"? Will the evaluation have more weight if they are allowed to make formal arguments? If so, consider conducting the process in a "moot court" format.
- Should the opinion be delivered in caucuses or during a joint session? If it is delivered to the disputants in each others' presence, the losers may feel humiliated, creating anger that will disrupt the process. If, on the other hand, the evaluation is presented in separate caucuses, the disputants may suspect that the evaluator is delivering different opinions to the two sides.

We strongly favor delivering evaluations in caucus, not because we wish to skew the results, but because doing so allows us to deliver the opinion using forms of phrasing and arguments calculated to help the listeners to accept our opinion. In that format one can, for example, piggyback one's views on bits of confidential information that each party has shared. The evaluator could, for instance, concede that an opposing witness might be lying as that party has been arguing but go on to say that the witness has a demeanor that would impress a jury. Proceeding in caucus allows an evaluator to more frankly acknowledge strengths in each side's arguments, and build on that foundation to deal with more controversial issues.

The problem of demonstrating that the evaluator is delivering the same opinion in each caucus is a real one. It can be addressed, for example, by writing the evaluation on a flip chart and carrying the chart from one caucus room to another. Putting the opinion in writing has the extra benefit of giving visual reinforcement to unwelcome news that parties may have difficulty in understanding and retaining, due to the "selective perception" problem mentioned earlier.

Consider language, culture and commonality. A mediator's choice of language, tone and cultural referents in presenting an evaluation will greatly influence its impact on the parties. One's individual and cultural background is what it is. But a bit of chameleonship in style and manner can increase the persuasiveness of the opinion, particularly when its content is critical. If, for example, one party (whose team may include a lawyer, expert and several client representatives) is informal, given to slang and colorful metaphor, it may be effective to use that style in their caucus. If the other party is more formal, deliberate and analytical, the mediator will do well to choose a tone and language likely to resonate with that group. In short, this advice on choice of style and manner is "When in Rome...," particularly when the substance of the message is relatively unfavorable. This is another reason to present evaluations in private caucuses with each side.

Emphasize differences in perspective. It is sometimes difficult for disputants to accept that someone who has the same information as they do nevertheless disagrees strongly with their judgments. One defense is to emphasize that in doing an evaluation, you are not giving your personal opinion about what is a fair resolution, but instead are predicting how other people (a judge or jury) would react.

We also note the special advantages of being neutral. Because we are not arguing the case and have no personal stake in its outcome, we are free to think about it from the perspective of an uninvolved person. It is difficult for disputants to admit that their judgment may be distorted by their roles in the case (although they readily see that the condition affects their opponents and perhaps their clients). Our practice is to mention the point but not to stress it heavily.

Distance yourself from the opinion. As we have noted, it is very important that the mediator not become personally identified with an unwelcome opinion. One method of doing this is to follow the guidelines set out above: empathize with the problem that this creates, note that you will never sit in judgment on the matter, use the language of prediction, and so on.

Another way for mediators to distance themselves is to use the technique known as decision analysis. Decision analysis is a mathematical technique that allows analysts to break down a case into a series of choices and chances (win on summary judgment or not; win or lose at trial; recover a high, medium or low verdict; etc.). The case is then "graphed out" in a way that lets the parties see the possible outcomes in the litigation and weigh the probabilities of each one. Individual choices and chances are then multiplied out, yielding an overall monetary value for the case. Decision analysis allows mediators to talk with disputants in a relatively dispassionate way about what could happen if a dispute is adjudicated. It allows both the neutral and the parties to "let go" of emotional arguments and consider litigation risks in a logical manner. Also, because participants are asked to give an opinion on individual issues before they see the ultimate result, they can talk about issues without feeling obligated to distort the percentages to produce the outcome they desire. For this reason, decision analysis often provides a good format in which to give a case evaluation.[9]

Conclusion

Evaluations rarely end cases themselves. Rather, they provide a strong "dose of reality" that helps break down differences in how the parties assess their no-agreement alternatives. Assuming an evaluation is necessary, therefore, mediators need to think in advance about how to use them to promote further negotiations.

1. Is reflection or consultation time needed? In simpler cases where the decisionmakers are present, a mediator can give an evaluation orally and then ask for a new offer. But when the case is complex, the results shocking to the listeners, or the evaluation calls for an offer outside a negotiator's authority to settle, an adjournment will probably be needed.

2. What kind of bargaining should occur after the evaluation? Who should make the next concession? Are inventive terms possible that would obscure or cushion one side's defeat in the

---

[9] For an explanation of how decision analysis can be used in mediation, *see* Marjorie C. Aaron, *The Value of Decision Analysis in Mediation Practice*, 11 NEGOTIATION J. 123 (1995) and M. AARON AND D. HOFFER, Chapter 11 *in* MEDIATING LEGAL DISPUTES.

> evaluation? Should the mediator make a compromise proposal (usually but not always mirroring the evaluation results)? If so, should the proposal be made on a "What if?" basis that allows each side to conceal its willingness to agree unless the other side has assented as well?[10]

Evaluations can help break through seemingly impassable merits-based barriers. A mediator should not use one, however, without some plan for what he or she will do on the other side to bring the negotiation to closure.

We do not advocate that evaluation be used in most cases, or even as a tool of first (or second) resort in those situations where it is likely to be helpful. Nor do we contemplate a model in which evaluation overshadows the facilitative aspects of mediation: quite the contrary. We do suggest that, despite the controversy that the phrase "evaluative mediation" has inspired in some quarters, it is no more than an extension of the practice of "reality testing" which has long been a part of mediation orthodoxy. When traditional techniques fail to persuade a party holding a deeply-held, but unrealistic, view of the merits, direct evaluation may be the mediator's only alternative to declaring an impasse. In these circumstances only, evaluation appears to us to be appropriate. Because of its inherent risks, however, evaluation should be undertaken only with skill and careful attention to its role within the mediation process.

---

[10] The essence of a "What if?" proposal is that the mediator proposes the same package of settlement terms to all sides, but under the ground rule that each side can tell the mediator in confidence whether the package is acceptable. If so, there is a deal. If not, the rejecting party will never learn whether its adversary was willing to compromise. This format makes it easier for a party to explore a compromise without endangering its bargaining position if an agreement is not reached.

IV. Risk Analysis

Practical Tips for Using Risk Analysis in Mediation

by James E. McGuire[*]

Sometimes a "reality check" is needed during a mediation when parties seem hopelessly deadlocked over the value of a claim. Risk analysis may be one answer, says the author. Its skillful use can steer the parties toward a realistic evaluation of a fair settlement range, as shown in this practical, by-the-numbers article drawn from an actual mediation.

This article discusses the use of risk analysis[1] as a tool for mediators. In money disputes, parties may be very far apart and a settlement seems unlikely. In such cases, a suggestion to "split the difference" rarely works and may leave both parties unhappy with the mediation process. Risk analysis provides a more structured approach the parties can use to re-evaluate their perceptions of the fair settlement range of the claim. The facts below derive from an actual mediation, although the names and certain facts have been modified to preserve confidentiality.

Background

Fifteen years ago, Peter Plaintiff's father died, leaving him $350,000 in blue chip stocks and a vacation home worth another $350,000. Peter was then 50 years old, married, with two adult children. He made

* The author is a member of the law firm of Brown, Rudnick, Freed & Gesner and is chair of its ADR Practice Group. He is on the mediation/arbitration panels of the American Arbitration Association, NASD Securities Regulation and the CPR Institute for Dispute Resolution. Mr. McGuire earned a B.A. from Harvard and a J.D. from Boston University School of Law.

1 As a mediator, I use the term "risk analysis" when introducing the concept. Litigators and trial lawyers are well- acquainted with the phrase and few have any exposure to terms such as "decision analysis" and "expected value." Howard Raiffa's book, THE ART AND SCIENCE OF NEGOTIATION (Harvard University Press, 1982), has introduced these concepts to business and management schools for many years. One of the seminal articles discussing application of these concepts to the world of mediation is Marjorie C. Aaron's *The Value of Decision Analysis in Mediation Practice*, NEG. J. 123-33 (April 1995). This article was prompted, in part, by a footnote in her article noting: "A separate article could be written on tricks and techniques for a mediator introducing decision analysis to parties and counsel unfamiliar with the approach." *Id.* at 133 n.5.

$40,000 per year as a technical writer and owned a modest home, with mortgage. Peter's knowledge of investments started and ended with managing the family joint checking and savings accounts. His wife, Mary, did not work outside the home and had less investment knowledge than Peter. With this inherited wealth, they wanted to have a little more money to spend and save for their retirement. "I also wanted to make more money, but not by investing in anything too risky," said Peter.

David Defendant ran a small suburban investment company in Peter's hometown. When Peter first came in, David remembers him saying, "Now that we're rich, I want to spend more time traveling with Mary. Can you make my portfolio of blue chip stocks perform better?" The portfolio would be one of the larger accounts in David's office. He agreed to handle the account and to make investment recommendations to Peter and Mary. David also agreed to make the financial information available to an accountant who did the tax returns for Peter and Mary.

Over the next five years, the blue chip stocks were sold. The proceeds were invested in various mutual funds and in limited partnerships, most of which were based on real estate investments. Peter and Mary sold the vacation house they had inherited because they didn't want to use it and didn't want to pay the taxes and other expenses of a second home. The proceeds were turned over to David to add to the portfolio.

From time to time, Peter would ask David if he could take money out of the account for various trips with Mary. David always told him that it was his money and that he could afford to take it out. Sometimes, David would report to Peter that money had been made through the sale of investments or from dividends. He would ask Peter and Mary if they wanted the cash or if they preferred to have it reinvested. They sometimes took the cash, but they never kept a record of how much they were withdrawing from the account.

Early last year, Peter and Mary were at a neighborhood party celebrating Peter's retirement. Peter bragged modestly that he and Mary were all set because of their investments. He mentioned that they had a great deal of money in limited partnerships. Someone mentioned that he thought limited partnerships were very risky. "They're very risky and provide lousy returns," said the local sage. "Why do you think the brokers get such a high commission for selling those things?" Following this discussion, Peter and Mary sought a second opinion about their investments.

The new broker looked at their portfolio and didn't recognize many of the mutual funds or the limited partnerships. He said he thought he could provide a better portfolio, one more suited to their current needs, and with an appropriate level of risk.

Peter and Mary wrote a letter to David, asking that the entire portfolio be transferred. The new broker quickly recommended that they sell as many as possible of the limited partnerships in the secondary market. He also recommended that they seek legal advice to evaluate whether they had any claims against the former broker.

Peter and Mary discussed their situation with a lawyer, Paul, who told them that he thought they had a good case. He said that David's investments weren't appropriate for them given their income, their lack of financial sophistication and their stated objectives that their investments not be "too risky." He agreed to take the case on a contingency basis, collecting his fee only if there was a recovery from the broker and his employer.

Approximately four months before the case was scheduled for trial and before the parties had exchanged information from their experts, the court recommended that the parties try mediation.

Mediation As Information Exchange

The parties described the background facts in the initial joint mediation session. There was a certain amount of tension in the air, particularly since it was the first time Peter and Mary had seen David following the transfer of the account. No formal demands or offers of settlement were put on the table by either party.

In the first caucus, David and his attorney both asked: "What are the plaintiffs complaining about? This account made money! We started with $350,000 in stocks and $350,000 in a house they didn't want and couldn't afford. When we transferred the portfolio, it had a market value of nearly $1,400,000. We doubled the value, not counting all the cash that was taken out. The case is frivolous and there aren't any damages, even assuming liability."

In the first caucus, Peter and Mary's lawyer stated that the other side was mixing apples and oranges. "No one is complaining about the mutual funds. Those investments made money. The limited partnerships, on the other hand, were not suitable and didn't make money. If the entire portfolio had been invested in conservative investments earning 8%, the portfolio would have been worth more than $2 million. Even at 4% and without compounding, which is worse than leaving it in a savings account, the money would have earned more than $400,000. Surely a jury is going to find that we should reasonably have expected more than savings book interest on these investments. Our damages, on an alternate investment theory, will be in the range of $700,000-$800,000, but we would settle today for $400,000-$500,000."

David and his lawyer pointed out: "An alternate investment theory must include the entire portfolio, otherwise the plaintiffs are simply cherrypicking. They liked the investments that worked and considered unsuitable those that did not. What's more, some of the limited partnerships performed exceptionally well. The plaintiffs now want to drop those from their suit! Even if one looks only at the limited partnership investments, this account does not look bad. The total of cash paid out, the residual value of the investments that were in the portfolio when it was transferred and the tax savings realized by the plaintiffs show that the plaintiffs didn't lose money on these investments."

The plaintiffs replied that David's numbers were all wrong. "We disagree on the amount of cash received and the value of the investments when we left. We didn't go into these investments for tax reasons and tax credits shouldn't be counted in valuing whether we lost money."

The parties had not exchanged expert reports because the experts had not completed their analyses. Both parties acknowledged that the basic facts about the portfolio performance would be relevant and admissible at trial. The parties agreed to an informal information exchange in connection with the mediation.

After some discussion in the second joint session, the parties had narrowed their disagreements on the facts to certain key points. The primary differences were:

1. Should portfolio performance include stock plus limited partnerships when the plaintiffs complained that only the limited partnerships were unsuitable?

2. Should portfolio performance be based on the market value of the partnership interests when the portfolio was transferred or on the actual proceeds realized when some limited partnerships were sold in the secondary market?

3. Should the two remaining limited partnerships be valued at current valuation or discounted for lack of liquidity since "value" will be realized only as part of the general partner's planned liquidation over the next year?

4. Should the remaining limited partnership interests be discounted because projections for distributions on liquidation may not in fact be achieved?

5. Should tax savings be an offset to the plaintiffs' claimed damages?

6. Have the plaintiffs been damaged in any amount?

The information exchanged eliminated significant areas of disagreement and sharpened the focus on the remaining issues. Resolution of these remaining issues by a further information exchange was not possible. The parties understood that their differences were fundamental. Even when they agreed on the facts, each side assessed the value of the case differently because of different assumptions about what a court would allow as damages. Both sides had plausible legal arguments and citations to prior cases that the court could decide either way.

Peter's counsel was not prepared to discuss specific damage calculations, but simply reiterated that, using an alternate investment model, his experts would prove damages in the $700,000 to $1 million range. He made a formal settlement demand of $600,000. David and his counsel formally countered at $25,000. In separate confidential sessions, each party indicated that there was some flexibility in its position. On condition that it be kept confidential, the plaintiffs said that they would accept a settlement in the $400,000-$500,000 range. The defendants said that they could go as high as $50,000.

As a device to assist the parties in evaluating their positions, I decided to discuss risk analysis with them.

Plaintiffs' Risk Analysis

I met first with Peter, Mary and their lawyer. I started by asking each of them what he or she thought the court should award as money damages at the conclusion of the case, assuming that the court found liability. The initial answers were: "I don't know"; "It depends"; and "In the range of $600,000 to $1.2 million." I asked each to write a dollar amount on a piece of paper. What should the court award as damages?

> This is a thought experiment. You are the judge. You have written a decision awarding the plaintiffs damages because limited partnerships were not suitable investments for them and

> the plaintiffs rightfully relied on representations of the defendant that they were. You have accepted the 'alternate investment' damage model proposed by the plaintiffs. Now write down the number to complete this sentence. 'Accordingly, I hereby award damages to the plaintiffs in the amount of $__________.'

Starting with Mary, I asked each of them to read the amount they had written down. Each had written $600,000. None of them could say exactly why they thought the court should find damages in that amount. At the end of the exercise, Paul said, "This proves my point. We've told you that we would settle in the $400,000-$500,000 range. The defendants have offered nothing."

We discussed the fact that before the court would consider how much to award as damages, the plaintiffs would have to persuade the court that they rightfully relied on the defendant's recommendations. All three stated that they understood this and that if the court found no liability the case would end: the plaintiffs would recover nothing. I then asked them to write down their belief of likelihood that the plaintiffs would win on the issue of liability.

Peter and Mary stated that they felt the question of liability was 50-50. Paul, the lawyer, said that his clients' case was 60-40 on liability. I suggested we use 50%, because the math would be easier to follow. I pointed out that the technique could be used with different assumptions and that their views of the likelihood of success could also change if new facts were learned or if developments warranted a re-evaluation of the assessment.[2]

I applied that risk assessment to the plaintiffs' own estimate of what they thought the court should award as damages.

> "Using your numbers and assuming no other variables, the risk-adjusted settlement value of the case is $300,000, less transactional costs." [$600,000 x .5 = $300,000]

---

[2] There is an obvious second reason to use 50%. Using 50% even as an illustration aids the parties in narrowing the perceived gap in valuation. Even though the attorney may have special expertise in assessing legal liability, the ultimate arbiter of risk is the client stakeholder who stands to lose or gain based on some future chance event. If the clients had estimated the likelihood of success at 70%, I would have used the attorney's estimate of 60%, with the same explanation that I was illustrating a technique that they could use with different assumptions of success.

I then asked the parties to focus on what they thought was the likelihood that the court WOULD award the damages that they thought the court should award. That concept required further discussion about the reasons why a court might find liability and yet not give damages—in the amount sought or in any amount at all—to the plaintiff. It didn't require that the plaintiffs agree on each reason or assign a separate likelihood for each variable. I merely requested that they review what they knew to be the practical risks of recovery of damages in the projected amount. Ultimately, the parties knew that an award of damages in the desired amount was an independent variable and did not follow automatically from a finding of liability.

I then asked the plaintiffs to repeat the same exercise as they had for liability.

> "What do you think is the probability that the court will award at least $600,000 in damages?"

I explained that the court could award any amount between $1 and $600,000 or more. In this exercise, I wanted to know only their judgment as to whether the award would be at least $600,000. This time the answers had a greater range: 40-60; 75-25; 50-50. I suggested that they should explore the reasons why their own views differed so greatly while I met with the other side. I explained that since liability and damages were independent variables, it was appropriate to consider $300,000 to be the lodestar[3] for calculating the risk-adjusted value of the claim based on the likelihood of a damage award in the amount requested. We then did the math.[4] A lodestar of $300,000 with a probability of 75% has a value of $225,000; a 50% probability—$150,000; a 40% probability—$120,000.

---

[3] Lodestar is a concept well known to securities lawyers and, particularly, class action counsel. In a fee application, the amount of time spent multiplied by the hourly rate is termed the lodestar. The court may award a multiple (greater or lesser than 1) of the lodestar based on various success factors. In this case, I borrowed the phrase to capture the concept of expected value. The word resonated with the plaintiffs' lawyer. There is nothing magical about the term, but sometimes it is easier to build on the familiar than it is to introduce the parties to new terminology.

[4] There are certain liberties taken in doing the math this way, but it captures the basic notion that liability and damages are independent variables and captures the basic notion of risk-adjusted settlement values. The purpose is not to determine rigorously the mathematical outcome, but to aid the parties in their internal assessment of their position.

Finally, I asked whether they thought they would likely spend any more money getting the case ready for trial. The plaintiffs quickly pointed out that this was on a contingent fee basis and that they would not spend any money. The lawyer, Paul, reminded them that they would be paying for the expert witnesses who would testify on suitability and an accountant who would perform the necessary calculations for the alternate investment scenarios. In addition, he said there were depositions to be taken, exhibits to be copied for trial, and other miscellaneous expenses. The estimated out-of-pocket expenses through trial were $25,000. Though some of these would be recoverable as costs if the plaintiffs were successful, I suggested that any calculation of the present settlement value should be adjusted to account for the costs to be incurred.[5]

I told Peter, Mary and Paul that I would be doing a similar risk analysis with the defendants. The plaintiffs suggested that I have the defendants perform a risk analysis starting with $800,000 as the lodestar. I knew that the plaintiffs were hoping that if the defendants analyzed the case with a higher initial value, that they would end with a higher risk-adjusted value.

Risk analysis, like any other tool, is subject to manipulation. As a technique to aid the parties in evaluating their interests, the exercise is useful even where different initial values are used. Theoretically, any initial value will be adjusted by the probability of that event occurring. The higher the initial value, the less likely that the plaintiffs will achieve that value. In practice, however, where one ends depends, to a certain extent, on where one begins. If the initial lodestar is hopelessly unrealistic, any value, other than zero, for the probability of that event occurring will produce a risk-adjusted settlement value as unrealistic as the initial lodestar.

Rather than point out the obvious fact that the plaintiffs were attempting to manipulate this tool, I told them that I would request the defendants to perform a risk analysis using $800,000 as the amount the plaintiffs believed the court should award to them. Since I wanted the plaintiffs to reflect on what risk analysis had suggested to them as the fair settlement value of their case, I believed that the plaintiffs would be

[5] Under the American rule, attorney's fees and expenses are not recoverable as an element of damages. Accordingly, the risk-adjusted settlement value should be reduced by the amount of attorney fees and expenses as estimated by counsel to be incurred through trial.

more likely to give greater credence to this tool than if we got sidetracked on this issue.

There was a real danger that in so doing I would violate one of the cardinal rules of mediation: avoid inconsistent actions or statements in separate meetings with each party. Though the plaintiffs' expert had indicated a preliminary range of values based on the alternate investment models and $800,000 was within that range, the plaintiffs' own exercise of predicting what the court should award as damages gave a value of $600,000. That information was obtained in private caucus, however, and the defendants didn't know how the plaintiffs had valued their case. I decided I could honor the request since it was likely that David and his lawyer would understand that the verdict lodestar was itself just another variable in risk analysis.

Defendants' Risk Analysis

David and his lawyer assured me that they were very familiar with risk analysis as an analytic tool. When I met with them, they readily agreed to help build a decision tree as an aid to a fair valuation of the case. I told them that the plaintiffs wanted to get $800,000 and that it would be useful for them to evaluate the case based on that fact. Significantly, the defendants agreed that the case was 50-50 on liability. Despite the positions taken in the first session, the defendants recognized that they could win or lose and had no strong basis for believing that the result, on liability alone, was anything more than a coin flip.

The defendants expressed their strongly held view that none of that mattered since the plaintiffs hadn't suffered any damages. Nonetheless, I asked them to test that view by assessing the probability that: "If the plaintiffs do prevail on liability, what is the possibility [probability] that the court will give them the damages they seek?"

The defendants ultimately conceded that the risk was real, but remote. "How remote?" After discussion, the defendants agreed that it was in the range of 10%-15%.[6]

I then asked them to consider the probability that, assuming liability, the court would award damages of $100,000. The defendants conceded quickly the intuitive proposition that a court is unlikely to struggle to the conclusion that the plaintiffs had been legally harmed, but had suffered

[6] Since risk analysis is a tool that falls within the general category of reality checks, when the parties give a range of values, I think it is appropriate to focus on one number at the upper or lower end of the range that will bring the parties closer together.

no damages.[7] The defendants thought it likely that damages of $100,000 would flow from a court decision on liability. "How likely?" The consensus answer was 80%. "How likely is it that you will win on damages, assuming liability?" The defendants conceded the likelihood was less than 10%; probably five percent.

The defendants didn't care for these projections, since the value suggested was higher than they were prepared to pay. They then presented their version of a decision tree, this time using $600,000 as the lodestar. (Damages = $170,000 [15% of $600,000 + 80% of $100,000 + 5% of $0]; liability @ 50% of $170,000 = $85,000.)[8]

David's lawyer wanted to continue the discussion by suggesting that even this value should be reduced because the defendant could appeal any plaintiffs' award and there is a certain probability that the defendant would prevail on appeal. He believed that by continuing this exercise we would arrive at a number below the amount the defendant was prepared to pay in settlement. Since risk analysis is only a tool and not a talisman, I was concerned that if he ran the numbers further his client would become increasingly rigid, even if the math was wrong and the assigned values open to debate.

I suggested that instead of further analysis that would reduce this value, the defendants should consider the cost of continued litigation. I suggested that those transactional costs should be added to the risk-adjusted value to arrive at a risk-adjusted settlement value.

The defendants then authorized a settlement offer. They would buy the remaining limited partnership units for the current value and pay $50,000 in cash, or they would pay $70,000 in cash in exchange for general release.[9]

---

[7] When the case is presented as an unsuitable investment case, it is possible that the court could conclude that the plaintiff was an unsuitable investor who, nonetheless, profited from the "unsuitable" investments. The court could then find liability, but award only nominal damages.

[8] This was the same methodology I had sketched out with the plaintiffs when I reviewed the possible damage outcomes. The math can be done left to right (reduce the lodestar at each chance node) or right to left (list all possible outcomes and calculate the expected value at each chance node). There is commercial software available to aid in risk analysis calculations.

[9] This was a significant move. Where the parties assign different values to the same asset, you can create perceived value to both by transferring the asset to the party who places a higher value on it.

Plaintiffs Explore Risk Aversion

I had left the plaintiffs comparing their differences in their own risk analysis, namely the divergence in their assessments of the court's possible damage award. When I returned with two different offers, they were forced to focus on a different aspect of risk: How risk-averse were they?

Before reviewing and discussing the defendants' offer, we considered the plaintiffs' risk analysis. In my absence they had decided that the lower range of damages was more likely. We reviewed the numbers and made a further deduction to the risk-adjusted values for the transactional costs yet to be incurred.[10]

To ensure consistent treatment, I then discussed the possibility of getting a damage award of $100,000 instead of the home run that the plaintiffs were seeking.[11] Paul agreed that it was possible to win on liability, lose on the particular damage model, and still recover something.

We then focused on the defendants' offer to buy the limited partnership units at the value assigned by the defendants as the current value. This offer created its own reality check: Did the plaintiffs really believe the units had no value? Even if they accepted the defendants' valuation, holding the partnership units would give the plaintiffs a greater upside potential. Since these were riskier investments than blue chip stocks, they were priced accordingly.

The offer also served as a reality check on the plaintiffs' basic theory of unsuitability. If the plaintiffs behaved consistent with the theory of their case, they would jump at the chance to get out of these risky, unsuitable investments. Peter stated that he believed that the limited partnerships would pay-out at maturity and that they would be better off holding on to these investments. The plaintiffs elected to reject the offer to sell and focused only on an all-cash settlement.

---

[10] The expected value is determined by multiplying the possible payouts by the probability and summing the total possible payouts. Where the parties state that the probability of winning at the liability stage is 50% and the likelihood of recovering damages in the full amount is 40%, the expected value is 20% of the lodestar ($600,000 x .20 = $120,000). This sketch ignores possible payouts at lower amounts.

[11] Manipulation of the process is a temptation for the parties and, I suspect, for the mediator. The temptation to manage expectations in pursuit of settlement is always present. It is better practice to deal with the gaps by addressing other considerations than to manipulate the numbers. My simple test is to suggest that if the parties got together after the mediation session and compared notes, they should find that the mediator acted consistently.

Any concrete cash settlement offer creates its own opportunity for parties to reflect on how risk-averse they are. This was the first concrete offer that had been made to the plaintiffs. As is usually the case in these types of proceedings, it was understood that the settlement offers now on the table were good only during this mediation session. The defendants' rationale for their settlement offer was avoidance of additional legal costs. The plaintiffs knew that there was no guarantee that this offer would be available in the future as costs continued to mount.

I asked Peter and Mary to consider the $70,000 as theirs to invest (or gamble) as they wanted. Would they gamble $70,000 at 10-1 odds in the hopes of making $700,000? Mary stated vehemently that she would not. "We might lose all of the money. This is for our retirement. We can't afford the risk." Peter agreed. I then asked them if they would invest $70,000 on the flip of a coin. If the coin came up heads, the payoff would be $700,000. If it came up tails, they would lose the $70,000. "We would be crazy to gamble it away like that," said Mary.[12]

At this point, the plaintiffs realized that the case should settle for an amount in the high five-figure range. They now understood that when the case was analyzed for risk, the expected value of the chance of recovering $800,000 or even $600,000 was substantially less than they originally believed. They also realized that they were more risk-averse than they had earlier thought. Peter and Mary asked that I convey an offer for an all-cash settlement at $75,000.

David was not surprised when I told him that the plaintiffs were more interested in exploring an all-cash settlement. Sensing that a settlement was in the wings, we discussed his alternative to a negotiated settlement, this time focusing on nonmonetary adverse consequences to his reputation, including regulatory reporting requirements of adverse judgments. He also recognized that he was more risk-averse than had been indicated by the pure mathematics of the expected value of the litigation.

The case settled at $75,000.

[12] The differences between objective risk analysis and subjective evaluation of risk can be a critical component in helping parties understand their true interests. A risk-averse decisionmaker will accept a settlement less advantageous than the mathematical risk. Differences in risk-aversion of the parties translate to settlement opportunities.

Conclusion

Risk analysis can be a useful tool to aid parties in their negotiations. The mediator should not, however, use it like a talisman that contains the "true" answer for the settlement value of a case. Like any other tool, it should be used when it is needed and not just because it is available. Even when the parties have had no prior experience with it, simple explanations of the basic concepts can be related to everyday experiences and terms that the parties will understand intuitively. When used to quantify the elements of risk and the alternative outcomes, this approach can help the parties reach a settlement where none seemed possible.

V. Mediation and Culture: A Five-Step Process

Bridging Cultural Gaps in Mediation

by Donna M. Stringer & Lonnie Lusardo[*]

A special technique exists in mediation that focuses on cross-cultural issues. The authors call it "cultural mediation." While cultural differences may not be the actual source of a dispute these differences can play a crucial role in the outcome of a mediation. For example, the simple act of listening or expressing one's opinion is manifested in different ways across different cultures. A mediator who is aware of these subtleties and is sensitive enough to act accordingly is most likely to succeed in helping parties with different cultural backgrounds achieve a satisfying resolution to their dispute. The following article outlines a five-step process and provides helpful insights on how to bridge cultural gaps during the mediation process.

At its core, culture is little more than "the way we do things around here." Most people are so programmed to respond to their environment that they tend to be oblivious to why and how they do what they do in relation to others. "It's just common sense" is a standard phrase for confirming our cultural roots. Common sense, however, is generally common only when it conforms to the speaker's experience.

At a time of conflict, especially when cultures collide, thoughtful, nonjudgmental questioning allows historical reasons to surface and be reasonably compared with the ways others do things to address similar issues.

Cultural anthropologist Morris Massey theorizes that humans form their cultural norms and values by the time they are ten years old. Those core values, Massey says, remain intact throughout a lifetime unless an

---

[*] Dr. Stringer is president of Executive Diversity Services, Inc., a consulting firm in Seattle, Washington. She is an adjunct faculty member on three campuses and a faculty member at the Intercultural Communication Institute in Portland, Oregon. Dr. Stringer holds a Ph.D. and is a social psychologist with over twenty years of experience in cross-cultural issues.

Mr. Lusardo is owner and principal consultant of The Diversity Collaborative in Seattle, Washington. He works with government agencies and national corporations, and he conducts strategic diversity management training and cultural assessments for numerous law firms and courts.

individual has a significant emotional experience that challenges them, such as falling in love with someone whose values are different, life-threatening illnesses, or significant losses.

In the absence of a reason to examine one's core values, cultural programming becomes subsumed in the context of a constantly changing environment. Interpreted as "human nature" or "common sense," cultural programming allows us to adjust to the challenges of everyday life. These differences are typically what lead to conflicts that require mediation. Cultural mediation offers a process to examine how and why people do the things they do.

While there are a number of mediation models, this article considers a five-step process. While these steps appear deceptively simple, they are not distinct steps and overlap as people move back and forth between them. We explore cross-cultural issues that can arise during each step and offer some tools for managing those issues.

A mediator is defined as an impartial third party whose role is to help parties identify needs, interests, and arrive at a mutually beneficial outcome. The final decision lies with the parties. The mediator is neither an arbitrator nor a counselor.

Defining cross-cultural issues in mediation does not mean that the dispute is regarding overtly cultural issues. That is, the parties are not accusing each other of racism, sexism, homophobia, or other culture-based behaviors. Rather, cultural differences between the parties—or between the parties and the mediator—often affect both process and outcome. To the degree that these issues are hidden to either of the parties or to the mediator, they are powerful contributors to the outcome of mediation.

An area where this can be seen clearly is how emotions are handled during mediation. Western models typically expect people (including the mediator) to separate feelings from issues—a concept very alien to people from cultures where emotions are overt, accepted, and considered integral to the issue. For people from such cultures, the more rational model of mediation can be both alienating and ineffective.

Being impartial, for example, does not imply that the mediator's own cultural expectations, styles, and approaches will not affect the process or the outcome of mediation. Consequently, as we explore cross-cultural issues involved in mediation, it is important that the mediator understand her or his own cultural patterns in order to be effective.

While few people leave their homes each morning with the aim of deliberately violating the sensibilities of friends and co-workers, many of us do just that. One challenge that separates the perceptions of another person's comments stems from the distinction between intent and impact. A person's positive intent can often have negative impact on the recipient of their behaviors, especially when the cultural experiences of the two people are different.

For example, an intended compliment like, "You speak English so well" (said to someone who looks "foreign") can have the impact of being insensitive, thoughtless, or even blatantly racist. The response might be, "Why shouldn't I? My family has lived in New York for three generations!"

Typically, when intent and impact do not match and lead to open conflict, the actor wants to focus on his or her intent while the recipient wants to focus on the impact the behavior has had on him or her. Notice that this process is one where each party is focused (and wants the other to focus) on their own feelings and experiences. The struggle over whether to focus on intent or impact can, in itself, lead to conflict and a feeling that the other is not listening. The mediator's role is to get the parties to listen to the other person's perspective—to be more other-focused, rather than self-focused.

This article will address cross-cultural mediation in its "simplest" form: between two individuals. The authors recognize that mediation involving groups expands the difficulty of mediation exponentially. The five step process addressed here will be useful for group mediation but will take on a much greater complexity.

Step 1: Opening

During the opening stage, the mediator sets the tone for the session. The goal of this stage is to put the parties at ease, establish mediator credibility, create a safe environment, gain an understanding of the process to be used, and clarify the mediator's role. Both parties agree to be open and honest in their comments, bargain in good faith, including not withholding information, and sign informal agreements to mediate. Mediators also gain agreement to confidentiality.

Early in this stage the mediator discusses a method for recording information with each party. Two options are: written notes taken by the mediator during the conversations or tape recording. Each of these options has advantages and disadvantages. Generally speaking, the mediator taking notes is less threatening to most parties, at least initially. Taking notes may, however, result in the mediator being distracted and not listening as well as she or he might otherwise. While the tape recorder is often most threatening to parties initially, it is typically forgotten pretty early in the process as parties get engaged in conversation.

One important consideration is for the mediator to explain that recording the conversation (either on tape or in writing) is for the purpose of helping the mediator keep track of the process and the agreements. Explaining that the records will be shared with no one else, and will be destroyed as soon as the mediation is complete, usually reduces initial discomfort and allows the parties to come to agreement regarding a recording process.

Cautions:

Trust

Perhaps the first caution is the degree to which the parties trust the mediator. Some cultural groups trust authority and will be willing to move forward in mediation with a relative stranger who is seen as the authority. Others have strong distrust of “outsiders” and authority, a reluctance to involve officials in disagreements based on historical experiences with authority. For example, many communities of color in the United States have experienced differential impacts of the criminal justice system.

If mediation has been court ordered, and the mediator is seen as an arm of that system, perceptions of the process and/or the mediator are likely to be valued less than a process seen as free of court-imposed intervention. Other individuals may come from another country of origin where officials were corrupt or abusive. If this is true for either party, trust in the individual mediator may be low at best. If the mediator does not manage this distrust effectively—or personalizes it—the process will be affected.

Recent examples of wavering trust levels surfaced during media coverage of the Elian Gonzales case—a scenario that shows how easily cross-cultural (and intra-cultural) conflicts may have an effect on mediation outcomes. Between the political perspectives of the child’s family members in Cuba and the U.S., views of court officials, legislators, diplomats, and a host of Justice Department and Immigration and Naturalization Service agents, the child’s ability to trust authority figures seemed to change as intermittently as did media reports.

Language

A second caution is language differences. Even if both parties speak fluent English, use of words can vary with sub-cultures, geographic areas of origin, educational differences, and any number of other influences. If English is not a first language for either of the parties, language can become even a greater challenge. When the mediator is uncertain about the specific use of a term or how it may be used, it is advisable to ask the speaker, "How would you define what you mean by…?" It is equally important to then ask the other party, "Is that your understanding of…?"

During a recent cultural mediation conducted by one of the authors, a dramatic conflict arose around various perceptions of "respect." One person was adamant that others were disrespectful of her culture by criticizing her arrival at meetings more than 15 minutes after the agreed upon start time. "They know I have a very busy work schedule and family commitments," she said. Others felt disrespected when late arrivals disrupted meetings, requiring time to "rehash issues we'd already discussed." Through dialogue, the disagreement became more focused on differences in time values, thereby facilitating a greater likelihood of resolution.

Disclosure

Another challenge in this initial stage is differences between the parties in what they consider appropriate for public disclosure. Many cultural communities keep conflicts within the community to avoid "airing dirty laundry." This expectation that some things are not discussed with outsiders may lead some parties to withhold some information in order to save face for both themselves and for their larger community. This may include issues around how religious practices are followed, child disciplinary practices, health care practices, allegations regarding the use of controlled substances, extramarital affairs, and other charges, however true or untrue.

Agreement

A final issue in the opening stage is whether the mediator asks people to sign an agreement to mediate. This is related to trust. Some cultures expect to "take a person at his or her word" and to have their own word trusted. Being asked to sign an agreement may be seen as implying that either the mediator or the other party does not trust the individual's word and may be an offensive, and conflict-producing, way to begin mediation. This can be exacerbated if there are literacy or interpretation differences between the parties.

Tools for Step 1:

Pre-Mediation Assessment

One tool, which would necessarily be handled with cultural sensitivity, would be a pre-mediation assessment of the parties. This assessment would obtain information regarding language history and skills, communication styles, conflict styles, values around authority, attitudes regarding disclosure, and any cultural or style issues each disputant feels may be relevant in the mediation process.

Cross-Cultural Co-Mediation

A two-person mediation team that uses individuals who are culturally similar to the parties can be enormously helpful. This is not to assume that being from the same culture implies that similarity will always be present, but that the perception of similarity on the part of the parties can be important to establishing trust and safety. To the degree that the mediator has an understanding of the parties' culture, however, this can begin to increase the mediator's understanding of hidden issues, create greater trust in the mediators, and reduce potential communication issues. It is also very likely that cultural patterns regarding authority figures, written agreements and feelings about public disclosure will be identified more accurately to the degree that mediators reflect cultural understanding of the parties.

Intent of Agreement

If a signed agreement is seen as necessary by the mediator, explaining the intent of this agreement could be helpful. Specifically, stating that the intent is to be sure that everyone understands the process and that the mediator has assured himself or herself that he or she has been clear in outlining the process. This explanation, then, is focused on the mediator's attempt to be sure she or he has been clear, not to question the trustworthiness of the parties.

Opening Statement

Include in the opening statement a very brief acknowledgment that each person's history, expectations, styles and behaviors might affect misunderstandings that have led to the dispute or that will affect the mediation. This is an opportunity to briefly educate the parties about how cultural backgrounds might affect misunderstandings and begin the process of listening to the other for greater understanding. This acknowledgment will allow the mediator to return to an exploration of potential cultural differences during the mediation if the mediator feels there are differences affecting either the process or the outcome of the mediation.

Step 2: Information Sharing and Issue Identification

During this step each party is asked to describe the conflict from her or his own perspective. The goals include having each person feel that she or he has been heard and for the mediator to identify the major concerns and issues to be resolved.

This is another opportunity for the mediator to conduct a brief teaching session regarding how to describe behavior in a nonjudgmental manner in order to increase understanding, rather than to interpret or judge the other person's behavior. A brief example of how to describe behavior will be helpful. It will also be helpful to get participant agreement that when either party moves beyond describing to interpreting or judging, the mediator will stop them and ask that they return to descriptions.

Cautions:

Speaker Sequence

One of the first decisions the participants will make is which party tells their story first. This can be critical to the development of trust. If either party feels that the mediator has given the other party an unfair advantage, trust is likely to be affected. The mediator's role here is to help the parties make this decision fairly and objectively. If the decision is problematic, the mediator may suggest criteria for making a choice.

One nonprofit organization that instructs mediation practices recommends that the individual who requests the mediation "go first" in explaining their perspective on the conflict. An additional option is to offer the opportunity for that person to allow the other person to speak first.

Communication Styles

A primary caution during this stage is differences in communication styles. Some people prefer communicating in a more rational/linear style—one that focuses on clear, succinct outlining of issues. Others are more likely to communicate in an emotive, circular manner focusing on feelings. The emotive communicator will often perceive the rational communicator as disengaged, cold, uncaring. The rational communicator on the other hand is likely to perceive the emotive communicator as "too emotional," out of control or even threatening.

Additionally, the emotive communicator may be more inclined to interrupt as she or he gets excited or engaged. This may be perceived as rude by the rational/linear communicator.

While there are many exceptions to cultural norms, it is very common for European Americans, northern Europeans, and some Asian populations to use a rational communication style. Many populations of color, notably African- American, Latin/Hispanic, Pacific Islanders, and Eastern Europeans are more inclined to use an emotive style.

This is a particular caution if the mediator also prefers a rational communication approach (which is the approach most mediators learn: one person talks at a time, no interrupting, stick to the issues). It can leave the emotive communicator feeling unheard, unappreciated, or disrespected. Adding communication style differences to any racial or ethnic differences can exacerbate a difficult situation.

A second communication style caution in this stage is that of pacing. Some parties will speak quickly, respond quickly, and make decisions quickly while others will be more reflective and take longer to respond. The former can perceive the latter as slow, stupid or withholding while the latter may see the former as "too quick to react" or thoughtless in their responses.

Objectionable Behaviors

Often, in the midst of mediating cultural conflicts, one party to the dispute may begin to grandstand or otherwise show some form of objectionable behavior. Behaviors that threaten to undermine the process must be addressed as quickly as possible. One way to prevent such behavior is to have a set of ground rules or norms that all parties agree to—then recognize when an individual's actions deviate from the accepted norms.

When practical, the parties may wish to set time limits for comments. The mediator's role is to ensure that such limits do not disadvantage a more reflective party, and to respond to behaviors that do not comply with the agreed-upon limitations.

One author was mediating a dispute when one party rose to her feet and proceeded to explain, "The real problem here is X and Y," naming names and surfacing personal details. When it was pointed out that this violated the ground rules established by the group, the speaker continued her tirade. The mediator gently interrupted her, reminded her of the ground rule again, and stated, "I will move to the next speaker now. Thank you." The woman quietly took her seat.

Disclosure

It is important to discuss the level of public or private disclosure parties are asked to make. A common expectation is that parties will be "open and honest." Honesty and disclosure can mean different things to different people. With no intent to be withholding or dishonest, a disputant may consider some information private and not relevant. This can lead to a perception of dishonesty if such information arises later in the context of an emotional confrontation.

Caucus

While some mediators use caucuses, these one-on-one talks require some caution. A caucus is an opportunity for the parties to leave the room and consult with the mediator before continuing the conversation with the other disputant. The caucus provides an opportunity for the mediator to speak candidly with each party, give recommendations and observations about how to address certain issues and, perhaps, respond to questions about the process.

Two cautions are important to emphasize: First, the caucus may be perceived by one or both parties as an attempt to keep secrets or unduly influence the mediator with private conversations. Second, information shared with the mediator outside of the mediation setting can undermine the trust that the mediator is attempting to establish.

Unless otherwise specified, a caucus implies an understanding between the mediator and all parties that what is said during the caucus is confidential and not to be shared by the mediator during the mediation process. If the mediator chooses to exercise the caucus option, it is imperative to explain the process prior to calling a break in mediation for that purpose.

Tools for Step 2:

Behavioral Language

A most difficult cross-cultural issue, discussed earlier, is the difference in meaning that individuals may place on a similar term. Teaching both parties to communicate both their own intent and the impact of the other person's behavior in behavioral terms is an important role of the mediator at this stage. In virtually every mediation one author has conducted, "being treated with respect" has been a primary goal of each party. Asking each person to translate "respect" into an observable behavior has resulted in significant insights about both self and other.

For example, one individual indicated that being called "Ma'am" by the other person was sarcastic and unnecessary. At this statement the other party was stunned: as a southern-raised male, with over twenty-two years in the military, he intended only respect. This simple piece of information was enough to begin a respectful mediation process. When each party understood that using non-behavioral words could result in such misunderstandings and conflicts, they were already along the way to better understanding and reduced conflict.

Communication Style Differences

If the two parties have different communication styles (e.g., direct vs. indirect; feeling-based or emotive vs. information-based or rational, formal vs. informal), the conflict will almost certainly be exacerbated by this difference—and it is highly unlikely that either person will recognize communication styles as a source of conflict. The mediator will facilitate understanding by conducting a "mini-training" about communication styles. The mediator can help each party identify his or her communication style preference and practice separating what the other person says from how she or he says it.

Listening and Paraphrasing

Another "mini-training," this time helping each party paraphrase both what the other person has said (content) and the feeling expressed in their statement (context) is an important role for the mediator. An individual cannot effectively paraphrase both content and context if he or she has not listened effectively. This explanation also helps reinforce the distinction between a speaker's intent and the impact on a listener.

As the reader can see, information sharing and issue identification cannot happen unless each party has good listening and communication skills. Many individuals who find themselves in mediation do not have these skills. Consequently, this step requires that the mediator assume the role of teacher and coach. Educating each party about behavioral language, communication styles, listening and paraphrasing—and then carefully coaching each party as they talk with each other, without embarrassment or loss of face for either individual, is the essence of this step.

Step 3: Exploring Interests

During this step the mediator reiterates what he or she has heard as to the issues and each party's interest(s). Each individual is asked to correct the mediator until each party agrees that the mediator and the other party understand her or his issues and interests. The goal of this step is to agree to the issues and understand each person's interest.

Cautions:

The first caution here is for the mediator to use the skills he or she has been teaching in Step 2: behavioral words, delineation of content and effect, and effective listening and paraphrasing. The mediator must be able to reiterate issues in neutral terms so that each party feels they have been heard without feeling that the neutral language has "watered down" their issue. Understanding and respect for differences in both pacing and communication styles are key to success in this step.

Pacing

There are real differences among people regarding pacing. Some individuals think and talk faster, while others are more reflective and may take longer to identify what they want to say and then communicate it verbally. It will be helpful for the mediator to (a) point these differences out to the parties if she or he has identified this as a difference before this step; and (b) demonstrate respect for both styles. A more reflective individual will need more time to think about issues and to communicate them. This can cause impatience in both the other disputant and the mediator if it is not acknowledged and the individual is not given the necessary time to state her or his issues. If this is not done, the more reflective disputant will be at a disadvantage.

Language is a second potential cultural issue that affects pacing. If either party is using English as a second language, they may need more time to respond to issues or questions because they may still be translating and back-translating in their first language. Parties will benefit if the mediator identifies this potential issue and allows sufficient time for each party to communicate without being rushed or treated with impatience.

Communication Styles

Some individuals communicate using more rational, information-based language while others use more emotive, feeling-based language. Deborah Tannen, a linguist who has studied gender communication differences, has labeled these "report talk" and "rapport talk." These differences can create misperceptions and potential conflicts.

The more rational communicator may perceive the more emotive communicator as emotional, and/or out of control. The emotive communicator, on the other hand, may perceive the rational communicator as being disengaged and/or uncaring.

Again, this is an opportunity for the mediator to quickly educate the parties regarding how they talk as a potential barrier to understanding. And, of course, the mediator will increase his or her own effectiveness to the degree that they recognize their own preference and demonstrate value for either style during mediation. The very process of mediation often leans toward the rational, objective approach which can put the emotive communicator at a disadvantage and which needs to be recognized and alleviated by the mediator.

Itemize and Prioritize Issue List

One option that helps the mediator and others move through the process is to itemize a list of issues to address during the mediation. Once the list is established, all parties are asked to agree to the list, including how each issue is articulated.

One caution is to create a list that notes each item in judgment-free context. It is helpful to note each item so as not to reflect a particular individual's perspective. That is, notes are written in a way that the issue would be of interest to all parties. For example, rather than listing what one person sees as another's "consistent tardiness," the mediator may list "time commitments." Generally, the fewer words the better.

Once the list is agreed to, it is useful to prioritize the list to ensure the most important issues are addressed first. This also requires agreement by all parties. If there is disagreement about which issues are most important, the mediator may ask each person to select his or her top issue first, selecting some neutral method for how to prioritize those two items (e.g., coin toss); then ask each person to list the second issue, etc. The creation of such a list helps both the mediator and others harness time during the mediation. One option the mediator may choose is to help the parties designate a realistic amount of time to devote to each mediation session and to an initial number of sessions, after which an assessment of progress will be made and new commitments sought if the issues have not been resolved.

Mediator's Cultural Competence

It is during this stage that the mediator's cultural competency may be most challenged. If the mediator is to help parties hear and understand each other, she or he will also need the ability to take time to listen without rushing either party or demonstrating impatience with pacing or style.

Tools for Stage 3:

Reframing of Issues/Feelings

The practice of reframing—taking a different perspective—can help avoid stereotypical bias in interpreting behaviors. Reframing requires interpreting a problem from a more positive perspective, generating all possible reasons for the behavior. The mediator can help each disputant generate all possible explanations for a behavior and what positive interpretations could be made for it. Both the parties and the mediator will want to guard against interpretations that are based on stereotypical assumptions about a behavior, including an assumption that one's own cultural point of view is "correct." Exhausting all possible interpretations helps move people from a blaming stance to a problem-solving stance.

Step 4: Negotiation

The parties brainstorm options for agreement, without evaluation. The mediator facilitates a discussion about the criteria for evaluating each option after which each option is evaluated based on the criteria developed. The goal is now to identify and agree to a resolution.

Cautions:

Brainstorming

Brainstorming may not be a natural process for some cultural groups. If an individual party in mediation feels particularly overwhelmed by fast-paced, "off the top of your head" idea-generation, she or he will not add many ideas during this step if brainstorming is the only tool available to the mediator.

One author conducted mediation where one party added virtually no ideas. The mediator stopped the process and asked how else they might develop creative ideas for resolution. The individual suggested that they take some quiet time alone to think about it. Another meeting was established and each individual was asked to bring as many ideas as possible. When this individual returned she had generated a rather lengthy, and quite creative, list of options—most of which would have been missed had brainstorming been the only method used to create options.

Tools for Step 4:

Brainstorming

The mediator can describe brainstorming as a single way to generate options and ask what other ideas each party may have. Caution is needed here not to assume that a direct request like this will be effective with indirect communicators.

Time-Out and Reflection

If any party to the mediation is more reflective and less direct in communication style, taking a break at this point and asking parties to return with as many ideas as they can generate allows for thoughtfulness and recognition of a more indirect or reflective individual.

Face-Saving

Mediation must allow all parties to save face. At this step, it is particularly important to attend to this. If one party's suggestions are responded to most positively by the mediator (verbally or nonverbally) and the other's less so, it can be an issue of face.

Further, if either party begins to hesitate, maintain long silences, change previous verbal or nonverbal patterns, the mediator will be well advised to explore with each party whether there are issues of face that have not yet been identified.

The mediator may want at this stage to discuss with each party who else might be affected by the outcome of this process. Face-saving may expand outside of this process to others in a disputant's family or community. Reluctance being experienced in the mediation may involve others. Knowing this will help the mediator identify ways to be most helpful to the parties at this time.

Step 5: Agreement and Closure

In its simplest form, agreement is the opposite of disagreement. Reaching a mutually satisfying resolution to differences is perhaps the most essential part of cultural mediation. This final step brings closure to the issues, sets a path to resolution and, ideally, includes options to avoid future cultural conflict. An agreement reflects upon future expectations by delicately recognizing past behaviors and actions.

This is one more opportunity for the mediator to clarify expectations and generate a clear, specific roadmap that is likely to be followed when one goes astray. If only a partial agreement is reached, it is important to identify the points that have been resolved and those that remain. Identifying options that allow parties to continue working on the unresolved issues also helps address the unaddressable.

Cautions:

As the cultural mediation process gears down, either party may agree to a behavior change that, in the mediator's observation, may be unreasonable for one to exercise through the emotions of a cultural violation. Pointing out such disparities, sensitively and with regard to each person's own style, helps all parties structure a more enduring agreement.

Written Agreement

It is not always necessary, or even advisable, to record an agreement. Some cultures, particularly many Asian and Spanish-speaking cultures, may find the notion of recording agreements to be a symptom of distrust. Formalizing an agreement in the context of distrust may further exacerbate an already fragile bond. For individuals from such backgrounds, word-of-mouth agreements may suffice. Written agreements are primarily used to check understanding, not to challenge trustworthiness.

Conversely, a written document, one that all parties may refer to from time to time, helps validate and confirm the outcome of mediation. Crafting a document that incorporates sensitive language and reasonable options for individuals to follow in responding to conflict often yields an abiding, rational approach toward equitable resolutions, even under the most stressful conditions.

Tools for Step 5:

Follow the Agenda

If a written agreement is recommended and all parties agree to the validity of such a document, one option is to note elements in the agreement in an order that follows the agenda used to discuss issues during the mediation. For example, if the parties chose to discuss "gender issues" as a top priority, it may be useful to begin the agreement with "gender issues."

Seek Common Ground

By this point in the dialogue, parties are likely to have demonstrated their respective passions around critical concerns. Common ground is often much easier for the detached person, the mediator, to recognize than for those involved in the disagreement. For example, individuals may dramatically disagree over the definition of a term like respect and how respect is extended to others. The mere use of the term by all parties suggests a common value for respect. In such a scenario, inclusion of specific ways both (all) parties can agree on to show respect for one another without violating cultural values would be an essential ingredient of an agreement.

Ask "What If" Questions

When a potentially unrealistic expectation surfaces in the context of an agreement, asking "What if" questions helps direct the parties toward a more collaborative result. It is often useful to reflect on the mediator's observations made about the styles, use of terms and language of the individuals involved.

"What if" questions may be voiced in a way that draws both (all) parties to their own reality and their own better judgment. For example, asking one party "Are you sure you'll be able to let the other(s) know when, how and why their behaviors affect you the way they do?" In so doing, the mediator may also explain, "This may be difficult, given what you've said about your tendency to avoid conflict. What do you think?"

To the other party (or parties), the mediator may also ask, "Recognizing the style differences we've discussed between you and the other(s), what if (the other/another person) brings a conflict to your attention in a way that triggers some unforeseen, possibly negative, emotion for you? Would you be able to discuss the conflict reasonably? What do you think?"

Offer a "Perhaps …"

In recognizing agreement articulated on what appears to be shaky or uncertain ground, the mediator may nudge the parties toward a more stable agreement, by using tact, diplomacy and sensitivity. This may also involve reflecting the styles of the persons involved.

It is often helpful for the mediator to offer options to each person, based on the mediator's understanding of that person's strengths as well as the mediator's repertoire of skillful approaches to similar challenges. "Perhaps the two of you can work out a code to use when either of you feels uncomfortable, dissatisfied or offended by someone else's actions or language. This may include saying one word like 'Ouch' or saying, 'Something isn't working for me here.' Is that possible?" In recommending such language, it is wise to reinforce the value of using a non-threatening, non-accusatory tone.

Another option is for the mediator to offer a way for either party to request revisiting an offensive or bothersome remark or conduct with a mutually agreed upon phrasing like, "I'd like to talk about this after I've had some time to think. Can we chat about this over coffee this afternoon?"

In discussing options to follow during the agreement step of the mediation, the mediator may sense that possible approaches toward resolving conflicts may involve language that the mediator recognizes as more sensitive (touchy-feely) or less sensitive (terse) than an individual would use in her or his normal discourse. In such a situation, it is wise to suggest alternative language.

Signing an Agreement

Should all parties agree to the value of a written agreement, having all parties sign the document adds further legitimacy to the words.

Occasionally an individual will object to signing an agreement while others insist upon signing. One option to exercise in such a situation is to probe the person who resists signing, by asking questions like, "What agreements would you feel comfortable signing, or if this language doesn't work for you, what words would work for you?"

What can you expect at the end of cultural mediation? By the close of a successful cultural mediation, all parties will have gained a clearer perspective on why and how others may respond to "the way we do things around here."

These dissimilar approaches are likely to present different ways of doing things than another person's cultural programming would see as "common sense." Rather than seeing someone else's way of doing what they do as baffling, wrong, or "just plain weird," participants are more likely to observe differences with empathy, sensitivity, and a series of judgment-free exploratory questions.

VI. The Trend Toward Med/Arb

Nuances of Med/Arb—A Neutral's Perspective

by Richard P. Flake[*]

Although arbitration as an alternative dispute resolution mechanism has existed for centuries, within the last several hundred years it has become ingrained into the dispute resolution conscience of several industries, such as labor and construction. More recently it has made significant inroads in other areas, including the securities and employment sectors. The continued growth of arbitration proves both its need and its popularity among users of all types.

By contrast, the use of mediation, which also has a long history, has exploded in the last several decades. In the private commercial sector, especially in the construction industry, which recently incorporated a mediation step into widely used form documents, mediation is often selected as the ADR process of choice. In certain areas of the United States, even a litigated matter cannot be set for trial without first undergoing mediation. It can fairly be said that mediation has changed the face of ADR in the United States.

Given the undeniable success of arbitration and mediation, it was inevitable that these two processes would be merged into what has been referred to by some as a "hybrid" procedure.[1] The singular point of definition of mediation/arbitration (med/arb)[2] is that the same neutral acts as mediator and as arbitrator. As a result, there is no question the dispute will be resolved; moreover it will be resolved

[*] The author is a principal in the Houston firm of Cokinos, Bosien & Young and is a municipal judge for the City of Friendswood, Texas. Mr. Flake serves on the American Arbitration Association's roster of neutrals and was named "Arbitrator of the Year" by the National Council of Better Business Bureaus for the southwestern United States. He earned a B.A. from the University of Texas at Austin and a J.D. from the University of Houston Law Center. He is the author if *Mediating Construction Disputes: What Counsel Should Know About Mediation Advocacy*, DISPUTE RESOLUTION JOURNAL (MAY-JUNE 2003).

[1] D. Van Duch, *Do 'Hybrids' Compromise ADR Benefits?*, NAT'L LAW J., Mar. 2, 1998.

[2] Other combinations exist, including "arb-med," shadow mediation and concilio-arbitration, each of which have their own distinctive characteristics. They are beyond the scope of this article, which focuses on standard med/arb.

more quickly than if an arbitration with a different neutral were to follow an unsuccessful mediation.

Is combining the two processes desirable? As current literature on the med/arb process is still largely anecdotal, the answer will depend on the perspective of the opinion-giver. Some have criticized the combination because of ethical issues raised by the dual role of the neutral and have charged that the process is flawed.[3] In my view, which is based largely on my own experience as a neutral in med/arb proceedings, the negatives of med/arb are outweighed by the positives. If the parties and their counsel understand the pros and cons of merging the two processes and the other nuances that result from their combination, med/arb can be an extremely effective method of resolving disputes.

A Single Neutral

At first blush, it seems logical to have the same person act as both mediator and arbitrator. Yet, the concept is a radical departure from "true" arbitration philosophy. Ethical rules governing arbitration prohibit an arbitrator from discussing or interacting in any way with the parties, except in an administered conference in which both parties and counsel are in attendance. In practice, an arbitrator being considered for appointment is usually requested to disclose prior knowledge of the case and contacts with the parties or their counsel. This is to prevent the purity of the arbitration process from being tainted by possible partiality on the arbitrator's part.

But in med/arb, because the arbitrator also acts as the mediator, he or she will meet with each side independently in private sessions out of the presence of the other party. The mere thought of a decision-making neutral discussing the facts of a dispute privately with one disputant is a major reason why the process receives less than universal support.

Yet, the process can give parties the chance they need to fashion a resolution on their own terms in mediation, and the assurance that if mediation fails, a rapid award will be obtained from a neutral with intimate knowledge of the dispute. Prior experience as a general counsel has convinced me that while the ultimate outcome of a particular ADR process is important to users, almost equal in importance is the ability to bring finality to the situation in a relatively inexpensive and time-efficient manner. The med/arb process without question favorably

---

[3] *See* n. 1 *supra.*

satisfies the desires of timely resolution and, if properly done, cost efficiency. As a result, some would say that med/arb combines the best of both mediation and arbitration.

Med/Arb Procedures

The parties may agree to participate in med/arb either before or after a dispute arises. Parties who agreed to arbitrate may choose to participate in a prior mediation with the arbitrator serving as mediator; similarly, parties who agreed to mediate may ask the mediator to become the arbitrator and decide their dispute.

In med/arb, the parties generally create the methodology that will be followed. As an example, the mediation portion of the proceeding may be scheduled for a definitive time period. A complete mediation can be scheduled for half a day, or one or more days, and a separate arbitration can be scheduled for a later time. Commonly, however, the arbitration immediately follows the mediation portion. Thus, in a one-day med/arb, a half-day arbitration immediately follows a half-day mediation; in a two-day schedule, the first day is devoted solely to mediation and the second, if necessary, solely to arbitration.

The arbitration hearing may be a "standard" arbitration, with a full presentation of evidence, including witness testimony. The parties should determine in advance of the med/arb whether a full evidentiary hearing will take place at the arbitration stage. In many, if not all cases, such a hearing will not be necessary. Typically, after the mediation session runs its course (assuming no resolution was reached), the parties, having fairly presented their case to the neutral in the mediation phase, are content with either a summary presentation of the case or simply closing arguments for the arbitration portion of the process. It is very important for the parties, who are the designers of the med/arb process, to reach agreement on methodology and to memorialize their agreement prior to the commencement of the med/arb.

Pros and Cons

Med/arb's most appealing attribute is the certainty that the dispute will come to an end, one way or the other. Ideally, the parties will resolve the dispute to their mutual satisfaction during the mediation, making arbitration unnecessary. If agreement does not occur, however, the mediator will put on the arbitrator's hat and ultimately issue an award, following whatever arbitration procedures the parties have previously agreed upon. The dispute ends at that point, allowing the parties to move on to other business.

Confidentiality. The speed and decisiveness of the med/arb process is not without sacrifices, however. One such sacrifice relates to confidentiality on the part of the mediator. In the mediation process, any statement made by a party to the neutral mediator is absolutely confidential unless the party has authorized its disclosure. This is a cornerstone of the mediation process. Further, in most jurisdictions, the entire mediation process is cloaked with confidentiality, such that the neutral cannot be subpoenaed to testify to what was heard or discussed with either party in the mediation. Concern regarding confidentiality in mediation is so great that some jurisdictions are in the process of creating ethical rules for mediators, most of which center around the issue of confidentiality. These rules, if violated, might lead to penalties being inflicted on the neutral.

How is confidentiality affected in the med/arb process? Essentially, the neutral's responsibilities relative to confidentiality do not change. Confidential information related by a party to the neutral during the mediation phase must be held in confidence by that neutral throughout the entirety of the process, including the subsequent arbitration, if any.

The difficulty arises, of course, when the neutral dons the arbitrator's hat and decides the issue, while in full possession of the confidential information. This information, if not brought forth by the party itself during the arbitration, will not be subject to challenge or cross-examination. This raises concerns about the information influencing the arbitrator's deliberation of the merits of the case, particularly since the information may be unreliable or, at least, untested.

As a practical matter, once a fact is put into the universe, the law of human nature usually dictates that it will be considered on some level. Because the arbitrator conducts private caucuses during the mediation phase of med/arb and may come into possession of information, even critical information, not known by the other party, there is a risk the arbitrator's decision may be based in part on that information. This risk cannot be stressed enough. However, it is not that different from a jury being instructed to disregard testimony by a witness during a trial.

Withholding of Information. A by-product of the concern that the arbitrator may be influenced by confidential information is that the parties, who usually feel more comfortable confidentially discussing the weakness of their case in the typical mediation, will be loath to do so during the mediation phase of the med/arb proceeding. It is simply human nature not to readily discuss any weakness with a potential ultimate decision maker.

One of the main activities of pure mediation is the honest and candid give and take regarding the strengths and weaknesses of the case in a confidential setting with the mediator. The mediator's ability to perform "reality testing" with the parties is a key ingredient of successful mediation. This activity is compromised in the med/arb process, and as a result the mediation part of the process may be more difficult, and ultimately may be unsuccessful.

The neutral should discuss these confidentiality-related issues fully with the parties in order to allow them to make an informed decision about what is potentially being compromised. After such a discussion, the parties may be content to compromise this issue for the sake of a speedy and decisive resolution. A well-drafted med/arb agreement covering the confidentiality issues is highly recommended.

Nuances

Neutral Selection. Another issue to be considered is the ability of the neutral who will act as mediator and arbitrator. Successful mediation techniques include an ability to obtain the confidence of the parties, hear what they have to say, and discuss the potential weaknesses of their positions. These skills can be critical to achieving a resolution at mediation.

In arbitration, the neutral should be able to sift through the critical facts and render an award.

The ideal med/arb neutral should have the necessary skills to perform both roles. There is always the possibility, however, that the individual selected may have more of an aptitude in one ADR process than in another. Parties may even desire a neutral with greater skills in one process.

Mediator Conduct. Combining mediation and arbitration may affect the mediator's own conduct. Whereas the typical mediation involves the reality-testing discussions referred to above, some neutrals may question whether to engage in opinion-giving when they may become the ultimate arbiter of the case.

After acting as the neutral in numerous med/arb proceedings, I believe it is not appropriate for the neutral to opine on particular issues during the mediation, and as a result I have become less probative and opinionated during the mediation phase of med/arb. While giving opinions or suggestions actually may hasten a mediated settlement, I would rather the parties mediate the case to a resolution based on their own feelings and understandings about the dispute, rather than mine.

So that the neutral in a pure mediation may avoid conduct that could later taint an arbitration of the dispute, it may be useful for the parties and the mediator to agree up front as to whether the mediator will later become the arbitrator in the case.

Effect on Costs. Because in med/ arb, a relatively short, binding arbitration by a neutral already fully familiar with the dispute will quickly follow a mediation that has not produced a settlement, the parties generally will not be worried about how long it will take to resolve the dispute or how much it will cost should the mediation not succeed. This distinguishes med/arb from pure mediation, where the mediator typically raises the specter of incurring these costs and expenses, and the time it will take to resolve the dispute through litigation or arbitration, in order to encourage the parties to settle during the mediation. The inability of the mediator to use this often successful mediation technique makes it all the more difficult for a resolution to be reached during the mediation phase of med/arb.

Conclusion

Despite these criticisms, med/arb should be looked upon as what it is: a singular alternative dispute resolution process that gives the parties the chance to resolve the issues on their own terms. It should not be considered "unsuccessful" simply because the parties were unable to resolve their dispute during the mediation phase. The ultimate goal of any ADR mechanism is resolution of the dispute. Med/arb, one way or the other, will mete out an efficient resolution, which is a primary goal of most parties.

CHAPTER FIVE

ATTORNEYS AND MEDIATION

I. Attorneys' Tools for Successful Mediation

Attention Attorneys! How to Achieve the Best Results in Mediation

by Karin S. Hobbs[*]

When a client walks into a lawyer's office and begins to recount seemingly endless details of a legal problem, the lawyer usually begins mediation preparation. Ten years ago, the lawyer may have set aside much of that information and transformed the "relevant" portions into an intricate web of legal claims and defenses. Today, a lawyer familiar with the mediation process will carefully note and discuss the client's interests and needs and may approach resolution of the problem from a different angle.

Lawyers are there to solve problems. Traditionally, lawyers have filed lawsuits as the expected mode of dispute resolution. However, lawyers and clients have learned that litigation often escalates emotions, increases costs, confuses the dispute, and delays resolution of the problem. Further, litigation almost always results in a win for one side and a loss for the other. Mediation, in comparison, is less expensive, significantly faster, and provides a solution that both sides agree upon. As a result, mediation has become an increasingly attractive method of resolving disputes.

Because the judicial process and the mediation process are vastly different methods of dispute resolution, mediation preparation differs dramatically from that of litigation. The judicial system is premised on the theory that if both sides present evidence to a neutral judge or jury,

---

[*] The author is the former Chief Appellate Mediator at the Utah Court of Appeals, board member of the Utah Council on Conflict Resolution, and chair of the Alternative Dispute Resolution Committee of the Utah State Bar. She teaches Negotiation and Mediation at the University of Utah and serves on the Board of Bar Commissioners at the Utah State Bar. Ms. Hobbs received her J.D. from the University of Utah College of Law.

the truth will surface, and the fact-finder will resolve the dispute fairly. In mediation, however, it is the parties who identify the issues, their interests, and their needs to determine whether—considering all the risks— they can resolve the dispute fairly. The parties are the decision-makers and are empowered to make decisions in the context of mediation. In litigation, however, the parties are asking attorneys to speak for them and for a neutral to decide the case. Judge-imposed solutions are often viewed as unfair, unjust, or legally flawed and often lead to appeals and a continuation of the dispute. Mediated settlements, on the other hand, are not consummated unless they are mutually satisfactory.

Preparing for mediation begins the moment the client begins to describe the problem. The attorney must understand the mediation process and the central importance of the client's interests, needs, and participation in the process. Zealous advocacy exists in mediation, but the form of advocacy is different because it is the parties themselves who reach a mutually acceptable agreement. Therefore, the client's interests and needs are of critical importance. Anticipating mediation as an option, attorneys may also treat each other with more civility to maintain open lines of communication and facilitate resolution of the dispute.

Direct and Honest Statement of Facts and Issues

Attorneys should prepare for the mediation conference by distilling the relevant facts into a concise, direct, and honest statement. Because the parties will likely exchange specific offers to resolve the dispute, both sides must come equipped with current information that will assist in proposing options for settlement. If attorneys and clients view mediation as an opportunity to openly share information and possibly avoid costly discovery, both parties' interests are served even if the case is not settled.

Although much of the factual preparation for mediation overlaps with preparation for litigation, notable exceptions exist. Unlike litigation, the attorney should prepare the factual statement using neutral language and should be mindful that it is the parties who need to reach a satisfactory solution. Concealment of issues will likely be unhelpful and may diminish trust between the parties. Also, because emotions run deep in most cases, attorneys and clients should avoid creating a contentious environment. At the same time, a statement of the facts that ignores the emotional backdrop may not honestly communicate the state of affairs. Thus, an attorney in a mediation conference is striking a balance between reciting the facts honestly, while carefully phrasing the facts in neutral language. If an attorney can empathize with the other side, concede weaknesses, and diffuse hostility, this will create a friendly environment and may expedite resolution of the case.

Identify Client's Interests and Needs

Prior to the mediation, the lawyer should ask the client to identify the interests and needs that are motivating the case. Interests are items such as fairness, justice, preserving relationships, and establishing legal parameters. Needs include minimizing costs, expediting resolution of the problem, paying pending bills, and terminating the emotional drain. During the initial consultation, the client may have revealed much of this information before the attorney transformed the client's statements into legal claims and defenses. Mediation focuses on not only the legal claims and defenses, but also the client's interests and needs. By satisfying the underlying interests and needs, parties can often arrive at a mutual resolution. Frequently, parties who have focused primarily on their legal rights and remedies are pleased to shift the focus to the remaining portions of the problem not articulated in legal documents and sometimes not capable of resolution through the judicial system. For example, a person bringing a wrongful termination action may accept a letter of recommendation from the former employer in lieu of regaining his former position or pursuing a protracted lawsuit against the employer. His underlying interest may be securing employment rather than rejuvenating his relationship with the former employer or fighting the employer in court. Similarly, a corporation may prefer to repair its relationship with another company rather than continuing to litigate terms of a contract between the parties.

Choosing a Mediator

In most settings, attorneys select the mediator. Different mediators have different styles, and lawyers should be aware of the three primary approaches to mediation: facilitative, analytical, and evaluative. A facilitative mediator attempts to facilitate discussions between the parties by keeping the process orderly or setting meetings. An analytical mediator assists the parties in assessing the risks in the case, while an evaluative mediator not only manages the negotiation process but also reveals an opinion of the offers. Some claim that the evaluative approach can undermine the client's ability to become empowered to resolve the dispute. In practice, many mediators adopt several of these approaches or progress from one style to another during the course of the mediation. Generally, attorneys assess the case and choose a mediator whose style and stated purpose will best assist in satisfactorily resolving the dispute.

Developing a Plan

Lawyers take seriously the duty to fully represent their clients. Mediation provides new opportunities for zealous advocacy, sometimes even greater opportunities than those available in court. Initially, attorneys should assess key evidence, and strengths and weaknesses of the legal aspects of the case. The attorney should analyze the best, worst, and likely case scenario along with approximate cost of each scenario. The lawyer should share this information with the client and determine the client's ability and willingness to fund litigation. The lawyer should discuss with the client the portion of the lawsuit not set forth in the pleadings. Many attorneys will be uncomfortable with exploring this aspect of the case, because it cannot be compartmentalized as a legal claim or defense, but perceptive attorneys realize that emotional underpinnings must be acknowledged before clients can begin to rationally address settlement. Once an attorney has obtained this information, he can formulate a plan. New information may emerge during the mediation process, and attorneys and clients should prepare to be as flexible as possible.

Understanding the Mediation Process

Once the facts, issues, interests, and needs are identified and a plan is developed, attorneys and clients must now become familiar with what to expect during the mediation process. The mediation process has approximately six distinct stages: opening statement by the mediator; opening statement by counsel and parties; private discussions or caucuses; brainstorming options for settlement; negotiation; and reaching an agreement.

1. Opening Statement of the Mediator

During the opening statement, the mediator introduces the process, and explains the basic rules regarding mediation. Typically, the mediator will explain that mediation is an opportunity for the parties to take control of the case and determine whether they can resolve the case in a way that suits their interests and needs. Parties will likely be informed that listening is critical in mediation, and they should creatively think of solutions to the problem. The mediator will also cover the parameters of confidentiality and may have the parties sign an agreement to mediate. The agreement will likely include a provision stating that communications during mediation are confidential and not to be disclosed in other settings. Confidentiality is an important component of mediation because candid discussions facilitate resolutions. The mediator may also set out rules of the mediation conference, such as using neutral language to avoid escalating the dispute and resisting the temptation to interrupt the other party. Finally, the mediator will explain the stages in the process.

2. *Opening Statement of the Parties*

The opening statement allows each party to present its version of the case. In the opening statement, attorneys should identify the players, articulate the relevant facts, and outline the legal and nonlegal issues. Attorneys should carefully prepare the opening statement, mindful that the intent is for the parties to reach an agreement, and that adversarial language, posturing, or entrenchment may either hurt or delay the process. Parties are also invited to make opening statements in most instances and usually take the opportunity to relay information regarding their interests and needs. A carefully crafted statement of a party can be extremely effective in notifying the other side of the interests and needs that are most important to that party. Clients should understand, however, that the opening statement is not the only opportunity to communicate with the other side and some of the more controversial or confrontational information may be best revealed during the private caucusing session and later communicated through the mediator to avoid inflaming the other side.

Verbal Communication

Word choice is critical—words that may seem harmless to attorneys, such as "liability," may carry negative connotations to the parties. "Role" or "involvement" may communicate the same message in neutral terms. Skilled attorneys have an ability to couch the facts, issues, and interests in language that communicates a willingness to examine the case closely, identify the risks, and attempt to resolve the dispute. Parties should also use language that communicates their viewpoint without creating a confrontational environment.

Nonverbal Communication

Body language also communicates. To convey your message, use effective body language. In American society, eye contact is important for credibility, persuasion, and communication. The rule of thumb is to look at the person who is speaking until they have finished, then look away. This creates the sense that you are interested in their message. Looking away can be perceived as not listening. If you are communicating with a person from a different culture, different body language may be preferable. In addition, a closed posture with arms folded across the chest may communicate a lack of openness, whereas relaxed arms may indicate a willingness to listen and negotiate. During telephone communication, pace, pitch, tone, volume, and voice inflection relay different messages. These nonverbal messages are often subconsciously heard.

3. Private Discussion Or Caucus

After the mediator has met with both sides in a joint session, the mediator may move the parties into two separate rooms. This stage of the mediation process gives lawyers an extraordinary opportunity to allow their clients to discuss the aspects of the case that are not found in the pleadings, whether or not they are legally relevant. This opportunity to vent personal emotions often leads to greater client satisfaction, because clients feel that someone has listened to them and has acknowledged their feelings. This portion of the process can make some attorneys uncomfortable because it departs from their area of expertise, and delves into the emotional basis of the legal action that does not fit neatly into any legal compartment. However, lawyers familiar with the mediation process have learned that this information is important to the client and must be addressed before the client can begin problem solving. The mediator then plays an important role of determining how much information should be shared, when it should be shared, by whom, and in what manner. The successful mediator strikes a balance between candor, relevancy, and deference to the feelings of both parties.

The mediator also reviews risks in the case with the parties, including the costs of the litigation, adverse rulings, personal and financial ramifications. Parties may need to consider the advantages and disadvantages of testifying as a witness and participating in the litigation process. Typically, the mediator will ask the attorney to describe the weaknesses in the case. This is an opportunity for attorneys to ensure that their clients understand the risks and have realistic expectations. A mediator may agree that an attorney's advice is reasonable or within acceptable parameters, and thus provide support for the lawyer's advice. Attorneys often use the process to fully inform clients who have unreasonably high expectations of the case. Thus, the mediator can be used to reinforce the attorney's statements, illuminate potential deficiencies, or temper a recalcitrant client.

4. *Options for Settlement*

After the issues are defined and the interests of the parties have been set, the parties will begin to explore options for settlement during caucus. Mediators will typically ask the parties to come up with as many options as possible and will discuss those options. The mediator will use the knowledge from both sides to attempt to formulate options that will appeal to both parties.

5. *Negotiation*

After the parties have created options, the mediator will take the options to the other side. At this point, attorneys discuss strategy with their clients and determine the manner in which they will negotiate with the other side. The negotiation then begins between the parties. As positive movements occur on both sides, the mediator will highlight areas of agreement, such as the interest of both sides to discontinue expending money on litigation, repair a relationship, or resolve this case. As momentum develops, lawyer and client should try to stay with the process to determine whether they can reach a mutually satisfactory resolution. During the negotiation process, attorneys shift between the role of advocating for the client to supporting the client's decisions. Seasoned lawyers recognize, at some point in the process, that the client has all the necessary information and is able to make an informed decision. At this time, the attorney's role shifts to that of supportive counselor.

6. *Reaching an Agreement*

In some instances, one party may request additional time to respond to an offer. In that instance, closure may occur at a later date or at a subsequent mediation conference. However, if the parties reach an agreement, they will likely gather in one room or telephone conference to discuss the terms of the agreement. In some instances, parties draft the agreement at that time. In other cases, the parties agree upon a person to draft the agreement. Attorneys should be prepared to discuss the terms of a final settlement agreement, including confidentiality clauses, releases of liens, or other provisions.

Client Satisfaction

When the parties are able to reach an agreement, both parties generally feel satisfied and sometimes elated. Often, both sides feel some discomfort but are pleased with their ability to resolve the dispute. In both instances, they have been empowered to solve their own dispute and have found a compromise that works for both sides. Personal or professional relationships may be restored, the emotional drain of the lawsuit or the fear of testifying is over, and the participants can move forward with their life.

In contrast, in litigation, the losing party may experience disappointment, frustration, anger, or other emotions. As one attorney commented, "The difference between mediation and litigation is that after litigation, my client walked down the hall with his head hanging down; but after mediation, my client was walking on air." Assisting clients to be empowered to make decisions in the mediation context is a skill that many attorneys are finding rewarding and necessary to practicing law.

II. Answers to Litigator's Questions About Mediation

Questions Litigators Ask About Mediation

*by David Grappo**

Lawyers are people who deal with disputes and hopefully resolve them. Legal scholar Karl Llewellyn wrote this description in *Bramble Bush*, a book often recommended to beginning law students. Legal literature abounds with strategies and techniques to help lawyers resolve disputes. In recent years, mediation has become a popular alternative to traditional litigation. This article briefly addresses questions that litigators frequently ask about mediation. Some of these questions could serve as topics of discussion for an entire seminar. The answers suggested here can serve as the starting point for such a discussion.

What Is Mediation?

Mediation is a meeting where the participants try to resolve their disputes. A neutral party, the mediator, presides over the meeting. If the parties reach a resolution, they may by agreement make it binding. One key feature of mediation is that the moderator remains neutral throughout the meeting. This distinguishes mediation from judicially supervised settlement conferences where the judge may actively pressure the parties to settle. Another key element of mediation is that no resolution is binding unless the parties agree to make it so. This ensures that there are no losers in the sense that there are winners and losers in conventional litigation. Until recently, all mediation was also voluntary. Some courts now compel parties to submit to mediation as a preliminary to arbitration or litigation. Whether compelled mediation will improve the court system, or corrupt the mediation process, remains to be seen. A possible problem in mandatory mediations is that one or more parties may not want to be there and thus may not cooperate in the process.

Is There Any Need for Mediation?

Our adversary system assumes that parties obtain the best results by vigorous advocacy. Some disputes in life may need such a resolution

* The author is a commercial litigation attorney in the San Francisco Bay Area and has frequently represented financial institutions in mediations.

system; many do not. A lawyer's advocacy skills can interfere with resolving some disputes, so lawyers seek out mediators, since mediators use non-adversarial techniques to resolve disputes. A lawyer shouldn't need a mediator in every case, but it is an alternative when the parties cannot find a way to settle their dispute.

Why Use Mediation?

Mediation is a faster, cheaper, alternative to litigation. It is faster because the mediation can be set at the convenience of the parties without waiting in the court system queues. It is cheaper because the parties avoid the cumbersome court forms and procedures which are intended to protect their right to a "fair fight" before an impartial judge. And in mediation, the parties can more easily preserve ongoing relationships than in litigation. The proceedings in mediation can be confidential, which may also be important to the parties.

Are There Downsides to Mediation?

If the parties fail to resolve the dispute, the mediation may appear to have been a waste of time and effort. However, the parties usually gain a better understanding of each other, which may aid a settlement later on. Compared to the cost and risk of litigation, the minimal cost of mediation justifies its use, even if the mediation fails and no settlement occurs. Some litigators complain that the opposing party gets too much "free discovery" in mediation. Cases rarely settle unless the parties exchange relevant information. Mediation encourages the mutual exchange of information, and this benefits both parties when they use the session to clarify their views of the dispute.

How Does a Mediation Session Work?

When attorneys are involved, the mediation typically follows this pattern:

- The attorneys usually prepare a short brief about the case for the mediator.
- The session begins with introductions and then everyone signs a confidentiality agreement.
- The mediator outlines the ground rules for the session, emphasizing the mediator's neutrality and explaining confidentiality rules. Everyone agrees to the ground rules.

- A round table discussion begins in order to identify the dispute. Each party speaks. In some cases, the parties can get quite emotional and do a lot of venting. The mediator will not express judgments or criticisms but will try to get the parties to focus on what they want and why they want it. The mediator will try to confirm that each side understands the other's position. When the mediator senses that the parties understand each other's position, the mediator will ask if there is anything else anyone needs to say. This is the time to speak up and get your "free discovery" on anything important that has not yet been covered. Terms of resolution may be discussed and concluded at the round table phase, but often are deferred to the next phase.
- As the round table session ends, the parties may go to separate rooms to meet privately with the mediator. This is a shuttle diplomacy phase where the mediator may go back and forth between the parties helping them to examine and confirm their understanding of the other parties' position. The terms of resolution will eventually be discussed.
- If a resolution is reached, a written agreement will be drawn up immediately for all parties to sign.
- If no resolution occurs, another round table meeting will occur where the mediator will not express any judgments, but will give suggestions to help the parties reach a resolution.

The mediation model differs from the traditional settlement conference model where the judge meets initially only with the attorneys, acts as an advocate against all sides, and meets with the parties only when the process stalls.

What Is the Role of the Mediator and What Skills Should the Mediator Have?

Ideally, the mediator should seem to be in the background so that the parties find their own resolution. But the reason people go to a mediator is because they can't solve their problems on their own. The mediator's proactive role is to help the parties overcome any attitudes or misconceptions that may have blocked resolution. This includes helping the parties find options and alternatives not yet considered. One of the mediator's skills is to be able to listen carefully in order to understand each party. The mediator must translate that understanding to the other parties if necessary. A mediator should not and need not express opinions; the thoughts and reasoning behind any opinion can be expressed as a non-judgmental question or comment to the party who needs to hear it. The mediator should not try to impose a resolution on the parties, and must be flexible enough to help the parties resolve their dispute even if he believes the resolution to be unfair to one of the parties.

How Successful Is Mediation?

There are no scientific studies on this question, but most mediators and mediation services claim a 65% to 90% success rate. These statistics seem incredible. But even if the true rate of success is only in the 50% range, mediation would still be an extraordinarily powerful tool for resolving disputes.

Why Is Mediation So Successful?

Most people prefer to settle their differences without resorting to hostilities. Mediation responds to that desire. Mediation encourages the expression and understanding of each party's feelings, motivations, and values, which otherwise might be ignored. Mediation also empowers people by enabling them to create and control the resolution to their disputes.

When Do You Mediate?

Mediation can be effective at any time during the course of a lawsuit or dispute. It is never too early to resolve a dispute. For example, in instances where a party wants more information, mediation can be substituted for the discovery process that occurs in normal litigation. An interim mediation solution is to identify what information is needed, agree on how to get the information, and then resume the mediation once the information is available. Likewise, it is never too late to resolve a dispute. Many lawsuits settle shortly before a trial. Mediation offers a neutral forum, which may be the best place for the parties to talk about settlement at the late stages of a lawsuit. The statistics on the success of mediation mean that the parties should try it as soon as possible, whenever possible, and at any stage of a dispute. Any time is a good time to resolve a dispute.

Where Do You Mediate?

The mediation should occur at a neutral site—not at the office of a party or a party's attorney. The mediator will usually provide or arrange for the neutral site. This avoids the perception of any home-court advantage, and it also avoids the distractions and interruptions which arise daily in any office. It is potentially disruptive when one party interrupts a mediation session to engage in other business activities. A mediator may, at the outset, ask the participants to turn off their beepers and cell phones or even to remove the batteries. The process works best when the parties are free to focus exclusively on their dispute.

Who Pays for the Mediator?

Mediators prefer that the parties share the fee equally. The parties may have more incentive to make the process work if they all pay for it. However, a party with limited financial resources should not be shy about asking other parties to pay the fee. This is always a negotiable issue.

How Much Does Mediation Cost?

The most popular mediators charge hundreds of dollars per hour. Some local governments sponsor low-fee, no-fee, and/or pay-if-satisfied mediation services. The cost ranges everywhere in between, but there is no direct correlation between price and quality of service.

How Do You Find Good Mediators?

This task is the same as finding any other service provider. Among the things you can do are:

- Ask your friends and colleagues for references.
- Ask for a résumé from your prospective mediator.
- Make sure that the mediator you choose has had mediation training.
- Ask for written materials, publications, or articles by the mediator, if available.
- Ask the mediator for references.
- Ask the mediator for statistics on number of mediations, successful resolutions, and types of matters mediated.
- Interview your prospective mediator. This concept surprises attorneys because of the bar on private conferences with a judge. A mediator is not a judge. You can and should interview your

prospective mediator. In addition to sizing up the mediator, you can share any insights you have about the problem which might help the mediator. You should also confirm that the prospective mediator understands the proper neutral role of a mediator. You probably won't get charged for your interview time if you keep it reasonable. It is a good idea to alert the other parties that you plan to interview the mediator as some parties may object to this practice.

Here are some general questions you may want to discuss with your prospective mediator:

- How do you see mediation as different from other types of dispute resolution?
- What is your view of the mediator's role in mediation?
- What mediation training did you have; did you find it valuable; why?
- Describe your experience as a mediator.
- What lessons has your mediation experience taught you?
- What are your strengths/weaknesses as a mediator?
- Do you have experience or preliminary thoughts on how to handle a problem such as (insert anything special about your situation)?
- Have you had any prior personal or professional contact with any other party? If so, what occurred, how would that affect you now, and what can you reveal about the other party?
- How can I best prepare myself, my client, and you for the mediation session?
- Do your unsuccessful mediations have common characteristics which the parties could have avoided? If so, please explain.
- If a dispute did not resolve at mediation, what initiatives have you taken afterwards to help the parties?
- What effort will you make to help me get another reluctant party to mediate?

What Do You Bring to the Mediation?

This question can be broken down into four categories: clients, witnesses/experts, documents/exhibits, and entourage.

Clients

If you represent a business entity, the person who comes to the mediation must have the authority to approve a settlement. When your client is only on phone standby, the risk of a failed mediation increases. The other party may infer a lack of seriousness, suspect other gamesmanship, and may be more likely to respond in kind.

Witnesses/Experts

Since mediation is not a trial, the presence and examination of witnesses is not appropriate unless the parties agree to it in advance.

Documents/Exhibits

Less is better. A skinny binder should be enough. Few documents get scrutinized at a mediation. Show that you know what is important and bring only that. The parties should also agree in advance if and when charts or visual aids should be produced and exchanged.

Entourage

Associates, paralegals, secretaries, etc. Mediation is supposed to be a peace gathering, not a show of force. If you have an army, leave it at home. The parties should also agree in advance on this issue.

What Code of Ethics Will the Mediator Follow?

In California, there are no generally accepted rules which all mediators follow, but some states do regulate mediators. Pay close attention to the mediator's opening statement about ground rules. Confidentiality will be discussed. Some mediators may advise you that they would relay any information from you unless told not to; others will not relay information unless a party requests this.

How Much Preparation Is Needed?

To achieve the best results in mediation, an attorney must be ready for anything that could come up. The mediator will tell you what you should submit in advance. Always exchange briefs and materials with the other party. Although you want the mediator to understand your client's position and to help you communicate it, the other party is the primary audience you are trying to reach. Anything private that you want the mediator to know should be said in private. Use your interview of the mediator for that.

How Much Settlement Authority Does Your Business Client Need?

Despite the importance of having a client with full settlement authority present, the person who attends from a large business will usually have strict limiting instructions not to settle the case either above or below a specified amount. Don't tell the mediator that limit, even if asked. An experienced mediator will usually regard such limits only as difficult obstacles, but not insurmountable ones. It is wise to urge your corporate clients to give liberal discretion and limits to the representative who attends the mediation. Information obtained at the mediation session may require a hasty reassessment of the proper resolution range for the dispute. You and your client must be ready to make such reassessments if new facts require it.

Who Makes the First Settlement Proposal?

This is a trick question. No one needs to make the first proposal, although anyone can do so. You will do well if you wait for the mediator to ask about this, either during the private conferences or at the round table. Many other issues usually need to be aired before a discussion of resolutions begins. A good mediator will know when to start talking about resolutions. Patience is the corresponding skill which the participants can practice.

Are There Common Characteristics to Disputes Which Don't Resolve At Mediation?

Not every mediation will be successful. One or more of the parties may be too emotionally or otherwise involved with the dispute to resolve it. Some parties may be unable or unwilling to reveal and discuss whatever keeps them from a resolution. Perceptions can differ irreconcilably. Sometimes the parties select the wrong mediator. Mediations can fail for any of the countless reasons that human relationships fail, but following the suggestions in this article can enhance your prospects for a successful mediation. With a clear understanding of how mediation works, you will more likely achieve the kinds of creative solutions which satisfy your clients and make mediation so popular.

How Long Should a Mediation Last?

Successful mediations often take longer than expected. Common scheduling is either for one half day or one full day. No matter how much time you initially schedule, make sure that you and your client keep the rest of that day free.

How Do Multiple Parties Affect Your Strategy?

Mediators often help the parties find unexpected resolutions in multi-party mediations. Your strategy should preserve the possibility of the unexpected. You should always try to maintain a courteous relationship with the other parties during mediation. The alignment of the parties can change dramatically during the session. Parties formerly opposed to each other may align against former allies. A hostile remark during the roundtable discussion can trigger such events. When you make a proposal to the group or to the mediator, limit it to what you want or to what you will contribute or do. Do not try to control what any other party must do. You preserve options if you discard the notion that each defendant must contribute a "fair share," or that a plaintiff must only receive a "fair recovery." Concentrate on getting what you really want or establishing what you will do. These general principles apply regardless of how your client fits into the alignment of the parties at the outset of the multi-party mediation.

Conclusion

Mediation is becoming popular because it is successful at resolving disputes. Clients, especially sophisticated clients, have seen these results and now frequently ask for mediation services from their attorneys. Litigators who adapt to the non-adversarial style of mediation will add new depth and versatility to their practice of law.

III. Preparing Clients

Preparing Your Client...for Mediation

*by L. Randolph Lowry**

Not all clients fully understand mediation. Drawing from his personal experience as a mediator, the author offers practical advice to lawyers on how best to prepare their clients. He recommends staging mock mediations, using proactive teaching techniques, and being creative wherever possible to help clients grasp the unique and unpredictable nature of what he calls the "negotiation dance."

The well-dressed corporate officials looked anxiously across the long mahogany table as the plaintiff's counsel described his client's age discrimination claim against their company. In the lawyer's mind the facts were clear, the liability certain and the damages substantial. As the corporate officers listened intently to the lawyer's presentation, they carefully considered the position they would take in response to the biting accusations.

Those business executives were impressed with the dispute resolution process in which they were participating. They saw how it encouraged the parties to communicate across the negotiation table with the assistance of a professional facilitator. In mediation, they were involved in listening, in sharing their perspective, and in working toward a solution they would help craft. It was a far cry from the formality of the courtroom that treated clients as little more than observers in the drama of litigation.

While real in appearance, atmosphere, and conduct, the entire process described above was only a staged enactment of what the lawyers for the executives expected would take place the following day when the case would be subject to actual mediation. It was a rehearsal undertaken to acquaint the business clients with the dynamics and strategies of what to them was a new and different approach to resolve conflict.

---

* The author is the founder and director of the Straus Institute for Dispute Resolution and a law professor at Pepperdine University School of Law in Malibu, California. Lowry holds a B.A. and M.P.A. from Pepperdine University and a J.D. from Hamline University School of Law. He is co-author of *Get Busy and Get Paid: Five Steps to Develop Your ADR Practice*, DISPUTE RESOLUTION MAGAZINE (Spring 2003).

Prepare a client for mediation? Pay a mediator to conduct a mock process and critique the performance of your client or the strategy of your negotiation? Invest time to anticipate an "informal" process? At first blush, such action might seem foreign to practitioners who already have too much to do, who are under pressure to avoid extra expenses, or who simply view mediation as an inconvenience on the way to litigation.

It surprised me when an excellent litigator from a large Los Angeles law firm called and asked if I would conduct a "mock" mediation—complete with hired plaintiff's counsel —to prepare his business clients for the mediation of an important age-discrimination case. Yet looking back, it made all the sense in the world. Such preparation is clearly a part of the evolution of dispute resolution activities in this country.

During the last decade, mediation—a process of facilitated negotiation—has emerged as a prominent avenue to settle legal disputes. Mediation has been defined as "[A] form of facilitated negotiation in which an impartial third party attempts to help disputing parties reach a mutually satisfactory solution to their problems, without the element of compulsion."[1] It is legislatively approved in many cases.[2] In some areas of the law, such as domestic relations, it is used extensively.[3] Mediation is court-mandated in many jurisdictions.[4] It is included in thousands of contracts.[5] While there are many views about mediation, its presence is

---

[1] David Plimpton, *Mediation of Disputes: The Role of the Lawyer and How Best to Serve the Client's Interest*, 8 ME. B.J. 38 (1993). For further definitions of mediation, see, for example, CHRISTOPHER W. MOORE, MEDIATION PROCESS: PRACTICAL STRATEGIES FOR RESOLVING CONFLICT 14 (1986), and WAYNE D. BRAZIL, EFFECTIVE APPROACHES TO SETTLEMENT: A HANDBOOK FOR LAWYERS AND JUDGES 17 (1988).

[2] *See, for example*, CAL. CIV. PROC. CODE § 1775 (West 1993 and Supp. 1994); TEX. CIV. PRAC. REM. CODE ANN. § 154.021 and 154.023 (Vernon Supp. 1994). *See also* Legislation on Dispute Resolution: 1990/1991 Addendum, 1992 A.B.A. Standing Committee on Dispute Resol.

[3] *See, for example*, CAL. CIV. CODE § 4607 (West Supp. 1994); 3 Del. Fam. Ct. R. 16(b) (1992). For a general discussion on the use of mediation in domestic relations disputes, *see* Leonard L. Riskin, *Mediation and Lawyers*,"43 OHIO ST. L.J. 29, at 32 (1982); Stephen J. Bahr, *Mediation is the Answer: Why Couples Are So Positive About this Route to Divorce*, FAM. L. ADVOC., Spring 1981, at 32.

[4] *See, for example*, TEX. CIV. PRAC. & REM. CODE ANN. § 152.001 to 152.004 (Vernon Supp. 1989); OKLA. STAT. ANN. TIT.12, § 1801 (West Supp. 1990). In general, see Andreas Nelle, *Making Mediation Mandatory: A Proposed Framework*,"7 OHIO ST. J. ON DISP. RESOL. 287 (1992).

[5] *See supra*, note 4, at 289. *See generally* ROBERT M. RODMAN, *ADR Contract Clauses*, *in* DONOVAN LEISURE NEWTON & IRVINE ADR PRACTICE BOOK 241 (J. Wilkinson, ed. 1990).

now part of society's dispute resolution fabric and one of the legal profession's most promising resources in settling disputes.

Lawyers increasingly use mediation to assist in settling their clients' cases. A recent survey of general counsel, deputy counsel, and chief litigators from 528 of the largest 1,000 corporations in America indicated that 85% had used mediation in the last three years, and 84% said they were likely or very likely to use mediation in the future. The survey also indicated that 81% of the respondents felt mediation provides a "more satisfactory process" than litigation, 66% said mediation provides "more satisfactory settlements" and 59% said mediation "preserves good relationships."[6]

Recently, when beginning the mediation of a construction defect case in southern California, I asked the eight lawyers in the room if any had been to mediation before. All eight raised their hands. In several California counties, virtually every case involving high emotion or ongoing relationships between the parties is being sent to a mediation process using a trained facilitator. The question is no longer, "Will lawyers and their clients use the mediation process?" but rather, "How can lawyers and clients prepare to maximize the resource of the mediation process?"

When I received the request from the Los Angeles law firm to prepare the lawyer and the business clients for mediation, I began thinking about what experiences might be most helpful and what information might be most useful. The following are a few ideas that should be considered by lawyers and clients alike.

Understanding the Mediation Process

Professionals in any field are familiar with their nomenclature and their forms of practice. They may fail, however, to understand how unfamiliar the client may be with such language and practice. Some clients have experienced litigation, and a smaller number have sat in on an arbitration proceeding. Even in the late 1990s, however, relatively few clients have been involved in mediation.

Of the growing variety of dispute resolution processes, litigation is most familiar to clients because of highly publicized trials and generations of television shows such as "Matlock," "Perry Mason," "The

---

[6] Gary Phelan, *Dispute Resolution the Mediation Way*, CONN. L. TRIB., Aug. 18, 1997. The survey was conducted by Price Waterhouse, Cornell University and the Foundation for the Prevention and Early Resolution of Conflict.

People's Court," and "L.A. Law." In the minds of most clients, the vision of processing any legal case probably includes a collage of what has been experienced and, therefore, what is expected.

As the lawyer knows, there are dramatic differences between the adjudicative processes of litigation and arbitration, and consensual processes of negotiation and mediation. It is imperative that the fundamental differences in these processes be understood so that the client can effectively join the advocate at the mediation table.[7]

For instance, many clients assume that whatever the process, sooner or later someone will "decide the case." They are more familiar with judges making decisions than with mediators facilitating the development of settlement options.

Recently I was explaining mediation to a prospective user. I was quite deliberate in describing each step of the process—convening the parties, opening statements, information sharing, reality testing, option generating, and closure.[8] After my elaborate and, I thought, accurate explanation, he asked, "And when do you make the decision?" I recognized that, even though I painstakingly explained the process, as I had done many times before, his expectations still involved some form of adjudication. One can seldom assume an accurate understanding of the process.

In addition, it is also important to recognize how difficult it is to verbally describe what is a dynamic and somewhat unpredictable process. Lawyers do not learn litigation skills by just listening to lectures; neither will clients understand mediation by hearing only verbal descriptions. Recognizing this reality, one prominent Los Angeles lawyer/mediator[9] created a videotape library so clients may observe an abbreviated mediation. In the era of video technology, such is a responsive attempt to help the client understand by seeing.

While such resources will be increasingly helpful, the law firm that asked me for assistance wanted the clients not only to observe the

---

[7] The consensual nature of mediation is implicit in its definition. *See supra*, note 1. Note, *Mandatory Mediation and Summary Jury Trial: Guidelines for Ensuring Fair and Effective Processes*, 103 HARV. L. REV. 1086 (1990). *See, for example*, NANCY H. ROGERS & CRAIG A. MCEWEN, MEDIATION: LAW, POLICY & PRACTICE 20 (1989). *See also* John B. Bates, Jr., *Using Mediation to Win for Your Client*, 38 Prac. Law. (March 1992) p. 24; Nelle, *supra*, note 4, at 287.

[8] For a more detailed discussion of the mediation process, *see* ROGERS & MCEWEN, *supra*, note 7, at 7-10 (1989); MOORE, *supra*, note 1, at 153 *et passim*.

[9] Forrest S. Mosten is the senior partner at Mosten and Wasserstrom in Beverly Hills, California.

process but also to actually participate in it. In response to the lawyer's request, I described the mediation process to his client, and then held an abbreviated mediation session with opening statements, information sharing, caucusing, and reality testing. The purpose was to have clients become so familiar with the process, they would be relaxed while it was actually conducted and be able to contribute confidently to its dynamics. The preparation process worked. Seeing and experiencing the mock mediation resulted in excellent questions by the clients, a modified strategy for their presentations, and the sense that they were full participants in the strategy that was offered to resolve their legal dispute. The clients' participation would not have been as effective without actually experiencing mediation. A wide body of recent literature proposes that adult education, as opposed to children's education, depends upon proactive rather than reactive teaching techniques.[10] Adult education is integral in any employee training scenario; and corporate training manuals often cite the efficacy of proactive teaching techniques.

Mediation Is a Continuation of Negotiation

Clients in the mediations I conduct often forget that the essence of the mediation process is negotiation—that give-and-take communication process we use to put deals together and resolve conflicts. In mediation, unlike adjudicative processes such as arbitration and litigation, the parties themselves attempt to reach a satisfactory settlement. The "real business" of a mediation session is the negotiation of a settlement.[11] The mediator merely facilitates the discussion.

While obvious to experienced lawyers, clients who do not recognize the application of negotiation strategies in mediation never reap the potential benefits of the process and often severely jeopardize their cases. For instance, a client entering the mediation room and directing comments to the mediator rather than the opposing party misses a tremendous opportunity to influence the only person in the room who can agree to settle the case.[12] A client making a "final offer" too early in the mediation process may demonstrate a lack of understanding of the

---

[10] *See*, *for example*, Malcolm Knowles, The Adult Learner: A Neglected Species (1990); Manuel London, Managing the Trainee Enterprise (1989); Thomas L. Quick, Training Managers So They Can Really Manage (1991).

[11] Charles Guitard, *Preparing for Mediation and Negotiation*, pt. 2, 37 PRAC. LAW., October 1991, at 66.

[12] "The mediator does not have the authority to write the terms of the agreement." FRANK Strelec, *A Trial Lawyer's Guide to Mediation*, FLA. B.J., July-Aug. 1991, at 70.

time necessary for the "negotiation dance" to function effectively.[13] A client with a single outcome in mind will not be open to the creative possibilities—even in acute, legal conflict—and may miss the very opportunity he or she seeks to resolve the case in a satisfactory way.[14]

Each of these mistakes may be innocently made. Nevertheless, they reflect a lack of understanding of what is happening in negotiation. Many times the most persuasive conversation is between the parties rather than between a party and the mediator. Most of the time, a series of negotiation moves will be necessary to reach agreement. Creativity, while not the key to resolving every case, is a highly recognized tool; but it is dependent on how the parties use it.[15] Effective negotiation strategies must be understood by the client (and lawyer) in mediation. When understood, such strategies can be carried out in a more effective way.

Several years ago I mediated a high-dollar employment discrimination case between a terminated executive and his former corporate employer. Midway through the first day of the lengthy mediation, the president of the company pulled me aside and asked if he could explain his perspective to the plaintiff. The president then explained to the plaintiff that he had come to the company after the incident involving the employee had taken place and that he wanted the employee to know that, regardless of the outcome of the employee's litigation, he regretted what had happened and was committed to its not happening to anyone else. In response to that explanation, did the plaintiff and his lawyer bringing the lawsuit pack up and leave? Of course not. After the explanation, did that direct and candid communication influence the nature of the negotiations, bringing the parties closer to settlement? Absolutely! The president was a client who saw the big picture, recognized that the legal positions did not reflect the entire conflict, and sought to influence the negotiation deliberately. He understood that negotiation is a communication process and used it to assist in the settlement effort.

---

[13] *See* Roger Fisher & William Ury, Getting to Yes: Negotiating Agreement without Giving In (1981) pp. 11-13.

[14] *See, for example*, Fisher & Ury, *id.* at 76-77. *See also*, William Ury, Getting Past No: Negotiating with Difficult People (1991) pp. 18-19.

[15] *See, for example,* Ross R. Hart, *Improving Your Chance of Success During Construction Mediation,* 47 ARB. J., Dec. 1992, at 14; Peter Lovenheim, *Mediate, Don't Litigate*, at 67.

Mediation Is a Participatory Process

Mediation is demanding of clients, but also responsive to them. To a large extent, clients sit on the sidelines in adjudicatory processes such as arbitration and litigation. Compare this with the mediation hearing, where it is the lawyers who often sit on the sidelines as coaches.[16] In adjudicative processes, clients speak only when they are asked, do so under the careful control of their counsel, and give up much of who they are in order to participate in a very structured process. While there may be great security for lawyers in forums that give them almost total control of clients' participation, it also may be very limiting not to have the energy, talent, and/or passion of the client involved in the resolution of the client's dispute. Mediation provides the opportunity to capture these elements for the client and have them contribute to the settlement.

Several years ago, while mediating an age discrimination case involving an older woman who was probably the victim of wrongful termination, the importance of client involvement became abundantly clear. The lawyers spent almost two hours describing the legal dimensions of their cases. Although artfully done, everyone in the room knew that neither side would convince the other nor could anyone totally predict the outcome at trial. That did not keep them from trying.

It was the client, however, who, frustrated by the ongoing legal argument, stated simply that what was most important was her lost medical benefits. She described her needs as sole provider of financial support for her son and daughter, both of whom had serious diseases, and her husband who was terminally ill with cancer. No lawyer could have described it as well nor provided as graphic a picture of her circumstances. Her somewhat spontaneous, but very human involvement in the mediation process caused the defendants to re-evaluate their case more objectively. The case settled that afternoon. In the confidential setting of the mediation room, important things happen when those who own the conflict participate in its resolution.[17]

---

[16] Compare this with the mediation hearing, where it is the lawyers who often sit on the sidelines as coaches. Martin Kobren, *Preparing for Mediation*, MD. B.J., Jan. 1993, at 46. Whereas the lawyer's role in litigation is generally seen as "a knight in shining armor, whose courtroom lance strikes down all obstacles" (Warren E. Burger, *Isn't There a Better Way?*, 68 A.B.A. J. 274 (1982)), it is the parties in a mediation session who are involved directly in the give and take of negotiation. ROGERS & MCEWEN, *supra*, note 7, at 20. For a good general comparison of the lawyer's role in litigation and mediation, *see* Curt Micka, *From Litigation to Mediation*, 23 MED. Q., (Spring 1989) at 87.

[17] In mediation, "those who are in the best position to determine the outcome do so." John B. Bates, Jr., *Using Mediation to Win for Your Client*, 38 PRAC. LAW., March 1992, at 25. *See also* ROGERS & MCEWEN, *supra*, note 7, at 22.

Mediation Is a Creative Process

Lawyers who expect legal disputes to be resolved in courtroom adjudication and clients who assume a decision-making model for dispute resolution generally adopt a "right" position for their case and seek to persuade the opposite party to accept it. It is quite likely, however, that even in a lengthy litigation process, there will still be only two solutions on the table or before the court—one advanced by the plaintiff, and one advanced by the defendant.

This is not surprising considering how lawyers are educated. From day one in law school, energetic students are challenged to take and advocate positions.[18] At times, the position taken is even less important than the ability to advocate persuasively for it in the context of "thinking like a lawyer."

Such skills serve lawyers well when conducting courtroom arguments in the 3% to 5% of cases that are fully litigated. Such skills are woefully limiting, however, when the focus is on problem solving at the mediation table. While persuasion is important, mediation affords the opportunity to change the dynamic, refocus the conversation, and capture the potential of more creative and innovative solutions—if the lawyers and the clients are prepared to pursue them.

In the case of the older woman described above, that is what happened. After the brilliant oral advocacy, the real question became, "How might the lawyers address her primary need for medical insurance during her retirement years?" The defendant company was quick to reject writing out a check for $187,000, the estimated cost of such coverage. One lawyer, in a creative moment, correctly pointed out that if the plaintiff had been able to retire, those benefits would have been automatically extended to her—and the cost to the company would have been so insignificant that "it would not be worth talking about." The ultimate settlement, in addition to some immediate consideration, included her "re-employment" so that the benefits could be extended to her. She was given the choice, however, whether she would return to work or, with her salary, stay home and take care of her dying husband. While obviously not possible in every wrongful termination case, in this instance it was far easier for the company to justify compensation valued at a few hundred thousand dollars being paid through re-employment,

---

[18] *See generally* Micka, *supra*, note 16.; Edward Sutton, *ADR and Law School Curricula*, (1984) VT. LAW SCHOOL DISPUTE RESOL. PROJECT; Burger, *supra*, note 16, at 275.

rather than through a much larger cash settlement. The creativity of that solution would never have occurred in court. It is not the least bit surprising as a result of mediation. Unlike litigation, which places primary emphasis on monetary damages, mediation enables parties to "fashion a creative solution to their disputes that will address their unique situation."[19]

Lawyers usually find it relatively easy to get business clients to think creatively—that is how businesspeople are trained in business school. They understand brainstorming solutions, free association, inventing options, and taking risks—their business success depends on it. Lawyers need to encourage businesspersons to use such skills in the mediation process and then join them in that creative and fulfilling work.

The Theater of Mediation

Every dispute resolution process is set up to deal not only with the substance of the dispute but also to provide some degree of satisfaction with the process of resolution.[20] In court, parties depend upon the integrity of the litigation process being high enough that even the losing party will accept the mandated result. Those who are satisfied with a decision are much more likely to comply with it.[21] In mediation, we depend upon the credibility of the process so that parties can work toward and find agreement which they can support.[22] Part of their ability to be supportive is related to how the "theater" of the process is performed.

Mediation is not a staged production that imitates reality, but rather a process that allows the parties—who are the ones "on stage" in mediation—to feel that their needs are truly met. For instance, it is important for clients to express, sometimes quite emotionally, their view of the conflict and its implications. The adversarial system stifles the ability of the parties to express their views of the conflict. It "may not

---

[19] Mary K. McLeod, *Preparing Your Client for Mediation*, 50 BENCH & BAR OF MINN. 26, (1993) at 26-27.

[20] For general information and psychological analyses of client satisfaction with the process and why procedural fairness is important, *see* Tom R. Tyler, *The Psychology of Disputant Concerns in Mediation*, 3 NEG. J. 367 (1987). Jessica Pearson, *An Evaluation of Alternatives to Court Adjudication*, 7 JUS. SYS. J. 420, (1982) at 431-33.

[21] *See, for example*, ROGERS & MCEWEN, *supra*, note 7, at 23.

[22] Some commentators cite the "coercive nature of adjudication" as the reason for noncompliance. Pearson, *supra*, note 20, at 420. In contrast, the "consensual process" of mediation "encourages more cooperative relations in the future." *Note*, *supra*, note 7, at 1092.

allow parties to resolve their underlying differences and often leaves their relationship permanently scarred."[23] Mediation, on the other hand, "provides opportunities for expression of feelings and discussion of legally extraneous matters.…Sometimes airing and acknowledging emotion facilitates the quest for settlement."[24]

While theatrical, this part of the mediation process is not always pleasant. It is necessary, however, to relieve clients of pent-up feelings that have festered for weeks, months, or years. In addition, it is necessary for lawyers to express, in front of their clients, their own indignation regarding the case—not because it is necessary for them to release their frustrations—but because the client needs to see the lawyers working as "zealous advocates."

Finally, it is critical, at times, for a client, such as a corporate defendant, to make the offer to the plaintiff personally. The corporate officer, not the company's lawyer, is a representative of the offending party. The satisfaction of hearing the settlement offer from the offending party provides value beyond the dollars exchanged. It becomes the emollient that allows the plaintiff to settle the case and get on with life. To achieve it, however, the company official must see and participate, sometimes after being coached in the theater of the moment.

Describing mediation as theater is not to suggest a contrived, dishonest, or artificial circumstance but rather to recognize the real human emotions and needs that must be met in effective dispute resolution. Responding to them through a carefully conducted process is key to more effective use of the unique mediation environment.

Good lawyers and helpful clients will discover, through repeated involvement in the mediation process, these observations that came from the mediation preparation experience at the Los Angeles law firm described earlier. Knowing the mediation process, understanding that mediation is continued negotiation, watching the participatory nature of the process, seeing the creativity possible in mediation, and appreciating the theater of mediation, comprise only a beginning list of items lawyers will want their clients to know to maximize the benefits of facilitated negotiation. The influence each of these items has in achieving a result acceptable to a client should not be underestimated.

While there were many reasons for the successful, real mediation that took place, the lawyer in the mock mediation described at the

---

[23] *Note*, *supra*, note 7, at 1091.

[24] ROGERS & MCEWEN, *supra*, note 7, at 21.

beginning of this article was gracious to attribute much of his client's success to the "hands on" preparation experience. The result the lawyer and his client achieved—a settled case—was the result sought by those choosing that dispute resolution process. It is most likely to occur when the lawyer and the clients prepare to take full advantage of the resource of mediation.

IV. Managing Clients' Emotions

Managing Client Emotions: How a Mediator Can Help

*by L. Therese White & Bill White**

Often, disputants are angry and emotional. Unfortunately, their lawyers and advocates are not always equipped to handle their emotions. A mediator may be needed before the party and its attorney or advocate can continue dealing with their opponent. In this article, the authors show some examples of how mediation effectively addresses emotional issues, provides reality checks, and paves the way for the resolution of disputes.

Anger. Sadness. Fear. Disgust. Shame. As you well know, disputes are often full of powerful, negative emotions on both sides. Sadly, these emotions can overwhelm good judgement and damage attorney/client relations, thereby reducing the possibility of a timely and successful out-of-court resolution. Sometimes, they even force an otherwise risky and unnecessary trial.

This article is about helping attorneys and other professional conflict managers reestablish order after the client's emotional brain has overpowered his thinking brain. It's also about the effective use of mediators to accomplish this task.

When Emotions Take Over

In his book, *Emotional Intelligence*, Dan Goleman says, "(emotions) are self-justifying, with a set of perceptions and proofs all their own ...When in control, the emotional mind harnesses the rational mind to its purpose, thus distorting past memories and current realities." What matters is what seems to be rather than what is, what is desired rather than what can be reasonably expected, and what is demanded rather than what can be negotiated.

---

* Ms. White is a mediator specializing in diversity-related employment disputes and conflict resolution training. She is an American Arbitration Association panelist.

Mr. White is an Associate Professor of Marketing at California State University, Los Angeles. He holds a B.S. from the University of Connecticut and a M.B.A. from Stanford University.

An emotion is defined as a feeling and its distinctive thoughts, psychological and biological states, and propensities to act. There are hundreds of emotions—good and bad. Emotions have their own variations and nuances, not to mention the ability to blend with other emotions.

Some people manifest their negative emotions in outbursts, others through quiet storms. But one thing for sure is that when people are acting on an emotion (be it for a split second or for a lifetime), they honestly feel it is the best thing to do, no matter how stupid it may appear later.

Most people act out because they prefer a conflict they know to the resolutions they cannot completely imagine. People also use emotion to keep from getting at the core of the conflict, which may be too painful to face head-on. In any event, emotional overreactions and underreactions are merely attempts to gain or regain control.

Experience has shown that given their left-hemisphere mindset, attorneys sometimes have great difficulty dealing with the emotions of their clients. Having been trained in the logic-driven rigors of fact-finding, analysis, and debate, it can become impossible to properly address highly charged matters of the heart and spirit. For that matter, attorneys often unwittingly feed the emotional fires of their clients. Here's how.

Conventional wisdom demands getting a "good, tough lawyer to protect your interests." Knowing this, some attorneys feel it's their duty to play that role to the extreme. The issues between the disputants then become subordinated to the increasingly complicated litigation process, and the "winner-take-all" battle between the attorneys.

Feeling overwhelmed, the clients are forced to hide behind their attorneys, and relinquish all control over the outcome. At this point, according to mediator Chip Rose in his Web site, "effective communication between the (parties) has been all but eliminated, and…the parties undoubtedly feel more not less fearful and experience greater not less anxiety."

This is where the talents of a good mediator and the benefits of the mediation process can put the attorney and client on the same page. This is how it is done.

Emotions Must Be Expressed

Like it or not, there is no official place for emotions in the litigation process. This is unfortunate in that a simple clearing of the air can move numerous conflicts to resolution. Only then can the unseen emotional complexities surrounding a case surface. This is especially true in situations involving diversity, persons with disabilities, the family, discrimination, and harassment.

One of the authors of this article recently mediated a seemingly impossible employment conflict pitting a "facts-only" corporate attorney against an abrasive, highly emotional plaintiff. The breakthrough finally came in caucus when the mediator validated the plaintiff's frustrations and asked her what could be done to make the process easier. That is when she confided that she had a mental disability (unbeknownst even to her attorney) that interfered with her ability to communicate civilly under stress. The mediator then decided to keep the two sides apart and to translate their respective points of view in a manner each could respect. That important finding made all the difference for a variety of logical and emotional reasons. The case settled quickly because the plaintiff finally felt heard and understood. And the defending attorney was able to appreciate the validity of the plaintiff's position.

Reality Checks

In an article in the March 8, 2000, issue of the Los Angeles Daily Journal (entitled "Is That All?"), mediator Jeff Kichaven gave some examples of what he calls the "climactic question." These are questions such as, "Is that all they're willing to offer, after all I've been through?" or "Why should we give that [expletive deleted] a dime?" It is the defining question that attorneys know will arise sooner or later, and that they had better be prepared to answer with conviction. Otherwise, cases that should settle won't, and the attorney is stuck with a continuing lawsuit and a client or boss with serious doubts about the attorney's effectiveness.

When faced with these and other troublesome situations, attorneys should take advantage of a good mediator's ability to safely deliver bad news to difficult, inflexible clients by expanding their perspectives.

Take, for example, a case mediated by one of the writers of this article. A delusional client wouldn't back off the "optimistic figure" his attorney quoted well before unexpected discovery suggested far less. The attorney feared to further press the issue with the client; so she pursued mediation.

The opposition agreed, and mediation followed. As it turned out, the mediator had done exactly as the attorney in question had anticipated. That is, the mediator presented (in caucus) the more modest outcomes of similar cases, talked about the inherent risks of a trial, and then invited them to re-evaluate their original position. Not surprisingly, the client quickly adjusted his stance, and was very happy accepting a more reasonable figure.

Non-Monetary Solutions

"When they say it's not the money, it's the money—but not every time." That old saying has been modified to recognize the fact that emotions aren't always driven by money alone. Mediation unlike litigation is excellent at finding the pivotal, nonmonetary needs that can sabotage an agreement. This is because skilled mediators are equally adept at dealing with the interests of the parties as well as the facts of the case. Getting away from win-lose debates over which side has the higher quality facts and moving toward creative, collaborative solutions are at the heart of the mediation process.

Think how often you've heard this statement or its equivalent from a distraught disputant: "I just don't ever want this to happen to anyone else." Concern for others is as much an emotional interest/need as are safety, greed, and revenge. Accordingly, a defending employer's offer to introduce a diversity-awareness and sensitivity training program might be just the thing to end a stalemate.

Sadly, if attorneys aren't truly sensitive to the significance of such seemingly innocuous statements, they miss out on the opportunity to really satisfy their most difficult clients.

Apprehension/despair, embarrassment/humiliation, and wonderment/shock are just a few of the numerous other misread, emotional deal-killers. Good mediators know how to identify them even in their most subtle forms, and then help discover effective solutions. And these solutions may have little to do with money. Sometimes nothing more is needed to make it all go away than a sincere apology and an enforceable promise to change.

In summary, this article explained how attorneys could use mediation as a tool to manage client emotions and to efficiently resolve more cases. When working at its best, the mediation process allows emotions to be expressed, provides reality checks, and addresses emotional needs that may not require a totally monetary solution.

Can mediation rein in every client with runaway emotions? No. But it's probably a better alternative than "just dealing with the facts."

Are You a Dangerously Good Mediator?

All mediators are not created equal. Like most other professionals, they vary in style and substance.

Ken Cloke, noted author and director of the Dispute Resolution Center in Santa Monica, Calif., is recognized as being among the elite of the mediation profession. He offers a fascinating look into his thinking about the field in his new book, *Mediating Dangerously: The Frontiers of Conflict Resolution* (Jossey-Bass, 2001). We have been fortunate to work with Ken, and to see him apply his nontraditional methods first hand. Here's our interpretation of what it takes to be a dangerously good mediator. (Caution: These are advanced mediation techniques, and should only be considered by those confident of handling the situation if things should backfire.)

Don't Settle

Don't settle for necessary change. If the goal is to settle rather than truly resolve a conflict, the mediator and/or the disputants may "settle for half measures, squelch honest ideas and true feelings, and undermine the values that lie at the heart of the (mediation) process." At what point does settlement for the sake of settlement become peace at any price? All too often, that price is tolerance of the unacceptable and the interruption of the personal transformation of the parties. So the question is: will you exert the extra effort to fully resolve conflicts by equalizing the negotiating power of the disputants, surfacing all underlying concerns, and promoting shared responsibility for the conflict and the outcome?

Forget Being Neutral

Neutrality implies objectivity, thus possessing a certain distance from the conflict and its outcome. This indifference—characterized by bland, safe language and demeanor—can paralyze the subjective interactions and the creative problem solving that are often needed to break an impasse. Why not become "omni-partial," which means being assertively, maybe even aggressively partial to both sides at the same time? If done properly, this approach will deepen understanding, empathy, and honesty between the adversaries and also within the mediator herself.

Be Unprofessional, When Necessary

In difficult mediations, the question often becomes, "Do you want to be professional or effective?" Sometimes mediators must let their hair down to gain the attention, trust and honest involvement of the disputants. The goal here is to be authentic, which can only happen if you are seen as truly mediating from the heart. When appropriate, will/can you wear your heart on your sleeve?

Don't Be "Too" Helpful

Helplessness does not necessarily mean harmlessness. Usually one or both sides in a conflict plays the role of victim, thereby believing "they will be supported only as long as they are in pain, unhealed, and oppressed…" Mediators must protect themselves from being used by so-called victims, and falling into the abyss of providing negative nurturing. This is where the mediator/rescuer does more harm than good by interfering with the responsibility and the potential of the victims to resolve the conflict themselves. Can your self-image handle the risk of being considered heartless?

V. When Clients Don't Disclose

The Phenomenon of Nondisclosure by Parties in Mediation: Observations on Party Nondisclosure As a Factor That the Mediator Must Deal with and Suggested Strategies to Bring About a Successful Settlement*

by Michael Redfern[*]

Having learned as a young lawyer that clients do not always tell their lawyers the whole story, I came to assess my clients and their problems always with this in mind. One of my earliest experiences was the representation of an elderly driver who had been involved in a motor accident collision with another motorcar. The other driver's insurer had made a settlement offer I considered inadequate. I advised my client to turn it down but he rejected my advice and firmly instructed me to accept the offer. I soon realized that he appeared to have his own very sound reasons for wanting to settle the case—reasons that had not been disclosed to me.

Experienced defense counsel know the impact of unknown and undisclosed facts. They sometimes counsel their clients to make a "cheeky" offer—one that is less than what might be regarded as reasonable or just bordering on the reasonable—"to test the water" and "see how serious" the plaintiff really is.

Because clients often do not tell their lawyers all they need to know to realistically assess the value of a case, I believe that every settlement offer, however unreasonable it may seem to counsel, must be presented to the client. For example, counsel may be ignorant of financial pressures or health problems plaguing the client or his or her family that make it difficult to take the case further. Thus, a less than satisfactory settlement proposal from the lawyer's point of view might be perfectly satisfactory, and sometimes a very good settlement, to the client.

At the end of the day it is the client's case, the client's money, and the client's decision. If counsel has thoroughly discussed the settlement

---

[*] Mr. Redfern is a mediator and a partner in Russell Kennedy, Solicitors, in Melbourne, Australia. He is co-author of the leading Australian law texts: *Australian Tenancy Practice and Precedents* and *Franchising Law and Practice.*

proposal and is satisfied that the client is fully informed of all consequences of accepting it—that should usually end the matter.

Nondisclosure also occurs in mediation. No matter how open a party may be with the mediator, he or she may not reveal all. A recent mediation in which I acted for one of the parties is a good example.

I represented the claiming party, which had received a notice of termination of its supply agency agreement with an overseas company. Legal proceedings were commenced claiming wrongful termination and requiring reinstatement of the agreement. The court ordered the dispute to mediation.

The facts were pretty clear. The supplier had acted unreasonably. My client was entitled to some type of relief. Soon after the mediation got underway my client was offered a short extension of the agreement and accepted the offer, although it appeared quite unreasonable. However, from the client's commercial perspective, it was in fact very reasonable.

My client wanted to retain the agency for a short time just to enable recent important orders to proceed. But beyond that it had reasons for wanting to terminate the agency as quickly as possible, without having to pay any compensation for early termination to the principal. The short extension provided by the terms of settlement proved the ideal way to meet all of my client's commercial needs without any compensation payment at all.

I knew these considerations were influencing the client's decision to accept the offer but many of them had not been disclosed to the mediator. Even without having this information, the mediator recognized that this offer might form the basis for a resolution of the dispute.

The mediator rarely has time to get to know all of the factors that may be important to the parties. Most if not all parties have other agendas, opinions, values and requirements that they are unwilling to share in confidence with the mediator (or even with their counsel). The mediator must accept that undisclosed factors usually will be present in a case. A mediator who wishes to be effective in mediation must develop practices that take these undisclosed factors into account and allow them to have an effect.

Some Mediation Strategies

At the earliest opportunity the mediator should work to gain a full appreciation of all issues in dispute and the dynamics of the situation. In the joint session, the parties should be allowed the freedom to tell their own stories and, above all, hear the other party's story in its own words. Only in this way can they learn what they are up against.

In private caucuses the mediator will discuss all of the legal and technical issues with the parties to ensure that they have fully considered their respective positions. It is often through this talking process that the mediator assists the parties to develop their own views of the case and formulate proposals that may ultimately lead to settlement. These discussions sometimes lead a party to reveal previously undisclosed information or wishes that may suggest the substance or direction of practical proposals likely to produce an acceptable outcome.

A well-established mediator technique is to stress the consequences to the parties if the dispute is not settled, such as the total legal costs that are likely to be incurred if the case goes to trial, the likely date and duration of the trial, the witnesses who may be called and other matters.

The party, and his or her attorney and expert, if any, should participate in the private caucus. Once all the issues have been fully discussed and considered, it can be helpful for the mediator to talk privately with the party. This assists the mediator in gauging whether the parties' wishes and interests are known, since often counsel may have prejudged the matter incorrectly or inappropriately or may not be aware of the factors that are most important to the party. It may be prudent in the particular situation to request counsel's permission before doing so, out of respect for the attorney-client relationship.

At the appropriate time the mediator should discuss with each party the full range of avenues of potential resolution. But far from putting out proposals or views, the mediator should seek to tease out proposals from the parties that may be consistent with what they say they want or appear to want. By listening very carefully the mediator may pick up on what might really be attractive to the parties as a possible settlement consideration.

The private sessions are usually critical. Once trust in the mediator has been formed, it is here that the parties often tell the mediator matters they would not tell their lawyers, let alone the other party. If both parties genuinely desire to resolve the matter it will be easier to float proposals for settlement.

In formulating the settlement proposals, the mediator should not decide what is best for the parties. Above all it should be made clear that the result of the mediation, including any settlement, is entirely in their hands, not in the control of the mediator or even the parties' lawyers or experts.

The parties should be encouraged to formulate their own proposals along whatever lines they consider workable for them. If and when a proposal is made, it generally should be communicated to the other side.

The parties may be strongly influenced by the mediator. At all times the mediator must be very conscious of this power. Therefore, the mediator should not endorse any particular proposal for settlement and should make clear that any proposals transmitted emanate from the other party.

Conclusion

Mediators must be aware that parties do not disclose all of the factors that may bear upon their decision-making processes. Thus, the mediator must develop the parties' trust and then engage the parties in full discussions that encourage these factors to be brought to light. Often these hidden concerns, interests and agendas may lead to creative ideas for settlement.

* This article is adapted from "Capturing the Magic—Nondisclosure as a Factor in Mediation Practice," Australasian Dispute Resolution Journal (May 1999). Details of the mediation discussed herein have been changed to preserve confidentiality.

VI. Using Expert Witnesses in Mediation

Experts in Mediation: Catalysts for Resolution

by Roger M. Deitz[*]

Experts have traditionally been regarded as credentialed spokespersons who endorse their client's position. To regard an expert as a catalyst for resolution in mediation may appear contradictory to the expert's perceived role as a paid advocate. However, experience demonstrates many instances in which an expert brings both knowledge and objectivity to a dispute and assists in a negotiated resolution. For example, an expert can significantly move the parties from emotion to reason and from expectation to reality. This article explores numerous ways experts can bring added value to the resolution of disputes.[1]

Prior to Mediation

A party to a dispute can retain an expert before a claim is filed to help identify issues, marshal facts, and bring key elements into focus. If counsel is unfamiliar with the client's business or with a particular product or service the client sells, an expert can be an invaluable resource, helping the attorney understand the facts and issues and identify the salient aspects of both.

An expert can help organize the case and provide a reality check. The expert may see potential weaknesses in the client's case or other facts the adversary may use which counsel has not recognized. For example, in a securities case, the expert may notice entries on the client's tax returns or trading in other accounts that could prove problematic. The

---

[*] Mr. Deitz is an attorney, mediator, and arbitrator based in New York and is the former Senior Trial Counsel of the U.S. Securities and Exchange Commission. He is a Special Master of the Supreme Court of the State of New York—Appellate Division. In addition he serves as co-chair of the Subcommittee for Commercial Disputes of the State of New York Unified Court System Alternative Dispute Resolution Advisory Committee. Mr. Deitz is a graduate of Brown University, Cornell Law School and Harvard Law School Program of Instruction for Lawyers.

[1] The author expresses his appreciation to Howard Berg, Hugh Cadden, Mary Calhoun, Robert Connor, Henry Ferguson, Ed Horowitz, Robert Lowry, Craig McCann, Sol Nirenberg, Jim Rothenberg, Patrice Stewart, Ross Tulman, and numerous other experts.

expert can help the client reach a balanced understanding of the issues, defenses and risks of litigation.

An expert with experience in mediation can aid in selecting a mediator. The expert's knowledge of different mediators and their mediation styles may help the party decide on the type of mediator, and even a particular mediator, appropriate for the dispute and the personalities of the parties and counsel.

During Mediation

The parties may retain their own experts after the mediation commences. Or they may agree to retain a single expert to perform a particular analysis or other tasks. This is especially useful in complex cases. However, the expert's role may change as the case progresses.

The parties are more likely to choose an expert who appears regularly in the type of dispute at hand. An expert who normally appears only on behalf of one side (on behalf of plaintiffs or defendants) will have to establish credibility with both sides to be a useful force for resolution.

Experts, whether retained by one or both parties, can help everyone, including the mediator, understand the disputed issues and how the circumstances of this case relate to other cases. Often an expert for one party helps both parties reach consensus on at least some of the facts.

Whatever the task, experts should be able to simplify complex issues and facts. They can explain the significance of pertinent facts without emotion or advocacy. They are particularly adept at presenting data in formats that can be easily understood. Experts often facilitate agreement on computational issues, freeing the parties to focus on other matters.

An expert can deflate puffery. Puffery may result from an overly zealous or inexperienced advocate who, for example, may claim punitive or other damages not supported by the facts, or advocate theories universally rejected by the courts. Without an expert's input, by the time the mediation takes place the client may be convinced that such damages are a certainty and will be recovered.

It is not necessary to establish all the facts in mediation. Nevertheless, the more experts help each side marshal and present its version of the facts and counter unfavorable facts, the more likely resolution will be achieved.

The ideal role for the expert is as an honest broker. The expert should opine only on facts or business practices about which she or he has expertise or experience. For example, in a securities case an expert can determine how often a particular account turned over, or whether the investments were consistent with an investor's stated objectives. But an expert cannot determine whether an investor knowingly ratified a transaction. An expert should not render an opinion on issues outside his or her sphere of knowledge.

An expert can play an even more significant role if the mediator lacks expertise in the subject matter of the dispute.[2] In that situation, the parties may look to a respected expert for a reality check of their respective positions. The expert can work collaboratively with the mediator, guiding the parties through the process and helping them place settlement options in context.

Even when the mediator's substantive knowledge is considerable, an expert may be an effective authority, especially on more subjective matters, such as custom and practice.

Experts with litigation experience bring a special strength to mediation—the ability to anticipate possible outcomes. This knowledge can be useful to the mediator and the parties. Counsel should respect the views of an expert retained by counsel's client, even if it conflicts with the client's expectations or with counsel's own prior assessment of a case.

Experts can participate in the mediation in many different ways. When two or more experts are retained, the mediator may suggest, with counsel's permission, that the experts caucus with each other and report on facts and issues on which they agree. Alternatively, each expert may present the facts and issues as she or he sees them. The mediator can use to advantage a good working relationship among party experts who know and respect each other. He or she can also make good use of experts even when they disagree.

In one very contentious employment mediation in which I served as mediator, the parties had exchanged expert reports prior to the mediation. It turned out that the experts reached vastly different conclusions based on the same data. I suggested that the experts confer on the telephone prior to the mediation session and counsel agreed to the idea. As a result

---

[2] There are experienced mediators in all fields. ADR providers, such as the American Arbitration Association, maintain panels of mediator with expertise in different areas, such as employment, labor, construction and intellectual property. The AAA, CPR, the National Association of Securities Dealers and the New York Stock Exchange have panels of mediators with experience in the securities industry. Many mediations are actually neutral evaluations where the mediator makes a determination of the outcome of the dispute and then attempts to sell his or her conclusion to the parties.

of their telephone conversations (conducted within the confidentiality of the mediation) the experts harmonized much of the data and many of their conclusions. This enabled the parties to turn their attention to the remaining issues, which were resolved during the mediation.

A mediator may suggest that it would be productive to meet privately with the parties' experts, outside the presence of the parties and counsel; this can achieve consensus on certain issues. However, such private meetings should be undertaken only with counsel's prior approval.

It may be very helpful for the parties and counsel to hear what all the experts have to say. In a mediation of a multimillion-dollar commercial dispute involving a sophisticated business strategy in a highly technical field, three experts conversed for several hours on a wide range of issues, including the parties' theories, the practice in the industry, and alleged damages. The parties and counsel listened and participated as the experts challenged each other's assumptions, methodologies and conclusions. By mid afternoon, the experts agreed on a methodology that the parties accepted. The case quickly settled after that. At the conclusion of the mediation, each party asked the opposing experts for their business cards.

The Neutral Expert

In particularly complex cases or in cases where the amount in dispute is substantial, the parties may suggest or may agree to a suggestion by the mediator that an expert be engaged to serve as an independent adviser. In these cases the expert will be chosen jointly by the parties and the mediator. The expert's fees and expenses are apportioned by agreement among the parties.

Neutral experts have been successfully used in complex cases involving highly intricate or scientific issues. But this practice has not migrated into all disputes. For example, a neutral expert is rarely used in securities mediation, possibly because many securities mediators have subject matter expertise.

Depending on the facts and circumstances, engaging an expert to assist the mediator is an option that may be considered.

Avoiding Problems

The expert should never displace the central role of the parties. Because an expert is an authority figure, it is possible that the expert's mere presence could polarize the parties. Sometimes an expert's behavior does not facilitate resolution. The expert may be unwilling to listen to the other side or may turn a blind eye to persuasive but unwelcome facts. Such an expert will be an obstacle to settlement. Indeed, these same characteristics would undermine this expert's effectiveness at trial.

Some experts feel compelled to read a lengthy, prepared statement in the joint session with the mediator. Counsel may think this will demonstrate the expert's prowess. But this, too, can have a negative affect on the mediation.

An experienced mediator will quickly recognize these problems and take steps to use the expert as a force for resolution. A private caucus between the mediator, counsel and the expert can avoid a presentation that will polarize the parties. Together they can craft a methodology better suited to productive negotiations.

Preparing the Client

Clients without experience in mediation, litigation or working with an expert are likely to have an incorrect and unrealistic expectation of the mediation process and the expert's role. It goes without saying that counsel should prepare clients for mediation. Counsel also should discuss the expert's role with the client and the expert in advance of the mediation. This discussion should be held first without the expert and then with the expert. It is important that the client understand that the expert is not an advocate but someone who will be forthright with facts, including facts that may be adverse to the client's interests. For example, after hearing the opposing side's view of the facts and issues, an expert may advise the client to settle based upon newly disclosed information. This may prove to be good advice.

An expert can justify the client's reassessment of a dispute so that she or he can accept a settlement without losing face.

Preparing the Expert

Counsel should not assume that an expert knows what behavior is appropriate in a mediation. Counsel should always prepare the expert and indicate what is expected. For example, the expert should not usurp the client's role. Since mediation is a collaborative process, counsel should also ask the expert for input on process issues. Many experts are qualified as mediators and can offer valuable assistance in fashioning the way in which the mediation will unfold.

An expert should never be brought into a case without advising all other parties and the mediator. To surprise the mediator and opposing counsel with an expert will undercut the mediator's ability to draw on the expert to achieve resolution.

Ethical Issues

Mediation raises some ethical issues that should concern experts.[3] Should an expert be disqualified from participation in subsequent court proceedings in a related matter because he or she heard confidential communications during the mediation? Can the expert change his or her opinion as a result of facts learned in the mediation? Is an expert precluded from using information acquired in mediation when testifying or advising in subsequent unrelated matters? Who is the expert's client? The party or counsel? And what is the duty of loyalty owed to the client? Does this depend solely upon who is paying the expert? These are difficult questions and are not easily answered. Contract, statute, court rules and other professional norms and rules may address some of these issues. Nevertheless, it is important that the scope of confidentiality in mediation be fully understood and agreed to by all participants, including the expert.

Conclusion

An expert can provide the independent impetus the parties need to resolve their dispute. Properly engaged, an expert can contribute enormously to the client's understanding of what happened and why a negotiated solution may be in the client's best interest.

---

[3] *See* Fields-D'Arpino v. Restaurant Associates, 39 F. Supp. 412 (S.D.N.Y. 1999). In this case, a law firm was disqualified from representing a corporate client in a dispute that an associate of the firm had attempted to mediate and discovery regarding the mediation was prohibited. While this case involved the ethical obligations of an attorney, the principles would appear to apply to a non-attorney acting as a neutral.

CHAPTER SIX

CONFIDENTIALITY AND ETHICS IN MEDIATION

I. Mediation Confidentiality

The Many Faces of Mediation Confidentiality

by Dennis Sharp[*]

Confidentiality is one of the keys to the acceptability and success of mediation among parties to a dispute. Yet, state statutes pertaining to such confidentiality remain inconsistent, when they address the issue. A model mediation statute may provide a solution, but at present a uniform approach to confidentiality provisions remains wishful thinking. This article reviews state statutes that deal with confidentiality and spins some interesting scenarios that highlight the need for any drafting or modifying body to incorporate flexibility and comprehensiveness into its mediation confidentiality laws.

Mediators agree that confidentiality is a crucial element of successful mediations. As reasoned by the Court of Appeals for the Second Circuit, "[I]f participants cannot rely on confidential treatment of everything that transpires during these sessions, then counsel of necessity will feel constrained to conduct themselves in a cautious, tight-lipped, noncommittal manner more suitable to poker players in a high stakes game than adversaries attempting to arrive at a just solution of a civil dispute."[1]

---

[*] Mr. Sharp is a full time mediator and arbitrator for Sharp Resolutions, Inc. He is also the former regional vice president for American Arbitration Association and has held leadership positions in several ADR associations including holding president or chair positions in the California Dispute Resolution Council, the ADR Section of the San Diego County Bar Association, and the San Diego Chapter of Society of Professionals in Dispute Resolution.

[1] Lake Utopia Paper Ltd. v. Connelly Containers, Inc., 608 F2d 928, 930 (CA2 1979), *cert denied*, 444 US 1076 (regarding mediation-like appellate preargument conference); this quote was drawn from NANCY H. ROGERS AND CRAIG A. MCEWEN, MEDIATION LAW POLICY AND PRACTICE, chapter 9 (1994), p. 4.

While most stakeholders—parties, attorneys, courts, legislatures, mediation programs, and mediators—agree to the principle of keeping everything said during a mediation confidential, codifying language to effectuate this intent has proved to be at best challenging and, at worst, seemingly impossible. The latest attempt to comprehensively address this slippery issue was made by the California Law Revision Commission.[2] After a year of wrestling with various contradictory statutory provisions and case law, the Commission completed its task of overhauling and consolidating California's confidentiality provisions. The new confidentiality provisions are housed in a revised California Evidence Code section.[3] These provisions replaced all previous confidentiality provisions found throughout several California codes: government; labor; evidence; insurance; welfare and institutions; and civil procedure. The only code not consumed by this new section was the family code. Because of the unique nature of divorce mediation, confidentiality provisions in this code were left unchanged.

The California Law Revision Commission is to be commended for its extensive efforts to redefine confidentiality protections. Likewise, efforts by legislators in Oregon and Colorado should be acknowledged for understanding and addressing needed modifications to their confidentiality protections. But despite these laudable efforts to comprehensively deal with the many faces of confidentiality, several issues remain.

Confidentiality in mediation is considered essential to allow the parties to candidly and thoroughly discuss all possible avenues of settlement. But can a mediator promise full confidentiality protections to the parties? What if a crime has been committed? Do the protections apply in subsequent arbitrations? Is a settlement agreement reached in mediation admissible? What if it is not written or signed? When does mediation begin and end for confidentiality purposes? Can or must mediators disclose threats of imminent death or harm? What about ethical violations attorney-mediators observe of a party's attorney?

---

[2] The California Law Revision Commission is a governor-appointed body which annually reviews selected California statutes and makes reports and recommendations regarding perceived needed modifications. The recommendations are then drafted into proposed legislation and authored by a sitting legislator. The revisions to the California Evidence Code regarding confidentiality were authored by assembly member Deborah Ortiz.

[3] Cal. Evid. Code § 1115-1128.

In an effort to address these and other related issues, this article sets forth various scenarios which pose these questions and provide an analysis comparing the new California confidentiality statute with similar statutes of six other states. This article does not attempt to answer these scenarios but instead highlights potential problem areas and provides guidance for practitioners and mediators alike.

Subsequent Proceeding

A mediation between the parties does not result in a settlement of their dispute. In subsequent civil litigation, the defendant's attorney on cross-examination asks the plaintiff about an admission made during the mediation. Plaintiff's attorney objects. How does the court rule?

All state statutes reviewed for this paper (California, Massachusetts, Colorado, Florida, Utah, Washington, and Oregon) deal with this question. Generally speaking, admissions made by parties and any settlement offers given during a mediation are inadmissible in subsequent civil court proceedings. Some exceptions are made for divorce proceedings and labor cases but for all other civil matters such statements, with few exceptions explored below, will be excluded by the courts.[4]

This is the heart of confidentiality protections—to allow parties to freely and openly discuss their disputes and make offers without worrying about having these statements used against them should full settlement not be reached. In almost all states, legislators and courts have balanced the interests and arrived at the same general conclusion: the interest in having society negotiate civil settlements through mediation outweighs the public's interest in having all relevant and probative evidence brought before the court.[5]

Twist #1: Instead of a court proceeding, the subsequent action is a private, binding arbitration. How does the arbitrator rule?

Because of the tremendous growth in the use of mediation, arbitrators are often faced with this dilemma: should I exclude testimony about admissions made during a preceding mediation or admit them and

[4] Cal. Evid. Code 1119; Mass. Gen. Laws. Ann. Ch. 233 § 23c; Colo. Rev. Stat. § 13-22-307; Fla. Stat. Ann. § 44.102; Utah Code Ann. § 78-31b-7; Wash Rev. Code 5.60.070; Or. Rev. Stat. §§ 36.220 and 36.222.

[5] *See* Nancy H. Rogers and Craig A. McEwen, Mediation: Law, Policy and Practice, Ch. 9 (2nd Ed. 1994) and John S. Murray, Alan Scott Rau, and Edward F. Sherman, Processes of Dispute Resolution: The Role of Lawyers (2nd Ed. 1996), pp. 379-418.

assign the weight they're worth? Arbitrators know that because they are rarely required to follow the formal rules of evidence, excluding any potentially relevant evidence is risky. Such exclusion of evidence may subject the award to vacatur for refusing to hear all material evidence.[6]

In the new California Evidence Code section pertaining to confidentiality, admissibility of such statements in a subsequent arbitration are specifically covered:

> "[n]o evidence of anything said or any admission made for the purpose of, in the course of, or pursuant to, a mediation...is admissible or subject to discovery and disclosure of the evidence shall not be compelled in any arbitration, administrative proceeding, civil action, or other non-criminal proceeding in which, pursuant to law, testimony can be compelled to be given."[7]

Without specifically citing arbitration, the Oregon statute also appears to address the question by applying the exclusion to "any subsequent adjudicatory proceeding."[8] It is likewise arguable that the Florida statute applies to arbitration because it establishes a privilege invokable by any party to prevent disclosure in any "subsequent legal proceeding."[9]

The statutes in Massachusetts, Colorado, and Washington are all more vague in their application to arbitration; these statutes make such communications inadmissible in "any judicial or administrative proceeding."[10] Utah's statute is even narrower, applying the exclusion to "any judicial proceeding."[11]

Many arbitrators feel more comfortable applying privilege laws than they do applying exclusionary rules to exclude evidence in arbitrations despite the potential probative value of such proffered statements. This comfort level is due primarily to the belief that courts will confirm awards where arbitrators have excluded such evidence for the same public policy reasons courts are required to apply privilege laws (i.e., to protect such relationships as attorneys/clients, husbands/wives,

---

[6] *See, for example*, Cal. Code Civ. Proc. § 1286.2(e).

[7] Cal. Evid. Code § 1119.

[8] OR. REV. STAT. § 36.222(1).

[9] Fla. Stat. Ann. § 44.102.

[10] Mass. Gen. Laws Ann. Ch. 233 § 23c; Colo. Rev. Stat. § 13-22-307; Wash. Rev. Code § 5.60.070.

[11] Utah Code Ann. § 78-31b-7.

doctors/patients, etc.). However, when faced with refusing to hear relevant evidence because of an exclusionary rule, such as hearsay, arbitrators generally tend to allow such evidence and give it the weight it is worth.

Therefore, in such states as Florida, which has treated confidentiality in mediation as a privilege that can be invoked, arbitrators are more likely to exclude communications made at a mediation. In those states that apply exclusionary rules, which is the case for most state confidentiality laws, arbitrators may be much more hesitant to exclude such mediation statements absent an agreement by the parties to do so.

Twist #2: What if the subsequent action is a criminal proceeding? Is the court's ruling the same?

All state statutes reviewed apply only to civil cases, not subsequent criminal proceedings. Therefore, mediation communications will not be protected from disclosure in any criminal actions involving the parties or others.

What happens if the mediator simply said, "everything said in this mediation will be confidential?" Does this expose the mediator to any liability? It is doubtful that a mediator would be found liable for failing to explain that statements could be compelled in any subsequent criminal proceedings. But the mediator may be seen in a different light if he or she did not disclose other exceptions to the confidentiality protections. A word to the wise to mediators: craft the confidentiality portion of your opening statement carefully to include clear exceptions to its applicability.

Twist #3: This time the case settled in mediation but the defendant is seeking to have the settlement agreement set aside by the court because the mediator did not disclose a previous professional relationship with the plaintiff. The defendant subpoenas the mediator who moves to quash the subpoena. What does the court do? What if the action is a lawsuit against the mediator for damages incurred because of the non-disclosure?

The Colorado confidentiality statute provides an exception to exclusion of mediation communications where the "[d]isclosure is necessary and relevant to an action alleging willful or wanton misconduct of the mediator..."[12] This statement appears to require

[12] COLO. REV. STA. § 13-22-307(2)(d).

disclosure of the mediator's previous relationship with the opposing party. The Oregon counterpart provides that, "[i]n any proceeding to enforce, modify or set aside a mediation agreement, confidential mediation communications and confidential mediation agreements may be disclosed to the extent necessary to prosecute or defend the matter."[13] While not explicitly stated, a party could argue that disclosure of the mediator's conflict is not precluded in any subsequent proceeding to set aside the agreement reached during mediation. The other five state statutes are silent on the admissibility of such evidence to set aside a mediation settlement agreement.

As to the question of compelling disclosure of the previous relationship in the party's lawsuit against the mediator, only the Colorado statute cited above and the Washington statute explicitly provide for such disclosure. The exception in the Washington statute sets out that such evidence is subject to disclosure, "[i]n a subsequent action between the mediator and a party to the mediation arising out of the mediation."[14]

In all of these jurisdictions, mediators would likely be compelled by the court to disclose previous professional relationships with the parties even absent statutory authority, provided the court believes that such an alleged relationship would be evidence of actual bias or the appearance of impartiality in a lawsuit against the mediator. Whether such nondisclosure subjects the mediator to liability or what potential damages might be awardable to a party are much less clear and vary greatly among jurisdictions.

Admissibility of Mediation Statement and Documents

Two of three parties to a mediation are involved in subsequent litigation regarding the same subject matter. These two parties agree that certain statements made during the mediation will be admissible in court. Can they do this?

The answer in California, Utah, and Colorado is no, unless the third party, who is not a party to the litigation, and the mediator agree to such disclosure.[15] In Oregon, Washington, and Florida only the other party to the mediation needs to agree to disclosure for the communication to be

---

[13] OR. REV. STAT. § 36.222 (5).

[14] Wash. Rev. Code § 5.60.070; *see also* Leonard L. Riskin and James E. Westbrook, Dispute Resolution and Lawyers, Ch. IV (2nd Ed. 1997).

[15] CAL. EVID. CODE § 1122; UTAH CODE ANN. § 78-31b-7(1); Colo. Rev. Stat. § 13-22-307(2)(b).

admissible.[16] The Massachusetts confidentiality statute is silent on the question of who must agree to the disclosure.[17]

The policy reason for requiring all parties to agree to disclosure of any mediation communication is simple and consistent: all parties expect that anything said during a mediation would be not disclosed in subsequent legal proceedings unless all parties agreed. Requiring the agreement of the mediator is more controversial. Critics of this requirement argue that confidentiality in mediation is designed to protect the parties' interests, not the mediator's; if they agree to disclosure in court, the mediator should have no say in the matter. Proponents contend that the sanctity of the mediation process will be compromised by not including them in the disclosure agreement, particularly where communications of the mediator are sought to be disclosed.

Twist #1: One of the parties submits a report prepared by its expert for the mediation to the mediator and all parties. Can a court in subsequent litigation admit this document?

The revised California confidentiality statute is the only codified state law among those reviewed that explicitly addresses this question. In their new Evidence Code Section, "[a] communication or writing...that is made or prepared for the purpose of, or in the course of... a mediation, is not made inadmissible or protected from disclosure...if... [t]he communication, document or writing was prepared on behalf of fewer than all of the participants, those participants expressly agree in writing ...to its disclosure ...and the communication, document, or writing does not disclose anything said or done or any admission made in the course of the mediation." The drafters of this language believed that when one or more of the parties prepares a document for use at a mediation, such as an expert report, there is no policy reason why the preparing party or parties should be prohibited from using this document to support their case in any subsequent adjudicative hearings.[18] The distinction they draw is that such a document was prepared before the mediation not during it;

---

[16] OR. REV. STAT. § 36.220(1)(b); WASH. REV. CODE § 5.60.070(1)(a); FLA. STAT. ANN. § 44.102(3).

[17] Mass. Gen. Laws Ann. Ch. 233. § 23c.

[18] CAL. EVID. CODE § 1122(a)(2); *see also* Comment to this section which states that "subdivision (a)(2) facilitates admissibility and disclosure of unilaterally prepared materials, but it only applies so long as those materials may be produced in a manner revealing nothing about the mediation discussion."

therefore, like any other document created outside of the mediation, it should not be excluded from evidence.

Twist #2: Plaintiff in subsequent litigation seeks to keep out an admission she made during the mediation. Defendant argues that this admission was also made at a dinner party two weeks before the mediation. How does the court rule?

This scenario is similar to the previous one and begs the same question: if a communication is made outside of the mediation, why should it be excluded? The Colorado and California statutes specifically provide that such statements are not subject to exclusion.[19] While the other five states' confidentiality statutes are silent on this question, it is well established that a party cannot invoke the protection of mediation confidentiality statutes to statements that were made outside the mediation. That of course, begs the next question:

When Does a Mediation Begin?

Defendant from an unsuccessful mediation subpoenas the intake coordinator from the mediation program to inquire about telephone conversations with the plaintiff that occurred when plaintiff called to inquire about using the program's mediation services. Plaintiff moves to quash the subpoena. What does the court do in this situation?

Under the revised California code, the court would be required to grant the motion to quash the subpoena.[20] Confidentiality protections cover not only the mediation session but also "mediation consultation" which is defined as "a communication between a person and a mediator for the purpose of initiating, considering or reconvening a mediation or retaining the mediator."[21] Further, a "mediator" is defined by the code as "any person designated by a mediator either to assist in the mediation or to communicate with the participants in preparation for mediation."[22] Presumably, these confidentiality protections would apply even if the mediator or mediation program is not ultimately employed by the parties. None of the other state statutes explicitly address such communications, leaving the courts in these states to judicially interpret whether to extend their confidentiality protections to employees of mediation programs.[23]

---

[19] COLO. REV. STAT. § 13-22-307(4) and CAL. EVID. CODE § 1120(a).

[20] Cal. Evid. Code § 1119.

[21] Cal. Evid. Code § 1115(c).

[22] Cal. Evid. Code § 1115(b).

[23] Other six state statutes are silent on this issue.

When Does a Mediation End?

Two weeks after a mediation session the mediator has a telephone conversation with the parties to try to further assist them in settling their dispute. This assistance fails to resolve the matter. In subsequent litigation can the mediator be compelled to testify about what was said during these conversations?

Only the California statute explicitly addresses the question of when a mediation ends. Under the revised code section a mediation ends when : "(1) The parties execute a written settlement agreement that fully resolves the dispute; (2) An oral agreement [that is reduced in writing] fully resolves the dispute; (3) The mediator provides the mediation participants with a writing signed by the mediator that the mediation is terminated or words to that effect; (4) A party provides the mediator and other mediation participants with a writing stating that the mediation is terminated, or words to that effect; or (5) For ten calendar days, there is no communication between the mediator and any of the parties to the mediation. The parties may shorten or extend this time by agreement."[24]

Presuming that neither the parties nor the mediator have executed a written statement that the mediation has been terminated, the mediator very well could be compelled to testify about the telephone conversations which occurred fourteen days after the last mediation session. Since this scenario is common, as are multiple sessions which take place more than ten days apart, mediators in California would be wise to have all parties agree in writing to extend confidentiality protections to include these situations. It is less clear how the other states would address this scenario, leaving it to the courts to determine if the protections apply. Likewise, mediators in those states should also consider drafting a confidentiality agreement covering interim periods between sessions.

Duty to Disclose

During a private caucus at a mediation, one of the parties reveals information which makes it clear to the mediator that the party has embezzled several thousands of dollars from the other party, her employer. Can or must the mediator disclose this information to appropriate authorities? To the other party?

In some jurisdictions, mediators may be required to report certain kinds of crimes. For example, a divorce mediator in Kansas, Utah, and

---

[24] Cal. Evid. Code § 1125.

Wyoming must report child abuse despite otherwise applicable mediation confidentiality provisions.[25] Likewise, the Oregon general confidentiality statute states that "any mediation communication relating to child abuse" is not considered confidential.[26]

While it is clear that mediation communications are not protected from disclosure in criminal proceedings, it is unsettled whether mediators who wear other professional hats are required to disclose information heard in mediation about crimes that have been committed. In gray areas like embezzlement, rarely are professionals (psychologists, doctors, lawyers, clergymen, etc.) required to report such crimes. In violent crime areas such as murder and rape, many are required to make such reports. Except for the area of child abuse, none of the state confidentiality statutes address this issue.

Twist #1: A party in a private caucus threatens to physically injure others in the company if he does not get what he's seeking in mediation. Can or must the mediator disclose this information?

Only the Oregon confidentiality statute explicitly deals with this question. The Oregon code provides that, "a mediation communication is not confidential if the mediator or a party to a mediation reasonably believes that disclosing the communication is necessary to prevent a party from committing a crime that is likely to result in death or substantial bodily injury to a specific person."[27] Additionally, most codes of ethics for doctors, attorneys, psychologists, and others allow, and in some cases mandate, disclosures where the professional reasonably believes severe physical harm or death may occur.[28]

Twist #2: An attorney-mediator learns in caucus that counsel for one of the parties has committed an ethical violation. Can or must the mediator notify the State Bar pursuant to his or her professional code mandate?

Attorneys under several state bar ethics codes are required to report evidence of code violations committed by fellow members of the bar. The Florida statute specifically exempts from the mediation

---

[25] KAN. STAT. ANN. § 38-1522(A); UTAH CODE ANN. § 78-31b-7; WYO. STAT. § 1-43-103; *see also* Rogers and McEwen, *supra*, note 5, at pp. 51-53.

[26] OR. REV. STAT. § 36.220(5) and § 36.222(6).

[27] OR. REV. STAT. § 36.220(6).

[28] *See* discussion in ROGERS AND MCEWEN, *supra*, note 5, at pp. 61-62.

confidentiality these types of disclosures made in state bar disciplinary hearings.[29] In other jurisdictions it is much less clear. Most mediators surveyed would keep such information confidential, especially where the violation is of a lower level.[30] When imminent harm or violent crimes are revealed, however, most agree that it is their professional responsibility to disclose such information to appropriate authorities.

Settlement Agreements

Parties to a mediation orally agree to settle their dispute during a mediation. A week later one of the parties decides the terms were not favorable enough to him and attempts to back out of the settlement. Can the other party submit evidence of the oral agreement reached at mediation in a subsequent court proceeding?

A new California Evidence Code section was drafted specifically to address conflicting California appellate court decisions in this area. One appellate division admitted evidence of an oral statement of settlement terms[31] while another applied the confidentiality statute to exclude such statements.[32] At the urging of the California Dispute Resolution Council, representing the consensus of the mediation community, the Law Revision Commission agreed with the appellate court which excluded such oral agreements.

New Section 1118 of the revised Evidence Code dictates that to be admissible oral agreements must satisfy all of the following conditions: "(a) The oral agreement is recorded by a court reporter, tape recorder, or other reliable means of sound recording; (b) The terms of the oral agreement are recited on the record in the presence of the parties and the mediator, and the parties express on the record that they agree to the terms recited; (c) The parties to the oral agreement expressly state on the record that the agreement is enforceable or binding or words to that effect; and (d) The recording is reduced to writing and the writing is signed by the parties within 72 hours after it is recorded."[33]

---

[29] FLA. STAT. ANN. § 44.102(4).

[30] Conclusion drawn from surveys and statewide dialogues conducted throughout the state of California by the California Dispute Resolution Council, an organization created to represent the ADR field's interests in the state legislature and other public policy making bodies.

[31] Regents of University of California v. Sumner, 42 Cal. App. 4th 1209 (1996).

[32] Ryan v. Garcia, 27 Cal. App. 4th 1006 (1994).

[33] Cal. Evid. Code 1118.

What began as a way to allow reliable audio recordings to be entered as evidence of a settlement reached in mediation was, in the eleventh hour, essentially subsumed by the final requirement that the agreement be in writing signed by all parties. All the other jurisdictions' statutes which were reviewed are silent on the issue of admissibility of oral agreements.

Twist #1: The parties reach settlement at the mediation which the mediator records in writing and has both parties sign before leaving. Is this document admissible in a subsequent action? Does it matter if the document is not signed by the parties?

Although it may seem obvious that written, executed settlement agreements resulting from mediation would be admitted into evidence by a court, this has not always occurred. To deal with this anomaly Florida, Utah, Washington, Oregon and California confidentiality statutes now explicitly provide that written, executed settlement agreements are admissible in subsequent court proceedings.[34] The Colorado and Massachusetts statutes remain silent on the question.

What if the parties do not sign the settlement agreement? Of the states providing for admissibility of written settlement agreements, only Oregon does not specifically state that they must be signed or executed by the parties.[35] All others require such execution.

Mediator's Reports and Recommendations

The parties are unable to reach accord during a court-ordered mediation. In subsequent litigation, the court requests that the mediator file a report with the court. Defendant objects to the admissibility of any report from the mediator. Can the court admit such a document?

All the state confidentiality statutes reviewed appear to imply by their language that such a report would be inadmissible absent agreement of the parties and the mediator. But it was precisely the concern of the California Law Revision Commission to assure that this implication is clear to the court when it provided in the new code section that "neither a mediator nor anyone else may submit to a court or other adjudicative body, and a court or other adjudicative body cannot consider, any report, assessment, evaluation, recommendation or finding of any kind by the

---

[34] Fla. Rev. Ann. § 44.102(3); Utah Code Ann. § 78-31b-7(3); Wash. Rev. Code § 5.60.070(1)(e); or Rev. Stat. § 36.222(4); Cal. Evid. Code § 1123.

[35] Or. Rev. Stat. § 36.222.

mediator concerning a mediation conducted by the mediator, other than a report that is mandated by court rule or other law that states only whether an agreement was reached, unless all the parties to the mediation expressly agree otherwise..."[36]

The policy reason behind prohibiting such reports is to prevent coercion by the mediator; that is, a mediator should not be able to influence the result of a mediation or adjudication by reporting or threatening to report why a mediation failed.[37] The other jurisdictions' statutes were silent on this issue, leaving it to the courts to interpret whether the general confidentiality protections include non-disclosure of any reports.

Attorney Fees

The mediator is subpoenaed to testify about admissions made by plaintiff at the mediation. The mediator moves to quash the subpoena and the court grants the motion. Can the mediator collect its attorney's fees and costs incurred for making such a motion?

There is good news for mediators in California where parties attempt to inappropriately compel them to disclose any communication made at a mediation: they can recover reasonable attorney's fees and costs. A new section of the Evidence Code provides, "if a person subpoenas or otherwise seeks to compel a mediator to testify or produce a writing...and the court or other adjudicative body determines the testimony or writing is inadmissible under this article...the court or adjudicative body making the determination shall award reasonable attorney's fees and costs to the mediator against the person seeking the testimony or writing."[38] This section is designed not only to fairly compensate the mediator for his or her costs but also to deter parties from subpoenaing the mediator in the first instance.

Uniformity

As the above scenarios and analyses illustrate, contradictions exist among many state statutes and several issues remain unaddressed in the area of mediation confidentiality. In order for mediation to be practiced more effectively and consistently, mediator confidentiality laws need to be overhauled to address the issues that remain vague or unanswered.

---

[36] Cal. Evid. Code § 1121.
[37] *See* Cmt. to CAL. EVID. CODE § 1121.
[38] Cal. Evid. Code § 1127.

Several practitioners in the ADR field are questioning the value of creating statutes that attempt to fill these gaps without regard to how other states have handled similar issues.

With this in mind, an effort has been established to develop a model mediation statute. This effort is being jointly undertaken by the National Conference of Commissioners of Uniform State Laws and the American Bar Association Section on Dispute Resolution.[39] This joint effort appears to be both timely and well-positioned to deal with the issues raised by the many faces of mediation confidentiality laws.

[39] *See* Nancy H. Rogers and Craig A. McEwen *Employing the Law to Increase Use of Mediation and to Encourage Direct and Early Negotiations*, OHIO ST. J. ON DISP. RESOL., VOL. 13:3 (1998), pp. 831-864.

II. Confidentiality in the Public Sector

Dispelling the Myths About Public-Sector Mediation and Confidentiality

by P. Jean Baker[*]

One of the myths surrounding mediation is the belief that anything said in the presence of a mediator will remain confidential. The reality is that in the majority of states, mediation sessions are conducted without any guarantee of confidentiality.[1] Moreover, in those states that have enacted legislation establishing confidentiality, the level of confidentiality differs markedly from state to state.[2] Even when a strong confidentiality statute governs mediation proceedings, nothing would prevent a state or federal judge from ordering disclosure in an individual case "in the interest of justice."[3]

If there is uncertainty in the private sector about the scope and nature of confidentiality, there is even greater confusion surrounding the issue when mediating a dispute involving the federal sector. This article will dispel some of the myths about this complex subject and identify the many areas of uncertainty.[4]

No Evidentiary Privilege

The first myth involves the existence of a federal mediation privilege. Federal Rule of Evidence (FRE) 501 provides the sole rule on

---

[*] The author is a vice president at the American Arbitration Association, in charge of its Washington, D.C. office.

[1] *See* May 1999 DRAFT, UNIFORM MEDIATION ACT, National Conference of Commissioners on Uniform State Laws.

[2] The application of a confidentiality statute may be complicated if a mediation proceeding is conducted telephonically or electronically among participants residing in different states. In such a case, counsel may wish to include in the agreement to mediate a clear statement concerning the confidentiality statute that shall govern.

[3] Rinaker v. Superior Court, 62 Cal. 4th 155 (Cal. 1998); Olam v. Congress Mortgage Co., 68 F. Supp. 2d 1110 (N.D. Cal. 1999). The decision in *Olam* sent shock waves through the mediation community when the judge ordered the mediator to testify, despite California's categorical exclusion of such evidence. *See also* Foxgate Homeowners' Ass'n v. Bramalea California Inc., 78 Cal. App. 4th 653 (Cal. Ct. App. 2d Dist. 2000).

[4] There are other confidentiality considerations not addressed here, including the impact of the Federal Privacy Act, which guarantees that certain information gathered by the federal government will not be made public.

evidentiary privileges in the federal courts. Except for one federal district court decision in California holding that there is a common law "federal mediation privilege" under FRE 501,[5] federal courts generally do not recognize a privilege that can be asserted to prohibit the introduction of evidence relating to mediation proceedings except in diversity cases when state substantive law supplies the rule of decision and the state recognizes a mediation privilege. Counsel are advised to not rely upon the holding of the California case given the reluctance of the Supreme Court in recent years to recognize new or novel federal privileges.[6]

Settlement Negotiations

The closest thing to a general federal statute protecting confidentiality is FRE 408 (Compromise and Offers to Compromise). Under this rule, conduct or statements made in compromise negotiations are not admissible "to prove liability for or invalidity of the claim."[7]

The last sentence of Rule 408 provides, however, that evidence of compromise negotiations may be introduced for another purpose, such as to prove bias or prejudice, obstruction of a criminal investigation or prosecution.[8] Thus, the protection offered by the rule is extremely narrow.

---

[5] *See* Folb v. Motion Picture Ind. Pension & Health Plans, 15 F. Supp. 2d 1164 (C.D. Cal. 1998).

[6] Jaffee v. Redmond, 518 U.S. 1 (1996); University of Penn. v. EEOC 493 U.S. 182, 189 (1990); United States v. Nixon, 418 U.S. 683 (1974).

[7] Rule 408 provides: "Evidence of (1) furnishing or offering or promising to furnish, or (2) accepting or offering or promising to accept, a valuable consideration in compromising or attempting to compromise a claim which was disputed as to either validity or amount, is not admissible to prove liability for or invalidity of the claim or its amount. Evidence of conduct or statements made in compromise negotiations is likewise not admissible. This rule does not require the exclusion of any evidence otherwise discoverable merely because it is presented in the course of compromise negotiations. This rule also does not require exclusion when the evidence is offered for another purpose, such as proving bias or prejudice of a witness, negativing a contention of undue delay, or proving an effort to obstruct a criminal investigation or prosecution."

The Advisory Committee Notes explain the reasons for the rule: "[E]xclusion may be based on two grounds. (1) The evidence is irrelevant, since the offer may be motivated by a desire for peace rather than from any concession of weakness of position. The validity of this position will vary as the amount of the offer varies in relation to the size of the claim and may also be influenced by other circumstances. (2) A more consistently impressive ground is promotion of the public policy favoring the compromise and settlement of disputes."

[8] *Quoted in n. 7 supra.*

Another deficiency is that the rule does not provide sanctions for violation of its provisions. Thus, courts must devise a remedy when a party or counsel reveals confidential mediation communications at a hearing on the merits.[9]

The ADRA

To continue encouraging federal agencies to use alternative methods of dispute resolution, in 1996 Congress amended the Administrative Dispute Resolution Act (ADRA). The ADRA governs the use by executive branch agencies of alternative means of resolving disputes relating to federal administrative programs.[10] The agency need not be a party to the dispute for provisions of the ADRA to apply to an ADR proceeding, provided the basis of the dispute involves an administrative decision that has had a substantial affect upon the parties.[11]

The confidentiality provisions of the ADRA reside in 5 U.S.C. § 574. Although broader in scope than FRE 408, § 574 offers only limited confidentiality protection. The scope of this protection results from balancing the concerns of private sector parties who wish to have a confidential process with the requirements of federal "sunshine laws" calling for governmental activities to be subject to public scrutiny except when compelling personal privacy interests are implicated.

The ADRA's confidentiality provisions also apply to ADR proceedings involving acquisition disputes subject to the Federal Acquisition Regulations (FAR).[12] Part 24 of FAR prescribes policies and procedures that apply requirements of the Privacy Act of 1974[13] and OMB Circular No. A-130, Dec. 12, 1985, to government contracts. It also cites the Freedom of Information Act (FOIA).[14] The 1998 amendments to Part 24 implement the confidentiality provisions of the ADRA.

Confidentiality and the ADRA

The ADRA's confidentiality rules prohibit disclosure of "dispute resolution communications" or any communication provided "in

[9] *See* e.g., Bernard v. Galen Group Inc., 901 F. Supp. 778 (S.D.N.Y. 1995).

[10] The Administrative Procedure Act of 1990 first authorized the use of ADR in the federal sector. 5 U.S.C. § 571 et seq.

[11] *See* 5 U.S.C. § 571(8)(B)(defining "issue in controversy"); § 571(2) (defining "administrative program" to mean one that protects and determines the rights privileges and obligations of citizens, whether by rule-making, adjudication, licensing or investigation).

[12] 48 C.F.R. Part 33.

[13] 5 U.S.C. § 552a.

[14] 5 U.S.C. § 522, as amended.

confidence" to the mediator, whether voluntarily or under compulsory process, except in the circumstances described below.

Notwithstanding the ADRA's mandatory confidentiality requirement, mediators and parties may disclose, voluntarily or involuntarily, "dispute resolution communications" when any of these conditions are present:

- All participants consent in writing to the disclosure.
- The information sought is already in the public domain.
- A statute requires disclosure. If the mediator is the person from whom the disclosure is sought, he or she may not make the disclosure unless no other person is "reasonably available" to testify.
- A court orders disclosure on one of the following three grounds: (a) to prevent a manifest injustice, (b) to establish a violation of law, or (c) to prevent harm to the public health or safety.[15]

In addition, parties may disclose, or be required to disclose, "dispute resolution communications" when any one of the following circumstances exist:

- The communication was produced by the party seeking disclosure.
- The communication is needed to determine: (a) the existence or meaning of an agreement resulting from the mediation, or (b) the enforcement of such agreement.
- The communication was distributed by a party to all other parties.[16]

"Issue in Controversy"

Before the limited protections afforded by the ADRA can begin to apply to mediation communications, there has to be an "issue in controversy" as defined in the ADRA.[17] This definition has two components. The first requirement is an issue material to a decision

---

[15] 5 U.S.C. § 574(a)(1)-(4), (b)(1)-(4). A mediator also may be forced to disclose a communication provided by a nonparty, but only if the parties to the mediation and the nonparty consent in writing. § 574(a)(1).

[16] 5 U.S.C. § 574(b)(1), (6), (7).

[17] 5 U.S.C. § 571(8), 574(c).

concerning an agency's "administrative program." The second requirement is that there must be a disagreement: (a) between an agency and persons who would be substantially affected by the decision, or (b) between persons who would be substantially affected by the decision.

In the only case involving this definition, the Fifth Circuit held that the ADRA did not apply to a state agricultural loan program financed with federal funds because there was no "issue in controversy" under the ADRA.[18] The government sought to subpoena records in the custody of the Texas Agricultural Mediation Program relating to mediation proceedings involving the Moczygembas. The Moczygembas sought to quash the subpoena, arguing that the documents were protected from disclosure by a federal mediation privilege under: (1) the federal Agricultural Credit Act, which authorizes funding for state agricultural loan mediation programs, and requires states to provide that mediation sessions "shall remain confidential," and (2) the Texas ADR Act, which granted broad confidentiality protection.[19] The government argued that the very limited confidentiality provisions in the ADRA governed, since the Texas mediation program received financial assistance from the federal government. The Fifth Circuit found that neither the Texas ADR Act nor the ADRA applied in this case.

In reaching this decision, the court set out the ADRA's very broad definition of an "issue in controversy" and without further analysis concluded that no such issue was involved in this case. Although the court reached the right conclusion about the need for disclosure in the face of potential fraud by a grant-holder, reasonable minds may differ as to whether there was an "issue in controversy" relating to an administrative program that would have made the confidentiality provisions of the ADRA applicable in this case.

This case suggests that the parties should mutually agree upon the nature of the "issue in controversy" in the agreement to mediate. In the case of a contract dispute involving a federal agency and a contractor, the parties must look to the definition within FAR. Section 33.201 defines "an issue in controversy" as "a material disagreement between the

---

[18] *In Re* Grand Jury Subpoena Dec. 17, 1996, 148 F.3d 487 (5th Cir. 1998).

[19] The court noted that the Texas ADR Act provides broad confidentiality protection for mediation communications in judicial and administrative proceedings. It also provides that if confidentiality provisions conflict with other disclosure requirements, then the issue of confidentiality may be presented to the court for an in camera determination whether the communications may be disclosed.

government and the contractor that: (a) may result in a claim, or (b) is all or part of an existing claim."[20]

To facilitate the threshold determination of whether a mediation will resolve an "issue in controversy," counsel may wish to include a statement in the agreement to mediate that describes the nature of the issue or issues to be decided. If the "issue in controversy" requirement is satisfied, then any "dispute resolution communication" that is disclosed in violation of the ADRA's confidentiality rules may not be admitted in "any proceeding relating to the issue in controversy with respect to which the communication was made."[21]

Application to the Mediator

Under the ADRA, a neutral is an individual who functions specifically to aid the parties in resolving an "issue in controversy."[22] Thus, the ADRA's confidentiality provisions would not apply to communications made to or by a federal employee while serving as a mediator if the dispute is unrelated to a federal administrative program or to a federal acquisition. Counsel would be well advised to question any guarantee of confidentiality by a federal employee-mediator in such a case. It may be prudent to ask the mediator to state in writing the legal basis for the confidentiality protection so that the guarantee can be evaluated.

Protected Communications

The confidentiality protections of the ADRA attach to communications made "in confidence" to the mediator and to "dispute resolution communications."[23] "Dispute resolution communications" are defined to mean both oral and written communications made for the purpose of mediation and specifically include memos, notes and work product of the neutral and the parties.[24] Expressly excluded are a written agreement to enter into an ADR proceeding, and a final written agreement reached as a result of that proceeding.

---

[20] 48 C.F.R. § 33.33.201.

[21] 5 U.S.C. § 574(c).

[22] 5 U.S.C. § 571(9).

[23] 5 U.S.C. § 574(a)-(c). "In confidence" is defined in § 571(7) to mean information provided: (a) with the expressed intent of the source that it not be disclosed, or (b) under circumstances that would create the reasonable expectation on behalf of the source that the information would not be disclosed.

[24] 5 U.S.C. § 571(5).

Thus, qualifying communications are protected from disclosure under the ADRA only after the parties have agreed in writing to mediate and a mediator has been appointed. Moreover, the protected communications include only those made to or by the mediator in private caucuses. Discussions and other communications shared in joint session with the mediator and among the parties are not protected.

Although the statute does not expressly say so, information that is otherwise available presumably would not be given "confidential" treatment under the ADRA. This may be inferred from the requirement that the communication be made "in confidence"—i.e., with an expectation of confidentiality.

Since mediation may be conducted under an agency ADR program, or by a mediator selected from outside the agency, there may be communications with an ADR program manager or with an ADR provider from whose roster the mediator was selected.[25] It is unclear, however, whether the ADRA protects these communications from disclosure. Thus, it would be prudent for counsel to proceed on the assumption that they would not be treated as confidential.

Because of the dearth of cases construing the ADRA and its confidentiality provisions, federal courts may seek guidance in cases involving private sector mediation. In one such case, a federal district court in Utah indicated in dicta that the first 30 minutes of a joint discussion to ascertain whether there were any conflicts of interest did not constitute protected communications.[26]

Preemption of Confidentiality

When the federal government is involved in a mediation (either by providing a federal employee as the mediator, or by participating as a party) unique disclosure rules may apply. Thus, even if confidentiality has attached to mediation-related communications under the ADRA, the statute's protections can be trumped in a variety of ways.

The False Statements Act makes it a crime for a person to make certain types of untruthful representations to government officials.[27] The act has been held to cover all false statements that might support

[25] The ADRA permits an agency to enter into a contract with a person for services as a neutral. 5 U.S.C. § 573(d). It also contemplates that an agency may use the services of public and private organizations that maintain rosters of neutrals. 5 U.S.C. § 583 (support services). The term "roster" is defined in § 571(12).

[26] Poly Software Int'l Inc., v. Su, 880 F. Supp. 1487 (D. Utah 1995).

[27] 18 U.S.C. § 1001.

fraudulent claims or that might pervert or corrupt the authorized functions of a government agency to which the statements were made. It covers oral as well as written statements and unsworn as well as sworn statements. The act applies to matters that involve a government agency's activity, even though the false statement is not made directly to the government. Theoretically, therefore, a federal employee serving as a mediator has an affirmative duty to report a false statement even when the inadvertent admission occurs during the course of a mediation.

Private sector participants in mediation should know that federal employees have a regulatory obligation to report fraud, waste or abuse. To encourage affirmative disclosures, Congress has enacted a number of whistleblower statutes.[28] These statutes protect an individual from reprisal following voluntary disclosure. One even authorizes the Attorney General to pay up to $250,000 if the disclosed information aids a possible prosecution under the Major Fraud Act.[29] To forestall a discovery inquiry, counsel might wish to include in the mediation settlement agreement an affirmative statement concerning the absence of any evidence of fraud, waste or abuse in the underlying matter.

The Inspector General Act of 1978 will also take precedence over the ADRA in the case of a pending audit or investigation. As amended, this act grants an inspector general the power to compel an agency employee, whether serving as the mediator or attending as a participant, to testify if an audit or investigation is pending.[30]

Congressional oversight authority also will preempt the ADRA's confidentiality protections if an enforcement or regulatory agency was involved as a participant in a mediation.

Disclosure also may be ordered, despite the ADRA's confidentiality provisions, when a party or nonparty participant has received notice from a neutral that a legal demand for disclosure has been made but fails to respond. Section 574(e) provides that the failure of the party or affected nonparty to respond within fifteen calendar days offering to defend the neutral's refusal to disclose constitutes a waiver to nondisclosure.[31] To

---

[28] *See* the Defense Acquisition Improvement Act of 1986, 10 U.S.C. § 2409.

[29] 18 U.S.C. § 1031.

[30] If requested, the inspector general can extend confidentiality "to the extent allowable by law" or to protect the identity of persons being criminally investigated.

[31] 5 U.S.C. § 574(e) requires the mediator to make reasonable efforts to notify the parties and any affected nonparty participant of any demand to disclose a mediation communication. Participants to mediations subject to the ADRA presumably would have to send change of address notices to mediators serving on completed mediations or risk exposure of confidential disclosures.

prevent activation of the waiver provision, the mediation settlement agreement should include a long-term mechanism for the expeditious handling of such requests.

Interplay with FOIA

The ADRA exempts dispute resolution communications between a neutral and a party from disclosure under FOIA.[32] Since the ADRA protects mediation communications made in private caucuses, these communications could not be discovered under FOIA. However, this protection will be lost if the parties agreed, with the mediator's knowledge, to alternative procedures that provide for greater confidentiality than is provided under the ADRA—for example, by protecting from subsequent disclosure trade secrets or proprietary information that was communicated to all parties to the dispute resolution proceeding. Section 574(d)(2) provides that to qualify for the exemption from FOIA disclosure, any agreed-to alternative procedures must not provide for less disclosure than is provided by the ADRA.

Mediation-related documents exempt from disclosure under FOIA could lose their exemption if they are considered "agency records." Take the case of a federal employee who, while serving as a mediator in a collateral-duty assignment,[33] retained copies of mediation-related documents. If this employee's work-related duties regularly involved him or her with the activities of any federal agency, the retained documents could be classified as "agency records." To prevent any such loss of confidentiality protection when a federal employee is appointed as a mediator, counsel may wish to obtain the mediator's written agreement to destroy all mediation-related documents at the conclusion of the proceeding.

Because communications in joint session in the presence of the mediator are afforded no protection from disclosure under the ADRA, they have no protection from disclosure under FOIA unless they separately qualify for the exception to disclosure in 5 U.S.C. § 552(b)(3).

---

[32] 5 U.S.C. § 574(j) makes § 552(b)(3) of FOIA applicable. Under § 552(b)(3), the disclosure requirements of FOIA are inapplicable to "matters that are specifically exempted from disclosure by statute…provided that such statute (A) requires that the matters be withheld from the public in such a manner as to leave no discretion on the issue, or (B) establishes particular criteria for withholding or refers to particular types of matters to be withheld."

[33] A collateral-duty assignment is unrelated to the federal employee's full-time function, and is generally undertaken voluntarily, without additional compensation.

Scope of the ADRA

Many hold the belief that all mediation proceedings associated with the federal umbrella are governed by the ADRA. This simply isn't true.

The ADRA may apply only if the mediation involves an administrative program of an "agency" as defined in the Administrative Procedure Act.[34] This limits application of the ADRA to agencies of the executive branch. In some cases, programs of executive branch agencies also may be subject to mediation provisions in statutes authorizing their creation, such as the Education Code under the Individuals with Disabilities Education Act, and the Farm Loan Program. It is not entirely clear how these provisions would work together. The only case to date is the Fifth Circuit decision in In re Grand Jury Subpoena dated Dec. 17, 1996, which provides little guidance.[35]

The ADRA does not apply to independent establishments or government corporations, such as the Federal Deposit Insurance Corporation, the Federal Trade Commission, or the U.S. Postal Service. Separate regulations govern confidentiality protections available during mediations administered by nonexecutive branch agencies. This is true of the Postal Service's REDRESS program.[36]

The ADRA also has no application to the federal courts. Thus, mediation-related communications in court-annexed mediation in the federal courts are not protected from disclosure under its provisions. Federal court-annexed mediation programs are usually governed by court rule, or in the absence of such a rule, by state statute.[37]

---

[34] 5 U.S.C. § 551(1).

[35] *See supra*, n. 18. On Nov. 9, 1999, the U.S. Department of Agriculture issued its proposed revision to the USDA Loan Mediation Program. The proposed revision would give federal officials access to mediation records in order to conduct audits of partially federally funded state mediation programs for agricultural loans. The proposed rule states: "Notwithstanding the confidentiality of mediation sessions, the State must provide the government access to its records in accordance with § 3015.24 of this title. State mediators will notify all participants in writing at the beginning of the mediation session that USDA, the Comptroller General of the United States, the FSA Administrator or any of their representatives will have access to mediation records to conduct an audit or evaluation of mediation services funded in whole or in part by USDA. The notice will be signed and dated by all participants and placed in the mediation file."

[36] Separate acts also govern mandatory disclosure when contractors or grant- holders are parties. These may be in addition to confidentiality provisions in the ADRA. Legal counsel should be consulted prior to the commencement of mediations involving such parties.

[37] The Federal Dispute Resolution Act of 1998 requires federal courts to authorize the use of mediation and other ADR procedures.

The lack of uniform treatment in mediation connected with the federal sector has created great confusion. To reduce this confusion, commentators have urged mediation participants to enter into confidentiality agreements. Granted such agreements can memorialize the intentions of the parties concerning future disclosures. But they also raise some problems.

One problem is that there is no "apparent authority" in the public sector. Federal agency personnel cannot bind the agency to any agreement without express authority to do so. If an employee signs a settlement agreement on behalf of the agency without having actual authority, then the agency would not be bound. Even if the agency were bound, affected third parties could seek disclosure, since they would not be bound by such an agreement. Thus, to be certain that a confidentiality agreement signed by an agency employee is enforceable against the agency, it would be prudent to obtain in writing from that employee the basis for the employee's authority to bind the agency. A related concern is that the protection afforded by a confidentiality agreement in the face of a third-party's civil discovery request or a grand jury subpoena would be suspect.

The other problem, which has already been alluded to is that if the confidentiality agreement provided for more confidentiality than the ADRA allows, the ADRA's FOIA exception would not apply.

Parties and their counsel should be aware that initiating a court proceeding to enforce a confidentiality agreement can prompt even greater public disclosure. Questions may also arise as to how to assess damages if the disclosure has already occurred, and how to collect a resulting judgment.

In light of the confusion surrounding confidentiality in public-sector mediation, guidelines need to be developed to provide a road map for attorneys and their clients. The American Bar Association's Administrative Law Section has just formed a working group to develop guidance on confidentiality in federal ADR programs. James Alfini, chair of the ABA Section on Dispute Resolution, called the effort "a very important initiative because some federal agencies have shown a lack of understanding of the issues surrounding confidentiality."[38]

Until those guidelines have been drafted and approved, know that there is no blanket confidentiality for communications made in public-

[38] J. Kelly, Administrative Law Group to Draft Confidentiality Guidance for Federal ADR Sector, ADRWORLD.COM (Mar. 10, 2000).

sector mediation. Also learn when the ADRA applies and when the exceptions to its explicit, mandatory confidentiality protections come into play.

III. Ethics in Mediation

Ethics within the Mediation Process

by Mattox Hair, Sharon Press & Brooks Rathet[*]

Mediation, a relatively young practice in the judicial system, presents an attractive alternative to the trial system in large part because it offers parties a simpler, less costly path to dispute resolution. The quality of the process depends heavily on the quality of the mediator, thus placing special importance on qualifications criteria, training and standards of practice for mediators.[1]

Yet, even well-qualified, trained mediators can face ethical issues in mediating a dispute. A study sponsored by the National Institute for Dispute Resolution and the Hofstra University School of Law, which addressed the ethical and professional concerns involved in the mediation process, revealed that mediators had ethical questions in such areas as the preservation of impartiality, the maintenance of confidentiality, the receipt of informed consent by parties to the mediation, and the separation of mediation from counseling and legal advice.[2]

---

[*] Mr. Hair is a former circuit judge for the Fourth Judicial Circuit of Florida and a member of Florida's House of Representatives and Senate. He is also a Diplomate of the Florida Association of Professional Mediators and is a certified mediator in Florida state courts the United States District Court, Middle District of Florida. He is also a member of Florida's Mediator Qualifications Advisory Panel. Hair received a B.S. from Florida State University and a J.D. from the University of Florida College of Law.

Ms. Press serves as Director of the Florida Dispute Resolution Center, a joint program of the Florida Supreme Court and Florida State University College of Law, where she is an adjunct professor. She serves on the Board of the Court-ADR Sector for the Society of Professionals in Dispute Resolution and on the committee re-drafting the Model Standards of Conduct for Mediators (Joint Standards).

Mr. Rathet is a shareholder at Anderson, St. Denis & Glenn and is an adjunct professor in Law and Ethics at the University of Florida College of Law. He earned a B.A. from the University of Virginia and a J.D. and M.A. from the University of Florida. Rathet is the author of *Survey of Georgia Privacy and Related Claims Against the Media, in* LDRC MEDIA PRIVACY AND RELATED LAW (1998).

[1] R.A. Baruch Bush, The Dilemmas of Mediation Practice: A Study of Ethical Dilemmas and Policy Implications, A Report on a Study for the National Institute for Dispute Resolution (NIDR 1992).

[2] *Id.* at 3, 9.

The need for ethical and other guidance for mediators in Florida is being met. For several years Florida has maintained standards for mediator conduct, having a rich history in the use of mediation. The use of this process in Florida has increased dramatically since its emergence in the 1970s. Beginning in the 1990s, 50,000 reported cases went to mediation, compared to about 34,000 in 1989,[3] and by 1996, over 3,600 mediators were certified by the Florida Supreme Court and approximately 8,000 individuals completed certified mediation training.[4]

In 1989, the Florida Supreme Court appointed the Standing Committee on Mediation and Arbitration Rules and directed it to recommend procedural rules and standards of professional conduct for arbitrators and mediators.[5] In 1992, the court adopted the Rules for Certified and Court Appointed Mediators recommended by that committee.[6] In 1994, the court amended its rules to place mediator certification exclusively within its jurisdiction and at the same time, with ethical concerns in mind, created the Mediator Qualifications Advisory Panel (Advisory Panel) to provide mediators with guidance and interpretations of the rules and their own conduct.[7] The Advisory Panel can be distinguished from Florida's Mediator Qualifications Board, which governs the discipline of certified mediators.

The Advisory Panel concerns itself with the ethical considerations that arise during the mediation process and with areas where the rules themselves cannot provide complete answers. The panel is composed of nine members, three from each of the northern, central and southern regions of Florida, who serve four-year terms. Members must include one county mediator, one family mediator and one circuit mediator from each geographic division with appointments made by the Chief Justice of the Florida Supreme Court.[8]

The Advisory Panel acts exactly as its name suggests, as a source of advisement for mediators.[9] When the Advisory Panel meets, it considers

---

[3] R.B. Moberly, *Ethical Standards for Court-Appointed Mediators and Florida's Mandatory Mediation Experiment,* 20 FLA. ST. L. REV. 701-703 (1992).

[4] Source: The Florida Dispute Resolution Center.

[5] Proposed Standards of Prof. Conduct, 604 So.2d 764 (Fla. 1992)(repealing and readopting FLA. R. CIV. P. 1.760 as FLA. R. FOR CERTIFIED AND COURT-APPOINTED MEDIATORS 10.010).

[6] Fla. R. for Certified and Court-Appointed Mediators 10.010 through 10.290. *See also* Fla. Stat. § 44.106 (1990).

[7] *In re* Fla R. Civ. P., 641 So.2d 343 (Fla. 1994).

[8] Fla. R. for Certified and Court-Appointed Mediators 10.300(a) and (b).

[9] Fla. R. for Certified and Court-Appointed Mediators 10.300(c).

requests sent by certified mediators seeking advisory opinions on a range of ethical issues. In offering ethical guidance, the panel often relies on its earlier decisions. Its opinions are formulated at panel meetings, which often are conducted by phone to reduce expenses. These opinions delete all references to the requesting mediator.[10] Once the Advisory Panel chair signs an opinion, it is sent to the Florida Dispute Resolution Center, which makes the opinion available upon request from any mediator or the public.[11]

The Advisory Panel will not delve into purely legal issues. For example, it declined to directly answer whether mediators were obliged to keep and maintain mediation files after the declaration of an impasse or final settlement, and if so, for what length of time, since it viewed the mediator's question as one involving legal matters not within its jurisdiction.[12] Instead, the panel offered direction to the mediator and pointed out the rules that were relevant to the mediator's legal question.

A mediator is not required to follow an Advisory Panel opinion. Although compliance with an opinion is not a defense in any disciplinary hearing against that mediator, it will be evidence of good faith and may be considered by the Mediator Qualifications Board in relation to any determination of guilt or mitigation of punishment. However, no opinion issued to one mediator will provide evidence of the good faith of any conduct taken by another mediator unless the underlying facts are identical.[13]

Need for Confidentiality

Advisory Panel opinions often emphasize the necessity of consent from the parties to a mediation and the preservation of confidentiality during the mediation process.[14] For example, in one opinion, the panel approved a mediator's continuing the mediation process after initial conferences ended without the parties reaching an agreement when the mediator sensed there was a chance to reach a compromise, only after the

---

[10] Fla. R. for Certified and Court-Appointed Mediators 10.300(f).

[11] Fla. R. for Certified and Court-Appointed Mediators 10.300(g).

[12] Mediator Qualifications Advisory Panel (MQAP) Advisory Op. 95-004 (Oct. 5, 1995).

[13] Fla. R. for Certified and Court-Appointed Mediators 10.300(e).

[14] *See e.g.*, MQAP Advisory Op. 95-001 (Jan. 19, 1995). It was the opinion of the panel that with the consent of counsel for the parties (or the parties alone if not represented by counsel) and a stipulation of confidentiality, a mediator may continue to help parties reach a voluntary agreement even after no agreement was reached at the initial mediation conferences.

mediator received the parties' consent, and all agreed to maintain confidentiality. The Advisory Panel's concern for maintaining confidentiality extends not only to the mediator's behavior but to the actions of the parties themselves.

In another opinion, a mediator asked the panel if it were consistent with the rules of confidentiality for a party to talk, telephonically or otherwise, with a non-participant to the mediation to seek advice or other information.[15] The panel's advice acknowledged the reality that, during mediation, a named party may want to contact an accountant, spouse or another person for guidance and emphasized the maintenance of confidentiality. The panel advised that, to comply with the statutes and rules governing the confidentiality of the mediation process, the mediator should remind the party making the communication of the privilege provided by statute and that any communication about the specific content of the mediation shall remain confidential.

The issue of confidentiality arises whenever a mediator must determine to what extent communications relayed during mediation will be revealed. Florida law provides general guidance and emphasizes the importance of confidentiality in the mediation process. A mediator must preserve and maintain the confidentiality of all mediation proceedings except where required by law to disclose information.[16] In a court-ordered mediation, all oral or written communications are confidential and inadmissible as evidence in any subsequent proceedings absent party consent.[17]

The Advisory Panel has demonstrated its strict adherence to confidentiality principles in response to a question regarding the mediator-attorney-client relationship.[18] The question arose out of a mediation involving the dissolution of a marriage, in which the mediator determined that one of the parties, who was present without an attorney, might not understand the law. The mediator suggested that the participants take a break and that the party call an attorney. Following the phone call, but before the resumption of mediation, the party told the mediator that the attorney could not be reached but that the attorney's secretary had offered legal advice. Knowing that this party had received legal advice from a non-lawyer and that the information was prejudicial, as well as possibly slanderous, the mediator was torn between the need to maintain confidentiality and the desire to relay this information directly to the attorney.

---

[15] MQAP Advisory Op. 95-003 (Oct. 5, 1995).

[16] Fla. R. for Certified and Court-Appointed Mediators 10.080(a).

[17] FLA. STAT. § 44.102(3)(1993).

[18] MQAP Advisory Op. 95-010 (Feb. 13, 1996).

The Advisory Panel reached two conclusions about this case. First, if a mediator believes that a party does not understand how an agreement affects legal rights, the mediator must advise the party to seek independent legal advice. Second, the mediator is not permitted to disclose to the party's attorney what the attorney's employee said to the party, but instead can encourage the party to relay that information to the attorney. A mediator who takes these steps would be working toward the furtherance of mediation and would not be violating the rules of confidentiality.

Some of the concerns of mediators involve party conduct. Mediators have little power to compel parties to act in certain ways. The underlying principle of mediation is that it is a consensual process by which individuals in conflict arrive at an agreement that is mutually acceptable. It is not based on the power and authority of the mediator.

One Florida mediator asked the Advisory Panel if the mediator could compel parties to attend the introductory statement phase of the mediation. The panel concluded that attendance at mediation is either by agreement of the parties or by order of the court.[19] It opined that an appearance at the mediation included, at a minimum, being present for the mediator's introductory orientation. Thus, while the mediator had no power to compel the parties to remain at the mediation, the mediator could report to the court the party's failure to appear at the opening statement but not the party's decision to leave after the mediator's opening statement.

Besides lacking the power to compel parties to behave in certain ways, mediators also are restricted in their ability to influence decisions because they are not supposed to offer legal advice. The mediator's role is limited to identifying issues, reducing obstacles to communication and maximizing alternatives to help the parties reach a voluntary agreement. In so doing, however, the mediator must maintain impartiality and refrain from giving legal advice. The Advisory Panel even has determined that a mediator cannot ask a question designed to advise a party about his or her legal options.[20]

Ethical issues concerning mediators can extend beyond the boundaries of the mediation process itself. The Advisory Panel has had occasion to render decisions on such matters as the substance of a mediator's advertisements and billing procedures. For example, the panel

---

[19] MQAP Advisory Op. 95-009 (Sept. 27, 1995).

[20] MQAP Advisory Op. 95-002 (citing Fla. R. for Certified and Court-Appointed Mediators 10.020(b)).

determined that a mediator would need to receive permission from the Department of State and the Florida Supreme Court to use their respective seals on business cards, advertisements, and promotional materials.[21]

In another advertising opinion, a mediator asked if it were ethical to advertise that a mediator will provide "a dispassionate evaluation." The Advisory Panel, offering a strict reading of the definition of "mediation," as provided by Florida statute, deemed the advertisement misleading since the statute does not describe a mediator's role as that of an evaluator.[22]

With respect to billing matters, the Advisory Panel has insisted that a mediator maintain the highest ethical standards when charging for mediation services. In a situation presented to the panel, the court had ordered a mediation and the parties elected to have a court-connected mediation program select a mediator, which placed the case on its docket with one of its contract mediators. One party did not appear at the mediation and everyone agreed to reschedule. After several reschedulings, the mediator informed the court that the parties had rescheduled the mediation privately. The panel was asked if it were ethical for the mediator to handle the case on a private basis at a fee consistent with a private mediation, which the mediator indicated could be as much as $100 per hour. The fee for the court-ordered mediation in question was $100 per case.

The Advisory Panel strictly interpreted the rules in reaching the opinion that changing fees represented an unethical act.[23] The Advisory Panel's focus remained on ensuring that the act did not compromise the mediator's integrity. Consistent with the reasons behind its creation, and with its other opinions, the Advisory Panel emphasized the need to prevent undermining public confidence in the mediation process.

The need to maintain public confidence remains the common theme throughout all Advisory Panel opinions. As the mediation process develops and grows, the Advisory Panel has recognized the need to uphold ethical standards strictly. The mediation process, with its relative informality when compared with the trial system, has come to demand the ethical policing provided by the panel. As the mediation process in Florida expands, so too will the panel's decisions.

---

[21] MQAP Advisory Op. 95-006 (Oct. 5, 1995).
[22] MQAP Advisory Op. 95-007 (Oct. 5, 1995).
[23] MQAP Advisory Op. 95-008 (Oct. 16, 1995).

IV. Conflict of Interest

Ethics and Mediation: Using Screening Walls and Advance Waivers to Manage Conflicts of Interest

by Paul M. Lurie[*]

A key element of the mediation process is a mediator's ability to receive confidential information from the parties. For mediation to be successful, mediators must be able to draw out this sensitive information. However, future conflicts of interest can arise as a result of a prior mediation.

The "conflicts" issue concerns attorneys who mediate and the firms that employ them. The attorneys worry that their mediation work might cause their firms to be "conflicted out" of some representations and may lead firms to exclude attorneys who mediate from their ranks. This would have a deleterious effect on the practice of mediation by attorneys. This article discusses this controversial issue and a practical approach to managing potential conflicts arising from mediation—using advance waivers and "screening walls."

Model Rules of Professional Conduct

Attorneys are obligated to comply with the applicable rules governing conflicts of interest, which generally are based on the American Bar Association Model Rules of Professional Conduct (ABA rules).[1] Several of these rules are designed to promote client loyalty on the part of all lawyers in the firm and to protect confidential client information.

---

[*] The author is a partner in the law group at Schiff Hardin in Chicago. He is a member of the American Arbitration Association's National Construction Dispute Resolution Committee. Mr. Lurie holds a B.A. from the University if Michigan and a J.D. from the University of Chicago Law School. He is a member of an Advisory Board of West Publications and is the co-author of OWNERSHIP TRANSFER: OPTIONS AND STRATEGIES, 3d ed. (American Consulting Engineers Council, 1966).

[1] The Model Rules along with state variations may be viewed on the Cornell Law School Web site: http://www.law. cornell.edu.

The ethical issues currently involve the interplay of Rules 1.6 (Confidential Information),[2] 1.7 and 1.9 (Conflicts of Interest), and 1.10 (Firm Attribution).[3] A lawyer can be disqualified under Rule 1.7 or 1.9 because of the acquisition of confidential information. If the lawyer is disqualified under these rules, the lawyer's firm will also be disqualified under Rule 1.10. The firm can take on the new representation only through a waiver permitted under Rule 1.7 or 1.9, as provided in Rule 1.10.

There is no provision in Rule 1.10 allowing the firm to resolve a conflict of interest by other means, such as by screening off the disqualified attorney from the matter that created the conflict.

Do these ethical rules apply to mediation proceedings conducted by lawyers who practice in law firms? There is a difference of opinion on this issue.[4] If they do apply to mediation, they would prevent a firm in which a mediator practices law from representing a party to a prior mediation, or another party whose interests are adverse to one of the parties to the mediation in which the mediator served as the neutral.

This raises a significant problem for mediators who practice law in large law firms. They are concerned that their mediation work may taint new business coming into the firm, and that the firm will react by restricting mediation activities by associates and partners.

Whether or not the ABA rules apply in this way, in recognition of the need to address ethical issues arising from the activities of lawyer-mediators, efforts are under way to revise the rules to eliminate all doubt that they apply to conflicts arising from mediation and arbitration. This development is no doubt the result of the tremendous growth of ADR

[2] In Comment 3 to the ABA's final November 2000 report recommending adoption of a new revised Rule 1.12 (discussed below), the ABA Commission on the Evaluation of the Rules of Professional Conduct observed that neutrals do not receive confidential information protected under Rule 1.6. However, the commission assumed that neutrals have a duty of confidentiality. Thus, the issue of imputation to the firm arises from laws or codes of ethics governing neutrals.

[3] Rule 1.7(b) provides: "A lawyer shall not represent a client if the representation of that client may be materially limited by the lawyer's responsibilities to another client or to a third person, or by the lawyer's own interests, unless: (1) the lawyer reasonably believes the representation will not be adversely affected; and (2) the client consents after consultation. When representation of multiple clients in a single matter is undertaken, the consultation shall include explanation of the implications of the common representation and the advantages and risks involved."

[4] Rule 1.8 (b) is pertinent to disclosure. It provides: "A lawyer shall not use information relating to representation of a client to the disadvantage of the client unless the client consents after consultation, except as permitted or required by Rule 1.6 or Rule 3.3."

and the increasingly important role attorneys play as neutrals in these proceedings.

The Proposed Rule Revisions

The ABA formed the Commission on the Evaluation of the Rules of Professional Conduct, known as the Ethics 2000 Commission, to revise the ABA rules. After proposing draft rules for public comment, in November 2000 the ABA released its final report recommending the adoption of a new Rule 1.12,[5] which specifically addresses the problems of mediators and arbitrators. Subsections (a) and (c) provide as follows:

> "(a) Except as stated in paragraph (d), a lawyer shall not represent anyone in connection with a matter in which the lawyer participated personally and substantially as a judge or other adjudicative officer or law clerk to such a person or as an arbitrator, mediator or other third-party neutral, unless all parties to the proceeding give informed consent, confirmed in writing.
>
> "(c) If a lawyer is disqualified by paragraph (a), no lawyer in a firm with which that lawyer is associated may knowingly undertake or continue representation in the matter unless: (1) the disqualified lawyer is timely screened from any participation in the matter and is apportioned no part of the fee therefrom; and (2) written notice is promptly given to the parties and any appropriate tribunal to enable them to ascertain compliance with the provisions of this rule."

This rule is a substantial improvement over earlier drafts, which did not allow the screening wall mechanism. Another improvement involves the subject of attorneys' fees. Existing rules and earlier drafts of the proposed rules prohibited screened attorneys from sharing in fees

---

[5] For commentary on the debate over whether mediation constitutes the practice of law, see Carrie Menkel-Meadow, *Is Mediation the Practice of Law?* 14 ALTERNATIVES 57 (CPR May 1996); Bruce Meyerson, *Lawyers Who Mediate are Not Practicing Law*, 14 ALTERNATIVES 74 (June 1996); *Symposium—Is Mediation the Practice of Law?* NIDR FORUM (June 1997); Geetha Ravindra, *When Mediation Becomes the Unauthorized Practice of Law*, 15 ALTERNATIVES 94 (July-August 1997); Menkel-Meadow (letter to the editor), *Is Mediation the Practice of Law? Redux*, NIDR NEWS 2 (Nov./Dec. 1997- Jan. 1998); *NJ Panel Finds ADR is Part of Law Practice*, 12 ALTERNATIVES 87 (July 1994). Proposed ABA Rule 2.4 (found at www.abanet.org/cpr/e2k-rule24.html), if adopted, would appear to end this debate.

attributable to the screened matter. Comment 4 to Rule 1.12 substantially relaxes the prohibition on salary sharing. It provides:

> "Paragraph (c)(1) does not prohibit the screened lawyer from receiving a salary or partnership share established by prior independent agreement, but that lawyer may not receive compensation directly related to the matter in which the lawyer is disqualified."

By accepting the screening wall device to insulate mediators, the proposed rule properly recognizes that the relationship between a mediator and the mediating parties (like that between a judge and litigating parties) differs from the normal lawyer-client relationship.

Screening Wall Cases

Ethical rules in several jurisdictions allow screening walls to rebut the presumption that confidential information has spread to the entire firm.[6] While there are no reported mediation cases involving the screening device, there is case law suggesting that screening walls are an appropriate mechanism to prevent confidential information from being communicated to other lawyers at the firm in which the mediator practices law.

For example, in *Chapman v. Chrysler Corp.*,[7] the court stated that the presumption of shared confidences could be rebutted by demonstrating specific institutional mechanisms had been implemented to effectively insulate against any flow of confidential information from the infected attorney to any other member of the firm.[8] Similarly, in *Cummin v. Cummin*,[9] the court remarked that the presumption that confidential information was shared could be rebutted where the

---

[6] Proposed Rule 1.12 can be found at www.abanet.org/cpr/e2k-rule112.html.

[7] Ill. Rule of Prof'l Conduct 1.10(b)(2)(e); Md. Rule of Proc. 1.10(b)(2)(d); Mass Rule of Prof'l Conduct 1.10(e); Mich. Rule of Prof'l Conduct 1.10(b)(1); Minn. Rule of Prof'l Conduct 1.10(b)(2); Wash. Rule of Prof'l Conduct 1.10(b).

[8] 54 F. Supp. 864, 866 (S.D. Ind. 1999). *But see* n. 11 *infra*.

[9] The court cited *Cromley v. Board of Educ. of Lockport Twnshp. High Sch.*, 17 F.3d 1059, 1065 (7th Cir. 1994). *See also* Portland Gen. Elec. Co. v. Weinberg, 986 P.2d 35, 49 (1999) (stating that establishing a wall in accordance with instructions of the court is sufficient to show no secrets or confidences passed through it); Actel Corp. v. Quicklogic, No. 94-20050JW, 1996 WL 297045 (N.D. Cal. May 29, 1996) (indicating that screening would have cured the conflict); G.D. Searle & Co. v. Nutrapharm, Inc., No. 98 CIV. 6890(TPG),1999 WL 249725 (S.D.N.Y. Apr. 28, 1999).

information previously acquired by a large firm, but never shared among its associates, could be physically isolated, such as by a screening wall.

The acceptability of a screening wall is highly dependent on its effectiveness. A screen that allows confidential information to leak to others in the firm will not prevent imputation under the rule.[10]

Prospective Waivers

Most law firms must have a procedure to identify when a new matter may be adverse to a prior representation. To identify conflicts arising out of the mediation and arbitration activities of lawyers at the firm, the "conflicts-checking" procedure should involve a search of the parties to prior ADR proceedings in which a firm lawyer has served as a neutral.

If a conflicts check discloses a potential adverse relationship, the firm, if it reasonably believes that representation will not be adversely affected, may undertake the representation under the existing ABA rules only if (a) it discloses the existence (but not the result) of the mediation, and (b) it obtains the informed consent from the affected parties[11] (which must be in writing under the proposed revision of the ABA rules).

As a practical matter, however, after a mediation proceeding has concluded, it may be difficult to obtain consent to the representation. Parties may refuse to consent to protect their own interests or for other reasons. Until proposed Rule 1.12 is adopted in the states where the mediator practices, it would be prudent for mediators to incorporate into their mediation agreements a waiver of prospective conflicts of interest, conditioned on the use of an effective screening wall to protect confidential information disclosed to the mediator during the mediation. The screening wall should give the parties to the mediation an incentive to waive future conflicts by providing needed comfort that their confidential communications to the mediator will be protected.

The ABA Standing Committee on Ethics and Professional Responsibility has concluded that seeking prospective consent to future adverse representation is permissible. But it expressed caution depending

---

[10] 695 N.Y.S.2d 346, 347 (N.Y. 1999).

[11] McKenzie Construction v. St. Croix Storage Corp., 961 F. Supp. 857, 859-861 (D.V.I. 1997) (disqualifying attorney and imputing disqualification to the entire firm after screening wall mechanism did not function correctly); Kassis v. Teacher's Ins. & Annuity Assoc., 93 N.Y.2d 611, 618-619 (N.Y. 1999) (stating that an inconsequential screening wall does not prevent attorney disqualification or the imputation of the attorney's law firm).

on the quality of the prospective consent.[12] The effectiveness of a prospective waiver will probably depend upon the adequacy of the disclosure that is made at the time of execution of the mediation agreement containing the consent. This issue will be of greater concern when the party whose waiver is sought is not represented by counsel since this person may not fully understand what is being asked.[13]

Conclusion

Identifying conflicts of interest is extremely important. But so is finding a practical way to deal with them. Screening walls ensure the integrity of the mediation process, encourage the free flow of confidential information to the mediator, protect the interests of the mediating parties and the mediator, while also protecting the law firm from unreasonable disqualifications from new representations. When used in combination with prospective waivers of conflicts of interest, screening walls should satisfy even current ethical requirements.

The author suggests this prospective waiver provision:

> The Neutral shall not subsequently provide professional services to a Party, regardless of the subject matter, until six (6) months after termination of his or her services as a Neutral. After this six-month period, the Neutral shall be permitted to represent a Party, provided that such representation does not involve the same matter to that of the Mediation.
>
> The Neutral's firm may provide services on matters for or against any Party in the Mediation during or after the pendency of the Mediation, including matters substantially related to the mediation on the condition that: (a) the Neutral does not participate in such matters; and (b) an effective and timely

---

[12] *See* Poly Software Int'l Inc. v. Yu Su, 880 F. Supp. 1487, 1494 (D. Utah 1995) (holding that a mediator who obtained confidential information in the course of mediation was precluded from later representing anyone in connection with the same or substantially related manner unless all parties to the mediation consented after disclosure). It should be noted that in some jurisdictions parties cannot waive a conflict of interest that arises when a party to a former mediation seeks representation by the mediator in a subsequent litigation involving the same subject matter. *See* Gilbert v. National Corp. for Housing Partnerships, 71 Cal. App. 4th 1240, 1258 (Cal. Ct. App. 1999); Florida Bar v. Charnock, 661 So.2d 1207, 1211 (Fla. 1995) (dissenting opinion).

[13] American Bar Association Formal Op. 93-372 (April 16, 1993).

screening procedure is established to insulate the Neutral from such matters and to ensure that other attorneys, support staff, and employees of the Neutral's firm do not have access to any Confidential Information obtained by the Neutral during the course of the Mediation.[14]

[14] Jacqueline M. Nolan-Haley, *Informed Consent in Mediation: A Guiding Principle for Truly Educated Decision-making,* 74 NOTRE DAME L. REV. 775, 777-778 (1999).

CHAPTER SEVEN

MEDIATION IN THE WORKPLACE

I. Ten Tips for Better Employment Mediation

10 Tips to Improve Employment Mediation: Valuable Advice for Counsel Representing Employees and Employers

by Rosemary Townley[*]

1. **Before the mediation explain to your client the basics of the mediation process.** While the mediator will spend time at the beginning of the session briefly outlining the process, your client should not be hearing about it for the first time at the mediation. Explain each step of the proceeding in detail so that your client will know what to expect at each step. Emphasize that *ex parte* conversations are common in mediation so that the client will not think that the mediator is "choosing sides." Also explain the duty of all participants, including the mediator, to maintain the confidentiality of the discussions during and after the mediation.
2. **Develop a "litigation tree" analysis for use during the course of the mediation.** In its simplest form, a decision tree is an analytical diagram showing the difference between the costs of litigation versus the costs of settlement. This tool enables the client to assess a settlement offer by comparing it with the cost of litigating the case through trial and the likely outcome. Moreover, these cost analyses are readily understood by those in management who usually make the ultimate decision on settlement.

---

[*] Ms. Townley is a full-time arbitrator and mediator in the New York City and teaches at St. John's University Law School. She is a member of the National Academy of Arbitrators and the AAA's National labor and Commercial Tribunals. She is also the past Chair of the Labor and Employment Law Section of the New York State Bar Association and serves on its Executive Committee. Townley is a contributing author to HOW ADR WORKS (BNA, 2002).

3. **Find out who should attend the mediation with the claimant.** Many times a claimant is not willing to settle without consulting with the person whose opinion he or she values most. Don't presume that person is the client's spouse or significant other. As claimant's counsel, you must question your client carefully to determine who the trusted friend or relative is. If this person cannot be present, be sure that he or she will be available via telephone in the event that a settlement is imminent. Or arrange to have this person meet with your client while the mediator is caucusing with the opposing party.
4. **Ensure that the employer's representative at the mediation will have full authority to settle.** Without this authority, the ability to reach a settlement will be severely handicapped. If the employer must obtain the approval of a board of directors or trustees to any settlement, be sure that the chair, or other person who can speak on behalf of the board, will be available by telephone to decide on the acceptability of a settlement offer. If there is a need to poll the board members, be sure that a mechanism will be in place to reach them, so that the lack of board input will not stymie the settlement.
5. **Direct the employee's opening statement to the executives or principals of the employer who are sitting on the other side of the table.** Some attorneys make the mistake of addressing all remarks to the mediator. The opening statement segment of the mediation is often the only chance you will have to address the employer directly. Take the time to show its representatives the strengths of your case. You should emphasize your willingness to negotiate a resolution and persuade the employer that a mediated settlement would be more desirable than the uncertainty of litigation.
6. **Allow your client to participate during the mediation if he or she is comfortable doing so.** Mediation is a participatory process. Your client should be allowed to do more than sit quietly. Mediators welcome party participation. Indeed, comments by the parties themselves often aid the mediator in understanding underlying issues that could become an obstacle to settlement—or provide a basis for complete resolution of the dispute. Many times the mediator unearths issues of utmost importance to a party through questioning designed to identify both emotional issues and potential non-monetary, creative means of settlement.

7. **Be on your best behavior**. An attorney who acts in an aggressive and obnoxious manner to prove to everyone that he or she can't be pushed around does not serve the client's interest. Such behavior will cost the client more money if the mediator is paid by the hour, since it will slow the process down. Faced with confrontational behavior, the mediator undoubtedly will be forced to spend additional time "calming the waters" before any meaningful progress can be made. The mediator will re-direct the focus of the sessions away from confrontation to mutual gain and urge the adversary not to respond in kind.
8. **Be positive in private caucuses with the mediator**. Although mediation ultimately involves a compromise in order to achieve a settlement, the parties must develop the feeling that they are going to get something out of it. Each can even conclude a mediation with a sense of having won. Whether the parties develop these feelings is highly dependent on the attitudes of their attorneys during private caucuses. If, instead of listening, the attorney immediately criticizes every suggestion the mediator makes, the client may begin to distrust the mediator, a development that can doom the mediation. Instead, make an effort to glean something positive for your client from the mediator's suggestions.
9. **Analyze the opposing party's position before and during the course of the mediation and educate your client about the strengths of the opponent's case**. This injects an element of realism into the discussions and will support the mediator's effort to do the same.
10. **At the end of the mediation, before anyone leaves the room, memorialize the settlement in some way**. Attorneys who leave the mediation without doing so make a huge mistake. Not only is it possible to forget the general intent of the stipulated settlement agreement and the points that were agreed to, the principals often change their minds once they leave the room. I prefer to have the full settlement agreement worked out and signed by all parties and counsel before the mediation is concluded. Many mediators bring sample settlement agreements to the mediation to aid counsel in drafting the terms of the settlement agreement. The parties' attorneys also should be prepared to offer language for the settlement agreement that will protect the interests of their respective clients. If it is impractical to draft the complete

settlement agreement, at the very least the attorneys should prepare a stipulation to the major points of settlement, leaving the full settlement agreement to be prepared when the mediation is over. Whichever is prepared, it should include language stating that it will be enforceable in court if one of the parties fails to live up to its terms.

What to Include in a Settlement Agreement

Every settlement agreement should include at least:

- the details concerning the monetary portion of the settlement, such as how and when it is to be paid, and whether taxes will be withheld;
- a mutual release of liability for all claims by the parties against each other and their agents or assignees;
- a statement that the settlement is voluntary and that the parties have been represented by legal counsel throughout the process;
- the details relating to the payment of attorneys' fees, including who will pay them and whether they will be paid out of the settlement amount;
- a statement that the settlement is confidential and an ADR mechanism for the resolution of any disputes arising out of the settlement agreement.

II. Perceptual Errors and Employment Disputes

In the Eye of the Beholder: Using Perceptual Errors to Resolve Employment Disputes

*by Melissa Janis**

Consider the simple problem of tardiness. How many times have we heard people attribute other people's tardiness to internal characteristics (she's just inconsiderate!) and yet blame their own lateness on external factors (the traffic jam was impossible!)? The author calls these fundamental attribution errors, one of two major perceptual errors that discussed in the following article. She shows how perceptual errors are often at the core of a conflict and offers practical mediation techniques in managing them.

In my undergraduate days, I was a lab assistant for a cognitive psychology class. Each week, I taught about a different aspect of perception, and conveyed the same message: our experiences and reality are not equal.

It was fascinating to demonstrate that color isn't real, that your experience of color is based on your perception of light rays bouncing off the surface of an object. Sound isn't real either; your experience of sound is based on your perception of vibrations (so if you were wondering, if no one is in the woods to hear a tree fall, it does not make a sound, only vibrations). Your perception of the world differs from mine, and neither is reality.

The possibility for two individuals to experience the same event differently is frequently acknowledged in employment mediation. The phrases "from my perspective" and "from your perspective" are invoked by counsel to respectfully recognize another's position and preface one's own.

Mediators use them to validate feelings and to encourage the parties to move off positions. Although the existence of multiple perspectives is routinely accepted in the employment mediation context, exploring the reasons for their existence is not.

---

* Ms. Janis is president of Dovetail Solutions, L.L.C., a consulting practice specializing in workplace conflict resolution services. She provides organization development, mediation, and training services in the New York area.

In resolving employment disputes, participants often look to the "merits," and accordingly, the reasons underlying differences in perception are regarded as irrelevant. Both counsel and the mediator typically fear igniting emotions and tend to view employment cases as statutory concerns. These preoccupations keep employment mediation on a legalistic path, which differs significantly from mediation in other contexts.

By and large, employment mediations are conducted like a settlement conference: the emphasis is on evaluating the strengths and weaknesses of each case and speculating about the likely outcome of litigation.

Indeed, in the employment mediation survey discussed by Robert Lewis in the *Journal of Alternative Dispute Resolution in Employment*, every employment attorney surveyed preferred a mediator who "forcefully and vigorously reviews with each party, in confidence, the mediator's opinion of the likely outcome of the case."[1] Movement toward settlement is achieved by evaluating each side's weaknesses combined with the time and costs associated with future litigation and then comparing this "package" to an outcome in the present.

In contrast, mediators who focus on resolving the conflict rather than settling the dispute can achieve both of these goals. Like the ubiquitous onion metaphor, we peel back the layers of the dispute to identify the root causes of the conflict. Often, the center of that onion contains a perceptual error.

As humans, we constantly perceive data and draw conclusions in order to explain our own behavior and that of others, and make errors in the process. A conflict may be created and then exacerbated by these misperceptions as each side becomes entrenched in its own interpretation of reality.

For example, when an employer's affirmative defense is poor performance; both parties formulate their perception of the employee's performance and attach reasons to the adverse action. Where the employee sees discrimination, the employer sees legal justification. The same event is perceived differently.

In discrimination claims, the parties typically disagree about the quality of employee performance. When performance appraisals are based upon subjective evaluations, perception is involved. The degree to

---

[1] Robert Lewis, *Staying Out of the Courtroom by Implementing ADR Procedures*, THE J. ALTERNATIVE DISP. RESOL. EMP., VOL. 2, NO. 4, 32-43 (2000).

which performance appraisals are ambiguous, are not provided to the employee in a timely manner, or are nonexistent heighten the possibility that a perceptual error has played a role in the conflict. By digging deeper in mediation, it is possible to discover a misperception at the source of the conflict that can lead to a quick, highly satisfying and durable solution.

Types of Perceptual Errors

There are several types of perceptual errors that contribute to interpersonal conflict. This article addresses two major errors I have identified in mediation: the fundamental attribution error, and the false consensus bias.

It is important to note that perceptual errors can occur alone or in combination, simultaneously or alternatively, necessitating special attention to the dynamics of the situation on the part of the mediator.[2]

Fundamental Attribution Error

We frequently make errors in judgment based on our perceptions. This isn't due to poor judgment or bad decision-making; perceptions and the resulting misperceptions are formed by an inherently faulty process.

Back in 1958, Fritz Heider postulated that in order to have a sense of control in our lives, we routinely explain our behavior and that of others. "Once we have determined the cause of some event, we can predict the occurrence of that event. In this way, life becomes controllable."[3]

Our explanations fall into two categories: (1) internal (disposition) attributions, in which the behavior is deemed to be caused by the individual's characteristics; and, (2) external (situational) attributions, in which the behavior is due to something outside of the person's control.

Heider coined the term "fundamental attribution error" to describe the tendency for people to attribute another person's mistakes to internal characteristics, but their own mistakes to external factors.[4]

Lateness is a classic example of the fundamental attribution error. Another person's lateness will be attributed to internal characteristics,

---

[2] John Ng and Sophia Ang, *Attribution Bias: Challenges, Issues, and Strategies for Mediation*, *MEDIATION* Q., VOL. 16, NO. 4 (1999).

[3] Anthony G. Munton, et. al. Attributions in Action: A Practical Approach to Coding Qualitative Data. (New York: John Wiley & Sons 1999).

[4] Fritz Heider, *Social Perception and Phenomenal Causality*, PSYCHOLOGICAL REV., VOL. 51, 358-374 (1958).

such as being inconsiderate. But when you arrive late for an appointment, you are likely to explain your lateness in terms of some external factor such as traffic. "Due to the fundamental attribution error, there is a tendency to attribute blame to the other's personality traits while justifying one's own behaviors as due to situational factors, resulting in an unhealthy win-lose approach."[5]

False Consensus Bias

"False consensus bias refers to the assumption that one's lifestyle, behaviors, and attitudes are the yardsticks of normality. Conversations tend to begin with 'she should do this and do that.'"[6]

Our judgments about another's behavior in terms of our own standards and assumptions that those standards are universally held interfere with accepting alternative perspectives. When we assume that ours is the right way, the other can only be wrong.

In a recent mediation, one party's efforts to prevent the circulation of a damaging memo were considered insufficient by the other. Even though she had advised the author of the memo that it was inappropriate and unnecessary, the other party held her responsible for the memo because she had not used the more forceful words he would have chosen. As long as he held her actions to his universal standards, he could not get past his conclusion that she had masterminded the event to hurt him.

Mediation Techniques

While focusing on perceptual errors can be a powerful and effective mediation tool, little has been written about the effect of perceptual errors in mediation and techniques to overcome them.

In their article on this topic, John Ng and Sophia Ang express their concern for the dearth of systemic empirical research and set forth a solid foundation for discussion based on their experiences and observations.[7]

Several of the techniques they suggest are standard fare for mediators—what is instructive here is framing them as a means to correcting perceptual errors. In this section, I will recount their suggested techniques and offer additional ones with specific examples from my mediation practice.

---

[5] John Ng and Sophia Ang, *Attribution Bias: Challenges, Issues, and Strategies for Mediation*, MEDIATION Q., VOL. 16, NO. 4 (1999).

[6] *Id.*

[7] *Id.*

Managing Fundamental Attribution Error

According to Ng and Ang, "maintaining impartiality is the key for the mediator to avoid becoming stuck if the parties fix blame on each other while justifying their own behaviors." They suggest that mediators maintain impartiality in three ways: being like teflon (reframing negative comments to neutral ones); focusing on common interests; and acknowledging feelings and interests.[8]

Another technique can be successful in managing the fundamental attribution error: asking the parties to switch seats and speak on each other's behalf. "Stepping into each other's shoes" invites parties to change their conclusions not through reason but through cognitive dissonance.

The theory of cognitive dissonance holds that people cannot simultaneously maintain two mutually exclusive beliefs. If our beliefs are in conflict, then we experience a discomfort that moves us either to change our beliefs or alter the reality to which the beliefs refer. In other words, each of us requires a consistency in our own beliefs; when our beliefs are not consistent, we are moved to rectify the inconsistency.[9]

In mediation, giving the parties the opportunity to "be each other" shifts their blame away from character and toward situational factors. As this technique corrects the fundamental attribution error, it creates cognitive dissonance as the parties validate each other's perspectives. The parties' need to reconcile their newly disparate beliefs creates movement toward resolution.

It is also possible to change the parties' attributions about their own behavior, from situational to dispositional. In addition to the movement gained by creating cognitive dissonance, the parties are encouraged to take some responsibility for their own roles in the conflict.

One possibility to consider is the use of videotape within mediation. In her April 28, 2001, presentation at the ABA Dispute Resolution Section conference in Washington, D.C., Gay Gellhorn showed videotapes of students conducting interviews. She said that videotaping students was the most effective way of getting them to accept constructive criticism. Until they observed their own behavior, the students were unable to take responsibility for their poor performance.

---

[8] *Id.*

[9] Doutooh, M. The Resolution of Conflict, Constructive Processes. New Haven: Yale University Press (1973).

Viewing their own behavior enabled the students to observe themselves as they would view others; watching the video lessened the fundamental attribution error by changing their perspective of their own performance from actor (with a tendency to attribute one's own behavior to the external situation) to observer (with a tendency to attribute others' behavior to internal characteristics).

Empirical evidence supports my hypothesis. Storms (1973) found that when people watched themselves interact on videotape, they tended to change their attributions about their own behavior from situational to dispositional.[10]

Videotape affords a unique opportunity for parties to consider their own contributions to a conflict. In the "right" scenario, videotaping the parties could be a valuable mediation tool.

Managing False Consensus Bias

Since what is considered normal is based on one's own experience, Ng and Ang propose that the mediator be an "angel of reality" to overcome the perception of universally accepted standards for behavior.

Reality checks expand a party's range of normality. Secondly, stating that "responsiveness to perspectives is a precondition for progress," they emphasize the need to ensure that the parties have an equal opportunity to express their perspectives and respond to the other party's perspectives, and to paraphrase and summarize the parties' perspectives.

The authors suggest that mediators float possibilities with examples of how similar situations have been resolved. "Floating possibilities means generating options without coercion or forcing. The solutions are suggestions."[11]

Taking the notion of floating possibilities one step further, mediators can offer alternative explanations for behavior. When one party's judgment of the other rests on a violation of some universal standard, mediators can float other possible explanations to open the door to other perspectives.

This may be accomplished directly, or through the use of an engaging story related by the mediator. The advantage of a story is its distance from the conflict; because it's about someone else, the parties

---

[10] M.D. Storms, *Videotape and the Attribution Process: Reversing Actors and Observers Points of View*, J. PERSONALITY & SOC. PSYCHOL., VOL. 27, 165-175 (1973).

[11] *Supra*, note 2.

are able to relax and hear in the story a message that challenges their assumptions about normality.

A related technique is using the mediator as evidence of false consensus. After establishing a great deal of trust and goodwill, it is possible for the mediator to illustrate how the yardstick of normality fails to measure up.

A story containing a minor self-disclosure, revealing something about the mediator that refutes the party's universal standard, can be highly effective in creating the cognitive dissonance necessary for the party to modify beliefs. The mediator can neutralize the false consensus bias by demonstrating its inapplicability to the neutral.

Identifying the Perceptual Error

After diagnosing the type(s) of perceptual errors that are occurring, the hunt is on for the actual misperception.

One of the most useful tools I've encountered is a shorthand for connecting feelings to needs. Simply put: if the party is angry, it's about respect; if the party is sad, it's about belonging; if the party is fearful, it's about safety.

Selecting the respect, belonging, or safety path, and asking each party questions about how they are affected by the situation will provide important clues. Listen for repeated phrases, especially ones both parties use. Follow the energy. Identify what produces more activity, passion, or participation in the discussion. Note changes in body language. Listen for the word "should."

The following examples are mediations I conducted as a contractor for the EEOC. In both cases, the employers cited poor performance in response to the charges of discrimination. Both cases were settled by addressing perceptual errors.

Fast Food Restaurant Case

In the "fast food" case, the employee was angry that she was fired despite her hard work in a difficult job situation. She was terminated after nineteen years of service that included being the cashier when the restaurant was robbed. She was convinced that her employer discriminated against her due to her ethnic background.

The employer maintained that the employee was not productive and presented performance appraisals bearing deficient ratings. Clearly, the progressive discipline followed by the employer was sufficient evidence to refute discrimination charges. Equally clear was that a mediation focused on the merits would have produced a winner and a loser. By searching for a perceptual error, the result was a win-win.

The clue surfaced when the employee characterized the current work environment as deplorable and the employer showed emotion for the first time. The employer, proud of the human resources initiative he had implemented, believed he had been successful in improving the workplace culture, and expressed anger when it was depicted as unchanged.

This revealed two clues. First, the energy around the subject of the new program was significant. Secondly, the parties' anger suggested that respect was an issue for both of them.

The employee attributed her poor performance to unfavorable and unchanged working conditions (situation) and the employer attributed poor performance to an inability to learn the new ways of doing her job (individual characteristics).

Since the conflict was so entrenched in situation vs. individual characteristics, I saw an opening to address the fundamental attribution error. By asking the parties to step into each other's shoes, I helped them reframe the alleged poor performance as lack of fit in the new environment and to value the good performance demonstrated in the old environment at the same time.

Feeling respected and appreciated for a job well done enabled the employee to accept the cause for termination. The employer took some responsibility for the employee's inability to succeed in the new culture, which motivated him to make various offers of assistance and career counseling that he might not otherwise have offered, and allowed him to feel respected as a manager.

Bridal Shop Case

In this case, a part-time employee charged age discrimination. In fact, the manager called her at home and told her not to return to work saying "we are retiring you."

Like the fast food case, she was a long-term employee who felt she had worked hard. However, in contrast to the previous case, it was generally agreed that the employee was one of their top performers and performance appraisals were lacking.

The employer's position was that even though the employee was a terrific salesperson, she was often incredibly rude to customers, jeopardized vendor relationships, and failed to comply with management directives. Management had decided they would "retire her" because direct methods of communication had been unsuccessful and they saw this as a way to avoid further unpleasantness.

There were two key clues to the perceptual error in this case. First, all five of the employer representatives were extremely angry and the employee was very sad, suggesting respect and belonging needs, respectfully. Then, both parties used the same phrase in caucus: the employee "didn't need the money." A false consensus bias was operating for each of the parties.

The employer's representatives believed that people who don't need money behave as they please. The employee believed that people who work but don't need the money are dedicated employees who demonstrate tremendous initiative due to their love for the job.

I addressed the false consensus bias in caucus with each party. With management, I inquired about their counsel's pro bono work (with his prior consent). Acknowledging that he approaches his work with the same dedication in the absence of compensation challenged their universal standard and created cognitive dissonance.

Since they were in a situation that necessitated confidence in counsel, it was critical that they continue to regard him as competent. They could not maintain their belief and regard their attorney as competent and unpaid at the same time. Reconciling these mutually exclusive concepts made them receptive to other reasons for the employee's undesirable behavior. Because these alternative explanations did not entail disrespect for management, their anger subsided and they felt sympathy for the employee instead.

As for the employee, "not needing the money" was integral in explaining her behavior in the workplace to others and to herself. She attributed her considerable effort, including ignoring management directives, to her devotion to the job. She harbored a belief that people who are not dependent on their salaries are superior workers who identify and act upon opportunities to prevent management mistakes.

When her universal standard was challenged through the use of a story about a person who worked to meet belonging needs instead of money (remember that this employee had expressed sadness), she was able to accept that people work in exchange for something they need, whether it be money or something else.

Once she realized that working in the bridal shop met her need to belong somewhere, to be a part of a group, the employee experienced cognitive dissonance. She could not simultaneously acknowledge that she benefited by working and conceive of herself as a superior employee who worked without regard to what she received. This cognitive dissonance enabled her to be receptive to the employer's perspective, and she ultimately understood how her behavior had been disruptive in the workplace.

Addressing the false consensus biases of the parties eliminated the misperception at the root of the conflict. As a result, they were able to quickly arrive at an integrative solution that the parties and their representatives deemed to be highly satisfactory in terms of both monetary and emotional outcomes.

At the Mediation Table

In addition to the attributions the parties make about the behavior that caused the conflict in the first place, there is a preponderance of attributive activity occurring in the mediation room itself. Parties and counsel attach meaning to their own behavior and to the behavior of those around them, and make perceptual errors in the process.

In a series of experiments, Morris, Larrick, and Su (1999) found that negotiators systematically misperceive their counterparts by interpreting their behavior in terms of character traits instead of situational determinants. "Although basic negotiation behavior is highly determined by bargaining positions, negotiators primarily interpret their counterpart's behavior in terms of the counterpart's personality, such as his or her level of cooperativeness or agreeableness."[12]

Finally, mediators make attributions about everyone else in the room as well. In our efforts to stay neutral, we must manage attributions of our own.

Conclusion

The fundamental attribution error and the false consensus bias are two types of perceptual errors that lead to misperceptions and ultimately conflict.

Without understanding the misperception upon which a conflict is based, it is possible for an employment mediator to resolve the dispute but not the conflict, or to fail entirely. When we invest time and effort to explore the underlying reasons for each perspective, a perceptual error

---

[12] M.W. Morris, R.P. Larrick, and S.K. Su, *Misperceiving Negotiation Counterparts: When Situationally Determined Bargaining Behaviors Are Attributed to Personality Traits,* J. PERSONALITY & SOC. PSYCHOL., VOL. 17, NO 1, 52-67 (1999).

may be discovered that can change the course of the conflict and the dispute.

It is my hope that this article will inspire researchers to explore and practitioners to reflect upon and write about their own techniques to reach the center of the onion. May all the onions be peeled and all our toolboxes be full.

III. Mediation and Workplace Discrimination

Discrimination in the Workplace: How Mediation Can Help...

*by Lamont E. Stallworth, Thomas McPherson & Larry Rute**

The following article discusses an insidious form of discrimination in the workplace—the kind that sneaks up on the individual and is hardly noticed by either the victim or the perpetrator because it is too subtle, if not unconscious. The authors maintain that acts of subtle or unconscious discrimination are prevalent and damaging. And, because these acts are largely unintentional, they usually do not fall under existing antidiscrimination laws. The authors discuss how the early use of mediation can be helpful and effective by describing the key features of the U.S. Postal Service's REDRESS program, and also explain the need for legislation such as the National Employment Dispute Resolution Act, still pending in Congress.

W.E.B. DuBois, an educator and author and a founder of the NAACP, said at the turn of the last century that "the problem of the 20th century is the problem of the color-line in relation of the darker to the lighter races of men in Asia and Africa, in America and the islands of the sea."[1]

This article posits that the words and underlying concerns of W.E.B. DuBois still persist today. However, the challenge facing our society in

---

* Mr. Stallworth is a mediator and labor arbitrator. He is a member of the National Academy of Arbitrators, a past president of the Society of Professionals in Dispute Resolution, and a professor at the Institute of Human Resources and Industrial Relations, Loyola University Chicago and founder and chair at the Center for Employment Dispute Resolution—an Illinois not for profit ADR Public Policy Research organization—initially established with a grant from the William and Flora Hewlett Foundation.

Mr. Rute is a co-founder of Associates in Dispute Resolution and is Special General Counsel and Legislative Liaison of the Midland Group and is the former General Counsel and Litigation Director of Kansas Legal Services. He earned a B.B.A. and J.D. from Washburn University and a LL.M. from the University of Washington School of Law.

Mr. McPherson is a consultant and trainer for the Conflict Resolution Academy. He is the former Co-chair, Employment Sector of the Society of Professionals in Dispute Resolution and a former Regional Director of the Equal Employment Opportunity Commission. Mr. McPherson holds a B.A. from Morris Brown College and a M.A. from the Interdenominational Theological Center.

[1] W.E.B. DuBois, The Souls of Black Folk (Gramercy Books, 1994) at p.12.

the 21st century is not solely identifying and eliminating the blatant or overt forms of discrimination contemplated by W.E.B. DuBois.[2] Rather, the real challenge facing our society is how to deal effectively, equitably, and fairly with two other forms of discrimination: unconscious discrimination and subtle discrimination.

Harvard professor and psychiatrist Chester Pierce was one of the first scholars and observers to recognize this phenomenon and its damaging cumulative effect. Professor Pierce referred to these forms of discrimination as "micro-aggressions."[3] MIT professor and ombudsperson Mary P. Rowe, building upon Professor Pierce's theory of "micro-aggression," coined the terms "micro-inequities" and "subtle discrimination."[4] Unlike Professor Pierce, however, Professor Rowe viewed the phenomenon of micro-inequities and subtle discrimination primarily within the employment context.

The authors of this article do not ignore the continued existence of overt and blatant discrimination in our society today. The incidents of hate crimes, police profiling and other documented acts of overt discrimination in the workplace unequivocally belie any such possible suggestion. The authors, however, assert that these forms of unconscious and subtle discrimination or "micro-inequities" (hereinafter the latter is referred to only as "subtle discrimination") often serve as the basis for many, if not most, claims of workplace discrimination.

The authors further assert that because these forms of discrimination are very difficult to prove, they are arguably not actionable under our various federal and state antidiscrimination laws. Consequently, the authors argue that such ADR processes as EEO/ employment mediation should, as a matter of public policy, be used as an effective tool to resolve these claims of unconscious and subtle employment discrimination. These processes along with internal conflict management systems may also be effective tools in inhibiting employment decisions unconsciously based on stereotypes.

In order to implement antidiscrimination laws and address the phenomenon of unconscious and subtle discrimination, the authors,

---

[2] *See, for example*, JOHN LEWIS, WALKING WITH THE WIND: A MEMOIR OF THE MOVEMENT, (New York, New York, Simon & Schuster, 1998).

[3] *See, for example*, CHESTER PIERCE, *Offensive Mechanisms in* FLOYD B. BARBOUR (ed.), THE BLACK SEVENTIES at pp. 265-282 (Boston, Mass.: Porter Sargent Publisher, 1970).

[4] For a review of research by other scholars, *see generally* Ann C. McGinley, *Viva La Evolucion!: Recognizing Unconscious Motive in Title VII*, CORNELL J. L.& PUB. POL'Y Vol. 9: 415-492.

borrowing from *Employing the Law To Increase the Use of Mediation and To Encourage Direct and Early Negotiations,*[5] by Professors Nancy Rogers and Craig McEwen, argue that the law must be used to increase the early negotiation and use of mediation in order to equitably and fairly resolve these claims. Accordingly, the authors recommend the enactment of the proposed legislation entitled the National Employment Dispute Resolution Act of 2000 (NEDRA).

This article shall define and discuss the phenomenon of "unconscious" and "subtle" discrimination. Within this context, the authors shall present the economic and psychological costs incurred by these types of disputes; the potential cost savings to both employers and complainant workers and the possible benefits to the public justice system derived from using mediation and other conflict management and dispute resolution processes.

Lastly, as a matter of good, sound and practical public policy, the authors advocate the need, for the federal government (and possibly various state and local governments) to require federal agencies and state contractors to establish and implement internal conflict management systems. These systems, as a voluntary option, would afford access to external professional mediators and other neutral workplace dispute resolvers to assist in the resolution of EEO and other employment disputes including those stemming from claims of unconscious or subtle discrimination. The authors suggest that the latter internal conflict management systems be fashioned after the proposed NEDRA and comport with the *Guidelines for the Design of Integrated Conflict Management Systems Within Organizations*, recently published by the Society of Professionals in Dispute Resolution.[6]

Urgent Issue

A candid and objective discussion and examination of the phenomenon of "unconscious discrimination" and "subtle discrimination" and the use of the law and public policy to effectuate the actual use of EEO and employment dispute resolution statutes and public policies is particularly timely and indeed urgent for three reasons:

---

[5] Nancy Rogers and Craig McEwen, *Employing the Law to Increase the Use of Mediation and to Encourage Direct and Early Negotiations,* OHIO ST. J. ON DISP. RESOL. Vol. 13:3 (1998).

[6] SPIDR's *Guidelines For The Design Of Integrated Conflict Management Systems Within Organizations* (August 2, 2000).

- The significant demographic change in the workplace, i.e., the inclusion of members of demographic groups who heretofore have been either excluded or not allowed to participate fully in the workplace.
- The constant increase in the filing of civil rights claims and lawsuits which are costly to employers and workers alike and unduly burden our public justice system.
- The avoidance or reduction of the substantial economic and psychological costs which these types of disputes create, particularly for workers who often cannot retain legal representation and whose claims are often dismissed as unprovable.

Economic Rationale

It has been estimated that it can easily cost an employer $96,000 to defend an individual claim of discrimination, whether overt, subtle, or unconscious, and that the majority of these unconscious or subtle claims of discrimination are either dismissed or settled but only after, in many instances, the incurrence of substantial economic and psychological costs by the disputants, particularly the worker.

Professor Wayne F. Cascio estimated the cost of the investigation and litigation of a single-plaintiff discrimination case at $96,370 and a class action at $462,430.[7]

Consequently, based upon these estimates by Professor Cascio, it is suggested here that as a matter not only of sound public policy but also from a cost-saving perspective, the focus of this country's ADR public policy and that of the federal government should be shifted to employing the law to increase the use of early mediation. Such a shift would resolve thousands of economically and psychologically costly workplace disputes which have as their basis "unconscious or subtle discrimination."

Furthermore, this shift in public policy focus would not only be a worthwhile and responsible use of the law, but it would also constitute a more cost-effective and humane method of resolving workplace disputes in a society where race and color are still a real barrier to equality. It is

---

[7] *See* WAYNE F. CASCIO, Chapter 4, *The High Cost of Mismanaging Human Resources*, COSTING HUMAN RESOURCES: THE FINANCIAL IMPACT OF BEHAVIOR IN ORGANIZATIONS, pp. 83 to 105 (Cincinnati, Ohio, South Western College Publishing, 4th Edition, 2000).

this public policy rationale which also serves as the basis for the most recently introduced legislative bill called NEDRA (H.R. 4593).

Unconscious Discrimination As a Barrier to Equality

A phenomenon called unconscious discrimination has come to the surface and has been the focus of considerable scientific research. Most recently this phenomenon has been arguably illustrated in the rash of claims of racial profiling and even unconscious disparate delivery of medical services and court decisions.

The existence of this phenomenon is generally not known and thus not appreciated by the majority, including human resources professionals, employment lawyers, and mediators. It is better said that the effects of unconscious discrimination are very well-known by racial minorities and in many instances women.

As is the case with subtle discrimination, the often-profound consequences of unconscious discrimination are just as damaging to the victim as is overt discrimination. In fact, the argument can be made that because unconscious and subtle discrimination are by definition essentially unintentional, it is worse than overt discrimination which is definitely actionable.

A victim of unconscious and/or subtle discrimination often has very little, if any, redress except where employers have implemented internal conflict management systems to deal with claims of unfairness. Increasingly, employer-sponsored internal conflict management programs provide for employment mediation and arbitration using outside neutrals.

Research and Studies

There is a considerable amount of scientific research and number of studies related to the nature of prejudice and specifically unconscious discrimination. One of the most informed and recent articles was published by Ann C. McGinley in *!Viva La Evolucion!: Recognizing Unconscious Motive in Title VII*."[8] In this article, Professor McGinley describes unconscious discrimination as:

> Persons whose acts result from bias and prejudice are often unaware of their subconscious motivations. Thus, it is likely that differential treatment of a female or minority employee in the

[8] *Supra*, note 4.

workplace is because of his race or her gender, even though the employer is unaware that race and gender motivated the differential treatment.

Professor McGinley further argues that:

A [evidentiary] rule limiting the definition of discrimination to cases where the employer 'consciously' treated an employee differently because of membership in a protected class ignores the social science evidence [related to unconscious discrimination] and narrows the effectiveness of the statute (i.e., Title VII).[9]

Professor McGinley also argues that:

The proof mechanisms serve the role of determining causation rather than conscious intent, assuring that the underlying employment decision is made because of the employee's protected characteristics, either with or without the employer's conscious awareness.[10]

According to her, this creates a dislocation between theoretical justification for the proof mechanisms designed to identify "conscious" discriminatory intent and the reality that these mechanisms could also identify unconscious discrimination. Professor McGinley criticizes and refers to this dislocation as a "counter evolution," resulting in a conservative shift in proof and evidentiary standards. In short, the "counter evolution" theory is based on a concept of discrimination narrowly limited to "consciously discriminatory acts."[11]

The question of whether a more comprehensive definition of discrimination should include differential treatment of members of protected classes resulting from conscious or unconscious motivation would better effectuate our antidiscrimination statutes is beyond the scope of this article. However, the tension created between the admissibility and consideration of social science evidence related to unconscious discrimination and traditional legal evidentiary standards is

---

[9] *Id.* at pp. 418-419.
[10] *Id.*
[11] *Id.* at p. 419.

often at the unspoken heart of many EEO disputes and invariably influences settlement decisions.

Notwithstanding, those who are interested and committed to promoting the early resolution of claims based on discrimination—unconscious or conscious—are in agreement that it is important to understand the concept and phenomenon of unconscious discrimination and how it works. Such an understanding might serve to prevent the filing of a number of EEO claims and better inform supervisors and managers, human resources professionals, employment lawyers, and even mediators of their unconscious biases.

Conscious Discrimination

The book PREJUDICE, DISCRIMINATION AND RACISM, describes experiments examining the "causes and consequences of contemporary forms of prejudice, discrimination and racism."[12] According to John F. Dovidio and Samuel L. Gaertner, although the percentage of whites with overt racist prejudices against blacks dropped dramatically between 1933 and 1988,[13] even whites who consider themselves to be liberal and egalitarian on race issues harbor unconscious racist attitudes and behave in racist fashion toward blacks. They often are unaware that their responses are race-based. This form of racism, identified as "aversive racism," results from whites' assimilation of an egalitarian value system with "impressions derived from human cognitive mechanisms that contribute to the development of stereotypes and prejudice, and...feelings and beliefs derived from historical and contemporary cultural racist contexts."

In brief, whites demonstrate an ambivalence toward blacks. While consciously holding egalitarian values, whites simultaneously harbor unconscious negative feelings toward blacks as a result of cognitive and motivational biases combined with socialization into a racist culture.[14]

---

[12] *See* John F. Dovidio and Samuel L. Gaertner, *Prejudice, Discrimination and Racism: Historical Trends and Contemporary Approaches in* DOVIDIO & GAERTNER (eds.) PREJUDICE, DISCRIMINATION AND RACISM, (Orlando: Academic Press) (1986).

[13] *See* John F. Dovidio and Samuel L. Gaertner, *Changes In The Expression and Assessment of Racial Prejudice In Opening Doors*, Perspective on Race Relations In Contemporary America, Harry J. Knopke; Robert J. Norrell and Ronald W. Rogers (eds.) (1991).

[14] *See* John F. Dovidio, et al., *On the Nature of Prejudice: Automatic and Controlled Processes*, J. EXPERIMENTAL SOC. PSYCHOL. Vol. 33: 510, 534 (1997).

In another study, Dovidio and Gaertner found that there was a difference between whites' conscious and unconscious attitudes:

> Even unconsciously, positive characteristics were associated more with whites than with blacks. For negative traits, however, there was a discrepancy between unconscious and conscious responding. Specifically, negative characteristics were responded to significantly faster following a black prime than following a white prime. Thus, even though at a conscious level whites reject negative attributions of blacks, at an unconscious level they do have negative associations. This study therefore provides direct support for our assumption that people who consciously and genuinely embrace egalitarian ideals may, out of their awareness, still harbor negative feelings toward blacks.[15]

According to Professor McGinley, the research of Dovidio and Gaertner strongly suggests that whites act on these unconscious negative feelings when they are able to justify their actions.

For example, in one experiment Professors Dovidio and Gaertner created an "emergency" situation in which black and white victims asked white bystanders for help. They found that whites normally helped black victims slightly more than white victims, if there was no one else present to help. They found, however, whites' helping behavior toward black victims dropped dramatically in situations where another potential helper was present.[16] Where others were present, whites helped black victims only about half as often as white victims.[17] Where there were no others present, whites could generally not refuse to help blacks without damaging their egalitarian self-image because there was no non-discriminatory reason for the failure to help.

Similar results occurred in tests conducted by Professors Katz, Wackenhutt and Glass. Their experiments demonstrated that white subjects reacted more strongly toward blacks than toward whites depending on the situation. For example, Katz instructed white male college students to give electric shocks[17] for errors made by white or black students working at learning a task. White students described the

---

[15] *Supra*, note 13 at p. 138.

[16] *See*, Irwin Katz, et al *Racial Ambivalence, Valve Duality and Behavior in* Prejudice, Discrimination and Racism, John F. Dovidio and Samuel L. Gaertner (eds.) (1986).

[17] The subjects were not really administering electric shocks, but they believed that they were.

black students receiving the severe shock in a much more derogatory fashion than their white counterparts.

There is not a universal school of thought explaining the nature of prejudice or for that matter, unconscious discrimination. However, it is generally concluded by psychologists that whites react to blacks differently than to whites, unaware that they were doing so. This phenomenon might explain the disparity with which black workers view their general and anticipated treatment in the workplace.

Strategies for Prevention

As it relates to conflict management and mediation, Professors C. Neil Macrae, Galen Bodenhausen and Alan B. Milne have found that the "heightened self-focus" of an evaluator (i.e., the alleged perpetrator) whose personal standards conflict with negative cultural stereotypes will permit the evaluator to inhibit the activation of the stereotype and to make decisions based on his or her more egalitarian personal standards.[18]

In sum, Professors Macrae, Bodenhausen, and Milne, conclude that "a heightened self-focus" increased the efficiency of the perceiver to regulate cognitive processing. In laymen terms, if the potential unconscious discriminator can be made aware of the tensions between his or her personal egalitarian standards and negative stereotypes, this will enhance the probability that his or her decision making, for example promotion decisions, will not be unconsciously motivated.

Professors E. Ashby Plant and Patricia G. Devine have also found that the source of motivation related to cognitive processing will influence whether the evaluator (i.e., potential perpetrator or discriminator) is able to inhibit his or her activation of the stereotype. Thus, if the motivation of a white subject is external, caused for example by the employer's EEO and diversity policy and training, the evaluator may process his or her decision-making realizing negative stereotypes related to blacks.

The fact that the persistence of unconscious stereotypes in evaluating group members may be inhibited, either by internal or external motivation, provides some hope that through diversity training, for example, employers may decrease the incidence of unconscious

---

[18] *Supra*, note 4, at 415.

discrimination. This has also been suggested by Professor Mary P. Rowe within the context of subtle discrimination.[19]

The authors further suggest that mediators using some form of "reality testing" or evaluation in a private caucus may also provide the "external motivation" for a supervisor or manager whose decision-making process is influenced by stereotypes.

Professor Thomas F. Pettigrew further recommends "macro" as well as "micro" changes to improve the workplace for racial minorities and presumably women. The authors suggest that the adoption and implementation of internal conflict management programs which afford employees access to external mediators or other workplace neutrals such as ombudspersons and perhaps fact finders constitute a "macro" change as recommended by Professor Pettigrew.[20]

These workplace neutrals might be able to shed light on the existence or effect of unconscious discrimination (or even subtle discrimination) and thus also facilitate the early resolution of such disputes within the confidentiality confines of mediation. For example, a sincere offer of an apology might bring the early resolution of such a controversy.

Whether the workplace neutral's role rises to the level of being an "evaluator" or "mediator-psychologist" is grist for some future theoretical debate. From a practical point of view, however, the authors believe that the early intervention or involvement of an outside neutral will be effective in resolving many disputes involving claims of unconscious and subtle discrimination.

Overt Discrimination Versus Subtle Discrimination

When the outside observers Alexis de Tocqueville and Gunnar Myrdal[21] visited this country during the early 19th and 20th centuries, respectively, the forms or types of discrimination which they observed were manifestations of a consciously and de jure segregated society. A society in which overt forms of both race and gender-based discrimination were commonplace and, in fact, often existed by law.

---

[19] Mary P. Rowe, Barriers *to Equality: The Power of Subtle Discrimination to Maintain Unequal Opportunity*, EMPLOYEE RESPONSIBILITIES & RTS J. Vol. 3, No. 2. (1990).

[20] *See* Thomas F. Pettigrew and Joanne Martin, *Shaping Organizational Context For Black American Inclusion*, J. SOC. ISSUES Vol. 43: 41 (1987).

[21] GUNNAR MYRDAL, AN AMERICAN DILEMMA: THE NEGRO PROBLEM AND MODERN DEMOCRACY, Vol. I and Vol. II, New York, New York, Harper & Row Publishers/ Pantheon 1972).

Indeed, many individuals today can recall when the concept and practice of "women jobs and male jobs" and "Negro jobs and white jobs" were commonplace and the order of the day. Many can also recall when there were no federal statutes in existence to prohibit age- and disability-based discrimination, much less sexual orientation and now genetic-based discrimination.

In retrospect, as a civil society this country has come a long way on the heels of the national public policies and laws which compel the inclusion of many formerly "excluded" members of various demographic groups or "outside groups" from the workplace. Parenthetically, we should be ever mindful that these changes came due to the compulsion of the law and court decisions and were not due to voluntary behavior.

Notwithstanding these advances due to workplace civil rights laws, the incidents of sexual and racial harassment and discrimination still exist today. Thus, in many ways, private internal conflict management systems and ADR processes such as mediation also serve as effective tools and mechanisms to further effectuate our civil rights laws and to manage better a diverse workforce. The role of the law and the courts in integrating our society and the workplace is a fact which is often not appreciated by the civil rights community.

In addition to the traditional forms of discrimination, it is argued here that the existence of "unconscious" or "subtle" discrimination is even more prevalent today and serves as the basis of many informal and formal claims of employment discrimination, as suggested by Professor Mary P. Rowe and other scholars. These types of discrimination may be unintended and even unconsciously perpetrated and therefore, not intentional and consequently not actionable under the applicable antidiscrimination laws. As asserted earlier, the economic and psychological impact and consequences of such unconscious and/or subtle acts of discrimination are just as pernicious and damaging to the subject of such acts as to the individual who is a victim of intentional and provable discrimination. It is not suggested here that these "unconscious" or "subtle" forms of discrimination should be cognizable under the law. It is, however, suggested that in many, if not most instances, academic researchers, employment lawyers and the media often speak in terms of our "litigious society" and the litigious worker but do not systematically inquire as to why workers file claims.

It is also suggested here that human resources professionals, managers, and employment attorneys can better understand the nature and profound anger of racial minorities and women complainants if they are also made aware of the lifelong experience of being subject to unconscious and subtle discrimination. In many instances, the basis of a claim of discrimination is equally based on the complainant's broader "social experience" of being the subject of unconscious and subtle discrimination as well as the immediate controversy at hand.

As suggested earlier, employing the early implementation and use of internal conflict management systems which provide the use of outside neutrals specializing in workplace disputes, including mediators, can effectively resolve these disputes. This would be to the economic benefit of both the employer and the employee and to the society as a whole, particularly given the realities of the changing demographics of the workplace. Many more employment relations would be preserved with the early use of mediation, if it were made an option.

Subtle Discrimination As a Barrier to Equality

Professor Mary P. Rowe, in her article entitled *Barriers to Equality, The Power of Subtle Discrimination to Maintain Unequal Opportunity,*[22] has described subtle discrimination as follows:

> ...Subtle discrimination is now the principal scaffolding for segregation in the United States.... This scaffolding is built of "micro-inequities": apparently small events, often ephemeral and hard-to-prove events, which are covert, often unintentional, frequently unrecognized by the perpetrator. Micro-inequities occur wherever people are perceived to be "different"; Caucasians in a Japanese-owned company, African-Americans in a white firm, women in a traditionally male environment, Jews and Moslems in a traditionally Protestant environment. These mechanisms of prejudice against persons of difference are usually small in nature, but not trivial in effect. They are especially powerful taken together. (As one drop of water has little effect, though continuous drops may be destructive, one racist slight may be insignificant, but many such slights cause serious damage.) Micro-inequities work both by excluding the person of difference and by making that person less self-confident and less productive.

[22] *Supra*, note 19.

Professor Rowe further suggests that "an employer may prevent such damage by developing programs on diversity, such as 'valuing differences' and team building."

In addition to the worthwhile suggestions of Professor Rowe, the authors also suggest that the establishment and implementation of internal conflict management programs with an optional access to an external corps of professional mediators and workplace dispute resolvers would be an effective tool for the early resolution of these types of disputes. This point is the overarching thesis of this article.

Is Subtle Discrimination Actionable?

Many of the cases involving claims of discrimination, particularly those arising under Title VII, employ some variant of the evidentiary framework set forth in *McDonnell Douglas* for establishing claims of discrimination when there is no direct evidence of discrimination. Under this framework, the plaintiff must initially establish a *prima facie* case. The elements of this *prima facie* case will vary somewhat depending upon the type of discrimination alleged. If the plaintiff is successful in doing this, the burden shifts to the defendant to come forward with some legitimate, nondiscriminatory reason for its challenged action. This is sufficient to rebut the plaintiff's *prima facie* case. The burden then shifts back to the plaintiff to show that the reason(s) advanced by the defendant for its action is pre textual, i.e., is not the true reason for its action, and that the defendant intended to act in a discriminatory manner. Issues of subtle discrimination typically arise when the plaintiff must demonstrate that the employer's proffered reasons for its actions are only a pretext for discrimination.

In determining whether or not to submit a matter to mediation or early settlement negotiations, the issue of whether a claim involves subtle discrimination versus overt disparate treatment might be a critical factor. Although it is beyond the scope of this article, it would be worthwhile to summarize the state of the law related to this issue as viewed by Professor Michael Selmi.

Professor Selmi, in *Proving Intentional Discrimination: The Reality of Supreme Court Rhetoric*,[23] argues that, although the Supreme Court has explicitly recognized that discrimination has become more subtle and therefore, more difficult to prove, and has acknowledged the fact that

---

[23] *See* Michael Selmi, *Proving Intentional Discrimination: The Reality of Supreme Court Rhetoric*, 86 GEO. L.J. 279 (1997).

subtle discrimination is no more permissible than overt or blatant discrimination, subtle discrimination is clearly actionable, at least in theory. According to Professor Selmi, the Supreme Court has affirmed this on many occasions. In fact, this is true almost by definition: it is "discrimination" that is prohibited. Whether it manifests itself in a "subtle" or "blatant" or "overt" form is ultimately irrelevant for purposes of liability, according to Professor Selmi.

Lower courts have also explicitly acknowledged the importance of recognizing subtle discrimination. In *Lynn v. Regents of University of California,*[24] a sex discrimination case, the court noted:

> The beliefs that women should not have the right to vote, practice law, or serve on the United States Supreme Court, were once reflective of the majority view, and the law. We now understand, somewhat belatedly, that these concepts reflect a discriminatory attitude. Today any person is free to hold to such concepts, but such concepts may not serve as the basis for job-related decisions in employment covered by Title VII. Other concepts reflect a discriminatory attitude more subtly; the subtlety does not, however, make the impact less significant or less unlawful. It serves only to make the courts' task of scrutinizing attitudes and motivation, in order to determine the true reason for employment decisions, more exacting. ...We are saying only what Title VII commands: when plaintiffs establish that decisions regarding academic employment are motivated by discriminatory attitudes relating to race or sex, or are rooted in concepts which reflect such discriminatory attitudes, however subtly, courts are obligated to afford the relief provided by Title VII.

EEO Mediation: Disputants' Experiences

There is now a considerable amount of literature and empirical research focusing on how employment mediation works and why it works and in some instances why it does not work.

Plaintiff attorneys Penny Nathan Kahan and Lori L. Deem in *Mediation As a Model For Resolving Employment Disputes In the New Millennium*[25] present three fundamental reasons why employment mediation works.

---

[24] Lynn V. Regents of University of California 656 F.2d 1337, 1343 n.5 (C.A.G. 1981).

[25] *See* Penny Nathan Kahan and Lori L. Deem, *Mediation As a Model For Resolving Employment Disputes In The New Millennium,* EMPLOYEE RTS. Q. (Spring, 2001).

The authors, noting that such disputes are always emotionally charged and recognizing the inherent imbalance of power between employers and employees, state as follows: First, it is a process in which both parties are engaged voluntarily. Unless part of a court-ordered mediation program, the parties submitting to mediation have acknowledged their desire, but inability to resolve the dispute on their own. In contrast to the litigation process, rather than turn over the power to determine the outcome of the dispute to a trier of fact, mediation allows the parties to retain the power to decide how best to resolve the problem. Importantly, each party retains the right to accept or reject the settlement and, where mediation is successful, there are no real winners or losers. The process is designed to be non-adversarial in focus and less about "who did what to whom" than "where do we go from here?"

Second, because mediation is far less an adversarial process than traditional litigation and the parties are focusing on problem solving as opposed to fault, it is often a positive and healing experience for the participants. Effective mediation of employment disputes provides an opportunity for both sides to tell their story, while the other side listens. This aspect of mediation is especially important for employee-plaintiffs because it provides them with the opportunity for an emotional catharsis. Allowing the employee to have a forum to work through the emotional component of the employment dispute helps to get it resolved. Additionally, in cases where the plaintiff is still employed with the defendant during the dispute, successful mediation allows the parties to move forward with their employment relationship, minimizing the animosity and resentment that so characterizes the litigation process.

Third, Kahan and Deem assert mediation is a much quicker and cheaper process than traditional litigation. In contrast to litigation, mediation prevents the parties from getting bogged down in the mind-numbing minutia of formal discovery, depositions, and motion practice. Indeed, many corporations are recognizing the high economic cost of litigation and are choosing mediation as an alternative in resolving all kinds of disputes.

These commonsense reasons for using employment mediation are particularly relevant for claims involving unconscious and subtle discrimination because mediation, at least in theory, does not focus upon who is necessarily right or wrong —or whether there exists a provable violation of applicable laws.

In these cases, a practical cost-benefit analysis prompts the disputants to examine the dispute at hand in more of a "problem solving" context, including why the complainant perceives that he or she has been the subject of either overt or unintended discrimination. It may also afford the involved supervisor or manager the benefit of examining their decision-making process through a "prism" which might indicate either that the decision-making process was unintentionally biased or the complainant has a reasonable basis to believe that he or she was subject to disparate treatment—whether intended or unintended.

In either case, where the disputants are given access to mediation early on, preferably prior to a formal charge or lawsuit, a candid explanation and exchange of views serves as a "day in court" for the disputants and might possibly conclude with an apology.

However, existing employment laws and ADR public policies (including that of the EEOC) do not provide a sufficient impetus to bring disputants to early mediation. More often than not, early mediation is only available where either the employer has instituted an internal conflict management system, which includes a voluntary or mandatory mediation, or where the dispute arises in a jurisdiction where the court "directs" participation in mediation as a precondition to a trial. In this latter situation, mediation at this stage is often considered "too little, too late."

Research and experience show that mediation works, especially when it is offered early on. Research further suggests that mandated mediation works even though it permits only voluntary settlement outcomes. Consequently, the authors suggest that there is an experiential basis to support legislation and public policy which would require participation in mediation, if not make mediation an alternative at an early stage of an employment dispute. This might be particularly true given the potential impact of Rule 26(a)(1) which will require litigants to provide certain information in the discovery process.[26] This is the underlying rationale, goal and objective of the proposed National Employment Dispute Resolution Act, i.e., the directed early participation in mediation where any settlement outcome is strictly voluntary.

EEOC's ADR Statement

As a matter of public policy, the federal government has "encouraged" the use of ADR, particularly the mediation of EEO disputes. Both the Americans with Disabilities Act and the Civil Rights Act of 1991 contain provisions which encourage the use of ADR,

---

[26] *See* Rule 26, "General Provisions Governing Discovery: Duty of Disclosure."

including mediation. The relevant provisions of these statutes read, in part, as follows:

> Americans with Disabilities Act: Alternative Means of Dispute Resolution:
>
> Where appropriate and to the extent authorized by law, the use of alternative means of dispute resolution, including settlement negotiations, conciliation, facilitation, mediation, fact-finding, mini-trials, and arbitration, is encouraged to resolve disputes arising under this Act.
>
> Civil Rights Act of 1991: Alternative Means of Dispute Resolution:
>
> Where appropriate and to the extent authorized by law, the use of alternative means of dispute resolution, including settlement negotiations, conciliation, facilitation, mediation, fact-finding, mini-trials, and arbitration, is encouraged to resolve disputes arising under the Acts of provisions of Federal law amended by this title.

These ADR provisions are designed to "encourage" the use of ADR. They do not mandate or direct participation in mediation, which may result in voluntary settlement outcome. In July 1995, the EEOC adopted a "Policy Statement on Alternative Dispute Resolution." In addition to providing a number of "Core Principles," the EEOC Policy Statement provided, in part, the following:

> The Equal Employment Opportunity Commission (EEOC) is firmly committed to using alternative methods for resolving disputes in all of its activities, where appropriate and feasible. Used properly in appropriate circumstances, alternative dispute resolution (ADR) can provide faster, less expensive and contentious, and more productive results in eliminating workplace discrimination as well as in commission operations.

The use of ADR is fully consistent with EEOC's mission as a law enforcement agency. It is squarely based in the statutes creating and enforced by the commission—Title VII of the Civil Rights Act of 1964, the Age Discrimination in Employment Act, the Equal Pay Act and the Americans with Disabilities Act.

Core Principles Governing Commission ADR Programs

Any use of ADR under commission auspices will be governed by certain core principles. Above all, any commission ADR program must further the agency's mission. It must also be fair, which requires voluntariness, neutrality, confidentiality, and enforceability.

Furthering the Commission's Mission

First and foremost, an effective ADR program must further the EEOC's dual mission: vigorously enforcing federal laws prohibiting employment discrimination and resolving employment dispute. ADR will complement current systems in operation by facilitating early resolution of disputes where agreement is possible, thereby freeing up resources for identifying, investigating, settling, conciliating or litigating other matters.

As of this writing, the EEOC has instituted mediation programs in all of its offices and the mediation programs appear to be working well.

By its very operation, the EEOC's mediation program necessitates, as a pre-condition, the filing of a formal charge of discrimination against an employer. EEOC then essentially determines whether the claim is appropriate for mediation as a "B" Case. Generally, cases classified as "A" or "C" cases are not considered appropriate or eligible for mediation. The authors suggest that a number of these "C" cases may involve unconscious or subtle discrimination and may be effectively resolved through employer-sponsored mediation programs, using outside professional mediators.

A Possible Precursor to NEDRA

The Supreme Court's landmark decision in *Brown v. Board of Education*[27] (1954) was some forty-seven years ago. The passage and enactment of Title VII of the Civil Rights Act of 1964 was some thirty-six years ago. In addition to *Brown* and Title VII being important from an historical and legal perspective, again we should be ever mindful that but for the legal impetus of the law and subsequent related public policies and statutes, it is doubtful that the workforce would have been voluntarily integrated with women and racial minorities today. The next

---

[27] *See* Brown v. Board of Educ., 374 U.S. 483 (1954); Steel v. Louisville-Nashville R.R., 323 U.S. 192, 15 LRRM 708 (1944); Rosenfeld v. Southern Pac. Co., 444 F.2d 1219, 3 FEP Cases 604 (9th Cir. 1971).

step following this integration of the workforce is the challenge of developing effective methods and processes to attempt to ensure the fair and nondiscriminatory treatment of all workers without regard to their membership in a particular demographic group.

In keeping with the concept of encouraging the early resolution of EEO disputes, the EEOC recently adopted, as a matter of public policy, the "Agency Program To Promote Equal Employment Opportunity," codified as 29 CFR Part 1614-Federal Sector Equal Employment Opportunity, as amended (November 9, 1999). Among other things, "1614" requires under Section 1614.603, the following:

> Voluntary settlement attempts: Each agency shall make reasonable efforts to voluntarily settle complaints of discrimination as early as possible in, and throughout, the administrative processing of complaints, including the pre-complaint counseling stage. Any settlement reached shall be in writing and signed by both parties and shall identify the claims resolved.
>
> In addition, Section 1614.102 requires federal agencies to:
>
> (2) Establish or make available an alternative dispute resolution program. Such program must be available for both the pre-complaint process and the formal complaint process.
>
> Section 1614.105, Agency Processing, also requires that:
>
> (2) Counselors shall advise aggrieved persons that, where the agency agrees to offer ADR in the particular case, they may choose between participation in the alternative dispute resolution program and the counseling activities provided for in paragraph (c) of this section.
>
> Lastly, Section 1614.109, Hearings, provides as follows:
>
> (c) Offer of resolution.
>
> (1) Any time after the filing of the written complaint but not later than the date an administrative judge is appointed to conduct a hearing, the agency may make an offer of resolution to a complainant who is represented by an attorney.

> (2) Any time after the parties have received notice that an administrative judge has been appointed to conduct a hearing, but not later than 30 days prior to the hearing, the agency may make an offer of resolution to the complainant, whether represented by an attorney or not.

As it relates to one of the central themes of this article, the EEOC's public policy arguably supports the position advocated by Professors Nancy Rogers and Craig McEwen in *Employing the Law To Increase The Use of Mediation and To Encourage Direct and Early Negotiations.*[28] Section 1614 also supports the extension of the requirement to "establish or make available alternative dispute resolution program(s)" to federal contractors (and possibly state and local governments) as suggested by the proposed NEDRA. Thus, Section 1614 may actually be a precursor to NEDRA.

Employers and EEO Mediation

Increasingly more employers recognize that the use of mediation makes good business sense. In a recent study by the Foundation for the Prevention of Conflict (PERC) at Cornell University and Price Waterhouse, LLP, 528 corporations (with reported sales of more than $1 billion each) were surveyed about their use of mediation.

The research showed that 88% said they would use it again. The employers surveyed were also asked why they preferred mediation to litigation and the study found 81% of the employers preferred mediation; 66% preferred mediated settlements; and 59% preferred mediation because it preserves good relationships. Moreover, many of the same employers who have used mediation successfully to resolve disputes with their customers and vendors, are now realizing that mediation can be used successfully to resolve employment disputes with their present and former employees.

The country's second largest employer, the U.S. Postal Service,[29] in 1994 implemented an internal conflict management program called "Resolve Employment, Reach Equitable Solutions Swiftly" or "REDRESS." REDRESS was implemented nationwide in 1997. A recent New York Times article entitled *The Very Model of Conciliation: Companies Adopting Postal Service Grievance Process*[30] reported that:

---

[28] *Supra*, note 5.
[29] Walmart is the country's largest employer.
[30] NEW YORK TIMES, Sept. 6, 2000.

> ...in the early 1990s, the U.S. Postal Service was plagued by angry, frustrated employees who filed complaints with the EEOC. The volume of informal complaints grew to 30,000 a year, more than any other single employer. Some of the complaints escalated into costly litigation, while others festered. But in 1994, as part of a settlement of a class action, the Postal Service created REDRESS to settle disputes using outside mediators, and tested it in a few cities before rolling it out nationally in 1997.

The results were spectacular: in the first twenty-two months of full operation, from September 1998 through June 1999, 17,645 informal disputes were mediated under REDRESS and of those, 80% were resolved. During the same period, formal complaints which peaked at 14,000 in 1997 dropped 30%.

Postal Service REDRESS Program

Under REDRESS, an employee who contacts an EEO counselor is offered the option of mediation in lieu of traditional EEO counseling. If mediation is chosen, a professional mediator from outside the Postal Service is brought in within two to three weeks. REDRESS is designed to be fast—so that mediation takes place early enough in the conflict to maximize the parties' ability to reach a resolution. The mediator provides a neutral environment in which the employee and the supervisor who are in conflict sit together at the table and discuss their dispute. The employee is permitted to have a representative at the mediation. The parties are not required to settle, and the mediator cannot impose any resolution. Most parties do, in fact, resolve their disputes at the mediation table. In addition, after mediation many employees withdraw, settle, or drop their complaints altogether.

Several aspects of the REDRESS program set it apart from dispute resolution programs at other federal entities. First, unlike most agencies which train their own employees to act as mediators, the Postal Service uses only outside professional neutrals as mediators. This eliminates a structural bias—real or perceived—that can undermine the credibility of a mediation program.

Second, the Postal Service is committed to the transformative approach to mediation as defined by professors Robert A. Baruch Bush and Joseph Folger, co-authors of The Promise of Mediation (1994).[31] Mediators practicing transformative mediation focus on engendering empowerment (giving the parties control over the process) and recognition (allowing the parties to understand and acknowledge each other), rather than influencing the parties to adopt any particular resolution.

The experience of the Postal Service and its REDRESS program has been systematically evaluated and reasonably leads to the conclusion and to the one overarching thesis of this article that internal conflict management programs using external professional mediators when offered early on do work. Consequently, the question and related challenge remains how best to get other employers to adopt and implement similar internal conflict management systems. The authors suggest that a law or public policy covering federal contractors would be the most effective and prudent route to follow.

Evidence on barriers and obstacles related to the use of mediation and good faith early negotiations have prompted a number of noted scholars and ADR practitioners to call for a public policy that would place greater emphasis on employing the law to encourage the early use of mediation and early negotiations to resolve civil disputes, including EEO disputes.

NEDRA

Based upon these realities and the urging of others, a recent congressional bill entitled the National Employment Dispute Resolution Act of 2000 (NEDRA) was introduced in the House on June 8, 2000. NEDRA requires federal contractors having contracts of $200,000 or more and 200 or more employees to establish internal dispute resolution programs which would, among other things, provide early opportunity to resolve EEO and other workplace disputes internally, and ideally prior to the filing of a formal charge or lawsuit.

Where the dispute is not resolved, the employee would have the option to use an outside professional mediator, similar to the REDRESS program of the U.S. Postal Service, to assist the disputants. The federal contractor would subsidize the cost of the mediator, i.e., mediator's fees and related expenses. The disputants would also be permitted to enter

---

[31] Robert A. Baruch Bush and Joseph P. Folger, The Promise of Mediation (San Francisco: Jossey-Bass, 1994).

into a private tolling agreement and reasonable attorney's fees may be part of any settlement.

There are a number of issues to be identified and addressed, related to NEDRA. It is contemplated, however, that these issues would be resolved in the adoption of any related rules and policies.

Mandatory Versus Voluntary Mediation

The cornerstone of NEDRA is the directed participation in mediation where after the exhaustion of certain internal steps, the worker will have the option to submit the matter to mediation. Any settlement, however, would be voluntary. Thus, mediation under NEDRA is not "voluntary" in the classical sense.

It is generally thought that "classic mediation" works best where participation in the process is strictly voluntary. This appears to be the underlying philosophy of the ADR provisions of the Americans with Disability Act, the Civil Rights Act of 1991 and the EEOC's ADR Public Policy Statement. There is not considerable legislative history related to the ADR provisions of Americans with Disabilities Act or the Civil Rights Act of 1991. Consequently, one cannot state with unequivocal certainty that the drafters of these provisions contemplated and if so, would have rejected the use of "directed" participation in mediation permitting only voluntary settlement outcomes.

However, there is empirical and anecdotal evidence that directed participation in mediation (with any voluntary settlement outcomes) is effective, using measures of satisfaction with the process and outcome as indicators.

Empirical research studies indicate that settlement rates and party perceptions of fairness are often comparable in both mandatory and voluntary programs. In a study on mandated participation in mediation by Professors Jeanne Brett and Stephen Goldberg,[32] the researchers found the following:

- Settlement rate (78%) and degree of satisfaction are similar for both voluntary and mandated mediations.
- Agreement in construction mediation was as likely in mandatory mediation as voluntary mediation.

---

[32] Jeanne M. Brett, Zoe I. Barsness, and Stephen B. Goldberg, *The Effectiveness of Mediation: An Independent Analysis of Cases Handled by Four Major Service Providers*, NEGOTIATION J., Vol. 12 No. 3, pp. 259-269 (1996).

- The distinction between "compulsion" to enter mediation and "compulsion" to settle mediation is crucial—only the latter is inconsistent with mediation.
- Mandatory settlement rates seem to resemble those of voluntary programs.
- Legal rules that emphasize voluntary use of mediation can reinforce barriers to access. While one party can force another to respond to a lawsuit, in the absence of a mandate to use mediation, one party cannot require the other to sit down and talk about settlement.

The empirical study by Professors Brett and Goldberg did not include EEO and employment disputes. Consequently, any inferences related to the effectiveness of mandated or "directed" participation in employment mediation must be made with this fact in mind. However, there is increasing experiential evidence that where federal and state courts have mandated participation in mediation as a pre-condition to a trial, mediation has not only proven to be effective, but the existence of mandated mediation effectively converted a number of "litigation cultures" into "mediation cultures" in resolving EEO charges and lawsuits.

Goals and Objectives of NEDRA

In light of the historical use of private dispute resolution processes in resolving race and gender disputes, such as labor arbitration; the public policy encouraging, if not favoring, the use of mediation; the economic and psychological costs related to EEO and employment litigation and given the positive experience with EEO mediation, NEDRA was introduced by Congresswoman Eva Clayton (D-North Carolina).

The fundamental goals and objectives of NEDRA are as follows:

1. To assist in the effectuation of the public policy and ADR legislation encouraging the use of ADR, particularly mediation of EEO and other employment disputes and "statutory-based diversity disputes."
2. As a matter of public policy and Presidential Executive Order, to require covered federal (and state) contractors to offer mediation to resolve EEO and other employment disputes at an early stage.

3. As a matter of public policy, to effectively require a covered federal contractor and disputing worker to attempt to resolve EEO and other employment disputes using the assistance of a third-party neutral, i.e., a mediator "where appropriate."
4. To promote the voluntary resolution of EEO and employment disputes using a legal concept similar to the "duty to bargain" but facilitated by the use of a third-party neutral, i.e., a mediator.
5. Participation in mediation may be required; however, all settlement outcomes are "strictly voluntary."
6. To promote the establishment and implementation of internal dispute resolution systems which are fair, regular, and cost-effective and recognize the traditional proximate relationship between employers and workers.
7. To fashion a cost-effective and fair dispute resolution system which does not place an "undue" burden on either employers or workers.
8. To provide an alternative to workers which permits them the real opportunity to resolve employment disputes internally without the necessity of filing external charges and pressure and/or lawsuits while still preserving their recourse under the public policies prohibiting discrimination and the public policy favoring ADR.
9. To decrease the number of charges and lawsuits filed with the administrative agencies and the courts.

Benefits of NEDRA

The authors offer the following top 10 advantages of NEDRA:

1. Applicable statute of limitations is tolled.
2. Enhance probability of continued employment relationships.
3. Certified and qualified private and federal (FMCS) mediators.
4. Includes "certified" Federal Mediation and Conciliation Service (FMCS), state and private mediators, and "certified" ADR providers, in a required public/private partnership.

5. Mediation provides a high degree of satisfaction both with the process and outcome.
6. Mediation provides early settlement at less economic and psychological cost to all parties, EEO agencies, and the courts.
7. Mediation provides confidentiality.
8. The mediator's fee is subsidized by the covered federal contractor.
9. "Required," "directed," or "mandated" participation in mediation will significantly increase the use of mediation, invariably increasing the number of voluntary settlement agreements, and decreasing the number of formal charges and lawsuits.
10. NEDRA would increase the early use of mediation and direct negotiations and thus decrease the number of EEO charges and lawsuits filed. It would promote judicial efficiency, by giving employers and employees an early opportunity to "problem solve" disputes, which in many instances are based on misperception, misunderstanding, and miscommunications and unconscious and subtle discrimination.

Conclusion

There are a number of documented reasons to support the early use of mediation to resolve EEO and other employment disputes. One of the major challenges facing us as a former industrial society and now a digital or "Y2K" society, is how to design cost-effective and fair private workplace dispute resolution programs. The purpose of these programs is not only to resolve overt or blatant forms of discrimination in the workplace, but also to resolve the many costly workplace disputes which stem from claims of unconscious and subtle acts of racial discrimination. Race and color remains one of the most emotion-provoking and divisive issues in our country today. This is another reality of the 21st Century.

It has been said that there are two fora in which racial minorities may seek redress of claims of unlawful discrimination: the court system and the Department of Justice. The authors suggest here that given the privatization of our public justice system a third forum has or will soon become employer-sponsored internal conflict management programs. This too is a reality of the workplace of the 21st Century. Accordingly, it is the responsibility and obligation of the government to encourage the use of such alternatives and to ensure that such internal conflict management systems are fair, effective, and timely, and do not supplant our traditional public justice system. It is also imperative that any internal conflict management programs and systems are inclusive and ensure the full and fair participation of racial minorities and women as workplace dispute resolvers. The absence of such assurances will raise serious questions and challenges about the integrity of these programs and systems and, indeed the ADR movement itself.

The authors would like to express their appreciation to Dr. Vida Stanius, Ruth E. Hollemans, and Lorraine Wolf, all of the Center for Employment Dispute Resolution, for their assistance in preparing this article.

IV. Addressing Race and Culture Issues

Addressing Race and Cultural Conflict in Employment Mediation

by Johnnie Scott Jr. *

In the new millennium, race and cultural differences continue to be a flash point for conflict in the American workplace. Employment discrimination disputes continue to be commonplace. Daily, we are reminded of this fact of work life by newspaper headlines chronicling huge judgments against some of the nation's largest employers. The Equal Employment Opportunity Commission received over 28,000 race-based discrimination complaints during fiscal year 1999, along with more than 1,800 religion-based charges and 7,000 national-origin-based charges.

Today, race- and culture-related disputes, especially in the workplace, are often addressed in mediation. In contrast to litigation, mediation has proven to be one of the most cost efficient and socially beneficial methods of resolving workplace disputes. Mediation is a problem-solving process wherein a third-party neutral assists the parties to the dispute through structured negotiations. The neutral endeavors to aid the parties in analyzing their problems and generating solutions through the exploration of options.

While disputes always introduce interpersonal dynamics, in disputes alleging racial discrimination or cultural differences, there is also an intrapersonal component. This denotes that, in addition to dealing with the parties' subjective feelings about each other, the parties must contend with their individual feelings and biases regarding the issues of race and culture. The intrapersonal component harbors the perceptions and stereotypical responses an individual has cultivated relating to other races and cultures. These perceptions and responses have sometimes been reinforced and fostered by social mores that either encourage such

---

* The author is a San Francisco-based mediator and arbitrator who serves on the American Arbitration Association's roster of neutrals. Previously, Mr. Scott served as an administrative judge with the Equal Employment Opportunity Commission and as a commissioner of mediation with the Federal Mediation and Conciliation Service. He also has worked as a mental health specialist and counselor.

beliefs, or at the very least, do very little to engender acceptance of other racial and cultural groups in the broader social structure.

Mediators who work with these disputes should not ignore the racial or cultural conflict. They must develop skills to confront the issues that arise and facilitate constructive problem solving. Although it is important to identify the racial and cultural conflict that may be the basis for the dispute, the mediator must recognize whether and when these issues are best discussed. The mediator must always respect the parties' wishes regarding discussion of these controversial issues.

Mediator From C. Moore, in "Mediating Across Cultures," a 1995 presentation to the annual conference of the Texas Association of Mediators in Houston, characterized eight dimensions along which racial and cultural differences may evince themselves in mediation. The dimensions are:

- relationship;
- views of cooperation and competition;
- problem solving;
- time;
- language and communication;
- impact of larger social structures;
- the role of third parties; and
- physical space.

These dimensions provide a helpful framework that the mediator can use to gather information and build rapport between the parties involved in the dispute. They provide a checklist of variables that the mediator should keep in mind whenever racial or cultural differences surface as an issue dividing the parties to a dispute.

In considering the relationship dimension, the mediator should be cognizant of the effect of hierarchy and power on the ability of the parties to speak directly to one another.

The mediator also should determine, in light of these factors, the extent to which the disclosure of feelings and personal perspectives should be encouraged or discouraged in a joint meeting. In most workplaces, the position of managers and supervisors in the employer's hierarchical structure suggests a degree of power over the individual employee. For instance, in a dispute in which a female employee alleges that a manager used his power or authority as a basis to engage in unwelcome sexual harassment, the employee may feel unable to speak directly to the alleged harasser during the mediation. Thus, when suggesting that a dialog take place between the parties, the mediator should be aware of the roles that subordination and power can play.

Under the second dimension the mediator should ascertain the parties' views regarding cooperation and competition and what form the outcome of the dispute will resemble (i.e., win/win; lose/lose; or win/lose). In cross-cultural disputes, social custom, cultural mores and folkways relating to communication, expressions of discontent, confrontation and religious practices influence the various types of possible resolutions. Western culture, for instance, views confrontation and the use of power as valid methods of addressing conflict (win/lose). In some eastern cultures, conciliation is the more prevalent form of resolving interpersonal differences (win/win).

The problem-solving dimension calls for the mediator to comprehend how the parties' feelings, interests or positions will affect their discussions. In transformative mediation, for example, the parties are encouraged to engage in "feeling"-based discussions designed to engender empowerment and eventual recognition of the other parties' concerns and interests. This contrasts sharply with positional bargaining where the parties negotiate from an extreme position in order to reach a middle ground. The mediator should be aware of whether the parties actually desire to resolve their differences, and whether they wish to center their discussion in the mediation on the presentation of feelings, interests or positions.

A key consideration when mediating disputes involving racial or cross-cultural issues is the amount of time the parties wish to commit to discussing the issues and the possible solutions, before moving up to a binding process (such as arbitration or litigation). In some instances, the party who initiated the mediation may believe that mediation is a precursor to litigation and should not be pursued indefinitely if an acceptable outcome is not forthcoming within a short period of time. Moreover, either party may determine that the issues have such social significance that legal precedent must be established or that the conduct of the other party is so egregious that it must be exposed.

The language and communications dimension calls upon the mediator to look at variations in nonverbal communication within the racial or cultural groups. How these variations are manifested can be significant. For example, does a "yes" response to a proposal mean there is agreement? Or does it signify that "we can keep talking?" In some instances, affirmation of the other parties' concerns does not always indicate agreement respecting the broader issues.

The impact of larger social institutions that may affect the parties, such as religion and the courts, are also important in understanding the racial or cultural conflict. The mediator should be aware of how the parties are influenced by their religious beliefs and should ascertain when beliefs regarding religion or spirituality are at issue. In addition, the mediator should know how the parties view the use of the courts in resolving disputes. In some eastern cultures, for example, parties view the courts as a last resort in resolving differences, while in western cultures, the courts are used more frequently.

With respect to the role of third parties, the mediator should be aware of how the parties view his or her presence in the dispute. For example, is the mediator viewed as an interloper or as a respected "authority" figure who will direct them through the course of mediation? In any event, the parties' perceptions of the mediator's role should be understood from the start.

In order to reach a resolution in mediation, the parties must build and cross over the bridges that divide them. In order to do this, the parties' discussions must lead each side to an understanding of the other's issues and concerns. The last dimension, physical space, addresses the parties' needs regarding the physical context of this discussion. First, the mediator should decide how to structure the mediation based on the needs of these parties. For instance, would they be most comfortable talking face to face initially or would they prefer to engage in a private caucus? The mediator should decide on a physical layout of the space that will facilitate resolution among these parties. For example, would the parties feel more relaxed intermingling or sitting on different sides of the table?

In order to assist the parties in their communications, the mediator should be alert to cultural mores and social forms of expression unique to the groups with which they are associated. How do these groups communicate, express discontent, confront adversaries? What are their religious practices, if any? To what extent do they value mediation as a form of dispute resolution? The mediator should be able to heed the cultural influences in the present dispute on the type of resolution the parties will agree to.

The mediator can adapt traditional mediation approaches when mediating racial and cultural disputes. One adaptation is to provide a more detailed explanation of the mediation process prior to the commencement of mediation. The mediator also can slow the pace of the mediation in order to level the playing field, facilitate understanding, and encourage constructive expression of differences.

Nothing takes the place of preparation on the part of the mediator. This includes becoming educated in racial and cultural differences in body language, views relating to confrontation, candidness in expression, and methods of devising solutions.

The mediator, above all else, should be aware of his or her own biases and should decline to serve as an impartial neutral when appropriate. The mediator who serves the parties in these disputes should take the time to reflect and evaluate his or her own assumptions even while providing assistance to the parties during the mediation. Ultimately, the mediator should serve as a model of respect for the different racial and cultural groups.

Finally, it is important to remember that not every dispute involving people of different races and cultures is the consequence of a racial or cultural problem. If the assessment is made by a skilled and experienced mediator that the racial or cultural issues are collateral at best, this analysis should be shared with the parties.

V. Mediating Disability Claims

Mediating Disability Employment Discrimination Claims

by Matthew W. Daus[*]

"The inability of already-overburdened courts to deal with the continuing increase in the filing of disability discrimination claims is a situation which must be addressed immediately," says Matthew Daus. One means of relieving the pressure of such an overwhelming caseload is greater reliance on alternative dispute resolution, and particularly mediation, he says. Mediation provides an informal environment in which the employer and employee can put their differences on the table and work toward a mutually acceptable solution.

The enactment of the 1991 Civil Rights Amendments to Title VII[1] and the Americans with Disabilities Act (ADA),[2] expanded the scope of the United States' civil rights laws. As a result, there will continue to be an influx of discrimination claims for years to come. Though Congress' passage of the ADA is a great accomplishment, its impact upon the judicial system, administrative agencies and employers is already tremendous. The inability of already-overburdened courts to deal with the continuing increase in the filing of disability discrimination claims is a situation which must be addressed immediately.

Since its enactment, ADA claims have resulted in a crippling caseload at the Equal Employment Opportunity Commission (EEOC). From 1992 through 1993, ADA claims caused a 22% increase in employment discrimination charges filed with the EEOC.[3] A total of

---

[*] The author is the commissioner/chairperson of the New York City Taxi & Limousine Commission. He is the former general counsel to the Commisssion and the New York City Community Development Agency and a former prosecutor with the New York City Commission on Human Rights. Mr. Daus received a J.D. from Tuoro School of Law and a Masters of Law from New York University School of Law. This article is solely the work of the author in his private capacity and should not be construed to represent the official views of the City of New York.

[1] 42 U.S.C. § 2000e, *et seq.*

[2] *See* 42 U.S.C. § 12101 *et seq.* (1990).

[3] *See* Howard A. Simon Yaroslav Sochynsky, *In-house Mediation of Employment Disputes: ADR for the 1990s*," 21 EMPLOYEE REL. L. J. 29 (1995).

20,210 ADA claims were filed with the EEOC during 1993, constituting approximately 25% of all charges filed.[4] The influx of ADA claims contributed to a 30.6% increase in the EEOC backlog from June 1993 through June 1994.[5] Currently, the EEOC reports the filing of more than 54,690 ADA claims,[6] accounting for a 25% annual increase in its workload and a backlog of approximately 24,800 ADA complaints.[7]

In order to curtail the impact of ADA claims upon governmental institutions, the use of alternative dispute resolution (ADR) should be intensified. One of the most popular, successful and cost-effective methods of ADR is mediation. Mediation has been defined as a "voluntary and informal process in which the disputing parties select a neutral third party to assist them in reaching a negotiated settlement.''[8]

Since pilot mediation programs have enjoyed such widespread success,[9] mediation may be one solution to the ADA litigation problem. In fact, the ADA itself contains a specific provision which encourages the use of ADR, including mediation, to resolve claims arising under the Act.[10] Mediation helps to achieve settlements and other dispositions

---

[4] *See* Jan O. Spalding, *ADA: Disabling Businesses for a Buck*, TRIB. BUS. WKLY–BUS. DATELINE, (vol. 5, # 27, sec. 1, p. 1) (Oct. 19, 1994).

[5] *See* Williams, Mullen, Christian & Dobbins, *ADA Charges Cause Increase in EEOC Backlog*, VA. EMP. L. LETTER (vol. 6, # 10) (Nov. 1994).

[6] *See* John R. Cashin, *Strategies Can Control Multiplying ADA Lawsuits–Corporate Strategies for Reducing Lawsuits Based on Americans with Disabilities Act.* BEST'S REV.-PROP.-CASUALTY INS. ED. (vol. 97, # 2) p. 86.

[7] *See Measure Fulfills Dreams and Nightmares,* CHICAGO TRIBUNE (Dec. 4, 1995) p. 8.

[8] ABCs of ADR: A DISPUTE RESOLUTION GLOSSARY, VOL. 10, # 8 ALTERNATIVES (August 1992) pp. 115, 116. The cited definition of the term "mediation" was derived from the Center for Public Resources. *See id.* at 115.

[9] In 1992, the EEOC instituted pilot mediation programs in four of its district offices for the voluntary use of mediation to resolve employment disputes. *See* PAUL STEVEN MILLER, *The Future of Employment ADR: EEOC Adopts ADR Methods*, DISP. RESOL. J. (vol. 50, # 4) (Oct.-Dec.1995) p. 17. The results of the pilot project were as follows: [M]ore than half of the charges mediated were resolved, and the mediations were completed in an average of 67 days. Fifty-one percent of the agreements provided for monetary relief, 17% received reinstatement or a change in employment status, 37% obtained positive references, and 5% received an apology. During confidential exit interviews, more than 90% of participants rated the mediation experience as "very fair" or "fair." Eighty percent stated that they would try mediation again.

[10] *See* 42 U.S.C. § 12212. The ADR amendment to the ADA was offered by Representative Glickman of Kansas in the House Judiciary Committee and was adopted and brought before the full House for floor action on May 17, 1990. *See* 136 Cong Rec H 2421, 2431 (101st Cong. 2nd Sess. May 17, 1990). Mr. Glickman remarked as follows concerning the ADR amendment: "This provision should serve as a reminder that rights and litigation are not one in the same. There are better ways to achieve the goals of the ADA than

while reducing governmental and private expense that would ordinarily arise from protracted litigation. Before implementing this purported solution to the ADA dilemma, the nature of the claims to be mediated should be explored and analyzed.

Fact-Specific Liability

ADA claims are fact-specific. The ADA has been interpreted by the courts to require a case-by-case analysis of each disabled person's job-related needs.[11] Whether an accommodation is "reasonable" or poses an "undue hardship" on the employer involves an inquiry best reserved for the finder of fact.[12] Because of the variety of businesses, jobs, disabilities and the numerous potential modifications which each distinct employer can make to the terms, conditions and privileges of employment, Congress evidently devised flexible standards to be further defined and applied by the courts.[13]

Because ADA claims are so fact-oriented, the outcomes are often unpredictable. As a result, such contingencies can enhance the probability of settlement. When parties to a disability discrimination suit realize that their destinies lie overwhelmingly with either a judge or jury, they are more likely to consider conciliation as an alternative.

Where there is a dispute as to whether a particular accommodation is reasonable or involves an undue hardship, mediation is the perfect forum to attempt the resolution of such differences. Because mediation is such an informal process, the mediator can spark discussion between management and the employee to search for a way to accommodate the disability.

Though approximately half of all ADA lawsuits claim wrongful discharge from employment, at least one-fourth of ADA claims are based

---

litigation and we should encourage cooperation in achieving those goals, not confrontation." *See id.*

[11] *See, for example*, D'Amico v. New York State Board of Law Examiners, 813 F. Supp. 217, 221 (W.D.N.Y. 1993); Coleman v. Zatechka, 824 F. Supp. 1360, 1369 (D. Neb. 1993). A similar case -specific approach was applied under the Rehabilitation Act of 1973 (the predecessor to the ADA). *See* McGregor v. Louisiana State University Board of Supervisors, 3 F.3d 850, 862 (5th Cir. 1993); Nathanson v. Medical College of Pennsylvania, 926 F.2d 1368, 1385 (3d Cir. 1991).

[12] *See id*; *see also, for example*, Lintemuth v. Saturn Corp., 1994 U.S. Dist. LEXIS 18601, p. 11 (Aug. 29, 1994).

[13] The Equal Employment Opportunity Commission's interpretive guidelines for Title I of the ADA support a flexible case-by-case approach. *See* 29 C.F.R. Pt. 1630, App. at 401.

upon a failure of the employer to provide a reasonable accommodation.[14] The ADA defines "reasonable accommodation" as:

> job restructuring, part-time or modified work schedules, reassignment to a vacant position, acquisition or modification of equipment or devices, appropriate adjustment or modifications of examinations, training materials or policies, the provision of qualified readers or interpreters and other similar accommodations for individuals with disabilities.[15]

These suggested accommodations are tools for the mediator to utilize to assist the parties in achieving a mutually desirable result. The mediator's suggestions may be the catalyst for the parties' consideration of a workable accommodation that was not contemplated beforehand. Yet, the mediator must be careful not to offer advice or opinion, but to instead guide the parties in the resolution of their dispute. The mediator may alert the parties to settlement options by subtly posing questions without actually advocating a particular solution. This less intrusive approach appears more appropriate within the context of the mediation format.

Further complicating the stability of the outcome of an ADA claim is the undue hardship defense available to employers. If an employer can demonstrate that a requested accommodation involves "significant difficulty or expense," a valid defense to an ADA claim has been established.[16]

The ADA sets forth a list of factors for the finder of fact to consider in determining whether a proposed accommodation amounts to an undue hardship on the employer.[17] The undue hardship factors provide the

---

[14] *See id.* at 36. *See also* Peter David Blanck, ADA *Study and Commentary: Employment Integration, Economic Opportunity, and The Americans with Disabilities Act: Empirical Study from 1990-1993,* 79 IOWA L. REV. 853, 921 (1994) ("[O]f the charges filed with the EEOC between the effective date of the ADA through June 30, 1994, 50% alleged illegal discharges, 25% involved failure to provide reasonable accommodations, and 11% charged hiring violations."); *see also,* CASHIN, *supra,* note 6 ("Nearly 27% of the complaints charged that employers had not made any accommodations for the alleged disability.").

[15] 42 U.S.C. § 12111(9).

[16] *See* 42 U.S.C. § 12111(10).

[17] *See id.* The following are the ADA's undue hardship factors: "(i) the nature and cost of the accommodation needed under this chapter; (ii) the overall financial resources of the facility or facilities involved in the provision of the reasonable accommodation; the number of persons employed at such facility; the effect on expenses and resources, or the impact

employer with the opportunity to explain the difficulties and costs of a proposed accommodation. Also, based upon the undue hardship factors, a mediator may inquire about the financial situation of the employer—information to which the disabled employee may not ordinarily be privy. The sharing of such information in confidence between the employer and the mediator during caucus—or directly between the employer and employee—may promote conciliation. Mutual recognition of the potential financial and other difficulties of a proposed accommodation is a starting point on the path to settlement.

Prior to mediation, the parties may be set in their legal and factual views until the mediator demonstrates, through posing questions, raising issues and exploring the merits of the parties' positions, that the disposition of an ADA claim is uncertain. Furthermore, since the ADA is still in its infancy, the fact-dependent nature of such claims will ultimately compel settlement at some point. Hence, mediation can serve as an alternate forum where parties describe their factual and legal theories underlying the ADA claim, to thereafter realize that regardless of the perceived merits of their respective positions, the costs of unpredictable continued litigation may not be feasible.

ADA Remedies

The damages recoverable under the ADA incorporate by reference those remedies available under the Civil Rights Act of 1964.[18] However, the nature of the relief requested in many ADA claims may be viewed as quasi-equitable. An otherwise qualified individual with a disability may request a very distinct accommodation, such as the physical alteration of the job site for access purposes or the purchase of equipment or devices to assist the employee in performing essential job functions. The costs of such requested accommodations can usually be easily assessed, in comparison to other forms of relief. For instance, the cost of constructing a wheelchair-accessible bathroom is relatively fixed while the monetary

---

otherwise of such accommodation upon the operation of the facility; (iii) the overall financial resources of the covered entity; the overall size of the business of a covered entity with respect to the number of its employees; the number, type, and location of its facilities; and (iv) the type of operation or operations of the covered entity, including the composition, structure, and functions of the workforce of such entity; the geographic separateness, administrative, or fiscal relationship of the facility or facilities in question to the covered entity." *Id.*

[18] *See* 42 U.S.C. § 12117.

worth of an injured employee's emotional distress resulting from discrimination is amorphous.

An ADA claim requesting a specific accommodation to the work site is settlement-conducive because the costs involved can be estimated, and a mediator has a set range within which to suggest solutions as a basis for compromise. Furthermore, in light of the fact that approximately 70% of all accommodations cost employers less than $100,[19] the likelihood of settling such ADA claims is augmented.

Continued Employment

In those cases where a current employee requests an accommodation, mediation may be more welcome than where a disgruntled former or prospective employee files an ADA claim. Where a disabled employee files an ADA claim and remains employed by the respondent employer, the reality that both employer and employee must face each other on a daily basis may often compel the need for dispute resolution. Hence, not only should both parties be more inclined to participate in mediation, but such claims possess enhanced settlement capabilities.

Certainly, a disabled employee's claim alleging the denial of a reasonable accommodation might be more amenable to settlement than an alleged denial of equal terms, conditions, privileges, or the termination of employment. The latter allegations are more likely to involve accusations of bad faith or the presence of discriminatory animus. However, where an employer makes a good faith effort to accommodate a disabled employee, or raises a genuine undue hardship claim, the level of hostility between employer and employee, if any, is diminished in comparison to cases involving allegations of discriminatory motivation in the terms, conditions, privileges, or termination of employment.

The Psychology of ADA Claims

Certain provisions of the ADA are pragmatically designed to encourage both employers and employees to reach amicable solutions. The ADA defines discrimination as not making a reasonable accommodation.[20] The use of the term accommodation itself implies a partnership between the employer and the qualified individual with a

---

[19] *See* Phillip M. Perry, *It Could Happen To You: Don't Be Sued for Disability Discrimination,* DOORS AND HARDWARE (vol. 58, # 11) (Nov. 1994).

[20] *See* 42 U.S.C. § 12112(b)(5)(A).

disability. The definition of discrimination under the ADA encompasses situations where there may be no intent to discriminate.

Though the ADA does contain provisions which seek to remedy disability discrimination after it has occurred, the accommodation partnership serves as an equally effective deterrent. By requiring employers to offer a reasonable accommodation to a disabled employee, the discrimination does not occur unless the employer either refuses to accommodate or does offer an accommodation which is, however, viewed to be unreasonable. In those ADA cases where an employer fails to hire a disabled job applicant or a disabled person's employment is terminated for discriminatory reasons, the remedial, compensatory and punitive measures of the ADA apply.[21]

Sometimes an employer does offer a disabled employee an accommodation, yet there may be a dispute as to whether it is reasonable or whether it poses an undue hardship upon the employer. In such instances, the employer may have acted in good faith. Where an employer does offer a good faith accommodation, this effort creates a different psychological mind-set between both the employer and the employee. Each party may be able to understand and appreciate the other's position, yet nevertheless respectfully disagree.

As a result of the unique psychology involved with ADA accommodation cases, mediation is the perfect settlement-promoting mechanism. The informality of a mediation conference provides both the employer and the employee with the opportunity to vent their differences and to work constructively toward a solution. The state of mind of the parties to a dispute is always a primary factor in facilitating settlement. ADA claims which are recently filed by current employees who seek an accommodation involve a more positive atmosphere than other discrimination cases. When such settlement-conducive ADA claims are coupled with an informal process such as mediation, extraordinary results can be achieved.

Mediation of Settlement-Conducive ADA Claims

Since certain ADA cases are, for the most part, uniquely situated for mediation, they should receive special attention. Special efforts should be made to streamline dispute resolution efforts and experiment with the use of mediation for the types of ADA claims discussed herein.

---

[21] The Civil Rights Act of 1991 broadened the scope of damages recoverable under both Title VII and the ADA to include compensatory and punitive damages. *See* 42 U.S.C. § 1981a.

All ADA claims are centralized due to pre-suit filing requirements with the EEOC, or state or local human rights agencies. As a result, the most logical place to commence the mediation process would be at the EEOC and/or its sister agencies. Claims that possess enhanced settlement propensities can be identified by the agency and referred to mediation on an expedited basis. In particular, pilot programs should be instituted which expedite mediation attempts for recently-filed ADA claims involving current employees who request an accommodation as the primary form of relief. If such a project proves successful, a permanent program can be implemented to streamline those particular ADA cases. The anticipated success of such a project may help to reduce the caseload at the EEOC and in the courts.

Although mediation will not work in all instances, government institutions can nevertheless attempt to ease the burden of litigation by attempting conciliation wherever possible. Because the development of the ADR field—including mediation—is still in its infancy, experimentation should be encouraged to see what does and does not work. The lessons learned from a mediation program involving select ADA claims can, hopefully, be applied to the resolution of other types of discrimination claims to add further strata to the ADR atmosphere.

VI. Overcoming Barriers to Mediating EEO Disputes

Barriers to Mediation: A Look at the Impediments and Barriers to Voluntary Mediation Programs That Exist within the EEO

*by Arup Varma & Lamont E. Stallworth**

Over the last two decades, there has been a substantial increase in the number of EEO lawsuits and charges relating to workplace disputes being filed. This has led to the search for alternative methods of resolving such disputes. Voluntary mediation, one such alternative, is underutilized in EEO and other types of disputes. This article shows the results of a survey conducted to find out why voluntary mediation is not used more often.

It has been said that "too few disputes settle, and too many that do settle drag on far too long."[1] Although this statement was made within the broader context of bargaining impediments and settlement behavior, the concerns expressed by those researchers are also applicable to the impediments and barriers related to the utilization of agency-connected voluntary EEO mediation programs. The purpose and objective of this article is to examine empirically those factors which EEOC disputants believe are significant impediments or barriers which might explain the underutilization of EEO mediation programs offered at the administrative agency level.[2]

---

* Dr. Varma is an associate professor at Loyola University Chicago, and Director of the Institute of Human Resources and Industrial Relations. He holds undergraduate and masters degrees from Xavier in Calcutta, India and a Ph.D. in Human Resources and Industrial Relations from Rutgers University.

Mr. Stallworth is a professor at the Institute of Human Resources and Industrial Relations, Loyola University Chicago, the chair of the Center for Employment Dispute Resolution, and a member of the National Academy of Arbitrators. He is a past president of the Society of Professionals in Dispute Resolution and currently co-chairs SPIDR's ADR in the Workplace Committee.

[1] *See*, Samuel Issacharoff, Charles Silver and Kent D. Syverud, *Bargaining Impediments and Settlement Behavior*, *in* DISPUTE RESOLUTION: BRIDGING THE SETTLEMENT GAP (Greenwich, Conn., JAI Press, Inc., 1996).

[2] This study was conducted in connection with a voluntary EEO mediation program administered by the Center for Employment Dispute Resolution, a not-for-profit organization, initially funded by the William and Flora Hewlett Foundation, Menlo Park,

Legislative and Public Policy Context

One of the most significant societal events and public policy changes which occurred during the last half of the 20th century was the racial and gender integration of the workplace.[3] The integration of the workplace, and indeed the general society was prompted, in large part, by the Supreme Court's decision in *Brown v. Board of Education*,[4] the civil rights movement of the 1960s[5] and the subsequent enactment of the Civil Rights Act of 1964, as amended.[6]

The cornerstone of Title VII was the principle that cases of discrimination were to be resolved by the use of "conciliation" prior to any court litigation.[7] Thus conciliation, as a matter of public policy, was foreseen by Congress as an effective method to resolve EEO disputes.

The period following the passage of Title VII brought with it the enactment of a number of other federal and state antidiscrimination and EEO statutes. These statutes included but were not limited to such legislation as the Age Discrimination in Employment Act (ADEA) of 1967, the Americans With Disabilities Act (ADA) of 1990, and the Pregnancy Act of 1978, just to name a few.

From the perspective of the federal judiciary, such antidiscrimination statutes as Title VII were of the highest importance and order in protecting individual statutory workplace civil rights. The growth of these workplace civil rights statutes also greatly changed how employment disputes would be resolved within organizations and through our public justice system. As two scholars observed, the resort of employees to these EEO statutes forever changed the nature of

---

California. *See*, *Illinois Human Rights Commission and CEDR Offer ADR for Job Bias Cases*, WORLD ARB. & MEDIATION REP., Vol. 5, No. 4 (April 1994, 75-78).

[3] *See*, *for example*, John A. Davis, *How Management Can Integrate Negroes in War Industries*, published by NEW YORK STATE WAR COUNCIL COMMITTEE ON DISCRIMINATION IN EMPLOYMENT (1942).

[4] Brown v. Board of Education, 347 U.S. 483 (1954). *Also see*, HERBERT HILL AND JAMES E. JONES, JR. (Eds.) RACE IN AMERICA: THE STRUGGLE FOR EQUALITY (Madison, Wisconsin: The University of Wisconsin Press, 1993) for a discussion of the impact of Brown and for a history of earlier struggles for racial equality.

[5] *See*, *for example*, John Lewis, Walking with the Wind: A Memoir of the Movement (New York, New York, Simon & Schuster, 1998) *and see* Philip A. Klinkover, The Unsteady March: The Rise and Decline of Racial Equality in America (Chicago, Illinois, The University of Chicago Press, 1999).

[6] Title VII of the Civil Rights Act of 1964, 42 U.S.C.A. § 2000e, *and see* The Civil Rights Act of 1991, Pub. L. No. 102-166, 105 Stat. 1081 (1991).

[7] Pursuant to Title VII of the Civil Rights Act of 1964, the EEOC is to participate in conciliation where there has been an agency finding of probable cause.

litigation.[8] Specifically, these scholars found that in the last two decades the number of EEO lawsuits filed in federal district court had increased 2,166%.

This substantial number of EEO charges and lawsuits filed created a substantial backlog at both the administrative agency level, for example the EEOC, and the judicial level.[9] This backlog or what is sometimes called "case inventory" has worked and continues to work to the disadvantage of defendant employers and particularly complainant employees. As we embark on the next millennium, there are clear indicators that racial minorities and women believe that they continue to be victims of disparate treatment in the workplace.[10] There is also increasing empirical evidence that women and racial minorities are the subjects of disparate treatment in the broader society, for example in medical and health care matters.[11]

Consequently, from both an administration of justice perspective, cost-efficiency perspective, and in light of the economic and psychological costs caused by these disputes, the EEO administrative and court litigation processes have fallen under considerable criticism and attack.[12]

These concerns and attacks, particularly of the EEOC, have led Congress and subsequently the EEOC to recognize the potential utility and effectiveness of employing ADR, particularly voluntary mediation, to resolve employment discrimination charges and lawsuits.

In both the Americans With Disabilities Act of 1990 and the Civil Rights Act of 1991, Congress incorporated provisions which expressly

[8] John J. Donohue, III, and Peter Siegelman, *The Changing Nature of Employment Discrimination Litigation*, STAN. L. REV., Vol 43 (1991) (hereinafter cited as Donohue III and Siegelman).

[9] *EEOC Chief Voices Frustration Over Case Backlog, Budget Cuts*, WASHINGTON POST, (February 11, 1996), *and see* BACKLOG OF CASES IS OVERWHELMING JOB-BIAS AGENCY, NEW YORK TIMES (November 26, 1994).

[10] *See, for example*, Philip A. Klinkover, The Unsteady March: The Rise and Decline of Racial Equality in America (Chicago and London: University of Chicago Press, 1999).

[11] *See, for example*, Chester Pierce, *Offensive Mechanisms* in FLOYD B. BARBOUR (Editor), THE BLACK SEVENTIES (Boston, Mass: Porter Sargent Publisher, 1970), at pp. 265-282. *And see*, GAVIN DEBECKER, THE GIFT OF FEAR: SURVIVAL SIGNALS THAT PROTECT US FROM VIOLENCE (Boston: Little, Brown and Company, 1997).

[12] For examples of research critical of government enforcement agencies, *see*, Alfred W. Blumrosen, Modern Law: The Law Transmission System and Equal Employment Opportunity (Univ. Wisc. Press, 1993); James A. Gross, Broken Promise: The Subversion of U.S. Labor Relations Policy, 1947-1994 (Temple Univ. Press, 1995).

encouraged the use of alternative dispute resolution processes such as voluntary mediation.[13]

With an ever-increasing caseload or case inventory, the EEOC subsequently adopted an ADR Public Policy Statement which further promoted the use of voluntary mediation and ultimately prompted the implementation of voluntary EEO mediation programs throughout the country.

In addition to these statutory provisions and public policy statements, Congress has attempted to promote further the use of ADR by enacting the Administrative Dispute Resolution Act[14] and most recently the Alternative Dispute Resolution Act of 1998.[15] The former requires federal agencies to design and implement alternative dispute resolution programs, the latter requires federal courts to encourage the use of and establish alternative dispute resolution programs in civil actions.[16]

ADR Underutilization

Notwithstanding these legislative and public policy attempts and initiatives on the part of Congress and the EEOC, experience to date indicates that the use of ADR, specifically voluntary mediation, has been underutilized in resolving EEO and other types of employment disputes and charges.[17] This, in large part, may be attributed to the under-funding

---

[13] Americans with Disabilities Act: Sec.513 Alternative Means of Dispute Resolution:

"Where appropriate and to the extent authorized by law, the use of alternative means of dispute resolution, including settlement negotiations, conciliation, facilitation, mediation, factfinding, minitrials, and arbitration, is encouraged to resolve disputes arising under this Act;"

Civil Rights Act of 1991: Alternative Means of Dispute Resolution:

"Where appropriate and to the extent authorized by law, the use of alternative means of dispute resolution, including settlement negotiations, conciliation, facilitation, mediation, factfinding, minitrials, and arbitration, is encouraged to resolve disputes arising under the Acts of provisions of Federal law amended by this title."

[14] Administrative Dispute Resolution Act and Negotiated Rulemaking Procedure Act, both at 5 U.S.C., § 581.

[15] Alternative Dispute Resolution Act of 1998, Pub.L. 105-315, 12(b)(1) 112 Stat. 2898.

[16] For an article discussing the provisions of the Alternative Dispute Resolution Act, *see* John Bickerman, *Great Potential: The New Federal Law Provides Vehicle if Local Courts Want To Move on ADR*, DISP. RESOL. MAG. (Fall 1999) at pp. 3-6.

[17] *See* Craig A. McEwen, An Evaluation of the Equal Employment Opportunity Commission's Pilot Mediation Program: Center for Dispute Settlement, Washington, DC (Contract no. 2/0011/0168). Under the EEOC Pilot Mediation approximately 58% of cases submitted to mediation were successfully resolved. It should be noted that a number of state EEO enforcement agencies implemented formal mediation programs prior to the EEOC's pursuit of its mediation programs. *And see* Lamont E. Stallworth and Linda K. Stroh, *Who*

of such ADR initiatives. However, the phenomenon of underutilization of voluntary EEO mediation programs at both the EEO administrative agency level and at the judicial level persists.[18] This phenomenon is particularly intriguing, given the general displeasure of the disputants and litigants with the EEO administrative process and the litigation process.[19] The authors suggest here that logic would dictate that EEO disputants would readily and voluntarily seize upon the opportunity to resolve an EEO matter using a mediator of their choice and maintaining control of any settlement outcome rather than incurring the costs and inefficiencies related to litigation.

This phenomenon of underutilization of agency-connected voluntary mediation programs, however, appears not to be unique to the EEO and employment ADR area.[20] The reluctance, or indeed, resistance of EEO disputants and their attorneys to use voluntary mediation have prompted a number of noted ADR scholars and practitioners to suggest some form of mandated participation in mediation. It has also been suggested that lawyers are one of the significant impediments and barriers to the use of mediation.[21]

Impediments and Barriers to Voluntary Mediation

The research in the ADR area has, thus far, focused on impediments or barriers to settlement.[22] There has been little empirical research into

---

Is Seeking To Use ADR? Why Do They Choose To Do So? Disp. Resol. J. (January-March, 1996).

[18] *Supra,* note at XXX. *See also for example*, Leslie Christovich and Lamont E. Stallworth, *The Equal Opportunity Act and Its Administration: The Claimant's Perspective*, PROCEEDINGS, ANNUAL MEETING OF INDUSTRIAL RELATIONS RESEARCH ASSOCIATION (1983).

[19] For articles on the benefit of EEO mediation, *see for example*, Donald B. Reder, *Mediation as a Settlement Tool for Employment Disputes*, LAB. L. J. (September 1992); Carol A. Wittenberg, Susan T. MacKenzie and Margaret Shaw, Chapter 15, *Employment Disputes* in DWIGHT GOLANN, ED., MEDIATING LEGAL DISPUTES: EFFECTIVE STRATEGIES FOR LAWYERS AND MEDIATORS (Little Brown, 1996). ; Lamont E. Stallworth and Carolyn Hernandez, *Labor Arbitration and Alternative Methods of Resolving Employment Discrimination Disputes*, WORKPLACE TOPICS (July 1992).

[20] Nancy H. Rogers and Craig A. McEwen, *Employing the Law To Increase the Use of Mediation and To Encourage Direct and Early Negotiations*, OHIO ST. J. ON DISP. RESOL., Vol 13 (1998) at pp. 831-864.

[21] *Supra*, note 1.

[22] *Supra,* note 1. *Concerns Raised About Trend Toward Using Alternative Dispute Resolution Process for Bias Claims, quoting* Professor Lamont E. Stallworth, DAILY LAB. REP. (BNA), October 31, 1994. *And see* Lamont E. Stallworth *Contract with the American Worker: Workplace Civil Rights and the Potential Role of Alternative Dispute Resolution,*

why EEO disputants and their attorneys do not use voluntary mediation to the degree or extent contemplated by Congress and other public policy makers. Similarly, there has been little empirical research to identify what the impediments and barriers related to the phenomenon of underutilization of voluntary mediation programs at the EEO administrative level. The identification of such barriers or factors would be helpful in assisting public policy makers in determining how to overcome these impediments and barriers in order to better design, implement, and more importantly, fund mediation programs so as to make them more acceptable and "user friendly."

In order to explore and examine empirically these public policy issues, the authors surveyed some seventy-one EEO disputants. These disputants had charges pending before the EEOC in St. Louis, Missouri and Kansas City, Kansas, and the Illinois Human Rights Commission, Chicago, Illinois, during the period of April 1994 to December 1997. The surveyed EEO disputants consisted of fifty-two charging parties; ten charging party attorneys and nine employer-respondent attorneys. There were a total of approximately 500 surveys mailed with a response rate of 14%.[23]

The questionnaire included eighty-five questions[24] related to the use or lack thereof of the EEO administrative agency-connected mediation program.[25]

Two of the questions in the survey were open ended and called for written open responses. These questions asked: "under what conditions,

---

Frank Sander Lecturer, Annual Meeting of American Bar Association (Chicago, Illinois), August 5, 1995.

[23] It should be noted that since the number of attorneys participating in this study was fairly small, the authors have used overall attorney responses in most cases. However, where necessary, the authors have provided attorney ratings broken up by charging party attorneys and respondent attorneys. It should also be noted that since this study was conducted, the EEOC has received funding to subsidize the cost of mediation which has permitted an increase in the number of cases submitted and resolved through mediation. *See*, *New EEOC Mediation Program* WALL STREET JOURNAL (December 28, 1999).

[24] It might seem that this study has a relatively small sample size, given that the total number of respondents was only 71 (52 disputants and 19 attorneys). However, it should be noted that the survey instrument contained 85 questions (including two open-ended questions). Such in-depth surveys, no doubt, lead to a decrease in the return rate—at the same time, such surveys allow the researchers to examine the questions of interest in depth and make the findings, inferences and recommendations more robust and meaningful.

[25] For the purpose of this article, the authors focused upon and analyzed the data related what factors were viewed and believed by EEO disputants as being the more, if not the most significant impediments or barriers to using voluntary EEO mediation at the EEO administrative agency level.

if any, would you support public policy or legislation requiring participation in mediation?" and "what are the key barriers to settlement and how can we overcome these barriers to arrive at mediated settlements more often?"

For the first question, a majority of the charging parties noted that they would support mandated mediation under certain conditions: (a) In cases where merit has been established, (b) in a clear case of discrimination, (c) only where strong financial gains for both parties existed, (d) in court-ordered cases, (e) only if internal procedures were not in place, (f) under situations of time and/or cost constraints, and (g) where only one party agrees to mediation. For the attorneys, a majority noted that they would support mandated mediation in all EEO cases, while some noted that they would support it only if there were no cost to the participants.

For the second question, many suggestions were given. The charging parties noted that (a) close-mindedness of the parties, (b) unskilled mediators, (c) lying on the part of either party, (d) lack of clarity in defining discrimination, and (e) lack of communication, were key barriers. Their suggestions on overcoming these barriers included (a) training, (b) having a competent mediator, (c) mandating mediation, and (d) giving mediator more power to make settlement decision. On their part, the attorneys believed that the major barriers included (a) limited availability of EEOC case workers, (b) charges without merit being filed, (c) unreasonable expectations of parties, and (d) the cost of the process to the disputant. Their suggestions for removing these barriers included (a) moderating both parties from extreme positions, (b) instituting court ordered deadlines, and (c) starting the mediation process much earlier.

At the outset it would be helpful to note and discuss here the respondents' perspective and opinions related to the role of the EEO administrative agency in effectuating the related EEO mediation program; the respondents' familiarity, training, and actual prior experience related to mediation and conflict management resolution, and also their opinions related to how effective mediation is "believed" to be in bringing final closure to an EEO charge.

The respondents indicated a general familiarity with voluntary mediation and also were of the opinion that the administrative agency made it clearly known that voluntary mediation was an option. However, when asked about their prior actual experience with voluntary EEO mediation and satisfaction with EEO mediation, the respondents indicated relatively limited experience with voluntary EEO mediation.

They viewed, however, that voluntary EEO mediation was only relatively effective in bringing final closure to EEO disputes.

Also related to the respondents' perception and opinion of mediation is their actual formal training in negotiations; mediation advocacy and actual EEO mediation. On this score, the survey responses indicated that generally, most of the respondents lacked training in any of these areas. The authors propose that this general lack of training in alternative dispute resolution methods and processes might explain their opinion about voluntary EEO mediation and indeed help to explain the underutilization of agency-connected voluntary EEO mediation programs.

Notwithstanding the respondents' less-than-enthusiastic support for and training in ADR and conflict resolution management, it is noteworthy that the respondents indicated considerable interest in submitting a matter to voluntary EEO mediation where the charge could be resolved within ninety days using a trained professional third-party neutral.

Interestingly, the respondents maintained essentially the same degree of interest in submitting a charge to mediation even where the matter could be administratively investigated by the EEO administrative investigatory agency within ninety days. The consistent degree of interest may be attributed to two factors. First, the respondents viewed the administrative investigatory process as "taking longer to resolve the dispute than expected" and that the "administrative investigative process currently being used to resolve their case was somewhat unfair."

This might explain the respondents' expressed interest in submitting their EEO dispute to mediation—a process under which they would have greater control. Parenthetically, the parties' control over the mediation process and any outcome has always been viewed as a major benefit of mediation, generally.[26]

This conclusion is particularly interesting in light of the less-than-satisfactory prior experience of some of the respondents with voluntary mediation. Again, control over the mediation process might be the determining factor here.

The analysis of these particular survey responses provides the context within which the surveyed respondents view voluntary EEO mediation; the EEO administrative investigatory process and the degree,

---

[26] Judith P. Meyer, *The Pros and Cons of Mediation*, DISP. RESOL. J. (Summer 1997): 9-14.

or lack thereof, of the respondents' familiarity and training they have with ADR and conflict management resolution.

The survey covered eight generally believed impediments factors related to using voluntary EEO mediation. These "believed" impediments and barriers are listed here in order of importance, as rated by the respondents:

A The cost of litigation;

B the clients financial situation;

C avoiding verdict and/or favorable decision on motion for summary judgment;

D avoid bad publicity;

E the need to maintain confidentiality related to the particular case;

F strength and weakness of the particular case;

G the likelihood that a particular judge would hear the case; and

H the likelihood that other damaging evidence would be unearthed

The surveyed respondents indicated that all of these items constituted, if not acted, as "somewhat of a factor or barrier to mediation."

These responses were not surprising, except for the response related to the "strength and weakness of the case." Clearly, no employer welcomes being the subject of an EEO charge or lawsuit; however, most charges and lawsuits do not garner the attention of the general public. For many employers, being the subject of an EEO charge or lawsuit has become an inevitable part of doing business. The exceptions, however, would be whether the employer is found to have been in violation of federal or state EEO law and particularly in those high profile cases involving, for example, pattern and practice instances of sexual harassment and racial discrimination. The bad publicity attendant with *Texaco* and *Mitsubishi* cases are two examples where the employers obviously would have preferred to avoid the national and international bad publicity created by those disputes.[27]

[27] The settlement involving Mitsubishi Motor Manufacturing and the EEOC pursuant to a court consent decree resulted in a $34 million settlement and adoption of sexual

In large part, the prosecution of the EEOC of these high profile cases is to signal to the general public, Congress, and other employers that the agency will vigorously pursue litigation in such matters as a public deterrent to other potential violators. Consequently, the concern over bad publicity or the need for confidentiality is probably not an important factor or barrier particularly where the respondent employer believes that it will prevail in an EEO or employment matter.

It is surprising and noteworthy that the strength and weakness of a particular EEO case does not act as a more important or significant barrier to using mediation according to the respondents. Specifically, it is generally thought that the strength and weakness of a case would definitely determine whether a party to a dispute having, for example, a weak case, would be more inclined to resolve the matter either through direct negotiations or mediation.[28]

There are a number of possible explanations for the weakness and particularly strength of a case acting as an impediment or barrier to using EEO mediation. For example, it may be the general practice and philosophy of the advocate or attorney to exhaust the administrative and litigation process particularly by substantiating the case has no merit and the employer respondent will prevail. There are some attorneys who are "litigious lawyers" and not "early settlers" and find it to their best interest not to settle, notwithstanding that it might be more cost-effective to settle. Similarly, certain clients, both employers and charging parties, want to have their "day in court" and want the matter in dispute adjudicated at any cost rather than settle.

Two of the other factors appeared to be more influential barriers to mediation. These were: the client's financial situation; and the related cost of litigation. The cost of litigation is of particular importance to both defendant attorneys and charging party attorneys.

Thus, it appears that there is some understandable rationale to explain why EEO disputants may or may not elect to use voluntary mediation. The potentially troublesome or problematic aspect of this essentially economic equation is that in many, if not most instances, the charging party is not as well financially situated as the employer-respondent; and thus, may not be able to pursue a matter in court, absent the EEO agency representing the charging party. Consequently, it is

---

harassment and diversity training. *See*, *for example*, MITSUBISHI WILL PAY $34 MILLION, (CHI TRIB., June 12, 1998).

[28] Cheryl Niro, *The Decision Tree: A Systematic Approach to Settlement Decisions,* ILL. B. J., 82 (March 1994).

suggested here that charging parties would be more inclined to seek voluntary mediation, primarily because of the proximate employer-employee relationships and the concomitant economics related to that relationship. Generally speaking, most employers can "out litigate" most employees.

Pre-Charge and Post-Charge Impediments and Barriers

The believed impediments or barriers to mediation might vary or change depending upon whether the voluntary mediation option were made available at the pre-charge filing stage versus the post-charge filing stage. The authors did not make a similar comparative inquiry related to post-lawsuit matters and relevant "believed" or perceived barriers or impediments. There is, however, a need to conduct a similar empirical investigation at the federal district court level, particularly in light of the Alternative Dispute Resolution Act of 1998.[29]

The respondents were asked to respond to the following questions using a "Likert-type" scale, e.g., "strongly disagree to strongly agree." Within this parameter, the respondents were asked to respond to some sixteen items which were believed or not believed to be a barrier to settlement prior to the dispute becoming a charge.

The authors initially contemplated that there would be a considerable, if not substantial, variance in responses related to believed pre-charge and post-charge impediments and barriers to settlement and mediation. This, however, was not the case. Generally, the responses of the respondents were consistent or similar to believed pre- and post-charge impediments and barriers to voluntary mediation.

The items posed to the respondents concerning believed impediments and barriers to mediation were taken from the major research in the area related to settlement and negotiation.[30] Of these items, the factors which appeared to be believed and viewed as having the least or little effect were: (1) the number of parties present at the negotiation table; (2) concerns or needs related to privacy and confidentiality; and (3) party's preference for formal adjudication. The factors that were believed and viewed as having the most effect were: (1) misrepresentation of facts by the other party; (2) the other party's refusal

---

[29] The authors plan to do an evaluation of an EEO mediation program which makes EEO mediators available to EEO litigants in the Federal District Court (N.D.IL). This program is being administered by the Center for Employment Dispute Resolution (CEDR).

[30] *See, for example*, Mnookin, Barriers to Conflict Resolution.

to moderate their extreme position; (3) the other party's refusal to negotiate in good faith; and (4) the other party misinterpreting motivation and intent.

As such, the items or factors that, in the respondents' opinion, are believed to act as significant barriers to settlement, and mediation may be grouped as follows:

A. Trust and motive factors, including distrust of motives related to why certain proposals are made.

B. Bad-faith negotiations, and inter-personal and personality issues.

The authors cannot present here as thorough a discussion and analysis as they would like. However, there are several factors which are particularly noteworthy and warrant some discussion, primarily because of their believed negative impact on settlement and the use of mediation.

The first factor relates to bargaining behavior and perhaps professional conduct. Specifically, the respondents generally believed that refusal to negotiate in good faith and refusal of the opposing party to moderate extreme positions was an important impediment and barrier. This position or belief is further compounded by the fact that the respondents felt that the opposing party "inherently misrepresented" the facts in negotiation. It is not suggested here that, as a general rule, all EEO and employment lawyer mediation advocates or representatives engage in such conduct with "ill will." However, this finding may merely reflect the lawyers' negotiation styles.[31]

This type of negotiation style, however, does not appear to enhance the probability of settlement or the use of mediation where the same parties have been unsuccessful in resolving prior cases involving the same EEO disputants and where there is an absence of a decision maker with settlement authority present at the negotiation table.

The dynamics of negotiations between the client and their principal also appear to be a factor related to believed impediments to settlement and mediation. These types of interpersonal or intra-organization bargaining behavior was explored by asking two related questions: The first question asked was to what degree the respondents believed that "the differing interests of lawyers and their clients" may be a barrier to a settlement or mediation prior to the dispute becoming a charge; the second was a similar question asked within the context of "after the

[31] *See* Dwight Golann, Mediating Legal Disputes: Effective Strategies for Lawyers and Mediators (Canada: Little, Brown & Co. Ltd. 1996).

dispute becoming a charge." The respondents generally agreed that this created "somewhat" of an impediment or barrier to settlement and mediation.

The respondents were subsequently asked "the degree to which you believe that your interests are different than your clients' interest in negotiation or mediation sessions?" It was particularly interesting to find that such a conflicting bargaining dynamic exists and, of course, that where such a dynamic exists, it is believed to create an impediment to settlement or the use of mediation, particularly where the client has a preference for formal adjudication and where the representatives or attorneys would prefer to settle. Although the EEO mediator may not be able to control the occurrence of such a situation, it is critical for the EEO mediator to be aware of such interpersonal or intra-organization conflicts and decide how they might best be handled.

Employing the Law to Increase the Use of Mediation

The study of negotiations, mediation, and conflict resolution is, in large part, an interdisciplinary endeavor drawing upon the fields of economics, the law, and the behavioral and social sciences.[32] The responses of the EEO disputants who participated in this study underscore this point. Indeed, one of the more interesting findings of this study was the role which conflicting personalities play in resolving disputes and the advocates' previous success or lack of success in resolving EEO cases involving the same parties has on the parties' future settlement behavior, including submitting matters to voluntary mediation.

One of the major challenges related to the use of voluntary ADR programs, particularly mediation, is how to effectively encourage the early negotiation and/or mediation of disputes, specifically EEO and employment disputes. It has been suggested that the law might be needed to encourage the early negotiation of disputes and the increased use of mediation.[33] Indeed, as stated earlier, the developing public policy in the EEO and employment area is to encourage the use of ADR, particularly mediation, to resolve the many thousands of EEO charges and lawsuits

---

[32] *See, generally* DAVID ANDERSON (Ed.), DISPUTE RESOLUTION: BRIDGING THE SETTLEMENT GAP (Greenwich, Conn. JAI Press, Inc. 1996).

[33] *See* Nancy H. Rogers and Craig A. McEwen, E*mploying the Law to Increase the Use of Mediation and to Encourage Direct and Early Negotiations*, OHIO ST. J. ON DISP. RESOL. (Vol. 13:3) (1998) at pp. 831 to 864.

filed annually. Thus, the critical public policy question is whether to mandate or not to mandate participation in mediation—and how?

This public-policy question was posed to the surveyed respondents by presenting a series of legislative or public policy proposals.

There were twelve questions related to employing the law to increase the use of mediation. These questions can be grouped or collapsed into four areas of inquiry: (1) legislation requiring training and certification of EEO mediators; (2) government funding of the cost of mediation, i.e., the mediator's fees and related expenses; (3) mandated participation in EEO mediation; and (4) whether attorneys should be legally required to advise their clients about EEO mediation.

The issue and debate to the job-related qualification and possible certification of mediators has existed for a considerable period of time is particularly critical given the potential exclusionary and disparate impact which qualification, such as being a lawyer, may have on certain members of protected classes.[34] Notwithstanding this and other related important concerns, the respondents clearly supported legislation or public policy which would establish qualification and training standards for EEO mediators. They also expressed a similarly high degree of support for the certification and licensing of EEO mediators. The respondents further expressed considerable support for legislation which would require that non-lawyer EEO mediators be familiar with EEO and employment law. Interestingly, they only moderately supported the use of training third-year law students serving as "sole" EEO mediators as long as they were supervised; however, the respondents indicated that they would not use EEO mediation if trained "non-lawyers" were presumably the only option.

Another recognized barrier or impediment was the cost related to retaining an EEO mediator and the payment of the mediator's fees and expenses. This cost is often cited as being particularly burdensome for the charging party, particularly in cases where the charging party is discharged and remains unemployed and is a racial minority[35] or a single parent.

---

[34] Given the decreasing number of minority law students, there will inevitably be a decrease in the number of licensed attorneys. This will lead to a decrease in the number of minority state and federal judges and also mediators and arbitrators, if being a lawyer is made to be a requirement. It should be noted that at the 1999 Annual Meeting of the ADR Section of the American Bar Association (Boston), a resolution was passed stating that being a lawyer in order to be a mediator or arbitrator is not required; "other professionals" may also be mediators and arbitrators.

[35] *Supra*, note 2.

Given this fact, the respondents were asked "to what degree would you agree with legislation or an EEO agency public policy which would provide 100% government financial support for mediation?" The EEO disputants' response to this public policy question was supportive, which is not surprising. Common sense dictates that most parties would prefer to shift as much as possible the economic burden for most services to the federal or state government. Furthermore, there are those, particularly plaintiff attorneys, who strongly believe that the cost of mediation should be borne entirely by the federal government. Without debating this philosophy, it should be noted that since this study was completed, the EEOC's mediation program has been sufficiently funded to subsidize the fees of EEO mediators. Early returns under the most recent mediation initiative of the EEOC indicate a greater percentage of disputants electing to use voluntary mediation.[36]

It should be further noted that in those situations where mediation programs and fees have been subsidized by the employers or the government the utilization of voluntary EEO mediation has increased. The recent mediation programs and initiatives of the U.S. Postal Service and the earlier programs of the U.S. Forest Service and Farm Service Agency of the Department of Agriculture and currently the Department of Navy support this proposition.[37]

The Question of Mandatory Participation

Mandated participation in mediation in which any outcome is strictly voluntary was presented as a central aspect of a series of possible legislative and public-policy options. These legislative and public policy mandates were posed within the following frameworks:

1. as a pre-condition to an administrative EEO investigation where both parties would be required to participate in mediation;
2. as a pre-condition to court trial where both parties would be required to participate in mediation;

[36] *See*, *New EEOC Mediation Program* WALL STREET JOURNAL (December 28, 1999) where it is reported that in the agency's year-end report for fiscal 1999, EEO mediation helped the agency cut its backlog by 23%.

[37] The EEO mediation initiatives sponsored and subsidized by the Forest Service and the Farm Services Agency of the Department of Agriculture in 1998, resulted in some 80% of the complainants electing to use EEO mediation. Seventy-eight percent of the cases were resolved. The Center for Employment Dispute Resolution administered these EEO mediation initiatives.

3. as a pre-condition to an administrative EEO investigation but where at least one of the EEO disputants expressed a desire to submit the matter to mediation. For the purposes of this study this is referred to as "modified mandated or directed" participation in EEO mediation;

4. as a pre-condition to a court-trial where at least one of the EEO litigants have expressed a desire to submit the matter to mediation. This form of mediation is also referred to as "modified mandated or directed" participation in EEO mediation. This option is similar to the Employment Dispute Resolution Act sponsored by former U.S. Senator John Danforth.[38]

In general, there was little support for mandated participation as a pre-condition to an administrative EEO investigation. This was also the case at the EEOC conciliation stage or post-probable cause-finding stage. The respondents support was even less for "mandated" mediation at the administrative investigatory stage.

The respondents appear to express the greatest degree of support for mandated participation in EEO mediation as a pre-condition to a trial court proceeding where "both" litigants must participate in mediation. However, the respondents expressed less support for "modified mandated or directed" participation in mediation as a pre-condition to a trial court proceeding.

The Obligation of Lawyers to Advise Their Clients About Mediation

From a historical perspective, it has taken a considerable amount of time to change a "litigation culture" to an "ADR culture" in which the use of ADR, particularly mediation, is the early, if not immediately contemplated means to be used to resolve a dispute.[39]

It has been suggested that ADR works where it is advocated and strongly supported from the "top down."[40] Within the context of the

---

[38] Former Senator John Danforth proposed S.B. 2327, the "Employment Dispute Resolution Act of 1994," in the 103rd Congress. S.B. 2327 mandated participation in EEO mediation as a condition precedent to a court trial where at least one of the disputants have expressed an interest in mediation.

[39] *Supra*, note 2.

[40] Todd B. Carver and Albert A. Vondra, *Alternative Dispute Resolution: Why ADR Works and Why It Does Not*, HARV. BUS. REV. (May-June 1994).

litigation of EEO and employment disputes, the attorney in many ways effectively takes upon the role of the "top down" person in advising his or her client about the existence of the EEO mediation alternative; the pros and cons of EEO mediation and, in fact, the appropriateness and effectiveness of using mediation generally for the resolution of specific EEO cases. Furthermore, with the enactment of the Administrative Dispute Resolution Act, the Alternative Dispute Resolution Act, and other various federal statutory ADR provisions and public policies, a legitimate argument can be made that now, more than ever, a lawyer has or should have a professional, ethical, and legal obligation to advise his or her client about the pros and cons of voluntary mediation and other ADR processes such as fact-finding and arbitration. Regretfully, the evidence suggests that this is not always the case. The absence of an attorney, or an attorney who is not an advocate of mediation and/or one who does not advise his or her client of the mediation alternative, acts as a major barrier or impediment to using EEO mediation. It appears that the surveyed EEO disputants agree with this statement and proposition.

The surveyed EEO disputants were queried as follows: "To what degree would you agree with legislation or an EEO agency public policy requiring attorneys to advise their clients of the availability of voluntary mediation in EEO disputes?"

The response yielded an unequivocal indication of strong support for legislation and agency public policy requiring attorneys to advise their clients of the availability and the pros and cons of EEO mediation. This is a significant finding, particularly if the attorney either has considerable "top down" influence with clients or actually has the authority to submit a matter to EEO mediation. Consequently, legislation or public policy requiring such client advisement is one generally recognized way, according to the surveyed respondents, by which employing the law may increase the use of mediation.

Conclusion

Several conclusions and recommendations can be made based on the responses provided by the surveyed EEO disputants.

Of all the "believed" or "expressed" factors related to the decision to use EEO mediation, the potential cost of litigation was indicated as a significant factor in deciding to settle or to submit the matter to EEO mediation. This was seen as a more important or controlling factor than the strength or weakness of a case. The other factor or barrier which was believed to influence the decision to use EEO mediation to settle a case was the high level of distrust between the advocates. This distrust, according to the respondents, stems from the assertion that advocates "misrepresent the facts in negotiations" and bargain based on extreme positions. Also related to this distrust issue was the apparent personality conflicts which exist between the advocates. According to the respondents, these personality conflicts create a significant barrier to settlement and, presumably, the successful use of mediation. In sum, the respondents were of the belief that "bad faith" negotiation was at the root of the failure to settle and to use mediation.

The purpose for posing public-policy questions was to attempt to find out how some of these barriers might be overcome by the increased use of the law and public policy. In order to enhance the acceptability of EEO mediation, the respondents expressed strong support for the proposition that EEO mediators be either certified or licensed. The respondents generally rejected the use of non-attorney EEO mediators.

The respondents also expressed strong support for federal and state governments to totally subsidize the cost of the mediator's fees and expenses. They rejected, however, the "modified or directed" mandating of EEO mediation at the agency stage. Interestingly, they supported the mandated participation of both parties at the trial-court stage. Lastly, there was substantial support for legislation or public policy which would require the attorneys to advise their clients of the pros and cons of EEO mediation and the availability of mediation.

A number of the above-detailed factors or barriers are not subject to change by the increased used of the law or public policy. However, the issue of bad faith negotiations, posing extreme negotiation positions, and misrepresentation of facts and contentious personalities, may be addressed by the use of an EEO mediator. This is one of the "value-added" of a mediator, i.e., to assist and guide the disputants through such dynamics, using such techniques as "reality testing."

The issues related to EEO mediator certification and licensing are issues which can be determined through the increased use of the law and public policy. The cautionary word here is that any such required qualifications should be "job related" and "validated" so as not to have a disproportionate effect on any protected class. The issue related to the funding of EEO mediation programs is critical, particularly given the financial constraints of many complainants and charging parties. Accordingly, it is recommended that Congress and state legislatures substantially increase the financial support for EEO mediation. It is also recommended that as a matter of public policy and law, attorneys be required to advise their clients of the availability of voluntary EEO mediation and the related advantages and disadvantages. Attorneys should be required that they certify such client advisement. Among other things, it is hoped that short of mandating the participation in EEO mediation, that this "client advisement" requirement would serve to make attorneys more knowledgeable about ADR. This may be the first step to increase the utilization of EEO mediation and to start changing the EEO litigation culture to an EEO/ADR culture.

Chapter Eight

Mediation in Specific Dispute Areas

I. Family Law Disputes

Family Law Disputes Cry Out for Mediated Settlements

by Roger C. Clapp[*]

Lawyers who practice family law know how important true compromise can be. A worthy objective in most domestic disputes is to reach an early compromise settlement, for a host of honorable and obvious reasons. Lawyers also know that in time some agreements erode, to say the least. Everyone in the business of family law knows that trial results don't always last either. We have all seen situations when one parent so bitterly resents a trial-court adjudication of child support or custody that he or she expends great energy and resources undermining the decision, always to the detriment of the children. But why after a settlement? Why do we see tragedy so often following a compromise, after the lawyers saved their clients from the uncertainties of a trial and obtained results that the parties agreed to in writing? Professional mediators know the answer if they have heard the cry.

A good family law practitioner understands that irrational or just plain mean behavior is less likely when there is real client acceptance of the ultimate resolution of a dispute of any kind. As a chancery-court judge, I knew that no amount of wisdom and fairness assured the parties' compliance with, much less their acceptance of, the court's "final" judgment. In fact, suits to modify court-ordered divorce judgments (and previous modifications) frequently result from non-acceptance, regardless of whether the terms were right or wrong, good or bad, big or small. Without real acceptance even compromise settlements don't really settle some things. Professionals must try for genuine client acceptance

[*] The author is an attorney in general practice in Florence, Mississippi, as well as a mediator and arbitrator. He is a member of the family law section of the Mississippi Bar as well as its ADR committee.

before we can hope for truly final resolution of most disputes, but this is tough duty. Lawyers need all the help they can get. Mediators need to let them know where they can get it.

Another worthy objective in most family law disputes is preservation of ongoing relationships. We know it's important in many business disputes, such as those between partners or vendors and customers. In divorce cases it is almost essential for parents and no less than critical to the short- and long-range interests of their children. Lawyers know this. Why is it then, that even carefully-negotiated compromises, to say nothing of hard-won judgments, are often merely preludes to decades of resentment and strife between former spouses and further damage to the chances of the children having successful marriages? Again, an experienced mediator could suggest an answer.

These goals of true compromise, acceptance and preservation of ongoing relationships actually can be achieved in some cases! Yes, it happens, but rarely if ever from a trial result, and seldom from a quick compromise where one party gives in "to end" the matter, and often not from tough negotiation even between relatively balanced powers. Frequently, however, all three happen through mediation. That is one reason mediation is a required step in family law matters in many states. In a few other states, such as Mississippi, lawyers can at least enjoy the advantages of mediation as an optional tool. If professional mediators everywhere would promote their services and increase their availability to the legal profession in response to the loudening cry coming from American families embroiled in disputes, we would meet these goals more often.

Not all jurisdictions offer mediation through the courts. I was one of only two trial judges in Mississippi who ordered opportunities for mediation in certain cases, using hand-picked mediators who cared. Both programs died when we left the bench. Without funding, official rules, state standards or general bar acceptance, it was impossible to sell the idea to enough practicing attorneys. Despite years of valiant efforts by our state bar alternative-dispute-resolution committee, annual American Arbitration Association training sessions and a slow increase in the use of mediation by insurance companies, we still have to push mediation without support from the top. We still rely on relatively few professionals to answer the cry.

If court-annexed mediation does not thrive where you are, it may be up to you to do something to increase use of this ADR technique where it can be most beneficial. Next time you have a chance, talk to a family law attorney. Respectfully suggest that any such attorney who has not repeatedly tried this method of dispute resolution in good faith is not using one of the best tools available. Part of the good news is that both lawyers and mediators can and should be paid for helping family law clients reach lasting resolutions of their disputes through mediation. It is less expensive in the long run and yet it really does not threaten any good lawyer's income.

How can you spread the news? As we sometimes admonish each other in my neck of the woods, "Get fired up!" Find out when the local bar association meets and volunteer to be a free speaker. Find out who teaches ADR in the nearest law school and ask to be a visiting lecturer. Find out about the family law or domestic-relations section of the state bar association and write a squib for their newsletter. Take out an advertisement that asks parents involved in divorce, "Has your attorney mentioned mediation?" Get permission to set up a booth at the next state-bar convention to hand out material on mediation of domestic-relations cases. Do something to help lawyers hear the cry.

What's the very practical essence of news they need to hear? The lawyers we are talking about are in the dispute resolution business, which requires an arsenal of sharp tools seldom all used in the same case. Hand them another tool. Tell them mediation is one of the best and least expensive dispute resolution tools. Urge them to mention it to their new domestic-relations clients in the first interview. Better still, their contract of representation should contain some innocuous words like "Client agrees that attorney may use mediation to resolve any disputed issues." This makes the attorney explain the term. Then, when they have a handle on the issues, they get opposite counsel to agree on a mediator. You and others are available—tell them how to find a good one. Point out that a good mediator is an impartial third party who uses techniques learned in training to help clients reach their own terms (not win their own terms) to really end their dispute (not give up under pressure), dealing with any power imbalances in the process. Clarify the lawyer's part, which is to make sure the client understands the legal ramifications of his or her initial and final positions. Remind them that the lawyers' presence during mediation sessions is seldom necessary or helpful, but is certainly proper billable work in some cases. Be sure to emphasize that they must approve, or advise against, any mediated settlement, and may have to prepare the final documents. They do not "lose control," as some fear, when they forget that it is, after all, the client's lawsuit.

Lawyers need to hear the statistics that show that spouses with problems who construct their own solutions through mediation tend to abide by them. Most sincere lawyers will listen. They will learn how mediation, by proceeding in a private settlement setting (where nothing presented is thereby admissible into evidence), usually builds (or at least preserves) respect and dignity, even when no agreement is finalized, so that future communication between the parties is enhanced, not cut off. Good lawyers will realize how, in such an environment, groundwork is laid for future problem solving, not for future battles. They can be taught that unless their client's main purpose is to punish and win at all costs (few lawyers intentionally take such clients), mediation is often the best approach to family law dispute resolution.

II. Business Disputes

Resolving Business Disputes: Fact-Finding and Impasse

*by Donald Lee Rome**

The mediation of business disputes can often result in impasse when the parties involved have polarized views often based on lack of information and misunderstanding, according to the author. Fact-finding, within the mediation framework, can be a useful tool to help the parties reach a compromise settlement while maintaining good business relations. The following article outlines the fact-finding process and its use in breaking impasses.

A typical impasse in a business mediation usually occurs when one party is demanding too much money, and the other is offering too little—or none at all. Furthermore, the impasse will generally not be broken if the mediator tries to "move" the parties in the direction of the traditional dollar-focused compromise settlement. This is because in many cases of an impasse in a business mediation, a resolution will only occur when mediator-assisted fact-finding is discussed with the parties as an option to help them reach a compromise settlement.

But some would say that fact finding is just what mediation is designed to avoid; that they are not trying to prove who is right and who is wrong; that they would rather not have discovery; and that they need to look to the future, not the past, for solutions. All of this is true. But for a large percentage of business disputes, when an impasse occurs or is likely, some degree of fact-finding is needed to enable the parties to break or avoid stalemate and to reach a fact- and situation-oriented business resolution of the dispute.

The Raison d'Être for Fact-Oriented Resolutions

When dealing with each other, businesspeople are not in the habit of giving away money, or making other concessions, without some basis for

---

* Mr. Rome is a mediator and arbitrator specializing in business, financial, and commercial disputes. He is retired from the law firm Robinson & Cole where he was senior partner. He is on the AAA's National Roster for Commercial Financial Disputes and the Mediation and Arbitration National Commercial Roster.

doing so, especially when in the midst of trying to resolve a controversy. Resolution does not require absolute certainty as to who is right or wrong, but it does require something more than the assertion of a claim. There may be good business reasons to compromise—and also not to. A criticism of some mediators in impasse situations in business mediations is that they seek an offer and counteroffer before any serious exploration of important issues is made. This is similar to the businessperson's aversion to "split the baby" arbitration results. To compromise for the sake of compromise irritates many businesspeople—and for good reason. Yet, many mediators and lawyers for the parties simply have not had enough involvement with business entities and businesspeople—particularly in the corporate environment—to understand what exactly is needed to avoid or break an impasse in a business dispute.

Compromise without Fact-Finding

Compromise only works to avoid or break an impasse in business disputes when each party, believing that the other is acting in good faith, decides voluntarily and without external pressure that good business relations require a speedy resolution of the dispute, even though the parties have not yet fully established the facts. A party-driven decision to compromise without fact-finding will in some cases be necessary to preserve a valuable business relationship. In other cases, it will be justified on business grounds simply to avoid losing money and time. Indeed, a skillful business mediator knows to explore this compromise option when the first signs of an impasse appear. But this must not be misunderstood as a push for compromise regardless of the facts. It must be presented to the parties as a business option.

Compromise without fact-finding usually requires understanding, as some form of "buy in," if not approval, by those back at the business ranch who have an interest and may be affected by the compromise outcome. They need to know the business objectives, the reasons for selecting compromise without regard to fault. That is not always easy. Internal departmental rivalry, chain of command decision making, internal allocations of the economic effects of a settlement are only some of the factors involved for many business entities in agreeing to a compromise that is not fact oriented. But mediators and lawyers must understand that before businesspeople agree to compromise without regard to fault, they must believe it is a good business choice and can be justified. It must also be understood as a mediation option, and not a mediator's mandate. Compromise in business disputes is usually a complicated matter and must be treated carefully.

Different Goals

Business disputes are usually associated with some type of contractual agreement. Thus, breach of a contract in one form or another becomes the issue.

This is quite different from a typical "fall down" negligence case involving liability, damages, and an insurance carrier. This type of case generally does not raise issues of performance by the parties in relation to each other, and traditional compromise is an accepted norm. But, if the defendant in an accident case does not believe the plaintiff did in fact fall down, then an impasse may result unless there can be some level of fact-finding. The plaintiff who really did fall down is not going to give up, and the company will not pay unless it is educated on the circumstances. Once the insurance company is given factual information to correct or create doubt as to the accuracy of the insurance carrier's information, settlement negotiations will follow.

The big difference between these two worlds is that in business cases, the contract creates a relationship between the parties, and the cause of the problem is not always readily apparent. Therefore, much more fact-finding—internal at each entity and jointly between them—may be needed before the parties are ready to negotiate for settlement.

The Dual Track

In many business disputes there exists a dual track in the dispute resolution process. One track is a dispute that needs to be resolved. The other is a business problem that requires fact-finding and solution.

An example of a dual track in business disputes is product performance.

Scenario: A manufacturer sells a machine to a customer. The machine does not perform as the customer expected. Regardless of fault and liability as a court jury might determine, normal business practice indicates that the manufacturer will want to try and answer certain questions.

- Did the sales representative make a product-performance representation to the customer of a higher level of machine performance than was appropriate for the equipment?

- Is a component—purchased by the manufacturer from a supplier, and installed by the manufacturer—in the machine defective?
- Did the customer fail to operate the machine in accordance with the manual supplied by the manufacturer?
- Does the manual contain specification or other errors in it that could have caused the problem if followed by the customer?
- Did the customer use the wrong products necessary for proper machine maintenance?
- Is there a basic design problem in the equipment?
- What other possibilities could cause the problem being experienced by the customer?

For the customer, in addition to some of the same issues of concern to the manufacturer, there are others.

1. Did the employees of the buyer who were involved in the equipment purchase fail to give the proper specifications for performance to the manufacturer's sales representative?
2. Did its employees improperly operate the equipment?
3. Can the problem be corrected by the manufacturer or by changing operational methods?
4. What information is available from its own people to identify exactly what may be causing the problem?
5. Will it be necessary to replace this equipment?
6. Is the manufacturer in a position to provide assistance in various business and financial issues caused by the problem, regardless of fault?

For both the manufacturer and the customer, none of these questions or business issues will be resolved through pre-trial discovery or trial. Yet, the parties have a mutual business interest in working together to find the cause of the problem, to see if it can be corrected, and to fairly allocate responsibility, economic and otherwise, for the problem.

The same mutual goals exist when a dispute arises from a letter of intent, a commitment letter, a joint venture agreement, a license agreement, a business acquisition, or other similar agreements where good-faith performance by the parties is essential. One party takes action based upon the belief that the other is in breach. Each then accuses the other of a failure to honor their agreement. Each thought it had the right to do what it did because of the perceived actions of the other party.

Yet, these actions and perceptions result from unclear and unknown facts. The result is misunderstandings by each party. Intent that is inconsistent with good faith may be assumed when in fact there may be acceptable reasons for certain actions—actions that unfortunately are unknown to the other party. This problem can be cleared up with some fact-finding. It is true that a court of law can decide the issue, but that will not necessarily resolve the business problem. It will not induce the parties to resume their working relationship.

The mediation challenge is to blend the two existing tracks into a single endeavor—the fact- finding that both parties really want, and the dispute resolution that is dependent on the fact- finding.

An impasse in negotiations will not be broken unless each party recognizes that some of the facts, circumstances, and assumptions on which their conclusions have been based may not be correct. Doubt and uncertainty usually will lead to risk analysis by the parties. Ideally they will ask themselves: What would the consequences be if we were wrong?

The mediator must help the parties come closer to understanding the root of the problem and to look at possibilities they may not have considered before entering mediation.

Fact-Finding to Break Impasse

A business-oriented mediator will be able to help the parties come closer to finding out what exactly happened, and how to assess responsibility. The critical ingredient for the parties, the mediator, and especially the lawyers is to recognize when a compromise settlement without a factual basis cannot be justified by the parties and their respective business organizations. Once this is realized, a skillful mediator can be the facilitator for dispute resolution.

The immediate goal of the mediation should be to have candid discussion with the parties as to how they can:

- share information;
- jointly employ a neutral expert if needed;
- conduct internal interviews based upon information provided by the other side; and

- pursue joint fact-finding efforts on the basis that it is important for business relations.

These elements are needed when key facts and circumstances are not fully known or are misunderstood by the parties.

It should be noted that this process need not necessarily be geared to a proof-positive conclusion. Neither party may need that. One party or both will usually know when the time is ripe for settlement negotiations to start. Sometimes negotiations can last a day, and sometimes they can take much longer. There is room for the mediator to provide significant assistance in the process. However, the parties themselves should be the driving force to the settlement.

Fact-Finding and Compromise As Business Choices

The most important aspect of breaking an impasse in a business dispute is to understand the choice between (a) fact-finding before undertaking serious settlement negotiation, and (b) pursuing a negotiated compromise without fact-finding. The option chosen must be oriented to business goals and practices. These are not theoretical ADR concepts, nor are they mediator-driven precepts to be taken by the parties on faith. A skillful mediator with experience in business disputes can be enormously helpful in bringing parties to a point where they can identify business goals, experiences, and practices in the context of these two options—or a blend of both—to bring about the problem-solving necessary to resolve the dispute at hand.

Unless the parties go through the exercise of choosing between compromise without fact-finding or some fact-finding, an impasse is likely to remain. The best mediation will be one where this choice is outlined, explored, and discussed with all parties—together and in caucus. The essential ingredient is to identify good business reasons for the choice to be made, not generalized concepts of why compromise is good. This process will often lead to creative business solutions to resolve a dispute.

Fact-Finding As a Flexible Process

A mediator should also point out the flexibility of the fact-finding process to the parties. He or she should show the parties that it is not an all-or-nothing process and that it is conducted in steps.

A party that is steadfast in its position, and driven to prove it is right, is likely to be receptive to fact-finding. After all, the mediator's argument to the no-compromise party will be that fact-finding will provide information that will help its position and let the mediator show the other party how reasonable the position is. That is the first step.

Then, once the mediator starts to explore the process of how this will be done—the cooperative effort needed the sharing of information—the no-compromise party may begin to see the merits of leaning towards a compromise. In effect, the process becomes a subtle form of reality checking.

The next step is to provide a schedule of who will do what and when. For example, which employees need to be interviewed? What documents are needed? What inspections will be required? This part of the process will test the parties, again without pressure from the mediator, to settle. The discussion will help each party to decide how much fact-finding will be needed.

The more matters are discussed, the more it is likely the parties will re-evaluate their position. They are likely to resist, privately, any lawyer-effort to convert this mediation fact-finding into pre-trial discovery. The mediator is therefore in a special position to see what changes are developing in the attitudes of each party once the nitty gritty of fact-finding is explored.

Once the fact-finding process is set in motion, then it is critical for the mediator to be involved so that the process does not take on a life of its own. The mediator is needed to help the parties move from this step to negotiations to resolving the dispute. For a skillful mediator, it will not be hard to see when the parties have had enough. Tight time schedules for the various fact-finding steps involved, interlaced with meetings of the parties and the mediator are needed to maintain momentum and to control the process. The mediator should work with the parties to follow the outline, to keep to the schedule, and to preserve the focus on the business objectives. At some point negotiations for resolution will flow naturally, based on the information then available to the mediator and the parties.

Business Considerations in a Mediation Impasse

What is it that businesspeople want from mediation when dealing with disputes where one business entity does not believe it is liable to another, and yet the claimant is equally certain that liability exists? This polarized posture of the parties and the impasse it creates cannot be dismissed on the basis that such polarity is always true at the start of mediation.

The following questions should be explored by lawyers for the parties and the mediator with the businesspeople involved.

1. Why is fact-finding so important in business mediation?
2. What questions and considerations can a mediator raise that will influence business thinking about dispute resolution, that will (a) influence how businesspeople react to an impasse, (b) affect the willingness or resistance to compromise, and (c) that will create fact-finding as an option in mediation where an impasse may be the alternative?
3. What is the principal reason for the impasse?
4. What are the credibility issues?
5. What are the different views of "what happened?"
6. What are the conflicting assumptions?
7. Is there good business reason to compromise, regardless of fault and liability? If so, will the other party have the same view?
8. If compromise without fact-finding, without a fact orientation to justify the result, and sooner rather than later is desirable, can the other party be convinced of this without a modest level of fact-finding?
9. Is fact-finding important to the parties for business reasons?
10. Will fact-finding help to restore trust where good faith behavior is in question? A typical business acquisition scenario provides an excellent example of how trust can be restored:

The Acorn and Zebra companies are in serious negotiations for Acorn to buy Zebra. Both parties expect the transaction to happen. Suddenly Squirrel Inc. makes an overture to buy Acorn. Word of that leaks to Zebra. Zebra thinks Acorn will make a deal with Squirrel and back out of its deal with Zebra. Zebra now tells Acorn it will not continue, based upon its information about Acorn/Squirrel negotiations. Zebra thinks Acorn is using Zebra simply to get a higher price from Squirrel. But Acorn thinks Zebra has found another company and wants to back out. A dispute develops under the letter of intent that had been signed by Acorn and Zebra. In fact, Acorn did not initiate the Squirrel overture, and told Squirrel that it was not able to pursue discussions.

Zebra doubts this. Good faith and trust—a critical element in a long pre-existing relationship between Acorn and Zebra—is now seriously damaged. Even if negotiations resume between Acorn and Zebra, a high level of mutual trust and good faith will be needed to consummate a very difficult deal. Fact-finding of some sort will be needed.

- Will fact-finding help the parties work together to solve a business problem, not simply the dispute at hand?
- Will fact-finding lead to awareness that more uncertainties exist than either party initially recognized?
- Will fact-finding cause tension among the parties and/or internally?
- Where preservation of a relationship is important, will some fact-finding help or harm that goal?
- Where relationship is not an issue, will some fact-finding be helpful to move the parties out of the impasse?
- Will some fact-finding be helpful, with the other parties and internally? If so, can it be done in a cooperative environment, with the other parties and internally?
- How can the mediator be helpful in the process?
- What are the business goals to be advanced through some fact-finding?
- If fact-finding really will not work to advance business goals and allocate responsibility, then why the impasse?
- Will a judge or jury fare any better?
- Does anyone have complete confidence in ascertaining all the facts and a just result in litigation?
- Given the foregoing, what will it take to break the impasse without fact-finding? What are the barriers?

With mediator assistance, businesspeople will begin to see the business issues in a new context. Hopefully these questions will highlight the key issues and decisions to be made to deal with the impasse in the negotiations.

Business Lawyers and Impasse

Business lawyers, whether outside counsel or in-house, usually know their client's business, the industry, and the people in it. They can be very helpful in dealing with business disputes that can give rise to an impasse as described in this article. Working with mediation counsel—usually trial lawyers—the business lawyer can assist the business client in the process. This should be encouraged.

Fact-Finding: Opportunities and Pitfalls

The great opportunity in fact-finding is that businesspeople can take the lead on business issues, objectives, and problems. The significant pitfall is that it can become a preparation for trial rather than mediation.

To explore what happened for the purpose of reaching a mediated resolution is not the same as trial preparation to reach a verdict. The trial lawyers involved in the process will need help from business clients and business lawyers, when appropriate, to provide assistance in a fact-finding process that is geared to mediation. It may not come naturally to trial lawyers. Some companies have employed settlement counsel as well as trial counsel, each performing their respective functions, in order to separate the mediation effort from the necessary pre-trial activity.

Let us take a look at fact-finding in litigation, and compare it to fact-finding in mediation. The judicial process is not geared to fact-finding in a methodical, organized, and objective manner when it comes to determining cause and effect in any situation. "Proof" is offered by competing interests to enable a third party—judge or jury—to reach a verdict. It is not a flexible process. Strict rules of presentation govern. Clients lack any control over the process. The court's rules and procedures are beyond the control of the participants.

What manufacturer of a product would rely on the verdict of a jury in a product liability case to determine whether a product was in fact faulty? For example, what governmental agency would rely on an adversarial judicial process to determine the cause of a fire or an airplane accident? Far more scientific methods are available if the goal is to ascertain whether a particular product malfunctioned, how and why an accident happened, and what the uncertainties were that might preclude a clear and certain identification of all relevant facts and circumstances.

Conclusion

A great opportunity exists for mediators who understand how business works, how business goals and objectives are important, and how to help businesspeople break an impasse. Business lawyers can and should help trial lawyers and mediators understand the issues businesspeople face in dealing with dispute resolution. When the businesspeople see that the "professionals" care about their problems, understand the barriers to settlement, and respect their input, and are flexible to meet client needs, the whole character of a mediation can change and lead to a successful resolution. It can offer a wonderful opportunity to all involved.

III. Bankruptcy Reorganization

Using Mediation in Bankruptcy Reorganizations: Experiments in Privatization

by Mary A. Bedikian[*]

> *"Bankruptcy reorganizations are important for our nation's economy—in terms of continuing viable and valuable business enterprises and in preserving jobs. How courts deal with bankruptcy is also important to the public's perception of our judicial system."*
>
> *—Ralph Mabey*[*]

Although bankruptcy reorganizations make up a relatively small portion of the bankruptcy courts' total caseload[1], Chapter 11 cases have a disproportionate impact on their work load because these cases tend to involve numerous attorneys, creditors and large sums of money.[2] For these debtors and their creditors, a Chapter 11 filing triggers a long, arduous process.

---

[*] Ms. Bedikian is the head of the Michigan State University-DCL College of Law's Alternative Dispute Resolution Program. She is a former regional vice president of the American Arbitration Association and former Chair of the Michigan State Bar Association on Alternative Methods of Dispute Resolution and was awarded its Distinguished Service Award in 1999. Ms. Bedikan earned a bachelors and masters from Wayne State University and a J.D. from Detroit College of Law. She is the author of THE MICHIGAN PRACTICE GUIDE—ADR (West).

[*] RALPH MABEY ET AL., "Expanding the Reach of Alternative Dispute Resolution in Bankruptcy: The Legal and Practical Basis for the Use of Mediation and Other Forms of ADR," 46 S.C. L. REV. 1259, 1313, n. 67 (1995).

[1] Judicial Business of the United States Courts 1998, App. F-2, p. 280, at www.uscourts.gov/dirrpt98/contents.html.

[2] The bankruptcy courts' overall caseload has been increasing. Bankruptcy filings rose 43% from 1993 to 1997. In 1997 alone, 82 out of 94 districts experienced a 20% or greater increase in caseload. In the 12-month period ending Sept. 30, 1998, bankruptcy filings increased 5.1% over the prior 12-month period, rising from 1,367,364 to 1,436,964. Administrative Office of the U.S. Courts, Statistics Div., Federal Judicial Caseload: A 5-Year Retrospective, www.uscourts.gov/publications.html.

Today, many bankruptcy courts are using mediation to offset the rigors of bankruptcy litigation and reduce docket congestion.[3] A number of bankruptcy courts have adopted their own court-annexed mediation programs, either through general orders or local bankruptcy court rules. Other courts are resorting to ad hoc mediation.

Despite objections by some to using mediation in bankruptcy cases,[4] mediation has been gaining acceptance by bankruptcy judges, who have been approving its use in Chapter 11 reorganizations, multiple claims resolution prior to confirmation of a reorganization plan, single creditor claims, adversary proceedings, contested matters, and other contexts. Why is mediation increasingly being considered? Some of the reasons are:

- The facilitated nature of mediation gives the parties control over the process and the resolution terms, consistent with remedies which the bankruptcy laws permit. The parties may "veto" a proposed settlement that does not satisfy their interests or needs.

- Chapter 11 proceedings are capable of exacerbating working relationships. At the very least, mediation can prevent those relationships from further deteriorating.

- Mediation encourages open discussion, allowing peripheral issues to surface. If these issues are effectively dealt with in the mediation, they are far less likely to arise again later.

- The process has proved its utility in resolving large, complex, multiparty cases. Chapter 11 reorganizations

---

[3] Nancy F. Atlas, *Mediation in Bankruptcy Cases (Part I)*, 41 NO. 6 PRAC. LAW. 39 *et seq* (Sept. 1995). *See, e.g., In re* Zale Corp., No. 392-30001-SAF-1 (Bankr. W.D. Tex., Nov. 4, 1992) (appointed mediator to resolve conflict); *In re* Public Serv. Co. of New Hampshire, 99 B.R. 177 (Bankr. D. N.H. 1989) (appointing an examiner); *In re* UNR Indus., 72 B.R. 789 (Bankr. N.D. Ill. 1987) (same); Kubick v. Apex Oil Co., 884 F.2d 343 (9th Cir. 1989) (court-appointed examiner recommended tiered ADR procedure, with mediation as the first step); *In re* Dore & Assoc Contracting, 43 B.R. 717 (Bankr. E.D. Mich. 1984); *In re* Eagle Bus. Mfg., 134 B.R. 584 (Bankr. S.D. Tex. 1991) *aff'd* 158 B.R. 421 (S.D. Tex. 1993); *In re* A.H. Robins Co., 89 B.R. 555 (Bankr. E.D. Va. 1988).

[4] Objectors cite the complexity and multiparty nature of bankruptcy proceedings, and the absence of a source of funding for the mediator's compensation. Cassandra G. Mott, *Macy's Miracle on 34th Street: Employing Mediation to Develop the Reorganization Plan in a Mega-Chapter 11 Case*, 14 OHIO ST. J. ON DISP. RESOL. 193 (1998).

typically involve a plethora of creditors. If mediation is used, the creditors can pool their resources early in the dispute transformation stage, accelerating agreement on an agreed reorganization plan or disputed claims.

Source of Authority

The bankruptcy court must have authority for its referral to mediation. There are a number of statutory and regulatory sources of authority. Among the most common are:

- *Section 105(a) of the Bankruptcy Code. 11 U.S.C. § 105(a).* Bankruptcy Code § 105(a) contains a broad grant of authority, empowering the bankruptcy court to "issue any order, process, or judgment that is necessary or appropriate to carry out the provisions" of the Bankruptcy Code.

- *Rule 16(c)(9) and (16) of the Federal Rules of Civil Procedure (FRCP*). Rule 16 governs the scheduling and management of pretrial conferences by district courts. Rule 16(c)(9) gives the district court authority to consider and take appropriate action with respect to "settlement and the use of special procedures to assist in resolving the dispute when authorized by statute or local rule." In addition, Rule 16(c)(16) gives the court the same authority with respect to "such other matters as may facilitate the just, speedy, and inexpensive disposition of the action." Although the FRCP by its terms applies to federal district courts, district courts confer this authority on bankruptcy judges when they refer bankruptcy cases to the bankruptcy courts. Moreover, FRCP 16 is expressly made applicable to "adversary proceedings" in bankruptcy by Rule 7016 of the Federal Rules of Bankruptcy Procedure.[5]

---

[5] Fed. R. Bankr. P. 7016 states: "Rule 16 F.R.Civ.P. applies in adversary proceedings." Fed. R. Bankr. P. 7001 defines an "adversary proceeding" as "a proceeding (1) to recover money or property, except a proceeding to compel the debtor to deliver property to the trustee, or a proceeding under § 554(b) or § 725 of the Code, Rule 2017, or Rule 6002, (2) to determine the validity, priority, or extent of a lien or other interest in property, other than a proceeding under Rule 4003(d), (3) to obtain approval pursuant to § 363(h) for the sale of both the interest of the estate and of a co-owner in property, (4) to object to or revoke a discharge, (5) to revoke an order of confirmation of a Chapter 11, Chapter 12, or Chapter 13

- *The Judicial Improvements Act of 1990*. 28 U.S.C. § 471 et seq. This Act, which is also known as the Civil Justice Reform Act of 1990, directs federal district courts to implement a civil justice expense and delay reduction plan to improve civil case processing. Plans may include the authority to refer cases to ADR programs designated for use in a district court, or that a court may make available.[6]

- *The Alternative Dispute Resolution Act of 1998*. 28 U.S.C. § 651 et seq. The 1998 ADR Act requires all district courts to authorize the use of ADR in civil actions, including adversary proceedings in bankruptcy.[7] It requires the federal courts, through local court rules, to create a system in which litigants may consider ADR options. Finally, it authorizes the district courts, and by extension, the bankruptcy courts, to require mediation or early neutral evaluation (as nonbinding forms of settlement), even without the parties' consent.

Bankruptcy courts also possess inherent power to direct the parties to mediation when it serves their best interests and furthers judicial economy. Since bankruptcy law is designed to rehabilitate the debtor, mediation is seen as a process whose goals serve the purpose of the bankruptcy proceeding.[8]

---

plan, (6) to determine the dischargeability of a debt, (7) to obtain an injunction or other equitable relief, (8) to subordinate any allowed claim or interest, except when subordination is provided in a Chapter 9, 11, 12 or 13 plan, (9) to obtain a declaratory judgment relating to any of the foregoing, or (10) to determine a claim or cause of action removed pursuant to 28 U.S.C. § 1452."

[6] Section 103 provides: "There shall be implemented by each United States district court, in accordance with this chapter, a civil justice expense and delay reduction plan. The plan may be a plan developed by such district court or a model plan developed by the Judicial Conference of the United States. The purposes of each plan are to facilitate deliberate adjudication of civil cases on the merits, monitor discovery, improve litigation management, and ensure just, speedy and inexpensive resolutions of civil disputes." Section 102, which contains Congress's findings, states that "an effective litigation management and cost and delay reduction program should incorporate several interrelated principles, including…utilization of alternative dispute resolution programs in appropriate cases." *See generally* Anne M. Burr, *Building Reform From the Bottom Up: Formulating Local Rules For Bankruptcy Court-Annexed Mediation*, 12 OHIO ST. J. ON DISP. RESOL. 311, 314-315 (1997).

[7] 28 U.S.C. § 652 (a).

[8] For an extensive discussion of the authority for the use of ADR in bankruptcy, *see* MABEY, n. *, *supra*.

Experiments in Privatization

For the last two decades, bankruptcy courts have been experimenting with various ADR processes in the bankruptcy reorganization context. The American Arbitration Association has administered many of these programs, which have involved "step" processes, combining the use of mediation with other forms of ADR. For example, mediation and arbitration were incorporated into the LTV Corporation Chapter 11 reorganization to resolve personal injury and property damage claims against the debtor. The Greyhound reorganization plan called for an "offer-and-exchange" negotiation, followed by mediation, and, if necessary, arbitration, to resolve personal injury and property damage claims. In the St. Johnsbury Trucking Chapter 11 case, the debtor proposed, and the bankruptcy court approved, a claims resolution procedure that included the use of mediation for all unsettled tort claims against the debtor, followed, if necessary, by arbitration or litigation, but only after the mediator had issued a report containing findings and recommendations.

Several major retailers who filed for Chapter 11 protection have also used mediation to resolve claims under reorganization plans. In the R.H. Macy "mega"-Chapter 11 reorganization, mediation was even used to facilitate the formulation of the reorganization plan itself.[9] When an agreed reorganization plan was not forthcoming two years after the filing of the bankruptcy petition in January 1992, Judge Burton Lifland of the Bankruptcy Court for the Southern District of New York appointed former Secretary of State Cyrus Vance as mediator to aid in the development of a consensual plan.

Complicating the process was the fact that Federated Department Stores, Macy's largest creditor, was attempting to acquire the debtor. After Federated and Macy agreed to a merger in principle, the two companies, with the assistance of the mediator, were able to formulate a joint reorganization plan that Macy's other creditors could approve. The reorganization plan incorporated mediation and arbitration to resolve claims by creditors.[10] Under the plan, the creditors secured $ 4.1 billion

---

[9] For a more detailed discussion of the Macy reorganization and mediation, *see* Mott, n. 4, *supra*. *See also* JEFFREY A. TRACHTENBERG, THE RAIN ON MACY'S PARADE: HOW GREED, AMBITION, AND FOLLY RUINED AMERICA'S GREATEST STORE 227 (Times Books 1996).

[10] Under the plan, the creditors' claims were divided into three categories: class A—claims under $100,000; class B—claims ranging from $100,000 to $500,000; and class C—claims in excess of $500,000. All class C claims were submitted to court-mandated mediation, while class A and B claims were submitted to arbitration. Over 100 creditor

for $6 billion in claims—which exceeded their initial estimates of recovery by $2 billion.[11] The court confirmed the plan 10 months after the mediator's appointment.

Because this Chapter 11 case was so large,[12] formulating an acceptable reorganization plan at first appeared elusive. By appointing a mediator to focus exclusively on the reorganization effort, financial restructuring occurred within a relatively short time, and at much less expense. The Macy experience confirms that mediation can serve the interests of all parties and that the size of a reorganization should be a lure, not a detriment.

Best Products and Venture Stores also incorporated mediation in their reorganizations plans. In the Best Products case, the bankruptcy court approved a reorganization plan that employed mediation to resolve disputed claims in the company's second reorganization.[13] Moreover, the court deferred ruling on motions by personal injury claimants seeking relief from certain stays, until the parties had at least attempted mediation under the plan.[14]

The mediation plan worked as follows: The debtor could schedule a disputed claim for mediation while a "claim objection" was pending but not yet heard. This two-track procedure prevented the debtor from misusing the mediation process. Discovery was allowed in the mediation consistent with the rights provided under the claims-objection process. If a claimant failed to participate in the mediation, which had to occur within thirty days after the debtor referred the claim to mediation, its claims were disallowed and extinguished. Eighty-five percent of the claims were settled under this program, avoiding lengthy personal injury and products liability litigation. This success rate is consistent with that achieved in commercial mediation.[15]

---

claims were filed in June of 1996. Many of these settled in mediation. *See* AMERICAN ARBITRATION ASSOCIATION, *Resolving Mass Bankruptcy Claims: Successful Dispute Resolution Systems*, 780 PLI/COMM 395, 399 (Nov.-Dec. 1998).

[11] TRACHTENBERG, n. 9, *supra*, at 227.

[12] The Macy Chapter 11 case is perhaps one of the largest. When the Chapter 11 petition was filed in January 1992, Macy's liabilities ($6 billion) far exceeded assets ($200,000).

[13] This national retailer originally filed a Chapter 11 petition in January 1991 in the Southern District of New York, but before payments to creditors were complete under its May 1994 reorganization plan, the company was forced to refile in September 1996.

[14] For a more detailed discussion see, H. Slayton Dabney, Jr. et al., *Bankruptcy Lawyers Better Tune Up Their ADR Skills: Best Products is One Case Where Mediation Really Worked*, 18 AM. BANKR. INST. J. 16 (June 1999).

[15] J. Feeley, *Bankruptcy Claims Head to Mediation: Delaware Judge Approves Use to Settle Personal Injury Cases,* THE NAT'L L. J. § B (Dec. 28, 1998-Jan. 4, 1999).

The Venture Stores Chapter 11 case turned into a Chapter 7 liquidation of 102 stores when suppliers cut off the debtor's credit. While overseeing the Chapter 7 liquidation, U.S. District Judge Roderick McKelvie ordered mandatory mediation for about 450 personal injury claims. This reduced the prospect of unjustifiably large awards and entirely avoided the grim reality of protracted litigation.

Initially, some claimants objected to mediation, arguing that the mediator's expenses and the time consumed by travel to the mediation session "chilled" the process of asserting claims. These concerns were addressed by permitting telephone mediations.

Conclusion

A primary goal of bankruptcy reorganization is to rehabilitate the debtor. Creditors look to the bankruptcy system as a way to resolve the financial affairs of the estate. Delays in resolution, combined with unnecessary expense, frustrate this process. Mediation, still the favored form of private ADR, has been used successfully on an ad hoc basis in a number of bankruptcy reorganizations. In the final analysis, it is less costly than litigation, and it fosters the preservation of business relationships, attributes which the drafters of the Judicial Improvements Act of 1990 recognized in the early deliberations of the Act. These attributes of mediation are good reasons why bankruptcy courts should look first to mediation when Chapter 11 filings occur. The likely result is that no other process will be required or desired.

Amy Weise-Ranspach assisted in the preparation of this article.

A Sampling of Bankruptcy Court Mediation Programs

California. Adversary proceedings, contested matters and other disputes (with certain exceptions), are eligible for mediation in all districts.[16]

Florida. In the Southern and Middle Districts, any civil action, adversary proceeding or contested matter may be referred to mediation at a pretrial conference or other hearing at the request of any party in interest, the U.S. Trustee, or on the court's own motion. The Northern District authorizes mediation in all adversary and contested matters.[17]

---

[16] N.D.: Local Bankr. R. 9040-1. S.D.: Local Bankr. Rule 7016-4 (mediation in pretrial procedures). C.D.: General Order 95-01. E.D.: General Order 95-1.

[17] M.D.: Local Bankr. R. 9019-2. S.D.: Local Bankr. R. 9019-2. C.D.: Local Bankr. R. 7016-1 Pretrial Procedures; Local Bankr. R. 16.3 sets out the procedure.

Indiana. Any adversary proceeding or contested matter may be referred to a nonbinding method of ADR.[18]

New York. In the Southern and Northern Districts, any adversary proceeding, contested matter or other dispute may be referred to court-annexed mediation upon motion by a party in interest or the U.S. Trustee, or by stipulation of the parties.[19]

North Carolina. All districts have authority to provide for mediation. The Middle, Eastern and Western Districts provide for a mandatory mediated settlement conference in civil cases, depending on the district rule.[20]

Oklahoma. In the Western District, any party to an adversary proceeding or contested matter may file a request for nonbinding ADR, or the court may direct such action. In the Northern District, the court may, on its own initiative or at a party's request, order a settlement conference or other ADR option, including mediation.[21]

Oregon. Oregon's Revised Statutes encourage court-annexed mediation in civil litigation. A judge of any circuit court may refer a civil dispute to mediation or the parties may stipulate to use mediation.[22]

Texas. The Eastern District provides for a court-annexed mediation plan, which is basically a supervised settlement conference. In the Southern and Northern Districts, the bankruptcy judge may refer a case to ADR on the motion of a party, agreement of the parties, or the court's own motion. The court may establish procedures for the implementation of an ADR program.[23]

Virginia. A court, on its own motion or on motion of a party, may refer any contested civil matter, or selected issues in a civil matter, to a dispute resolution evaluation session to encourage early settlement of disputes. This includes mediation.[24]

---

[18] The parties may agree to be bound by the results. N.D.: Local Bankr. R. B-919.2. S.D.: Local Bankr. R. B-9019.2.

[19] S.D.: Civ. R. 83.12, General Order M-117, General Order M-143, Amended General Order 143. N.D.: Local Bankr. R. 9019.1.

[20] N.C. St. Mediated Settlement Conf. R. 1. M.D.: Civ. R. 205 Mediated Settlement Conferences Pursuant to Local R. 601 et seq. E.D.: ADR R. 32. W.D. ADR R. 32.

[21] W.D.: Local Bankr. R. 7016 Pretrial ADR and Local Bankr. R. 16.3 ADR and Settlement. N.D.: Local R. 16.3.

[22] 1998 Ore. Rev. Stat. § 36.100-36.210.

[23] N.D: Local Bankr. R. 9019.2. E.D.: Tex Order 99-507 with General Order 99-2, amending App. H, providing for court-annexed mediation. S.D.: Local R. 20.

[24] Va. Stat. § 8.02-576 *et. seq*.

IV. Environmental Agency Mediations

Mediating with an Environmental Agency

*by Elissa Tonkin**

In many ways, particularly in the context of environmental enforcement, disagreeing with the government is different from disagreeing with a business or an individual. Accordingly, mediated negotiations of disputes involving an environmental enforcement agency are distinct from mediated negotiations of environmental disputes solely among private parties. This article describes a few of the key differences and the impact that they can have on the participants in the mediation. Understanding the dynamics of mediating with regulatory agencies helps the parties with the process.

Difference #1: The government decision-maker is seldom at the table.

Irritating though this often is to non-governmental parties, it is an immutable fact of the way the government does business. This does not mean that the government negotiator with whom you are dealing has no settlement authority or influence over the outcome of the case. Typically, the agency case lawyer enters into a negotiation with a bottom line that is either pre-approved or that the lawyer is reasonably certain will be acceptable to agency management. This bottom line, which may consist of not simply a dollar amount but also a set of remedial requirements, will be premised upon the private parties' acceptance of the terms of the agency's standard settlement documents.

If agreement within this zone of settlement authority is not possible, a daunting series of approvals may become necessary. Exactly who needs to approve what request varies from case to case and issue to issue. For example, a one-word departure from the standard contribution-

---

* Ms. Tonkin is a senior attorney and mediator with the U.S. Environmental Protection Agency in Boston, where she is the director of the New England ADR Program. She has served as a Superfund section chief and a Superfund case lawyer. Ms. Tonklin received a B.A. from Amherst College and a J.D. from the University of Michigan School of Law. The views expressed in this article are solely those of the author and do not necessarily reflect the official position of the EPA.

protection provision in a consent decree may have national implications and require high-level approvals from agency headquarters and the Department of Justice. On the other hand, approval of a seemingly fundamental change to the agency's authorized proposal might be accomplished through a quick phone call to an available supervisor.

Private parties struggle to understand and endure the approval procedures that are triggered as new settlement options are put forward. They have little grasp of the mysterious organizational structure through which their request will be wending its way. And they have little interest in the agency's institutional concerns about hypothetical cases that stand in the way of solving their actual problem. They want simple answers to simple questions. How likely is it that the agency case team's recommendation will ultimately be accepted? When? What aspects of a recommended settlement will be subject to the greatest scrutiny? To what extent does the case team have control over how long it takes to get an answer to a proposal? Misunderstandings and conflicting expectations regarding agency approvals are a frequent cause of negotiation setbacks, if not complete breakdowns.

While private parties are hungry for information that will help them evaluate the risks associated with future agency decisions or approvals, agency staff are wary of creating false expectations and tend to err on the side of saying less. Government negotiators are especially reluctant to speculate about the internal deliberations of their office when a particular issue or proposal is under review. This reticence fuels the fears private parties have that information is being withheld, that they are at the mercy of an arbitrary process, or, worse yet, that they are being manipulated by an invisible decision maker who is trying to extort yet another concession out of them. Mediators can help parties anticipate and avoid some of these misunderstandings through early (i.e., before any approvals are pending) clarification of the agency's decision-making process, including realistic time frames for agency actions.

At later stages, when agency decisions may be unexpectedly delayed or inconsistent with what the negotiators had anticipated, disappointed parties are likely to leap to cynical conclusions. During these reactive junctures, parties benefit by involving the mediator and resisting the impulse to make quick, dramatic decisions. The mediator can help the private parties accurately interpret whatever information is available so that they can differentiate between minor glitches and major problems. The mediator also may be able to provide the necessary assurances to the agency negotiators to allow for more information to be exchanged. In this way, if a realistic possibility of achieving a desirable settlement remains, it is less likely to be squandered in a moment of frustration.

Difference #2: The government's objectives are essentially different from those of private parties so that the same incentives and disincentives do not apply.

Private parties generally have an interest in avoiding litigation costs, especially when the magnitude of those costs begins to approach or exceed the sum that is at stake in the litigation. They have other interests as well but, as a rule, losing money on a case is bad business. It is not necessarily bad government, however.

While agencies are seldom indifferent to the resources involved in pursuing litigation, they do not experience their involvement in lawsuits as an expensive distraction from their real work. Enforcing the law through various mechanisms, including litigation, is their real work. Their litigators' salaries are already paid. Many of their experts are on staff.

In pursuing a penalty claim against a party that it believes has failed to comply with an environmental regulation, the government does not determine its settlement range by simply taking the amount claimed, adjusting for litigation risk, and deducting the litigation costs. Rather the government decision makers ask themselves questions like: What result is necessary to ensure that the law has been properly and consistently enforced? What are the likely environmental consequences of different settlement options? By what settlement criteria are we bound as a matter of law and agency policy? What message will a particular result send to the regulated community? The public? What result will inspire confidence in the integrity of our enforcement program? Are there environmental justice concerns that would be better addressed by certain settlement options?

All this is to say that, from the standpoint of the government's key interests, it may be advantageous to spend $50,000 pursuing a $10,000 penalty claim.

The cliché that productive negotiations occur when parties understand and take into account their adversaries' interests is nowhere truer and nowhere more elusive than in environmental enforcement negotiations. Mediators help parties achieve this ideal, first, by helping them understand their own interests. This can be deceptively difficult for the government, which typically has multiple competing priorities, each with its own set of advocates. The agency's project manager may be primarily concerned with getting the remedy implemented before a contaminated plume migrates to other areas; the agency's litigator may be more intent on securing a good legal precedent; and the community-involvement coordinator may be focused on public perceptions of a particular enforcement strategy.

Meanwhile, the private parties have competing internal agendas of their own. Outside counsel may be convinced that an aggressive litigation posture will get the best result, while corporate management and in-house counsel may believe that a low-risk, low-profile strategy is more in the company's interest.

The extent to which a mediator can help parties understand and address one another's issues depends partly on the extent to which the parties help the mediator truly understand their own perspectives, and partly on their willingness to receive the mediator's input with an open mind. The trick to getting the most out of mediation is for parties to find a mediator whom they trust and then really involve that mediator in the process.

Difference #3: The enforcement setting is uniquely fertile ground for provocative moral judgments running in both directions.

Government enforcers typically believe that they have justice on their side, that they are working on behalf of the public good, and that they are redressing a wrong that has been committed. Respondents against whom an enforcement action is being taken often believe that they are hardworking Americans who are being persecuted for obscure technical violations by bureaucrats who are abusing their authority and have no clue what it takes to run a business. They feel that the agency should be going after real polluters instead of responsible citizens.

Neither mind-set accurately captures the full picture, though each perspective has an undeniable reality. As with many disputes, the filters through which each side interprets the other's behavior routinely interfere with the parties' attention to their own interests. Because of the perceived moral content of the judgments being made in enforcement cases, the levels of righteous indignation may escalate to a blinding pitch more quickly than in other settings.

Parties must recognize, first, that the mediator cannot change the essential points of view of their adversaries and, second, that the mediator's grasp of the adversary's perspective does not constitute bias. With this awareness, parties are encouraged to use the mediator to anticipate how their communications and positions will be received by the other side, to minimize unnecessary provocations, and to frame discussions in ways that are calculated to advance the negotiation rather than awaken the distracting outrage that is never far below the surface.

Mediation of an enforcement action with a public agency may call for a fuller expression of the creative power of all disputants, as they each seek to maximize their interests, minimize their burdens, and be respected along the way.

V. Medical Malpractice

A Medical Malpractice Litigator Proposes Mediation

by Sheila M. Johnson[*]

"At the commencement exercises for St. Louis University, after the medical graduates received their degrees, they took off their gowns to reveal they were dressed in green surgical scrubs. When the School of Law was called to stand and receive their degrees, the new doctors stood up on their chairs, began howling, growling and hooting, while throwing wads of paper and other objects across the aisle at the graduates about to be lawyers. I was appalled. The new lawyers did not even turn around." A warfare mentality has sprung up around the issue of medical malpractice. As in most wars, there are no winners, only losers, says the author. Her solution for a lasting peace is the imposition of a true mediation model that can provide satisfaction to all parties.

When patients are injured by medical negligence, mediation is not on their minds. The modern and customary methods of resolving disputes in cases of medical negligence fall into two general categories: the patient sues or the patient does not sue. There are serious problems with both categories. Our system of jurisprudence provides one solution, trial by jury, for the redress of wrongs against citizens who have been injured by medical negligence. Unfortunately, there is growing dissatisfaction with the results: Too many patients who are injured by medical negligence do not seek redress, and when they do, the result is not satisfying. On the other hand, many physicians believe they should be protected from lawsuits. They believe that juries are unreasonable and punitive. There has been a concerted effort to "fix" the doctors' perceived problem by legislative tort reform. It has not been successful. There has been no legislative effort to stop physicians from negligently harming patients.

---

[*] The author is a partner at Johnson & McLoyd where she has practiced medical malpractice litigation for twenty-five years. She is an active member of the Michigan Trial Lawyers Association, ATLA and the Women Lawyers Association of Michigan. She has served as chair of the State Bar Committee on Advertising, Certification and Specialization and the Medical/Legal Committee, a joint committee of the Oakland County Bar Association and the Oakland County Medical Association. Ms. Johnson holds J.D. and LL.M. degrees.

Patients, however, are becoming more aware of their rights and their ability to gain access to the courts.

When a patient's condition has been exacerbated by medical negligence, instead of relieved by good medical care, his or her response will vary along a continuum. At one extreme of the continuum is the injured patient who takes no action to confront the problem, not even raising concerns with a trusted family physician. The patient limps away and copes with the injury as an extension of the initial illness. The other extreme is the injured patient who wants to sue the doctor, the nurses, the hospital and anyone who happens to be in the way with an anger and vengeance that cannot be satisfied. Some patients entertain physical violence as a solution to their pain. As patients gain more information and sophistication, they will be less likely to limp away when injured by a physician. The answer is not to decrease their access to the court through more tort reform legislation. The mediation of medical negligence claims is a feasible middle ground between the two extremes. The legal profession also should become involved in the process of mediation and take the lead in fostering its growth.

The Failure of Litigation

It is estimated that there are over 150,000 deaths and 30,000 serious injuries per year caused by physician and hospital negligence in the United States.[1] Medical malpractice litigation has not been an effective tool for compensating patients for the injury caused by physician negligence because it rarely identifies health care providers who are negligent and it rarely holds them accountable.[2] If litigation was the sole response to negligent medical care, we would have 180,000 meritorious lawsuits filed every year. In fact, litigation is the least likely response to medical negligence when it occurs. According to the Harvard Medical Practice Study III (*The Harvard Study*), only 1.53% of the patients injured by medical negligence filed claims against their tortfeasors. The researchers in this huge undertaking matched the medical records of a random sample of 31,429 patients hospitalized in the State of New York in 1984 with actual medical claims that were filed against physicians and hospitals.[3] The Danzon Study,[4] an extensive study in California,

---

[1] Paul C. Weiler, Medical Malpractice on Trial. (Harv. U. Press, 1991) p. 12.

[2] A. Russell Localio, J.D., M.P.H., MS., et. al., *Relation Between Malpractice Claims and Adverse Events Due to Negligence. Results of the Harvard Medical Practice Study* III, 325 NEW ENG. J. MED. 245 (1991).

[3] *Id.*

estimated that there were ten injuries due to medical negligence for every claim that is filed.

Paul Weiler, professor of law at Harvard University, and one of the researchers and authors of *The Harvard Study*, is of the opinion that the system of litigation not only fails to compensate patients, it further undercompensates those claims with minor injuries while overcompensating the major injuries.[5] Professor Catherine Meschievitz arrives at the same conclusion in reviewing several studies including *The Harvard Study*, the "Sloan Study," the large empirical study conducted by researchers at Vanderbilt University, and a recent observational study conducted by researchers associated with the American Bar Association. She concluded that "...the present system of providing compensation for medical injuries due to malpractice is hardly equitable."[6]

It was the increasing frequency of patient complaints and the increasing size of jury awards beginning in the 1960s and 1970s that provoked the declaration of a medical negligence insurance crisis. In almost every state, legislatures passed tort reform statutes to ensure medical negligence insurance for physicians and inhibit the rise in claims.[7] Patricia Danzon concluded in her study that the tort reforms of the 1970s had little or no effect on the frequency or the severity of claims.[8] Using empirical studies, Paul Weiler concluded that legislative tort reform has been relatively ineffective in changing litigation performance and only temporarily has made changes in insurance rates. In the long term, he predicts it will be an ineffective factor in the future in determining whether or not patients will assert claims when they have been injured.[9]

Neil Vidmar, professor of social science and law at Duke University, used empirical evidence from several sources to conclude that contrary to the prevailing fears among health care providers, medical malpractice

---

[4] Patricia M. Danzon, Medical Malpractice Theory, Evidence, and Public Policy. (Cambridge, Mass.: Harv. U. Press, 1985).

[5] *Supra*, note 1, at 53, 54.

[6] Catherine S. Meschievitz, *Efficacious or Precarious? Comments on the Processing and Resolution of Medical Malpractice Claims in the United States,* 3 ANNALS HEALTH L. 123 (1994) p. 130.

[7] Patricia M. Danzon, "The Frequency and Severity of Medical Malpractice Claims: New Evidence," 49 LAW & CONTEMP. PROBS. 57 (1986).

[8] *Id.*

[9] *Supra,* note 1, at 33-36; DENNIS J. RASOR, *Notes and Comments: Mandatory Medical Malpractice Screening Panels: A Need to Reevaluate,*" 9 OHIO ST. J. ON DISP. RESOL. 115 (1993) p. 138.

juries do not favor plaintiffs. He also found that juries are conservative regarding the plaintiff's burden of proof, generally are competent to decide the issues, and tend to award reasonable and justifiable verdicts when they do find in favor of the plaintiffs.[10]

Although tort reform was driven by the fear of unreasonable jury verdicts, high insurance rates and the increase in the number of claims, tort reform has failed to deliver relief and has discouraged patient access to justice.

Medical negligence is a fact of life just like other forms of negligence. Physicians will continue to make mistakes in the care and treatment of patients. In reality, physicians do high-risk work. It can and does injure patients. Some mistakes will meet the legal definition of medical negligence. Some physicians will be negligent often. Litigation also is a fact of modern life. Some patients will want to sue when they are disappointed, hurt or grief-stricken at an unexpected result, whether or not it was caused by negligence. But litigation has not worked well to compensate injured patients or to curtail negligence.

More Litigation to Come?

There are an increasing number of cases being filed against doctors and hospitals and the rate of medical negligence lawsuits per physician is increasing.[11] Patients who have been injured by medical negligence are becoming more educated about their rights and are more aware of how to find a lawyer. As distasteful as lawyer advertising is to many, it is still legal and can help guide prospective clients to the right legal specialist.

As more hospitals and medical centers acquire private physicians' medical practices, they also will acquire the liabilities for the physicians' negligence. These hospitals are better able to pay the damage claim in its entirety. This change in the practice of medicine is encouraging to lawyers because it means there will be a larger source of funds to pay for damage done to patients instead of settling within the policy limits of an individual physician's insurance.

Health maintenance organizations (HMOs) market themselves to the public with a promise to provide high-quality medical care. Instead, they

---

[10] Neil Vidmar, *The Unfair Criticism of Medical Malpractice Juries*, 76 JUDICATURE 118 (1992) p. 121; NEIL VIDMAR, MEDICAL MALPRACTICE AND THE AMERICAN JURY (University of Michigan Press, 1995); Randall R. Bovbjerg, et. al., *Juries and Justice: Are Malpractice and Other Personal Injuries Created Equal?* 54 WTR LAW & CONTEMP. PROBS. 5 (1991) p. 7.

[11] *Supra*, note 7.

control costs by refusing to authorize tests and procedures that physicians believe are necessary. This has formed the basis of several lawsuits. Consequently, large managed-care organizations are expecting a great deal of future litigation.[12]

The litigation system of resolving disputes is burdensome. It is costly for everyone involved: the courts, the parties, the attorneys and insurance companies. Because it is costly for insurance companies, rates go up for physicians. When rates go up, physicians lobby legislatures to change the rules of litigation in their favor. Tort reform has resulted in more expense for plaintiffs and for defendants. In states that have medical malpractice tort reform with caps on pain and suffering, malpractice insurers have less incentive to settle meritorious cases with large or moderate damages, depending on the amount of coverage. For instance, if a case has a value of $500,000, and the cap on non-economic damages is $500,000, insurers will not settle for a figure near that amount because they know that no matter how high the jury verdict is the most they will pay is $500,000. They know the chances of winning at trial are more in their favor than in favor of the plaintiffs.[13] They may as well roll the dice, even in cases they know to be meritorious. The plaintiff trial lawyers are not going to give up just because the system has become more difficult. They simply will work harder to get more cases. According to the Harvard and Danzon studies, there is no shortage of medical negligence cases.

The cap on non-economic damages also has caused an economic disincentive for attorneys to represent patients whose injuries are small or moderate. Consequently, plaintiff attorneys are declining cases where the potential for recovering a large amount of money is low, even when the liability of the health care providers is clear. This is unfair to patients who have been harmed by the negligence of health care providers.

Litigation is disruptive to the practice of medicine. Even when physicians prevail at trial, they often feel it's a Pyrrhic victory. They are emotionally spent. Their lives have been disrupted. They feel personally and professionally attacked. They have lost time away from their office, but still have overhead to pay. If they are uninsured, attorney fees and litigation costs are astronomical. Insurance for medical negligence remains very expensive and tort reform will not come to the rescue. Before the dust settles on a verdict in their favor, they get angry at the

[12] Robert Pear, *HMOs Asserting Immunity in Suits Over Malpractice,* N.Y. TIMES, Nov. 17, 1996.

[13] *Supra*, note 10.

system, at plaintiffs and at lawyers in general, even their own. There is no satisfaction in a victory like this.

When plaintiffs have a verdict in their favor, they cannot rejoice for very long. If it is a substantial verdict, it is likely to be appealed by the defendant. If the verdict is lower than reasonable compensation, the plaintiffs are dissatisfied. Then, they must reduce their verdict further to pay their attorney.

In addition to the actual monetary costs, both parties must face time expended and lost from work. Delays, such as the repeated adjournment of trials, waste everyone's time. Physicians believe their professional reputation has been publicly maligned and patients rarely get their day in court. The uncertainty and arbitrary nature of the outcome forces parties to settle and feel unsatisfied with the resolution. At the end of the trial, at the very best, only one party will believe justice has been done. This causes everyone, plaintiffs and defendants alike, to be mistrustful of the system.

Most of these problems can be resolved with mediation, a dispute resolution practice which has been practiced formally and informally for centuries.[14] In China, for instance, there are ten million mediators compared with 15,000 lawyers.[15] In the United States, we have come to rely on the system of trial by jury as a first response. As we become educated to other forms of dispute resolution, we can begin to see the merits of a process that allows the parties to resolve their own disputes with a mediator who facilitates the process.

A Problem with Definition

In the dispute resolution community, mediation is generally understood to mean a process by which parties resolve their dispute to their mutual satisfaction with the facilitation of a neutral person who has no interest in the outcome and no authority to impose a solution or make a ruling. The statutorily mandated medical malpractice mediation programs that have been established in several states[16] bear no resemblance to this definition. "Medical malpractice pretrial screening panels" is the more descriptive and more accurate name. These panels were legislative responses to a perceived medical malpractice insurance

---

[14] Susan S. Silbey, *Mediation Mythology*, 1993 NEGOTIATION J. 349, p. 350.

[15] Lemoine D. Pierce, *Mediation Prospers in China*, 49 DISP. RESOL. J. 19 (1994) p. 21.

[16] Peter S. Chantilis, *Mediation U.S.A.*, 26 U. MEM. L. REV.1031, (1996); NANCY H. ROGERS AND CRAIG A. MCEWEN, MEDIATION, LAW AND PRACTICE (Clark Boardman Callaghan, 2nd ed., 1995) Appendix C.

crisis in the late 1960s and early 1970s.[17] They were never meant to serve as mediation because the purpose did not contemplate the peaceful and mutual resolution of claims to the mutual satisfaction of both parties. They were legislatively mandated procedures established to reduce medical malpractice costs and insure the availability of malpractice insurance to physicians by screening all medical malpractice cases and getting rid of those considered to be frivolous.[18]

Mediation is a process. In the tort reform screening/evaluation procedure by contrast, panel members do not facilitate dispute resolution to the mutual satisfaction of the parties. They give an opinion on the settlement value of the case. Michigan and Wisconsin are typical of several states that have mandatory, medical malpractice pretrial screening/evaluation procedures, officially named "mediation."[19]

In Michigan, every medical malpractice case must be evaluated by a panel of five "mediators" before trial. The statute requires five panel members, three of whom are lawyers, two of whom are health care providers.[20] One of the health care providers is selected by the plaintiff and one is selected by the defendant.[21] The attorney panel members have no training, but are required to attend an orientation session. The physician panel members have no training or orientation. Each party submits a brief in advance and each party is limited to a 15-minute oral presentation. The actual parties do not attend the session. They are represented by their attorneys. The panel members deliberate and present an "award" that represents the opinion of the panel members on the settlement value of the case. Within twenty-eight days of the award, each party is required to either accept or reject the award without benefit of knowing the decision of the other parties. If all parties accept, the case is settled and an order is automatically entered with the court. If any party rejects the "award" and the case proceeds to trial, the rejecting party must better his position by 10% or face sanctions which include costs and attorney fees. If the panel members unanimously agree that the action is frivolous within the meaning given in the statute, they are required to so state. The "frivolous" plaintiff is required to post a cash or

---

[17] Morris v. Metriyakool, 309 N.W.2d. 910, 107 Mich. App. 110 (1981) at 916.

[18] *Id.*

[19] E. Scott Henley, Ph.D., J.D., *The Use of Pretrial Mediation and Arbitration in Medical Negligence Cases,* 1994 MED. TRIAL TECH. Q., pp. 524, 529.

[20] Mich. Comp. Laws. Ann. 600.4905 (1986). In actuality, this requirement is honored mainly in the breach. Physicians rarely attend and the procedure continues to be conducted by attorneys.

[21] Mich. Comp. Laws. Ann. 600.4901, *et seq.* (1986).

surety bond before trial in the event he loses at trial. The bond will then be used to pay sanction costs and attorney fees. In effect, any party who loses at trial could be punished twice, once by the verdict and once by the sanctions.

There is nothing in the Michigan procedure that resembles mediation. It was not intended to encourage opposing parties to resolve their differences with the assistance of a facilitator. Predictably, it is not successful in resolving cases or weeding out frivolous cases.[22] In actual practice, attorneys vigorously advocate for their clients in this "mediation" and do not view it as a cooperative process meant to settle the case. The procedure is just another competition which somebody wins and somebody loses. Plaintiff attorneys often consider it just another hoop for the plaintiff to jump through to get to a trial on the merits. It is also a starting point for negotiation, often to the detriment of one of the parties, especially if the award does not reflect an accurate value of the case. By definition, the Michigan system cannot be successful as mediation. What it has done is mislead lawyers in their understanding of the mediation process.

Wisconsin's procedure, also called mediation, is different in form but similar in purpose and intent and similar in its failure to mediate. The panel consists of an attorney, a health care provider and a member of the public appointed by the governor. Mediation is a prerequisite to filing a lawsuit. The parties are present but they speak through the attorneys and have very little participation unless encouraged by the mediators. The panel members are supposed to facilitate a compromise so that an agreement can be made and a lawsuit avoided. They have little training. They do not actually render a decision. If there is no compromise, the panelists are free to advise the parties of their opinions of the future outcome. In actual observed practice, the attorney member tends to control the procedure. Research conducted by Catherine S. Meschievitz, assistant dean of the Office of International Studies and Programs at the University of Wisconsin-Madison, has revealed that medical mediation panels rarely reach a settlement at the mediation stage.[23] "By almost any measure of program settlement rates, the MMPS settlement rate must be considered extremely low."[24]

---

[22] Statistical information provided by Mary Jane Rigonen, Assignment Clerk, Oakland County, Michigan.

[23] Catherine S. Meschievitz, *Mediation and Medical Malpractice: Problems with Definition and Implementation,* 54 LAW &CONTEMP. PROBS. 195 (1991) p. 206.

[24] *Id.* at 207.

Michigan and Wisconsin have mediation panels typical of panels used around the country. They are erroneously referred to as "mediation"[25] in the literature. The discussions regarding their success, failure or usefulness is misleading. Lawyers have the word "mediation" in their lexicon but it is not the same definition as a dispute resolution professional would use. Consequently, lawyers believe that mediation is a failure as a system for resolving lawsuits.

The Traditional Model

In legal and dispute resolution journals, there has been very little reported voluntary medical negligence mediation. Professor Leonard L. Riskin attempted a project at the Center for Dispute Resolution at the University of Missouri-Columbia School of Law where traditional mediation techniques were applied to medical negligence cases. No cases were referred to the program.[26] In his report to the National Institute for Dispute Resolution, Riskin describes his exhaustive efforts in promoting the use of mediation by contacting plaintiff and defense lawyers, the university medical center and insurance companies, all to no avail. He also was unable to discover many cases that had been voluntarily mediated, nationwide.

The Private Adjudication Center, an affiliate of the Duke University School of Law, has developed and provides alternative dispute resolution services in medical negligence cases. The director of the center, Thomas Metzloff, is of the opinion that mediation for the large majority of medical negligence cases is inappropriate because he believes that the parties require a decision on the merits. The minority of cases that involve emotional issues, which need to be explored and recognized much like a psychotherapy session, are the only ones he would recommend to mediation. The program has conducted only a few mediations in medical malpractice cases.[27]

---

[25] Charles W. Ehrhardt, *One Thousand Seven-Hundred Days: A History of Medical Malpractice Mediation Panels in Florida,* 8 FLA. ST. U. LR. 165, (1980); Lawrence C. Mann, *Mediation of Civil Cases: Neither Panacea Nor Anathema,* 67 U. DETROIT L.R. 531, (1990); Leonard J. Nelson, *Medical Malpractice and Alternative Dispute Resolution,* 10 AM. J. TRIAL ADVOC. 345 (1986); Note, "Medical Malpractice Mediation Panels," 46 Fordham L.J. 322 (1977).

[26] Leonard L. Riskin, *Final Report to the National Institute for Dispute Resolution on Innovation Fund Grant for Medical Malpractice Mediation (1992).* On file with the author.

[27] Thomas B. Metzloff, *Alternative Dispute Resolution Strategies in Medical Malpractice*, 9 ALASKA L. REV. 429 (1992) note 87.

Mediation of medical malpractice is still theoretical, but it merits more than just further discussion.[28] It merits implementation. Even though programs in Michigan, Wisconsin and other states are not working to settle cases, many authors believe the basic components of mediation fit the needs of medical malpractice litigation.[29] We cannot draw the conclusion that mediation has failed in medical malpractice. Screening/evaluation panels have failed,[30] but true facilitative mediation has not been tested in a significant number of cases. There is no particular or practical reason why malpractice claims cannot be satisfactorily resolved by mediation any more than any other complex issue.

The Merits of Mediation

Litigation is based upon a war model. The parties muster an army (the firm), appoint a general (the lead trial lawyer), choose a battleground (the court with jurisdiction), stockpile the ammunition (discovery), engage in battles (the motion practice), participate in a required peace effort (pre-trial settlement conference), blow each other to bits (trial) and declare a victor (the verdict). One side "wins," but all it wins is money or the right to keep it. Unfortunately, money, and a great deal of it, is what is spent to win. Medical negligence litigation has been referred to by prominent scholars as "war"; one calling it "law's Vietnam."[31] Our combative language is similar to the way the lay person often talks. There is a litigation vocabulary in popular culture that reveals a need for vengeance and a search for power over others. It is common to hear expressions like "slap him with a lawsuit," "drag her into court" and "take him for everything he is worth."

For lawyers who have chosen to be litigators, trials make great "war stories." Litigators love the excitement of trial but clients do not. In actuality, an attorney's first duty to clients is to solve their problems in a responsible and professional way. Most cases are only settled when the

---

[28] *Supra*, note 23, at 213.

[29] Andrew McMullen, *Comment, Mediation and Medical Malpractice Disputes: Potential Obstacles in the Traditional Lawyers Perspective,* 1990 J. DISP. RESOL. 371; Meschievitz, *supra,* note 23, at 215.

[30] Meschievitz, *supra*, note 23. *See* note 22, *supra*. Leonard J. Nelson, *Medical Malpractice and Alternative Dispute Resolution*, 10 AM. J. TRIAL ADVOC. 345 (1986) p. 351; RASOR, *supra*, note 9.

[31] Thomas B. Metzloff, *Understanding the Malpractice Wars*, 106 HARV. L. R. 1169 (1993) (reviewing PAUL C. WEILER, MEDICAL MALPRACTICE ON TRIAL, *supra*, note 1).

burdens of trial become a reality. Once there is a jury trial, nothing is guaranteed: certainly not justice, only theoretical justice.

Mediation, by contrast, makes no determination of who is right and never declares a winner.[32] This seems like an alien concept to lawyers, who are educated to think only in terms of winning and losing. Just as we have evolved from Saxon and old English law of trial by ordeal,[33] it is time to evolve to a more civilized and fair method of resolving our differences.

There are many advantages to taking the medical malpractice dispute out of the war model. Mediation gives the power to the parties themselves, to resolve disputes at an earlier and less expensive point in the process[34], before the specter of trial forces a settlement. It is a generally recognized fact that most lawsuits settle before trial, but usually only "on the courthouse steps." By then, years have gone by, money has been spent, emotions have been exhausted and wounds are still open.

Because of the passage of time, events can and do occur that are detrimental to the case and parties are arbitrarily harmed. This author has been involved in cases where the plaintiff has died, the defendant doctor has died, or a witness has died. Time also can be detrimental to the survivors of the decedent in a wrongful death suit. The litigation has the effect of holding open their grief. They cannot finish accepting the death until all the business is finished. Usually, the only business left is the lawsuit. In addition, the longer a case continues unresolved and the more personally invested the attorneys and the parties become, the more entrenched become their positions.

Cases destined for settlement will do so earlier with mediation. Lawyers have difficulty bringing up the subject of settlement. Under the war model, settlement seems like a behavioral contradiction. An offer to settle is often interpreted as a sign of weakness by the opposing counsel. Defense attorneys have a particular disincentive to settle a case because they work by an hourly rate. For this reason, mediation would appeal to the insurance carriers of physicians, because a third party, the mediator, facilitates the discussion of settlement. In a pilot program in San

---

[32] *Supra*, note 23, at 198.

[33] BLACK'S LAW DICTIONARY, Revised Fourth Edition (West Publishing Co., 1976).

[34] William A. Quinby, *Why Health Care Parties Should Mediate Rather Than Litigate*, 1 HEALTHSPAN 13 (1994) p. 13.

Antonio, Texas, mediating general claims is entirely underwritten by insurance companies.[35]

There can be considerable savings if a lawsuit can be avoided, especially in the case where the actions of the health care providers are indefensible, the facts are emotionally charged and the damages are not astronomical.

Another type of case which is perfect for pre-suit mediation is the one where there is no professional negligence but there is an injury. What is present is some inexcusable mishap that injured the patient and is poorly handled by the health care providers. Since patients often have an incomplete understanding of their medical care, they can easily misinterpret the meaning of events.

For example, a 59-year-old man was injured during his coronary angioplasty. During this delicate procedure, while the cardiologist had a catheter in the man's coronary artery, the camera that was videotaping the procedure fell off the ceiling and hit the patient in the face. The cardiologist was able to give the camera a shove before it hit his patient with full force. It glanced the patient's eyebrow, broke his glasses and the glasses cut the man's forehead. Needless to say, there was a lot of excitement and some swearing going on in that procedure room. Minutes later, the surgeon informed the patient that one of his coronary arteries had ruptured and he needed an emergency coronary artery bypass graft. The patient made the assumption that the falling camera had caused the rupture. What he did not know was that the rupture had already occurred and the bleeding was under control before the camera fell. He also did not know that angioplastic procedures carry a five percent risk of rupture. The surgery was successful and the patient, being a reasonable man, was just glad to be alive. He asked for his glasses, since he couldn't see at all without them. He was promised that his glasses would be repaired immediately. They were not. For five days he begged for his glasses. The hospital personnel did not fix his glasses, but they did call a plastic surgeon to repair the laceration on his forehead and a neurologist to make sure he did not have a concussion. He went home with bent and crushed glasses. He was still steaming about this when he received the bills from the plastic surgeon and the neurologist. That is when he made the transformation from patient to client. He wanted to sue the hospital for unnecessary bypass surgery. Once the hospital heard from his lawyer, it

---

[35] Edward J. Rice Jr., *Pre-suit Mediations: A Win-Win Situation for Everyone*, 63 DEFENSE COUNS. J. 454 (1996).

dug in its heels and started defending itself. It charged the man $300 for a copy of the angioplasty film. Eventually, the matter was negotiated to a settlement, money was paid, but nobody was satisfied. This man needed a sincere apology[36] and not just for the camera falling on him. He also needed an explanation from a doctor, not a lawyer. His trust was shattered along with his glasses and he will not return to that hospital again. Although the hospital settled this case and technically won on the issue of professional negligence, it certainly lost good will. Hospitals and other institutions of medicine cannot afford to take customer good will for granted.

One of the benefits often ascribed to mediation is that it maintains relationships. That would not normally be an important consideration in determining whether a client should mediate because the patient's relationship with the physician is usually severed at the time of the negligence. But maintaining the physician-patient relationship is becoming important to hospitals as they are increasingly incorporating individual physicians into the institution as employees. The same is true for HMOs that administer ERISA health plans. As employers lock large groups of employees into a particular provider system, the HMO will want to maintain customer satisfaction or risk losing many clients at once.[37]

Mediation can resolve many of the issues underlying the dispute,[38] as in the "case of the broken glasses." Patients often need to discharge certain emotions. They also need an opportunity to ask questions, and sometimes just to be able to pose questions for which there may not be an answer. My clients often have expressed disappointment at the conclusion of their deposition. Their main complaint is that they did not have the chance to express the extent of their pain. Unless they go to trial, they never get this opportunity. One of my clients was inconsolable because her defendant doctor was inept in communicating what had transpired. Because they were personal friends outside of their patient-physician relationship, the lawsuit caused the loss of two relationships valuable to both of them. My client has repeatedly said to me, "I just want to ask her why she treated me that way. She was supposed to be my

---

[36] Ann J. Kellett, R.N, *Healing Angry Wounds: The Roles of Apology and Mediation in Disputes Between Physicians and Patients,* 1987 J. DISP RESOL. 111.

[37] Nelson, *supra,* note 32, at 346; Armand Leone, Jr., *As Health Care Enterprise Liability Expands...Is ADR the Rx for Malpractice?* 49 DISP. RESOL. J. 7 (1994).

[38] Elaine A. Wohlner & John A. Rymers, *Civil Mediation: Where, When And Why It Is Effective*, 24 COLO. LAW. 2161 (1995) p. 2162.

friend." What is interesting about this is that the event she wants to ask the doctor about has nothing to do with the liability in the case. I also got the impression from the doctor's deposition that she also wants to explain her actions very much. The litigation is keeping them from the satisfaction they both might gain from face-to-face communication. The satisfaction that this plaintiff could derive from an encounter with her former friend and doctor could be enough for her to give up her need to go to trial. She then might think in more reasonable terms about a settlement. It also could focus the issues for her by relieving the most emotional one.

Mediation should not be considered the only answer to the inefficiency of litigation. I am not advocating the abolition of trials. Trials can serve some cases well. The trial system also provides the legal and procedural safeguards that are cherished in a free society. But it does have its inherent faults and it is not a good solution for the vast majority of malpractice claims. Mediation can address those faults and resolve many more claims.

The Mediation Proposal

Very few medical negligence cases are as simple or as obvious as the ones described above. Most are complex whether or not the damages are great. Medical issues compound legal ones. Emotional issues on both sides of the controversy overlay each case. Cases that have real merit still involve a tremendous amount of proof to prevail. There is no written standard of care that guides physicians in how they should practice or the jury in how they should decide. Experts can and do differ widely on proximate cause even when the breach of the standard of care is obvious. Damages are always fertile grounds for expert opinions because the patient came to the doctor sick or injured in the first place. The communication that mediation allows gets people off on the right foot as they establish a framework within which to work in resolving the real issues. As they continue the discussions, they can narrow their case down to the most relevant issues that will be decided by a jury, if not by themselves. Leonard Riskin points out the wide variety of activities that fit within the broad definition of mediation.[39] The broadness of definition has allowed it to function well in many other areas of dispute at least as

[39] Leonard L. Riskin, *Understanding Mediators' Orientations, Strategies and Techniques: A Grid for the Perplexed,* 1 HARV. NEGOT. L.REV. 7 (1996) p. 33.

complex as medical negligence.[40] The flexibility of the process is what recommends it to medical negligence. Each case can be mediated in a different way depending upon the particular circumstances.

Principles of Mediation Malpractice

Certain principles must be honored in every medical malpractice mediation in order to insure that the rights of the parties are respected and the integrity of the process is maintained. The four main principles are: self-determination, impartiality, fairness, and confidentiality.

Self-determination. The American Bar Association, The American Arbitration Association and the Society of Professionals in Dispute Resolution have developed and published "The Model Standards of Conduct for Mediators" (the Standards). The first standard is self-determination and mediators are instructed to recognize the importance of this principle. "Self-determination is the fundamental principle of mediation." It means that the parties must have the ability to voluntarily reach their own agreement. They also must be allowed the decision to end their participation in the mediation at any time.[41] Litigators, unfamiliar with mediation, will have a difficult time with this concept. The mediator must take responsibility to educate the lawyers as well as the parties on this concept. It should be pointed out to the participating lawyers that they have a duty to allow the principle of self-determination to rule the proceedings.

Self-determination can only occur if the parties are well-informed.[42] The participants should be advised that the decision to end the mediation is entirely theirs, that they have certain rights and alternatives, and that they may not be coerced or sanctioned if they refuse to participate.[43] One of the benefits of the self-determination principle over a judicial decision is that the judge can only rule on the issue before the court. Creative or personalized solutions are never addressed during litigation.[44]

Impartiality. The impartiality of the mediator is what gives the mediator the necessary credibility to guide the participants. If there is

---

[40] ROGERS AND MCEWEN, *supra*, note 16, at chapter 12.

[41] John D. Feerick, *Standards of Conduct for Mediators*, 79 JUDICATURE 314 (May-June 1996) p. 316.

[42] Robert B. Moberly, *Ethical Standards for Court-Appointed Mediators and Florida's Mandatory Mediation Experiment*, 21 FLA. ST. U.L. REV. 701 (1994) p. 5.

[43] *Id.*

[44] *Supra*, note 41, at 2.

favoritism, then there is no trust.[45] The parties must be able to perceive that the mediator has no interest in the outcome and that his or her primary responsibility is to encourage the best interests of all parties. The Standards consider impartiality to be central to the process and oblige a prejudiced mediator to withdraw.[46]

Fairness. People come to the court system in search of justice. They are powerless to help themselves and seek the assistance of an attorney to right wrongs that have been done to them. They rely on the ideal of being able to obtain justice and that they are entitled to justice. This basic principle of fairness must be maintained in mediation or the process will lose its legitimacy as a dispute resolution choice. When there is an imbalance of power between the parties, there is the potential for injustice.[47] The opposing parties in a medical malpractice cause of action are inherently in an imbalance of power. The relationship begins that way. The patients are ill or injured and do not have the power to heal themselves. They look to the physician and the medical institution to take care of them. They will even submit to great physical pain (e.g., surgery) to get well. Sometimes it is the abuse or neglect of this enormous power that causes an injury. Upon first complaining that the doctor did something wrong, the patient is challenging a social and cultural bias in favor of the doctor. Patients are not likely to be able to do this on their own and should not be expected to. Add to this fact that plaintiffs in medical negligence cases remain injured or ill. They come to the table from a position of weakness, literally and culturally.

There are two ways that this imbalance of power concern can be addressed and are critical to the concept of fairness. First, each party must have an attorney, and second, each party must understand that either one of them may unilaterally discontinue the negotiation and choose adjudication instead.

Each participant in a medical negligence mediation must be represented by an attorney who holds the client's best interests in high regard. This requirement is equally important to an individual physician. Physicians can be just as bewildered and naive about their rights and the alternatives as their patients. "Uninformed self-determination is

---

[45] Joseph B. Stuhlberg, Taking Charge/Managing Conflict (Lexington Books, New York, 1987) p. 37.

[46] *Supra*, note 43.

[47] Jacqueline Nolan-Haley, "Court Mediation and the Search for Justice Through Law," 74 WASHINGTON UNIVERSITY LAQ. 47 (1996) p. 89.

hollow."[48] There is nothing in medical school that prepares physicians for negotiating their way through the legal system. Their only exposure to the concept or practical reality of medical malpractice litigation is the attitude that filters down to them through their teachers, who are physicians themselves. They learn nothing in medical school about law. This fear of the unknown causes them to feel threatened and frightened by the prospect of litigation.[49] They would be naive to believe that a hospital where they have staff privileges or are employed or an insurance company will represent their interests.

Each party should be properly advised that: They may not be coerced into a settlement; there are consequential effects of the settlement they are contemplating; there are alternatives to settlement; and they have a right to a trial by jury. Professor Trina Grillo argues persuasively that when settlements are forced in a mediation process, it loses all its virtue. This is true in general but particularly for those who have subordinate positions in the society.[50]

Confidentiality. It is a basic tenet of mediation that confidentiality is critical to its success because it encourages the participants to speak freely.[51] Medical negligence litigators involved in mediation will be concerned that clients will say something from the heart that will be of great detriment to their case, something that will take away their leverage in the negotiation, or worse, something that will prejudice them at trial. In litigation, plaintiffs' attorneys carefully prepare their clients not to reveal thoughts such as: "No amount of money can bring back my father. I know this. It's not the money. It's the principle of the thing. I just want to hurt that doctor the way he hurt me." Attorneys for defendants carefully prepare their clients not to testify to real feelings either. There would be a tremendous loss of leverage in negotiation, not to mention an evidentiary faux pas, if a doctor blurted out: "Can't we just get rid of this thing? What do I pay all that insurance for? Just pay them and get them off my back." Yet these are the very sentiments a mediator needs to hear to move the parties forward toward a resolution. The parties need to feel

---

[48] *Id.* at 91.

[49] This is an assumption I make based upon my professional and personal experience. I also have had the opportunity to periodically teach a class in medical malpractice to residents. The level of anxiety and anger at the beginning of the class is palpable and not easily diffused. By the end of the class, the physicians seem more open to discussion.

[50] Trina Grillo, The *Mediation Alternative: Process Dangers for Women,* 100 YALE L.J. 0(1991) pp. 3, 28.

[51] John S. Murray, et. al., Mediation and Other Non-binding ADR Processes (Foundation Press, Westbury, New York, 1996) p. 159.

confident that if these things are said in private to a mediator, they will not be revealed to the other side without the permission of the speaker. The parties' confidence must be kept after the completion of a mediation. If the parties were assured by the mediator and their attorney that it was acceptable to reveal confidences during the mediation, then the mediator has essentially stepped into the shoes of the attorneys and has agreed to adopt the attorney-client privilege. Attorneys for the parties need the same assurances. A mediator must never reveal settlement statements made by an attorney in confidence unless the protection of the confidence is waived.

The issue of confidentiality must be distinguished from the issue of privilege. They are similar but are not the same. A mediation privilege created by the courts or by statute exists in some jurisdictions.[52] Like the attorney-client privilege and the physician-patient privilege, it protects the confidences held by a mediator from subpoena. The confidentiality agreed upon during mediation is contractual, but if the mediator is subpoenaed the contract is unenforceable.[53] It is generally against public policy to contract to withhold evidence, but evidence can be withheld by asserting a privileged relationship. The concern usually arises when a mediation has not resulted in a settlement of the case and someone attempts to discover or admit into evidence what was said during the mediation. Federal Rule 408 offers some protection but is limited to only one type of conversation. It excludes from evidence offers to compromise or settle,[54] but it is not as broad as the kind of privilege that would allow the parties the confidence to be candid. The most compelling argument against privilege is that the law is jealous of relevant evidence. It is a basic evidentiary principle that all relevant evidence is admissible. The question becomes, "Do the confidences between a mediator and the participants serve an important enough purpose that they warrant protection as great as a privilege?" The answer probably lies in the degree of protection.[55] Clear rules need to be established stating: (1) who has the right to assert the privilege, (2) the subject matter to be protected, (3) whether or not third parties are harmed

---

[52] *Id.* at 173.

[53] Alan Kirtley, *The Mediation Privilege's Transition From Theory to Implementation: Designing a Mediation Privilege Standard to Protect Mediation Participants, the Process and the Public Interest,* 1995 J. DISP. RESOLUTION 1, p. 10.

[54] Federal Rule of Evidence 408; Murray, *supra*, note 53, at 161.

[55] *Supra*, note 53, at 161.

by the privilege,[56] (4) carefully crafted exceptions (e.g., criminal matters or child abuse matters) and (5) whether or not there is a public policy interest.[57] Forty states and one territory have enacted mediation privilege statutes, some more expansive than others.[58]

The four principles: self-determination, impartiality, fairness and confidentiality are necessary to all mediations and are what drive the process toward legitimacy.

Effective Mediation

The following is an analysis of how the typical elements of an effective mediation program apply to medical negligence cases.

1. Court-ordered attendance. A court order is the only way that most cases of medical negligence will get to mediation. Attorneys are neither familiar nor comfortable with the process and are suspicious of it. Linda Mulcahy, an advocate of mediation and an evaluator of the London, England, program of voluntary medical malpractice mediation, considers it very important that the process be voluntary so that it gains its own credibility.[59] Between September 1995 and April 1996 the program had only three cases to mediate. Leonard Riskin went to enormous effort to attempt to get malpractice cases to voluntarily mediate and was unsuccessful. I found it interesting, but not surprising, that even though some lawyers agreed to mediate, they did not follow through in practice.[60] Admittedly, voluntary mediation would be better, but if a voluntary program does not get people to the table then there is no program at all.

Our culture is so invested in the trial system that it is unlikely that a significant number of lawyers would advise their clients to voluntarily try mediation. It is more common and more comfortable to put ourselves between the client and the courthouse. We protect clients from the process by fighting their battles for them. In mediation we are giving our clients more responsibility for the solution and thereby giving up control.

---

[56] In some jurisdictions there is a duty imposed upon professionals to protect third parties who are in danger. Tarasoff v. Regents of University of California, 551 P.2d 334 (1976); Rogers, *supra*, note 42, at 62.

[57] *Supra*, note 53, at 161.

[58] *Supra*, note 43, at 64 and Appendix B.

[59] Joanne Easterbrook, *Resolving Health Care Disputes*, 140 SOLICITORS J. 410 (1996) p. 411.

[60] *Supra*, note 26.

As attorneys become more familiar with the process they will presumably trust it more, especially when they experience the benefits through their clients. Whatever initial economics-based resistance there is to mediation will be replaced with the realization that the clients are more satisfied.

The attendance requirement should include the plaintiff, the spouse of the injured plaintiff if he or she is a party, the defendant physician, the attorney for each party and a representative from a defendant hospital or insurance company who has authority to settle the claim.

The requirement of the attendance should include the understanding that the parties are free to speak their mind in any way they need to. Commentators have pointed out, especially in divorce mediation, that mediation can be a dangerous process for those who do not naturally speak in an unfamiliar setting and that "orthodox patriarchal rules" inhibit the free flow of expression.[61] An example is the remarkable statement made by one commentator that "tirades should not be allowed in mediation."[62] I could not disagree more. First, we do not know what the author means by "tirades." Second, there is actually nothing technically wrong with a tirade as long as there is no inappropriate name-calling or violence. Third, discouraging anger in mediation sends the wrong message. Anger is often seen as an inappropriate emotion. The message is that the anger, and perhaps the person expressing anger, are unacceptable.[63] It has been my experience that patients who have been victimized by the negligence of a trusted doctor are often at a loss to find the "right" feelings. They often express feelings of guilt until they give themselves permission to feel anger. That anger may not come out until mediation. The mediator should allow it and prevent others from discouraging it.

2. Voluntary agreement. "Referral to mediation does not necessarily diminish the importance of law for those parties who sought its protection when they first came to court."[64] Although parties may be forced to try mediation, they must never be required to settle or feel pressure to settle. The developing case law on the issue of mandatory mediation supports this concept. Courts have specifically ruled that a

---

[61] *Supra*, note 52, at 1550.

[62] Paul Fisher, *Tips to Attorneys and Mediators: How to Successfully Mediate a Case,* 46 ARBITRATION J. 59 (1991).

[63] *Supra*, note 52, at 1572.

[64] *Id.* at 64.

state statute requiring mandatory referral did not require settlement,[65] a state mandatory mediation statute does not require parties to make an offer,[66] and that attendance at mediation but refusal to move from a pre-mediation position satisfies the statute.[67]

Some cases just need to go to trial, either because the attorney believes it is best for the client or the client insists on the right to see the judge and have his day in court.

Other cases have important issues of law that should not be negotiated away. A coerced agreement would violate the fundamental principle of fairness. When a program starts out with a court order, it is this principle of fairness that needs to be zealously guarded.

3. Formality. Mediation should be as formal as possible.[68] By this I mean respect must be shown for the process, the procedures and the parties. Because mediation is in a less structured setting than the courtroom and the strict rules of the court are not enforced, there is the risk that participants may not take it as seriously. One of the advantages of mediation is that it is less formal than the strict rules of the courtroom environment. A well-trained mediator will know how to balance this advantage of mediation with the obligation to protect the rights of the parties and, therefore, the integrity of the process.

4. Skilled mediator. A mediator for this area of the law must be well-trained in effective mediation technique and have expertise in the subject matter to be credible to the parties and their attorneys. In addition, an effective mediator will be "intelligent, articulate, persuasive, skeptical, resourceful, imaginative, empathetic, reliable, honest, patient, persevering, optimistic and have a good sense of humor."[69] Most lawyers, in my experience, already possess many of these attributes valued in an effective mediator. But by their education, training and experience, most lawyers have not developed the ability to be "neutral, impartial, objective, flexible, an effective listener and non-defensive."[70] The very attributes that make an effective trial lawyer are the opposite of what make an effective mediator. Professor Riskin theorizes that lawyers follow a "standard philosophical map" that contains two guiding

---

[65] Decker v. Lindsay, 824 S.W.2d 247, 252 (Texas App. 1992).

[66] Avril v. Civilmar, 605 So.2d 988, 989-990 (Florida App. 1992).

[67] Graham v. Baker, 447 N.W.2d 397, 401 (Iowa App. 1989).

[68] Stephen Meili & Tamara Packard, *Alternative Dispute Resolution in a New Health Care System: Will It Work for Everyone?* 10 OHIO ST. J. ON DISP. RESOL. 23 (1994) p. 7.

[69] *Supra*, note 47, at 41.

[70] *Id.*

assumptions: 1) disputants are adversaries, and 2) a third party, applying a rule of law, will resolve the dispute.[71] To function as mediators lawyers will have to be able to change this way of looking at controversy. A mediator who advocates or provokes adversarial responses is not impartial and will destroy the credibility he or she gains in the beginning. A mediator who attempts to impose a general rule of law on the parties also will lose credibility. Mediation training must be comprehensive and include techniques that show a mediator where personal bias may lie and how to create a mediation that is bias-free.[72]

Subject matter expertise is very important to the attorneys who represent the parties in a mediation. Lawyers who are known in the community of medical malpractice litigation will be the most credible mediators. Litigators in this field are usually identified as either a plaintiff specialist or a defendant specialist. If two mediators, one of each specialty, serve together, the process may have more credibility to the parties and the advocates.

5. Finalize an agreement. An agreement to settle the case should be memorialized as soon as possible, preferably when the parties are present. Ideally, the agreement should be placed on the record in the courtroom as soon as it is mutually decided. If this is not possible, the mediator should create a settlement agreement that will record the result of the mediation.

Conclusion

It should be of great concern to both the professions of law and medicine that there is a large client population whose grievances are not being addressed. That it can negligently injure people with impunity reflects badly on the medical profession. This causes physicians to lose respect in the community. The same is true of lawyers. The public trusts us to champion their causes and to correct personal injustice. We cannot accomplish our responsibility under the present system. It also should be of great concern to both professions that we are losing respect for each other through our adversarial system of justice. Mediation is a solution that does not strike back. Mediation is a middle ground between patients suing their doctors and patients being discouraged from suing. The goal

---

[71] Leonard Riskin and James Westbrook, Dispute Resolution and Lawyers (West Publishing Company, 1987) p. 58.

[72] Meili, *supra*, note 70, at 9.

should be to resolve these disputes and still protect the rights of the individuals involved.

The judicial system should remain involved in the process. It has a highly developed system with safeguards against injustice and must remain available to parties who want it or need it.

Lawyers must form the core of the process. They are central to the litigation of medical negligence and they will be central to the success of mediation. It is a specialized area of law that requires a mediator with subject matter expertise in medical and legal issues. Medical negligence litigators, as mediators, will lend credibility to a process that has very little credibility now. While guiding clients through mediation, lawyers can protect client rights and interests so that their hope for justice is not sacrificed.

VI. Mediation in School Settings

Conflict Resolution in America's Schools—Defusing an Approaching Crisis

by Kay O. Wilburn & May Lynn Bates[*]

This country is currently experiencing a "violence epidemic," say the authors, particularly among young people. Left unchecked, this wave of aggression could lead to disastrous consequences when these adolescents become adults. A potential solution with a proven success rate is mediation at the elementary, middle and high schools levels. Peer mediation programs enable disputants to vent frustration or anger in a controlled setting and "concentrate on identifying the problem instead of establishing blame or seeking revenge," and formulate their own solution to the conflict.

Innumerable statistics pronounce this country is suffering a violence epidemic. Too often, the violence is being committed by children against children. According to the National Center for Health Statistics, shootings represent a leading cause of death for children under nineteen. James A. Fox, dean of the College of Criminal Justice at Northeastern University, states that murders committed by adolescents aged fourteen to seventeen have increased by 165% in the past decade and that the number will continue to rise dramatically as children grow into their teens. Fox predicts that unless measures are taken now, this country will experience a "blood bath in ten years when all these kids grow up."[1]

---

[*] Ms. Wilburn is adjunct professor of business law at the University of Alabama at Birmingham (UAB). She has served as past vice-chairperson of the Alabama State Bar Committee on Alternative Methods of Dispute Resolution and past chairperson of the ADR Task Force subcommittee on Mediation Model. She is an AAA-trained mediator and has been appointed to the Violence Prevention Consortium of the Alabama Center for Law and Civic Education. She initiated a conflict resolution pilot program for urban primary and secondary schools in collaboration with UAB's School of Education.

Ms. Bates is chairperson of the Alabama Center for Dispute Resolution and is an attorney in private practice in Birmingham, Alabama. She previously served as assistant general counsel of Sonat Inc. and as vice president of Sonat Mobile Bay Inc. She has been trained as a mediator by the AAA and was instrumental in developing a conflict resolution pilot program for urban primary and secondary schools in collaboration with UAB's School of Education. In addition, she has been a peer mediator trainer in various K-12 schools.

The authors are members of the UAB Violence Prevention Grant Steering Committee.

[1] The Birmingham News, February 19, 1995.

While the problem seems overwhelming at times, many communities are beginning to take proactive approaches to deal with the crisis, including the initiation of conflict resolution programs in kindergarten, middle and high school (K-12) classes. These programs often are not originated by the school board or administrators; rather, various community segments are stepping in to encourage the implementation of K-12 conflict resolution training. The programs are producing benefits in the schools and the communities. Attorneys trained in alternative dispute resolution can, by forming partnerships with their communities, provide invaluable support for programs that can make significant inroads against the rise in violence by and against America's children. Further, the tools given to adolescents to handle conflicts during their school years will be carried into their adult lives to handle disputes on the job and in their neighborhoods. As a result, the current generation of children as they mature into adults may be more likely to employ ADR measures rather than to rely exclusively on the court system to resolve all their disputes. Accordingly, attorneys can help accomplish these concomitant goals by their involvement in K-12 conflict resolution programs.

Peer Mediation in the Classroom

The process of peer mediation used in K-12 schools is similar to that used in mediating a legal dispute in that it involves third-party neutrals—mediators—to assist the students in resolving their dispute. The mediators do not issue a decision as to how the students should handle the problem, they guide the students in exploring solutions to resolve the dispute. Since students typically serve as the mediators for K-12 disputes, two mediators are typically recommended for each session so that no one student will shoulder the full responsibility of moving the process along. Furthermore, if any serious problem were to arise during the mediation session, one student could go for assistance while the other would remain to keep control. Also, in the relatively small world of a school, one mediator who will be perceived as neutral by both parties may be hard to find, but two mediators with opposing perceived biases may together form a neutral team. While an adult is not present at the mediation, one must be accessible during the session. Using students as mediators brings other students to the table who might not otherwise discuss the particular problem with a teacher or administrator.

As in the legal arena, submission to the peer mediation process should be voluntary. When a dispute arises, the teacher or principal can give the students the option either to use mediation or be subject to the decision of the intervening adult. The latter course could include disciplinary measures. Most students will prefer the mediation option. Peer mediation is appropriate for most types of disputes except those involving weapons, drugs or physical or sexual abuse. While many school systems permit mediation of disputes where fighting occurred, some do not. Each school must establish its own policy about what disputes can be mediated.

To begin the mediation, the mediator introduces the disputants and describes the process.[2] The peer mediators also explain the rules that each participant must agree to follow in order to use the process. Common rules for mediation (depending upon the curricula adopted) include: (l) maintain confidentiality of what is stated during the session; (2) show willingness to resolve the dispute; (3) show respect to the other participants; and (4) promise compliance with the agreement reached during the mediation session. The mediators do not take sides but must ensure that the rules are followed and that one disputant does not take unfair advantage of another. The disputants are typically seated across from each other (to avoid contact), and the two mediators usually sit at opposite ends of the table.

After the process is explained, the peer mediators allow each disputant to "tell his/her story" in an uninterrupted manner. The mediators ask about each disputant's feelings to allow the parties to vent frustration or anger in the controlled setting. As the accounts are told, the mediators attempt to identify the problem and the real interests of the disputants. Peer mediators are trained to practice effective listening skills and to paraphrase each disputant's account to obtain a better understanding of the disputant's concerns. The mediators guide the parties to concentrate on identifying the problem instead of establishing blame or seeking revenge.

Once the problem is identified, the disputants are asked to "brainstorm" for all possible options to resolve the conflict. The parties are limited only by their imagination and creativity in devising possible solutions to the problem. Implementation, of course, will depend on school rules. The mediator lists each proposed option, withholding judgment until all options are given. If the parties initially find it difficult

---

[2] The typical process described in this article is more fully described in most existing curricula on K- 12 conflict resolution. The UAB Pilot Program (referenced in this article) utilized materials created by Peace Education Foundation, Inc. for its initial training session for participating teachers and administrators; thus, the process described herein primarily reflects the Peace Education Foundation, Inc. curricula.

to create options, the mediator can assist in the brainstorming process but the mediator does not impose a solution on the parties. The disputants, in analyzing each option, discuss their feelings and concerns. Based on the discussions, the mediators assist the disputants in devising a mutually acceptable solution which then may be written down and signed by the disputants. Peer mediators are encouraged to have the participants discuss ways to avoid similar conflicts in the future. Finally, the mediators congratulate the disputants on resolving the conflict through mediation and encourage the disputants to tell others that the process was successful (while maintaining confidentiality as to what was said). Most schools provide mediator report forms to indicate whether the dispute was resolved through mediation.

Selection and Training of Mediators

Students selected as peer mediators in elementary school are usually in the fourth or fifth grade. They can serve as mediators for their peers and for the younger children in the school. Peer mediators in the middle and high schools can be from any grade, but selecting the older students lends credibility to the program as the older students can serve as role models for others. The counselors or teachers typically select the mediators based upon various criteria. The top academic students should not automatically be chosen. Many schools have discovered that the average student frequently "steps up" to the responsibility and gains more confidence and self-esteem as a result of being involved in the mediation program. In fact, some student mediators with a history of disciplinary problems have significantly improved their behavior after training in peer mediation. Most schools dismiss peer mediators if they are involved in fighting so the program provides an incentive to students to adopt non-aggressive ways to resolve conflicts.

Some of the criteria used in selecting mediators are:

- Ability to respect others and be neutral
- Ability to gain the trust and respect of the participants
- Ability to maintain self-control
- Ability to listen effectively and process nonverbal communications
- Ability to understand the real problems and issues

- Ability to communicate (frequently through paraphrasing) each disputant's concerns
- Ability to help create options
- Ability to guide the disputants to a successful resolution
- Ability to maintain confidentiality

While it is helpful if the students already have such skills, the students selected are trained in the peer mediation process before they provide any mediation services. Age-appropriate curricula have been developed by various organizations (see the side bar), and many of these organizations also provide training programs in designated cities or where a trainer comes to the school. Most of the training programs involve a "train-to-train" format where the principal, a counselor and at least one lead teacher are trained in the principles of conflict resolution and peer mediation and this "team" goes back to the school and provides training (or support as in the case of principals) for other teachers and students.

Ultimately, all teachers and students should receive instruction. Conflict resolution techniques can easily be incorporated into most, if not all, subjects. For example, math teachers could require students to calculate how much the parties owe when a dispute arises after several families rent a condominium together for a summer; history teachers could have students mediate historical disputes or current disputes between countries; English teachers could have the students write essays on conflict resolution. The drama department of the Alabama School of Fine Arts, with the assistance of a local attorney trained in mediation, instructed its students in the principles of conflict resolution and peer mediation in preparing for a collaborative drama project requiring an unusual degree of cooperation among competing talents and interests. The instruction has proved useful to student stage managers and to the entire drama company. When the play was not "coming together," the students initiated problem-solving sessions to focus on the conflicts and brainstormed for solutions utilizing the peer mediation skills they had learned.

Community Role

Lawyers and business professionals familiar with mediation and its advantages in the legal setting should recognize the benefits that peer mediation and conflict resolution training can produce in schools and, in turn, support the development of these programs. For example, Ben and Jerry's Ice Cream business, in conjunction with the Resolving Conflict Creatively Program (RCCP) in Cambridge, Massachusetts, awarded each participating student a free ice cream cone for essays about an act of peace they initiated or witnessed. Massachusetts Attorney General Scott Harshbarger won the 1994 Innovation in State Government Award for his commitment to conflict resolution/mediation programs in the state's schools.[3] The Ohio Commission on Dispute Resolution and Conflict Management coordinates the implementation of various forms of alternative dispute resolution in the state, including school peer mediation programs and community education programs. The New Mexico Center for Dispute Resolution initiated a school mediation program which requires the parents of the disputants also to be involved in the problem-solving session when their teen-agers have been in serious fights. One principal is quoted as stating that the program was "without a doubt the most effective conflict resolution process that has ever been implemented at this site."[4]

Judges, too, can offer significant credibility to peer mediation programs. For example, as a result of the encouragement of a state judge and several attorneys from the Alabama State Bar's Alternative Dispute Resolution Committee, one high school in Montgomery, Alabama, initiated a "drop everything for peace" program which involved an extensive two-day training in conflict resolution and peer mediation for every student in the school. The Alabama State Bar Center for Dispute Resolution, assisting with the implementation of the program, provided the facilities for the earlier teacher training.

Attorneys can bring the business, legal and academic sectors together to promote K-12 mediation programs on a local basis. For instance, the authors initiated a peer mediation pilot program involving urban schools with the School of Education of the University of Alabama at Birmingham (UAB) and obtained initial "seed" funding from the business and legal community. The School of Education will compile data on the effectiveness of the program and will seek additional funding through grants for the expansion of the program. In connection with the pilot, members of the Birmingham Bar Association's Community Education Committee and other local attorneys trained in mediation recently provided a five-day (two hours per day) training program for

---

[3] NIDR News, November/December 1994, at 6.

[4] *Id.*

fifteen fifth grade students at North Birmingham Elementary School. The training was so well-received by the school that the committee anticipates similar requests for assistance from other schools in the area. Responsibilities for the training were divided among the attorneys so that no one attorney had to attend more than a session or two, but some did anyway! The clear consensus among the participating attorneys was that they received much more than they gave. The appreciation of the students in the forms of hugs and heartfelt "I'll miss you" remarks is a reward not easily attained within the confines of the typical law practice. As more attorneys begin to provide assistance to peer mediation programs, communities will benefit from the ripple effect of their efforts for years to come.

Conclusion

Initial research indicates that peer mediation programs are successful in reducing disciplinary problems and in improving overall school climate. One middle school, almost immediately after implementing conflict resolution programs initiated by the Ohio Commission on Dispute Resolution and Conflict Management, began to see suspensions (for fighting, unruliness and truancy) decline dramatically. A decrease in violence, physical fighting and other serious conflicts is commonly reported by schools. Just as encouraging, school administrators and teachers are reporting that the programs have had a general positive impact on adolescents by improving their attitudes, behavior and even grades. Teachers are afforded more time to teach instead of having to handle disruptive conduct such as name calling, intimidation and threats.

Mediation can resolve conflicts without further exacerbating the tensions among disputants. The process affords the disputants an opportunity to fashion a more workable and satisfactory solution to the conflict than the typical alternative of suspension or even detention. Peer mediation programs are needed for all schools as today's children grow up in a society which glamorizes violence and aggression. The programs have been utilized successfully in suburban communities, inner-city schools and even in gang prevention and intervention programs. Teaching non-violent ways to deal with conflict is a priority that must not be ignored by parents, schools and community leaders.

Organizations Providing School Dispute Resolution and Mediation Curriculum

NAME (National Association for Mediation in Education)
205 Hampshire House
Box 33635 University of Massachusetts
Amherst, MA 01003 -4802

Peace Education Foundatio, Inc.
2627 Biscayne Blvd.
Miami, Fl. 33137-4532

National Institute for Citizen Education in the Law
711 G Street SE
Washington, DC 20003

National Crisis Prevention Institute, Inc.
3315 -K N. 124th St.
Brookfield, WI 35005

Educators for Social Responsibility
23 Garden Street
Cambridge, MA 02138

Children's Creative Response to Conflict
Box 271
523 N. Broadway
Nyack, NY 10960

Johnson Institute
7205 Ohms Lane
Minneapolis, MN 55439

New Mexico Center for Dispute Resolution
620 Roma NW, Suite B
Albuquerque, NM 87102

Illinois Institute for Dispute Resolution
110 West Main Street
Urbana, Il 61801

VII. Family Business Mediation

Business Mediation: All in the Family

by Lawrence I. Drath[*]

As a practicing mediator, the author has seen first-hand the benefits of employing the process to "prevent all-out war" between disputants and to "[preserve] the equity of a viable enterprise." This article recounts one such experience in which mediation successfully resolved a potentially devastating commercial dispute between the children of a trio of hotel owners on the verge of retirement.

The three patriarchs of the Benson, Miller and Reisler families had jointly developed, nurtured and supported a successful group of hospitality properties. Their portfolio consists of fifteen hotels and four restaurants located along the eastern seaboard. They pooled capital, know-how and guts and in 1965 acquired two Holiday Inns located in Virginia. More recently they were considering entering into an areawide franchise for a new budget concept. During their thirty years in business they delegated among themselves responsibility for operations, finance, purchasing, maintenance, administration and particular locations. From time to time, changes of responsibility were implemented without resentment or rancor.

Each patriarch had three children who were invited to and accepted positions in the business. As each "junior" came on board they were introduced to the operations and, by design or chance, were assigned responsibilities for specific geographical areas. As the juniors reached their late twenty and early thirties, certain resentments arose. Some didn't want to travel monthly to their assigned properties. A few didn't want the company to enter into an area franchise for a new budget concept and instead argued for the purchase of a luxury hotel. Others felt that they were making a greater contribution in sales, operations or financing than others and were therefore entitled to a greater slice of the

* The author is a partner in the law firm of Holm & Drath in New York City. He has lectured at seminars and conferences dealing with management and joint venture relationships, has been an adjunct professor at New York University's Hotel and Restaurant Administration Program and is an arbitrator on numerous panels at the American Arbitration Association. The names of the parties mentioned in this article have been changed in the interest of confidentiality.

pie. Arguments over who was, or was not, carrying his or her own weight or was "getting in the way" of the others became frequent. It got to the point that business issues were determined along family lines.

The patriarchs tried unsuccessfully to respond to the resentments and concerns. Meetings resulted in heated diatribes and shouting matches. While the silent treatment became the main weapon during office hours, employees could not avoid getting caught in the crossfire of countermanded instructions.

I had recently spoken at a hotel seminar attended by two of the fathers. During the course of my discussion I had mentioned the success I had achieved resolving a disagreement between a hotel owner and its management company through the use of the mediation process. Later, the patriarchs asked me to consult with them for what they described as their sorry state of affairs.

As a practicing attorney my traditional reaction to such a narrative of the facts would have been, in the past, to offer to represent one family and attempt to achieve a "winning" outcome for them. However having experienced enough battles and witnessed the damage that most often results from traditional posturing and antagonistic confrontations in business relationships, I have enthusiastically become an advocate of alternative dispute resolution as a means of preventing all-out war and preserving the equity of a viable enterprise. Clearly, this family situation cried out for such relief.

Moving Toward Mediation

I met with the fathers on a number of occasions during which they briefed me about the evolution of the business, peculiarities of each property, specifics about geographic areas and local conditions. They shared with me the relative strength of the staffs and how they saw the personality clashes. I had just facilitated a resolution of a commercial dispute with which they were familiar and they were hopeful that I could suggest a method to resolve this dispute so that each of them could retire with a feeling of closure as to the continuity of the enterprise.

I proposed to the fathers that we send a letter to the nine children suggesting a new format to attempt to resolve their business differences. The letter introduced the children to the basic concepts and goals of mediation, including a clear message that the parties, not the mediator, formulate the agreement and that the focus would be on their specific interests and needs rather than legal principles. Unlike arbitration, mediation is a compromise procedure and is non-binding until the agreement is executed by all parties. I also emphasized the benefits of alternative dispute resolution: economy, speed, confidentiality and control. We wanted to assure each child that they held a veto as to the outcome, since I had the feeling that such assurance would be essential here. Finally, they were asked to commit to the following:

- Each would stick with the process as long as the mediator believed that it was worthwhile.
- Each would conduct themselves in good faith.
- Each would respect the confidentiality of the proceeding. The letter provided them with details of my professional background as it related to commercial transactions and alternative dispute resolution proceedings in order to gain their confidence and allay any concern as to impartiality. Ultimately, they all agreed to participate in the process.

Mediation Strategy

While an initial joint meeting is often preferable in the mediation process, I chose to meet with each group separately in order to evaluate whether the greater need was to assist in the process of communicating and issue defining or in formulating substantive concepts for the terms of a deal. Often the mediator's greatest worth is to unblock the process and allow the parties, who are already familiar with the business, to decide the issues.

I began by asking them if they thought the business could be divided into three independent businesses. If so, three separate packages of properties (including the new area franchise under consideration) would be developed. They were also asked to rank their preference by areas, to describe the extent to which they would need the cooperation of the other two groups to accomplish this process and what restrictions against competition would be necessary or desirable. I also wanted to know how they perceived and reacted to the grievances of the other groups. Finally, I asked them whether they would choose to keep the business intact as one unit (notwithstanding the current levels of antagonism), rather than work out a separation with the inherent financial risks of spinoffs. There was unanimity for a breakup. Their answers enabled me to evaluate a number of substantive and relationship issues, the relative strengths and weaknesses of each group, and where the blockages existed.

To get the ball rolling we needed to focus on:

- The parties' lack of ability to "listen" to each other (this can be overcome through the use of a mediator).
- Their mutual respect for all of the "patriarchs" (to be used as a "melding agent").
- Their resentment that some work harder than others (no longer an issue after separation).
- Sibling-like rivalries that evoke a "we against them" or clan behavior (to be recognized as a cause and then mutually discarded).

In due course, I would apply various concepts to overcome these barriers.

I reviewed the written responses, and with the assistance of the patriarchs as well as the accountant, began to assign values or points to such assets as preferable geographic areas, condition of each property and equipment, comparable profitability of each operation, book values and mortgage debt.

The next step was another series of individual group meetings to discuss what they would "pay" to purchase the segment of the business they indicated as their first choice. I obtained authority from them to allow me to show the other groups the various "purchase prices" without identifying the bidder. This allowed each group to "throw darts" at other proposals without a hostile response. It also allowed me a chance to question some of their exaggerated notions of any aspect of the business.

Two of the groups were primarily interested in the same package, so I asked each of those what they would "pay" to purchase their second choice if the first one couldn't be delivered. Their responses were encouraging since there seemed to be a consensus as to the values of particular assets, the relative degree of competition, and the potential for growth in a particular market area. The result was the production of three "packages" of assets and businesses, not currently identified with any branch of the families. I asked each group to indicate whether they thought the packages were materially different.

It was now time to hold joint meetings to refine each "package," agree on dollar adjustments, time periods for payments, and terms of restrictive covenants against competition. The parties subsequently agreed that each group's selection of one of the packages would be made by picking lots out of a hat.

With the assistance of their counsel, an agreement was drafted and 90 days from the time we first met, the deal was done.

Why Mediation Worked

Most family business relationships are not formed by consensual negotiations. The parties are appointed successors in interest to the originators of the business or have been encouraged to take a position by family members. Under such circumstances parties are often hesitant to openly question business decisions. A disagreement over the purchase of a truck can culminate in a battle along family lines, while a critical comment concerning a sales approach may be squelched in order not to embarrass a cousin.

It was quite clear to me that this particular family business dispute was the result of years of hostility and lack of communication which raised barriers to a dialogue about their interests, needs and concerns for the business.

In this case the disputants were hesitant to disclose their ultimate interest and instead employed various positional bargaining devices, attempting to arrive at a "win-win result." This attitude usually leads directly to adversarial processes in the courtroom where rules and customs allow and encourage the parties to exercise combative techniques (even though 95% of those who take a dispute to trial leave the courthouse disappointed). The object of mediation is an agreement by parties resulting from "interest-based" bargaining. Mediation tends to focus on the "interest" and how to satisfy the perceived rights of the parties. The goal is to get the parties to agree and, unlike arbitration, not to impose the mediator's standard of fairness.

By highlighting each party's exaggerated claims, mediation provides feedback which is not tainted with emotions or history. Since the mediator is not empowered to render a decision, the parties can openly disclose facts that they would otherwise conceal from a decision-maker. Yet, mediation allows the parties to uncover underlying interests that may shape resolutions far broader than those available in an adversarial win-lose process.

In this case study, each group needed to cooperate with the others to maximize the value of the assets created before the separation. For example, the people who now oversee the North Carolina properties would be at a loss if not for an open line with those who had previously been responsible for that area. This cooperation would not have happened had they been forced to litigate their dispute in an adversarial form.

Parties often remain locked in positional bargaining merely because they are not aware of the alternative means available. Hopefully, more and more decision-makers will turn to the mediation process as a means of settling their grievances.

One year later each of the separate businesses is functioning with some success and growing pains, while the patriarchs remain in happy retirement.

CHAPTER NINE

MEDIATION AND THE LEGAL SYSTEM

I. Is Mediation Constitutional?

Mediation and the Constitution

by Jay W. Stein[*]

The inspiration for this paper was a conversation between the author and consumer advocate Ralph Nader at a legislative committee meeting on tort reform. Nader's comments to the assembled lawmakers and other citizens left some of them thinking that he believed one may question the constitutionality of mediation.

"***Supreme Court to Rule on Constitutionality of Mediation.***" That was the news headline my fantasy raised after a conversation with Ralph Nader. The noted trial lawyer and consumer advocate had appeared at a state legislative hearing on a tort reform bill. He criticized several items, including proposed ceilings on the dollar amount which courts could order a defendant to pay in a case of personal injury or other wrongful act. One of Nader's remarks led several members of his audience to believe that he had serious reservations about the propriety of mediating disputes and perhaps about other alternative dispute resolution (ADR) procedures. Afterward I asked him whether he opposed or favored mediation. His immediate answer: "I can accept it, but not if it is unconstitutional."

In studying and discussing mediation and ADR for many years, I had never considered a constitutionality question. Nor have I encountered colleagues who gave it any thought. Mediation is part of a growing movement in many states. The federal government has long utilized it in

---

[*] The author is a principal of Research and Resolution (Mediation, Research, and Education), in Columbus, Ohio. He has a Ph.D. from Columbia University's Department of Public Law and Government, along with other graduate degrees. His university teaching and administrative posts included dispute resolution. Mr. Stein is the author of THE HOBGOBLIN DOCTRINE IN LAW, LIFE, AND WAR: CONSISTENCY AND INCONSISTENCY, WISE AND FOOLISH (Resolution Press, 2002).

its labor relations and personnel (human resources) departments. Mediators, whether or not they have taken law school courses, accept the constitutionality of the process. How or why would anyone seriously raise the question?

As a first approach toward an answer, one may note the historical and textual interest of constitutional fundamentalists or literalists.[1] They promote an "originalism" position which seeks to discover the timeless and permanent truths of constitutional content and to determine the one true meaning of each provision. Impliedly, then, through historical study and textual analysis, a judge who exercises discretion in formulating an opinion or judgment may regard it as a determinate answer for any question of constitutionality.

An opposing controversial picture in the American constitutional discourse is the modernist idea of a "living constitution" that means its adaptation to the various crises in societal development. The nature of the Constitution is one of constantly changing meaning.[2] Its very history is one of change, as with any other developing organism. This view challenges the aspects of legal method that for some once purported to endow law with a permanent quality of objectivity. Meanings of the words, philosophical interpretations, and the sociology of knowledge enter in with a host of flexibilities which support and rationalize change.

Along either path, permanent or changing, one may argue that mediation justifies itself as constitutional. If mediation is regarded as part of a trend (change) toward modernism, it marches alongside the arts, sciences, and religion as they respond when inventions and innovations overwhelm them, and social pressures raise new expectations from their cutting edges. Mediation is respectable also in practice because it responds to a societal need when the courts are overloaded or when they encounter individual and public disenchantment.

In the instance of court overload, the courts must face long delays in distributing justice, sometimes to the extent of depriving citizens of judicial services for an indefinite period. Another reason for court inadequacy may be budget downsizing in the justice system much as downsizing occurs in many government offices and in commercial ventures. A judge would seem to have no recourse but to order, or at least encourage, parties in appropriate conflict situations to resort to

---

[1] Morton J. Horwitz, *The Constitution of Change: Legal Fundamentality Without Fundamentalism,* 107 HARV. L. REV. 44 (1993-94).

[2] *Id.* at 67.

alternatives. Constitutional or not, court resort to mediation becomes a pragmatic necessity.

In the instance where increasing numbers of citizens are criticizing the justice system, and are suspecting less than competence or even honesty among attorneys and judges, they may seek alternative avenues in times of conflict. Many persons also find that courts do not give them resolutions in their best interests. Even where money awards may be potentially large, the real desires may be for the preservation of relationships or other satisfactions destroyed in litigation. For many persons the uncertainty of what a judge or jury will decide and the long delays and bureaucratic maze of litigation turns them against attorneys and the courts. Society finds the courts wanting in expeditious attention to the real basis of a petition or claim.

The criticism, uncertainty, and dissatisfaction regarding the courts may be linked to a changing socio-economic milieu, one that is far different from that of the founders of the new republic in a transition from Colonial America. Contemporary influences on court actions range from technology in its broad scope, to the information explosion, to its availability to increasing numbers of citizens, to the individual expressions of freedom which stretch the First Amendment, to thousands of new laws and regulations every year. The result is crises and conflicts in variety and volume unimagined in 1787. The established institution for hearing and resolving them is the justice system. Its engine is the legal profession solidly entrenched in traditions of pretrial and trial, discovery, evidence, precedent, judgment, and appeal.

It is out of crisis circumstances that serious commentary or discussion about the constitutionality of mediation might suggest itself. A widely recognized example is the medical profession in situations involving the high cost of insurance. In medical malpractice cases, attorneys have often succeeded in winning a battle for inordinately large money awards for their injured clients. When the defendant insurance company loses the litigation, it responds with higher premiums, sometimes to prohibitive heights, and with preclusion of some insurance applicants.

Malpractice claims against physicians and hospitals brought to a crisis level the widespread dissatisfaction with litigation. The promise of large awards motivated many persons to hire attorneys to seek the maximum possible awards, often regardless of consequences. Medical insurers of the defendants had to raise premiums to meet the costs of soaring money judgments that were sometimes so high that heavy losses and even bankruptcy were the result. Facing payment of huge claims, the insurance industry asserted: "Our highly litigious culture has finally produced a group of attorneys who make their living filing the largest kind of lawsuit imaginable, ...making careers of targeting the deep pockets available: the insurance industry."[3]

The mass media communicating to the millions fan the flames of the crises by publicity in the news and on talk shows concerning outlandish sums in settlement for claims. In effect they play a role in the resolution of disputes not only through litigation but also through alternatives. It is a role which media representatives themselves decry.[4] The media impact is tantamount to a fourth "branch" of government,[5] although the word "branch" is not in the Constitution. One scholar reviewed the authority of the judiciary's interpretation of the Constitution. He asks: "Whose Constitution is it anyway?"[6]

Not only the losing party, but also physicians, employers, employees, the courts, and the general public suffer when the judiciary under media influence loses temperance. The crises grow as the court-honored procedures allow for drawing out a case to indefinite, and seemingly interminable lengths of time, with accompanying mounting costs and invasion of individual lives. Courts also then accommodate increasing numbers of litigants. At all levels, some courts near the verge of becoming incapable of fulfilling their purpose. One study predicts that by the year 2020 one million cases will be filed annually, compared to 281,740 filed in 1994.[7]

Docket overload grew increasingly critical as more and longer case law ensued. Legislative bodies became vulnerable to pressures for new laws and regulations.[8] They encouraged standards to enable courts to order disputing parties to participate in a mediation hearing whereat the parties would arrive at their own settlement voluntarily.[9] Laws and

---

[3] Bill Coffin, *Elephant Hunt: Big-Game Attorneys Target Insurers*, BEST'S REV., V. 97 (Mar. 1997), p. 43.

[4] George Freeman, *The Media Shouldn't Arbitrate Disputes*, L. A. DAILY J., V. 4 (June 10, 1988).

[5] Jay W. Stein, *The Fourth Branch of Government*, 117 USA TODAY, p. 26.

[6] Gary Apfel, *Whose Constitution Is It Anyway; The Authority of the Judiciary's Interpretation of the Constitution.* 46 RUTGERS L. REV. 771 (Winter 1994).

[7] Randall Samborn, *Judges Foresee Federal Courts Caseload Crunch*, NAT'L L. J. (Jan. 9, 1995). p. A1.

[8] Michael H. Moore, *Constitutional Standards of Review for Medical Malpractice Panels*, OHIO STATE JOURNAL OF DISPUTE RESOLUTION 200-02 (1985).

[9] David S. Winston, *Participation Standards in Mandatory Mediation Statutes*. OHIO ST. J. ON DISP. RESOL., V. 11 (1996), p.189.

regulations in some jurisdictions now mandate mediation and list standards for participation.[10] They determine that the public has a strong interest in a means for encouraging and facilitating the settlement of claims in a reasonable time and at a predictable cost.

At the same time, nongovernmental entrepreneurs arose to offer mediation services. The acknowledgment of alternatives coincided with a national plea in the 1980s for legislative committees to recommend tort reform. With a cap on personal injury awards, a statute could stem a presumed underlying tide of "litigation explosion and colossal verdicts."[11] More and more disputants heard an encouraging call to consider mediation.

Mandatory Mediation

Where the legislation, rules, or judicial discretion provide that a court may mandate mediation, that is, require the parties to mediate, the critics' voices grow louder and call for a closer examination of its procedure. Ordering parties to undergo mediation, critics argue, is to destroy the generally underlying principle that each party voluntarily decides to mediate. The mandate deprives a party of his/her right freely to access the courts for a full menu of trial, discovery, judgment, and appeal. The assumption is that under a court order the parties are able to confront each other, with or without representation, and arrive at a resolution which satisfies them both.

The fear which brings trial attorneys to legislative hearings on strengthening mediation services is that established traditions and principles of justice are at stake. Their questions are penetrating. Are the underlying premises of a "litigation explosion" and "colossal verdicts" accurate? Have evidence and its examination no place in unlitigated settlement procedure? What of limits on the award in personal injury cases, which an insurance company should pay? Do not all of these questions at legislative hearings risk meddling with the constitutional rights of citizens?

During his 1996 election campaign for the presidency, Ralph Nader appeared on the television program "Democracy Now" over KPKF in Los Angeles. If not giving direct answers to these questions, he at least affirmed his concerns underlying mediation legislation and showed its

---

[10] *Id.*

[11] Larry S. Stewart, *The 'Tort Reform' Hoax: Will the Tort System Take the Fall for the Insurance Industry?* XXII TRIAL 91 (July 1986).

political nature. He held that consumers are losing power to negotiate and bargain, finding themselves stripped of their rights to go to court, as banks and insurance companies force them to accept alternative means of resolving their disputes.[12] He adds:

It's pretty simple. Most people will tell you that if they're ripped off, defrauded or injured by someone's negligence or worse, they should be able to go into court, get compensation, get refunds, get justice against the wrongdoers—against the manufacturers of defective products like automobiles, flammable fabrics, untested pharmaceuticals for side effects, asbestos, Dalkon Shield, Pinto fuel tank, you name it. And the insurance industry and its clients—the manufacturers and other companies—basically say, look, we don't want to fight this out in the courts of law before a civil jury and the judge; we want to grease legislation in Washington and state capitols and take away these rights, make it very difficult for people to get adequate damages, to introduce evidence in court, to get a competent lawyer. And this is what's called "tort reform." That is why we call it "tort deform."

In constitutional terms, what the critics with these concerns seem to suggest or imply are mainly due process (discovery, trial, and appeal) and its equal application for both parties. Thus it is appropriate to look at the Constitution itself.

In its Preamble, the Constitution lists its objectives: "to establish justice, insure domestic tranquility, and promote the general welfare." Thus at the very outset of any movement against mediation, would not its proponent need to demonstrate that mediation fails to meet these objectives? Would not the critic be implying that constitutionally legal justice, tranquility, and general welfare can exist only through a symbiosis between the judiciary and its established procedures of trial advocacy? Do they not ignore the fact that mediation services which try to avoid trial and which function outside the courts may be highly successful in assuring the Preamble's objectives? To the extent that mediation does succeed, as daily illustrations indicate, would not legislative (or judicial) restrictions of the process thus be questioning whether the very objectives may also be unconstitutional, an absurdity, indeed.

A lawyer critic may also raise the question of whether a legislature is not crossing the line separating it from the judiciary. Article III of the Constitution gives Congress the power to set up courts; it has power also

---

[12] Broadcast on KPFK FM 90.7, Los Angeles (Mar. 27, 1996).

to enact rules supplementing and extending those which the courts have developed. If a legislature in turn mandates compulsory mediation, it hardly violates any separation doctrine.

The amendments, especially the first ten under the rubric of a "Bill of Rights," offer the framework for enumerating just which ones might impinge on the process and purposes of mediation. Amendment I is most directly related. Congress shall not make a law abridging the right of parties (disputants) peaceably to assemble, or inhibiting their freedom of speech in doing so. The justice system, the legal profession, and society generally accord to this First Amendment a hallowed status. Its unequivocal declaration of freedoms to speak, write, and assemble would seem to preclude even the slightest suggestion that mediation, which at its core utilizes these freedoms, could be unconstitutional. Tied closely to the commercial world and its foundation in marketing for profits, today's Internet demands that the individual be sovereign, creating his or her own speech and associations, free of governmental oversight.[13]

While several of the other amendments are expressly, but not exclusively, in the domain of criminal law, their repetition of basic freedoms has values for the law generally. Amendment V emphatically precludes deprivation of life, liberty or property without due process of law. Amendment XIV extends the letter of Amendment V to laws enacted by the states. It reads: "...nor shall any state deprive any person to life, liberty, or property, without due process of the law, nor deny to any person within its jurisdiction the equal protection of the laws."

In Amendment VI, an accused enjoys the right to a speedy trial by an impartial jury, to be informed of the nature and cause of the accusation, to confront witnesses against him and obtain witnesses in his favor, and to have the assistance of counsel for his defense. These are basic attributes also of civil litigation. At the same time one must recognize that the right to a civil trial by jury depends on a legal construct called "Equity."

Amendment IX declares that the enumeration of these rights cannot be construed to deny or disparage others retained by the people. Amendment X declares that powers not prohibited by the federal constitution to the states are reserved to the states respectively, or to the people. As if in anticipation of these rights, the Declaration of Independence had asserted earlier that "life, liberty, and the pursuit of

[13] Robert H. Posch, *Keep Privacy Laws Out of Cyberspace II*, DIRECT MARKETING, V.59 (Jan. 1997), p. 58.

happiness" are "among" inalienable rights; the use of "among" implies that there may be others. It is no mental stretch to imply the right to mediation.

Conclusion

Mediation falls under the umbrella of ADR, which in some circles has taken on the quality of a buzz word. For many persons, its definition implies a rather recent, increasingly popular procedure characterized by an intention to be free of court control. In actuality, the roots of mediation are deep.

Several professions, such as social work and psychology, offered forms of mediation services long before courts began to refer parties to it, and long before professional mediators arose. Clergy and other religious personnel and psychologists have long brought disputants together to help explore and settle differences which divide them.[14] Historically, mediation has been used to resolve disputes throughout the world for centuries.

Numerous writings now describe how the process works and how almost any intelligent person can learn how to conduct mediation, regardless of training in any one professional field. The widespread ascribing of dispute resolution dominance to the legal profession has weakened. Such mediation precedents and accompaniments as negotiation are well-established among many professions and in many administrative agencies. It is widely taken for granted that alternative means of dispute resolution accord with the United States and state constitutions.

The profession of a mediator as such has arisen to meet the needs of parties who have found dispute resolution through the courts to be lengthy and costly, commercial and unpredictable, formal and indifferent. Many parties believe that the court system construes every need into monetary terms which are often far afield from the "life, liberty, and happiness" they pursue. Professional and lay persons alike experience the justice system as an atmosphere that is formal and hostile, indifferent and uncontrollable.

The concept and process of mediation and other ADR procedures favor a setting which is quite the opposite of formal and they follow procedures and set goals that are more amenable to the parties' needs and

---

[14] For English history of ADR, *see* Valerie A. Sanchez, *Towards a History of ADR...in Anglo-Saxon England and Today*, XI OHIO ST. J. OF DISP. RESOL. 1-40 (1996).

desires. The contemporary search for alternatives to the courts is a movement throughout society. Major rules and formalities of litigation, built up over generations, have been relaxed, including discovery, examination, and formal evidence. No longer is a judge or other outsider typically vital in deciding a dispute. No longer need the parties feel themselves imprisoned in an entrenched adversarial mode. For many persons a place for values other than monetary awards has assumed greater significance than before. For some time, the impartial third party involved in meeting party interests has not been judged primarily by having completed law school.

A weakening of an attorney's promise of high monetary reward as a "constitutional right" threatens to make his or her services much less in demand. The attorneys' precedents of case decisions and the judges' respecting and expanding the cited precedents become awkward, if not unmanageable. A cap on personal injury awards as sought by legislative committees for tort reform has impacted litigation.

Attorneys themselves are adding mediation to their services as they register for training courses available through bar associations and mushrooming mediation centers. They suddenly find their names listed in ADR directories, alongside the names of nonlawyers. Attorneys could realize another avenue for obtaining clients and a few shifted their businesses away from litigation. At the same time, many officers of the court could criticize some mediation training programs as lacking in standards. They might assert that in the absence of litigation protections and practices some basic constitutional rights of parties may well be in jeopardy. ADR authorities, however, are aware of this possible risk as they engage in vigorous efforts at production and revision of standards.

When parties choose mediation, they are exercising inalienable constitutional rights, mainly those in the Preamble and the First Amendment. Mediation can help disputants sharpen an issue, reduce misunderstandings, establish priorities, vent emotions, find points of agreement, and ultimately negotiate an agreement. In the broader perspective, it helps to facilitate the life, liberty and the pursuit of happiness promised in the Preamble.

If Nader and company argue that mediation may deprive the parties of constitutional rights to full discovery, evidence, and trial, it is appropriate to counterargue that mediation enhances the parties' constitutional rights to life, liberty, and the pursuit of happiness as the parties themselves envision them. If the mediation alternative helps them move in that direction, it is the very instrument of happiness. A more acceptable view for critics of mediation is a balance between the literally described entitlements allegedly or presumably compromised and the benefits of resolution alternatives.

The mediation process, conducted under conditions of privacy and confidentiality and as efficiently as the parties desire, may conceivably risk modification of a party's rights and privileges and recourse to full discovery information. Yet, one may note that this is also possible under litigation and that unbridled discovery can yield torrents of often useless information at great cost to the parties. With appropriate mediator guidance the parties must determine the trade-off value of diminished rights, privileges, and information opposite more expeditious settlement for both parties.

Most of all, while resort to mediation in some jurisdictions may be compulsory by a court order, constitutional rights still prevail. This is true so long as the mediation settlement itself leaves open the path to revision through further mediation or, if either party desires, through litigation. To the question of whether mediation reflects the originalist or the "living constitution" test of constitutionality, the answer lies in its passing both tests.

II. Enforcement of Mediation Agreements

Enforcing an Obligation to Mediate Or Negotiate

by James H. Carter[*]

Two-step dispute resolution is becoming more popular. Agreements providing for "step" ADR procedures typically include at least one nonbinding step, followed by a binding process to resolve the dispute if the nonbinding effort is unsuccessful. Thus, a modern "step" clause might provide for binding arbitration as the ultimate remedy but require prior good faith negotiation for a specified time period or formal mediation, or both. Such agreements show awareness of the fact that mediation, in particular, successfully resolves many disputes without need for further action; but a binding arbitration backstop may be useful to promote meaningful settlement negotiations.

But what happens if no settlement is reached during the first ADR step because one of the parties refuses to participate in a nonbinding process, or frustrates it? What if that party believes it would be futile to engage in contractually specified formal negotiation? Should those responsible for the binding step (i.e., arbitrators or a court) engage in "policing" the first step? Should they compel the reluctant party to negotiate or mediate?

If so, then what? Should they evaluate the conduct of the reluctant party in the negotiation or mediation, and if so, what remedy should they prescribe for bad conduct?

At least some U.S. courts are willing to undertake an evaluation of the quality of negotiation under the rubrics of "good faith" or "fair dealing." Although arbitrators also face the question of whether to engage in an evaluation of the parties' conduct in a failed prior proceeding, there is as yet little or no precedent to which we can look.

---

[*] The author is a partner at Sullivan & Cromwell in New York. He is a Chairman of the Executive Committee of the American Arbitration Association's Board of Directors and past Chair of the American Bar Association's Section on International Commercial Arbitration. He is also Vice President of the North American Council of the London Court of International Arbitration. Carter holds a B.A. from Yale University and a LL.B. from Yale Law School. This article is adapted from a paper presented at the International Federation of Commercial Arbitration Institutions.

Compelling Participation in Nonbinding Processes

Mediation. Court-annexed ADR programs often require parties to participate in mediation and other non-binding ADR proceedings.[1] For example, the Commercial Division of the New York Supreme Court in Manhattan established a court-annexed ADR program for commercial cases in 1995, under which the court may order the parties to participate in mediation. The parties are required to attend the mediation session together with their attorneys, and only parties who show good cause and have the permission of the mediator may be excused. Since its inception, the Commercial Division's ADR program reportedly has achieved a 59% settlement rate through mediation.[2]

When the agreement to mediate is contained in a contract, some U.S. courts have found that the Federal Arbitration Act empowers a court to order the parties to participate in mediation. Most recently, a federal court in New York entered an order compelling mediation of a dispute involving waste removal from commercial properties pursuant to a general contract clause in which mediation was agreed.[3] The court reasoned that FAA § 2, which makes the full body of U.S. arbitration law applicable to commercial contracts to "settle" disputes by arbitration, also includes contracts to "settle" disputes voluntarily by mediation.[4]

Negotiation. The situation with respect to enforcing a contractual agreement to negotiate is more complicated. In the absence of a contract, U.S. courts traditionally assume the parties have broad freedom with regard to their conduct during the precontractual, negotiation period. As Professor Allan Farnsworth, a leading contract-law scholar, has written: "As a general rule, a party to precontractual negotiations may break them off without liability at any time and for any reason...or for no reason at all. The only cost of doing so is the loss of that party's own investment in the negotiations in terms of time, effort and expense."[5]

---

[1] *See generally* Edward J. Bergman and John G. Bickerman, Court-Annexed Mediation: Critical Perspectives on Selected State and Federal Programs (Pike & Fischer 1998).

[2] Ann T. Pfau & Daniel M. Weitz, *Court-Annexed ADR on the Rise*, N.Y.L.J., Apr. 12, 1999, at 10.

[3] CB Richard Ellis, Inc. v. American Environmental Waste Management, 1998 WL 903495 (E.D.N.Y. 1998). *See also* AMF, Inc. v. Brunswick Corp., 621 F. Supp. 456 (S.D.N.Y. 1985).

[4] For criticism of that argument, *see* 10 W.A.M.R. 59 (No. 3) (March 1999).

[5] 1 FARNSWORTH ON CONTRACTS 346 (Aspen Law & Business, 2d ed. 1998). Courts nevertheless do impose precontractual liability for (a) unjust enrichment resulting from the negotiations; (b) a misrepresentation made during the negotiations; and (c) breach of a specific promise made during the negotiations. *Id.* at 349-61. They also impose liability for

But sometimes the courts hear requests to enforce a written agreement in which the parties purport to obligate themselves to undertake further negotiations. These commitments may be contained in a preliminary "letter of intent" or a "commitment letter," an agreement that usually contemplates a final, formal contract. Such a preliminary agreement also may be embedded in an initial contract as a clause providing for negotiation with respect to options for renewals or other related contracts. Because these agreements often contain "step" ADR clauses that include nonbinding and binding steps, arbitrators may face the problem of policing the conduct of the parties during the first ADR step.

Preliminary agreements are of two principal types, broadly described as nonbinding and binding. But both types create obligations. The former is an agreement to negotiate that requires good faith efforts[6] by the parties but does not obligate them to reach agreement on anything. The latter is an agreement that resolves essential terms but is preliminary either because the parties wish to complete a more formal document or because some open terms remain to be negotiated.

In the first type of preliminary agreement, parties may list specific substantive terms of the proposed deal but express an intention not yet to be bound to them; the terms are "settled only for purposes of negotiation."[7] In this situation, the parties are obligated to proceed in good faith with their negotiations (from which certain obligations and liabilities may flow), but with the knowledge that they will not be bound if they fail to reach ultimate agreement.

If the preliminary agreement is of the second type, some U.S. courts have held that the parties are obligated to go forward with a transaction in the framework of the agreed terms, even when they are unable to agree on the open terms.[8] Those terms will be supplied by a court if necessary. The second type of preliminary agreement also has been said to impose a general obligation of "fair dealing" in the negotiation of the open terms.[9]

---

breach of a specific agreement to negotiate in good faith, which is discussed below. *See also* STEVEN J. BURTON & ERIC G. ANDERSEN, CONTRACTUAL GOOD FAITH § 8.3 at 335-347 (Little Brown 1995).

[6] *See* Arcadian Phosphates, Inc. v. Arcadian Corp., 884 F.2d 69 (2d Cir. 1989); Channel Home Centers v. Grossman, 795 F.2d 291 (3rd Cir. 1986). *See* BURTON & ANDERSEN at 349-350.

[7] Burton & Andersen at 352.

[8] *E.g.* Borg-Warner Corp. v. Anchor Coupling Co., 756 N.E.2d 513 (1958).

[9] FARNSWORTH at 227. Professor Farnsworth prefers the term "fair dealing" to "good faith" because the latter term is used in the Uniform Commercial Code to denote "the sort of

Whether a preliminary agreement is binding or not depends on the parties' intent, which is ascertained primarily from the language of the agreement. However, American courts have varied widely in their reading of the language of such preliminary agreements. Indeed, Professor Farnsworth states that "it would be difficult to find a less predictable area of contract law."[10] And even if an agreement states clearly that the parties intend it to be binding, U.S. courts will not enforce it unless the contract is sufficiently definite to allow a court to supply any open terms on which the parties fail to agree. There must be a "fall-back standard" such as a market price or other reference point to which a court can direct its attention.

Preliminary agreements of the first type—i.e., contractual promises to negotiate in good faith but without even a preliminary commitment to be bound to specific material terms—are "nonbinding" yet carry some obligations. Courts have been of two minds about whether parties are free to impose upon themselves a binding obligation to negotiate that the courts should enforce. Courts that have refused to enforce such an obligation have given two reasons: (1) a court cannot determine the scope of the obligation of good faith under the agreement, and (2) a court may have difficulty in fashioning a proper remedy for bad faith conduct.[11]

Although some U.S. courts have refused to enforce such agreements, increasingly the trend has been to take the first enforcement step and order the parties to engage in negotiation. Courts that have done so may have assumed (perhaps naively) that compliance will not be difficult to police because "a general duty to negotiate simply requires that a party be seen to make some reasonable effort to reach agreement."[12]

Courts also will enforce exclusivity provisions in preliminary agreements of the first type, barring negotiations with third parties if contract terms so provide.[13] Arbitrators applying the same body of law and authorized to issue injunctive orders are likely to do so as well.

---

honesty that makes one a good faith purchaser," which is mostly inapplicable to the present context. Id. at 377.

[10] *Id.* at 231.

[11] *See* Ohio Calculating Corp. v. CPT Corp., 846 F.2d 497 (8th Cir. 1988), and Ridgeway Coal Co. v. FMC Corp., 616 F. Supp. 404 (S.D.W. Va. 1985), *cited in* FARNSWORTH at 372, n. 11.

[12] BURTON & ANDERSEN at 360. The authors note, however, that "[t]he better view is that a general duty to negotiate, without more, is too indefinite to be enforced."

[13] *See* VS&A Communications Partners v. Palmer Broadcasting Ltd., 1992 WL 339377 at *9 (Nov. 16, 1992)(Unpublished opinion); A/S Apothekernes Laboratorium v. I.M.C.

But enforcing an agreement to negotiate or mediate raises more difficult questions at the second step, when courts or arbitrators may be asked to police the results of the failed negotiation or mediation. The problems of the scope of that obligation and the remedy for breach deserve further consideration, particularly as regards the role of arbitrators in that effort.

Is it possible to define "good faith" and "fair dealing" in the context of negotiating an agreement or participating in a mediation, so that a party could be held responsible for violating these implied contractual duties if they frustrate the ADR proceedings? Of course, any contractual agreement can be invalidated when it has been induced by improper means, such as fraud or duress. But the question here concerns a failed negotiation or mediation, after which one party charges the other with using unfair means to obstruct an agreement.

Policing Party Conduct During Negotiations

In an attempt to organize U.S. precedents[14] in this field, Professor Farnsworth has identified seven different types of allegations of obstructive conduct that courts have treated or might consider unfair dealing during the negotiation process. One may wonder how well arbitrators could apply these criteria.

Refusal to Negotiate. What if a party simply refuses to participate in a negotiation that it had agreed to join? Or what if, as a device to mask an intention to refuse to participate, a party conditions its participation on terms that cannot reasonably be imposed on the other party? Some courts have held that conditioning participation in negotiations on concessions as to matters that are "arguably far removed and unrelated"[15] is unfair dealing. But how far removed or unrelated must the subject be? And

---

Group, Inc., 873 F.2d 155 (7th Cir. 1989), and other cases cited in BURTON & ANDERSON at 350, 351. ns. 8 & 11.

[14] FARNSWORTH at 380. *Compare* the UNIDROIT Principles of International Commercial Contracts, Art. 2.15 (Negotiations in bad faith):

(a) A party is free to negotiate and is not liable for failure to reach an agreement.

(b) However, a party who negotiates or breaks off negotiations in bad faith is liable for the losses caused to the other party.

(c) It is bad faith, in particular, for a party to enter into or continue negotiations when intending not to reach an agreement with the other party.

(d) Professor Farnsworth says European courts have been more willing than American courts to endorse scholarly theories supporting a general precontractual obligation of good faith. FARNSWORTH at 359.

[15] *A/S Apothekernes Laboratorium, supra,* n. 13, *cited in* FARNSWORTH at 382, n. 28.

should we assume that arbitrators would be able to recognize unreasonable conduct when they see it?

Improper Bargaining Tactics. Some U.S. cases have attempted to define when "hard bargaining" becomes "unfair." As Professor Farnsworth writes, "Courts have recognized the difference between justifiable tenacity intended to encourage concessions and unfair stubbornness as a pretext for avoiding any agreement at all."[16] Some courts have held that insisting on conditions beyond the scope of a preliminary agreement can become unfair dealing when it is a "pretext" for walking away from previously agreed terms due to an unfavorable change in market conditions or similar events.[17] But as in the case of defining what is a proper reason for refusing to negotiate at all, determining what is merely a "pretext" for walking out requires a close examination of the particular factual setting in which the bargaining occurred.

Unreasonable Proposals. Should a court or arbitrator sit in judgment on the substantive "reasonableness" of what a party tables as its position? At least one U.S. court has suggested that "injecting new demands, such as an increase in price, late in the negotiating process can constitute bad faith in some circumstances."[18] One might agree with this approach, but articulating a general principle to guide arbitrators in this area is not easy.

Nondisclosure. How far must negotiators go in disclosing their cards to each other? Wholly aside from deception, some U.S. courts have said that the failure to disclose facts on which a party's bargaining position is based may constitute bad faith or unfair dealing.[19]

Negotiation With Others. Suppose the ADR clause provides that one party will negotiate exclusively with the other for a fixed period of time. This is purely a procedural matter and thus seems relatively straightforward. As noted above, exclusive negotiation clauses in preliminary agreements now commonly are upheld.

Reneging. What if a party takes the position late in the negotiations that it will not abide by a term on which earlier agreement had been

---

[16] *Id.* at 384.

[17] *See* Teachers Ins. & Annuity Ass'n v. Ormesa Georthermal, 791 F. Supp. 401 (S.D.N.Y. 1991), and Ashland Management Inc. v. Janien, 624 N.E.2d 1007 (N.Y. 1993), *cited in* FARNSWORTH at 384, n. 37.

[18] Venture Assocs. Corp. v. Zena Data Sys. Corp., 987 F.2d 429, 433 (7th Cir. 1993). *See also* BURTON & ANDERSEN at 379-380 (parties may have limited their discretion to the range of "objective reasonableness").

[19] FARNSWORTH at 386-388 (citing cases under the National Labor Relations Act.)

reached, unless the other party makes a concession on a matter still to be negotiated? In the view of some courts and commentators,[20] this conduct also may show bad faith.

Breaking Off Negotiations. Suppose a party's patience becomes exhausted and it concludes that there is no chance that the negotiations will be successful, so it walks away from the table. Should a court or arbitrator second-guess whether impasse actually has been reached? Some courts have required that the party proceed "reasonably" in exhausting the negotiation process before walking away.[21] Indeed, Professor Farnsworth says it "seems reasonable" to expect the party who wishes to withdraw to inform the other party of relevant proposals from third persons so that any impasse would be based on a full evaluation of alternatives.[22]

Bad Mediation Conduct

There is little case law concerning liability for bad conduct during formal, voluntary mediation.[23] Courts may believe that conduct that might be subject to criticism and sanctions in a non-mediated negotiation should not be the basis for liability when mediation fails. This view may arise out of deference to the right of the mediator to control the mediation. It also may be the result of mediation rules that ordinarily limit a party's ability to reveal what happens in mediation to outsiders.

Indeed, an attempt by a court or an arbitrator to police and sanction bad conduct during a mediation may be contrary to the fundamental principle of confidentiality that ordinarily attaches to certain aspects of a mediation. Mediation-related confidentiality provisions have been

---

[20] American Seating Co. v. NLRB, 424 F.2d 106 (2d Cir 1970), and Teachers Ins. & Annuity Ass'n v. Tribune Co., 670 F. Supp. 491 (S.D.N.Y. 1987), *cited in* FARNSWORTH at 389-390, ns. 63 & 65. BURTON & ANDERSEN at 372, *discussing Arcadian Phosphates*, n. 6, supra.

[21] *See* Chevy Chase v. Consolidated Foods Corp., 744 F.2d 566 (7th Cir. 1984), *discussed in* FARNSWORTH at 393. *Compare* UNIDROIT Principles, Art. 215(3) (liability for breaking off negotiations in bad faith), *supra*, n. 14.

[22] Farnsworth at 393.

[23] This is not the case for violations of judicial mandatory mediation rules. These rules usually provide for sanctions in the case of violations by the parties or their attorneys. *For example*, *see* Few v. Hammack Enterprises, Inc., 511 S.E.2d 665 (N.C. Ct. App. 1999) (court allowed confidential evidence from a court-ordered mediation conference, including mediator testimony, to be admitted in a proceeding before the judge who was determining whether the parties had agreed to settle their dispute). State statutes also address this subject. *See generally*, D. Sharp. *The Many Faces of Mediation Confidentiality*, 53 DISPUTE RESOL. J. 56 (Nov. 1998).

enforced by a number of courts in the United States and abroad. In a recent Belgian case, one party unsuccessfully sought to raise the other party's conduct in a failed mediation as a basis for relief in a subsequent arbitration. The ADR clause stated:

> The parties shall loyally and in good faith participate in the mediation proceedings...Any position papers or proposals drawn up or exchanged in the course of the mediation process shall not be admissible as evidence in any legal proceedings...

The mediation occurred under the mediation rules of the Centre for Dispute Resolution, which make confidential "all statements and all other matters" produced in the mediation. These rules also provide that the mediation procedure is to be treated as privileged and that the mediation "shall be conducted on the same basis as without-prejudice negotiation in an action in the courts or similar proceedings." Faced with this language—which is typical of mediation rules—a Brussels juge des référés held that the provisions barred assertion of claims based on bad faith in the mediation.[24]

While confidentiality clauses and rules may not shield all mediation-related conduct from disclosure, they obviously make inquiry into bad faith acts in mediation highly problematic.

Potential Remedies

Cases and commentators agree that it is difficult to formulate a remedy for breach of an enforceable obligation to negotiate in good faith or to participate in mediation.[25] The straightforward sanction for failure to negotiate in good faith in most cases is an award of reliance damages, which conceivably would be the cost of preparing for and participating in the failed negotiation. A party's loss of some other commercial alternative that can be shown to have occurred as the result of participation in a frustrated negotiation also might constitute an element of damages in an appropriate case.[26]

The recovery of "expectation" damages, such as lost profits and the benefit of the bargain, is rare. Except in the unusual case of a preliminary agreement with open terms that can be related to objective external

---

[24] Ashanti Goldfields Co. Ltd. v. Mindev & Associes S.A., (R.K. 38/99, Feb. 5, 1999).
[25] *E.g.*, FARNSWORTH at 372-376.
[26] FARNSWORTH at 372-373. *See* UNIDROIT Principles, Art. 2.15, Cmt 2.

criteria, U.S. courts are reluctant to complete a bargain for the parties when they have failed to agree. They are also reluctant to award damages based on a prediction about how successful the hypothetical relationship would have been.[27]

Some Observations

Although the traditional reluctance of U.S. courts[28] to determine what it would have been reasonable for parties to do in their bargaining may be changing to some degree, arbitrators, in my view, should remain as conservative as courts traditionally have been. They should not be quick to consider themselves experts in the "proper" outcome of contract negotiations and should avoid engaging in "gap filling" unless the parties expressly authorize them to do so. Arbitrators may help parties maintain long-term relationships by serving on request to fill in missing terms in situations such as price renegotiations. However, they should not supply terms for an agreement that the parties have not made in the absence of strong evidence of an intent that the parties wished for them to do so, and without an appropriate external reference point.

The temptation to enter this area may be greater for an arbitrator than for a judge, since the arbitrator, who is likely to be a commercial lawyer or business executive, may know what he or she probably would have done in the circumstances. This is a temptation that should be resisted because that usually is not the only possible outcome of a two-sided negotiation. Unwarranted gap filling is a particular risk in an international case, in which part of the contract (such as a license agreement) might require future specific performance in a country with different cultural assumptions.[29]

In addition, there is a risk that pursuing the issue of bad negotiating conduct may distract the arbitrator from the substantive issues in a case. Bad faith conduct is not to be approved, but trying to determine what type of offer might be "reasonable" could be a poor use of the parties'

---

[27] *Accord*, UNIDROIT Principles, Art. 2.15, Cmt 2 (party "may generally not recover the profit that would have resulted"). *But see* FARNSWORTH at 374 and n. 19 (noting that some courts have indicated a willingness to consider awarding expectation damages).

[28] Courts in Australia and England also have addressed these issues. *E.g.*, Coal Cliff Collieries Pty. Ltd. v. Sijehama Pty. Ltd., [1991] 24 NSWLR 1; Walford v. Miles, [1992] 2 AC 128.

[29] *See generally*, Troy E. Elder, *The Case Against Arbitral Awards of Specific Performance in Transnational Commercial Disputes*, 13 ARB. INT'L 1, 32 (1997) (meaningful enforcement of an award of specific performance would effectively require conscripting foreign courts to supervise the implementation of an arbitrator's decree).

resources. It might also lead to criticism that commercial arbitration focuses too much on process and not enough on justice.

The distinction between negotiation and mediation should also be considered in determining whether courts and arbitrators should address, if at all, the issue of bad party conduct. Negotiations (other than settlement negotiations to resolve a lawsuit) normally occur without any expectation of confidentiality in the event of a dispute. Thus, negotiating conduct can be examined by a court or an arbitrator without the risk of invading a confidential process. Mediation stands in a different posture from ordinary commercial negotiations. Mediation is about potential settlement, and most mediation rules provide an expectation of confidentiality for bargaining that occurs within a mediation. Were this type of negotiating conduct to become subject to policing by courts or arbitrators, parties might be deterred from using mediation. As the law now stands, however, most mediation communications are protected from disclosure, so parties who wish to avoid having a court or arbitrator second-guess their choices would be well advised to include a mediation clause, rather than a negotiation clause, in their contract.

We should not overlook the fact that mediators are in a position to police a party's bad conduct through informal sanctions, such as moral condemnation. In view of the limited punishments usually available to courts or arbitrators policing failed negotiations, such sanctions may be appropriate to the offense.

Even if arbitrators do decide to evaluate party conduct during negotiations or mediation, I believe they should not award an expectation remedy. The wide range of transactions to which parties may agree in commercial transactions suggests that no one possesses special expertise in forecasting how a failed negotiation would have turned out if one party had not decided to abort the talks. Reliance damages typically will suffice.

Before taking any steps toward enforcing agreements to negotiate or mediate, arbitrators should examine closely the particular context in which courts have been willing to police the bad conduct of negotiating or mediating parties[30] and the limited remedies that are available.

---

[30] Some of the cases in which there has been identifiable unfair dealing during the negotiation process have involved administrative procedures and special circumstances, not general commercial transactions. For example, some decisions involve U.S. labor law. FARNSWORTH at 378-80. This body of law imposes statutory bargaining obligations on employers and unions who are in continuing, long-term relationships with one another. This relationship provides a context against which to judge various negotiating tactics. Cases

Arbitration will be best served if arbitrators avoid actions that would put them in the position of awarding remedies based on questionable "might-have-beens" or slapping the wrists of negotiators when there may be more important issues to resolve.

---

involving statutes that require good faith bargaining and empower decision makers expert in the subject to fill in terms when the parties are unable to do so also differ considerably from the customary contractual setting in which commercial parties ordinarily negotiate. *E.g.*, the U.S. Telecommunications Act of 1996, which obligates certain telephone companies to "negotiate in good faith" with other industry participants "the particular terms and conditions of agreements to fulfill the duties described" in the statute, including "rates, terms and conditions that are just, reasonable and nondiscriminatory." 47 U.S.C. 251(c). *See* AT&T Corp. v. Iowa Utilities Board, 119 S. Ct. 721 (U.S. 1999).

III. Using Mediation to Expose Fraudulent Claims

ADR and Suspected Fraudulent Claims

by Jeffrey Krivis[*]

Rather than tying up suspected fraud cases in the drawn-out, and often unprofitable process of litigation, the author recommends using mediation as a way to get to the heart of a case quickly and effectively. By allowing for strategic sharing of information and enabling disclosure of that information in a non-threatening environment, an investment in mediation may produce healthy rewards.

If you were a conservative investor who was looking for a modest return on your dollar, would you invest in unusual penny stocks with no track record? Of course not; the risk would be too great, though the reward, if one of the equities turned out to be the next Microsoft, could be tremendous. My sense is that most disputants are like investors; they are not looking to achieve fame and fortune in litigation, but are looking for conservative investments (risk) with reasonable returns (reward).

Recently, I had occasion to mediate a stream of disputes for a large department store, ranging from slip-and-fall to false imprisonment. Each case was unique in its own way. The one thread that seemed to run through the risk analysis of defense counsel, in which liability was seriously in question, was whether or not there were actual injuries, and if there were, were they related to the incident in question? I wondered why there was so much concern about each case. Was I so naive as to think everyone was being truthful? Then a pattern started to emerge that was striking. Many of the claimants either did not disclose to their lawyers previous injuries which were identical to those claimed, or the lawyers were not disclosing the injuries to the other side.

For example, consider the case of the woman who claimed that a clerk ran her over with a shopping cart. Though the clerk said the woman

[*] Jeffrey Krivis is a private mediator and arbitrator in Los Angeles and teaches mediation at Pepperdine Law School/Straus Institute for Dispute Resolution. He is also on the board of directors of the International Academy of Mediators. Krivis received degrees from San Diego State University and Southwestern University School of Law. He is the author of IMPROVISATIONAL NEGOTIATION: A MEDIATOR'S STORIES OF CONFLICT ABOUT LOVE, MONEY, ANGER... (Jossey-Bass, forthcoming 2005).

did not fall, was fine after the incident, and continued to shop, the woman claimed massive lower-back injuries that would necessitate surgery. Also, she claimed that during all the commotion, she lost her diamond wedding band worth approximately $12,000, which was just one of many red flags for the defense. The demand to settle was in excess of $250,000, with no offer presented by the defense. A huge amount of written discovery requests, depositions, and other related litigation tactics occurred—and then it was the eve of trial.

Unfortunately for the woman, she forgot to tell her lawyer that she had a 15-year history of ongoing back problems and was addicted to narcotics. As a drug addict, she needed money from this case to maintain her habit. This information was presented to me outside earshot of the plaintiff and her counsel. I urged the defense to disclose this information to plaintiff's counsel. Initially, they resisted, claiming that they would rather save it for trial unless the plaintiff would get realistic in this case. I advised the defense that without the tools to do a reality check, we had no chance at settlement. After some discussion, I was eventually permitted to share this information with plaintiff's counsel, who was stunned when he saw the medical records of his client for the first time. Needless to say, the case was resolved quickly.

How many lawyers have had similar promising damage cases turn into time-consuming, unprofitable pieces of litigation, only to find out late in the game that the defendant has hunkered down because of suspected fraud? Wouldn't it be nice to know early on in the case that the defendant has questions about the legitimacy of some aspect of the case, so that it can be properly evaluated?

Despite the obvious answers to these questions, many lawyers find themselves stuck, never knowing why certain cases are log-jammed in the system with no way out except through the litigation maze.

Drawing the lines in the sand are the defendants who naturally are concerned about paying a woman who loses her diamond wedding band in a fall; a medical facility that is on its "watch list"; a low-impact case with "excessive" medicals; examinations going far beyond the range of the injuries involved; questionable treatment cycles; and the like.

Strategy or habit often dictates that until the eve of trial, neither side will communicate to the other the real reasons the case is stuck. Not until the trial will the judge require that the parties discuss openly and candidly the various elements of the case.

The Dividends and Returns

An early investment in disclosure of information can provide dividends for counsel that will far exceed the returns from pursuing the standard path. Though I'm biased, I think using mediation to share that information is the safest avenue to get from point *A* to point *B*. The biggest dividend is that before a huge amount of financial resources is spent, the lines of communication will open so that informed decisions can be made about how to resolve cases. Consider the tangible opportunities available in mediating the suspected fraud claim for both plaintiff and defendant.

Mediation:

- provides a place for an early evaluation.
- allows for a strategic exchange of information.
- allows for dialogue in a "safe, non-threatening environment."
- requires complete confidentiality.
- enhances the probability of settlement.
- eliminates wasteful litigation—a great time-saver for counsel on both sides.

1. Early Evaluation

In the mediation which occurs early in a case, the mediator serves the function of an agent of reality. By listening closely to the evidence available, or not available, the mediator can explore the consequences to all parties if their positions are taken to court. The ability to observe the plaintiff and the insured, and review the facts of the case, may provide both sides with information that was desperately needed to put a reasonable proposal on the table.

In addition, the mediation setting provides each side with the chance to review:

- the demeanor of the other;
- the veracity of each other's story based on their own version;
- new documents not previously discussed in litigation, i.e., medical bills; and
- the veracity of counsel from his demeanor.

On the other hand, the evidence might also reveal facts about which counsel was not aware. Consider a typical personal injury case and the following might become known:

- previous injuries not disclosed to the doctor;
- violations of the chiropractic code;
- inconsistencies between medical bills and records; or
- unsubstantiated examinations/treatment.

Armed with this "new information," all parties are then able to more intelligently communicate, with the aid of the mediator, different ways to resolve the case.

By introducing the resources of a third-party neutral, the parties are afforded a rare opportunity to strategically manage the flow of information in a way that benefits their case. Faced with new information and the potential need to re-evaluate a case, mediation may be the most useful forum in which to explore methods of changing direction.

2. *Strategic Exchange of Information*

In managing the flow of information, the mediator capitalizes on the strengths and weaknesses of the parties by surveying information that each side thinks might make a difference in its case. The typical dilemma in a mediation of this kind is how much of the investigative efforts to allow the mediator to reveal to the other side. While insurers might be armed with information such as a witness statement, questions about the medical clinic, or even proof that the plaintiff wasn't at the accident scene, they may be reluctant to share it with the plaintiff for fear that if the case doesn't settle, they would lose the impact at trial or arbitration.

While the value of using the fruits of the investigative effort at trial are in theory very sensible, the necessary transaction costs and attorneys' fees to prove the case, as well as the reality that most cases don't get to trial, are rarely taken into account. The costs and fees to prove the case could be completely eliminated by offering to share the information during the mediation session. In so doing, the mediator can be the conduit for making the kind of recommendations about settlement or dismissal which the parties and counsel are prepared to accept. By strategically revealing information at certain stages in the mediation, the mediator can slowly assist in communicating each side's position in such a manner that protects each side in the event they decide to go to trial.

Each party maintains control of the flow of information and decides when to reveal evidence based on calculated decisions about the impact of the evidence, and how it might be received during the mediation. This is accomplished through close consultation with the mediator, who gauges the temperature of the parties and recommends the appropriate time to exchange or disclose critical information.

For example, if the defense has an undercover film showing the plaintiff in compromising activities that completely undermine the case, the defense would explore with the mediator the right moment to allow the plaintiff to know about this information. When the mediator senses that the information would have an impact on the evaluation of the case, and that resolution could be made possible by revealing the information, the mediator would get permission from the defendant to discuss the information with the plaintiff. This analysis holds true if the plaintiff presented evidence to the mediator that would undermine the defense position.

In short, the power in the mediation of this type of case is in the information available to the parties. If one party chooses to bargain by keeping its cards close to the vest, the other party will not likely make a concession or even consider the outcome contemplated by the party with all the information. By systematically controlling the flow of the information through a seasoned mediator, the ice can be broken and a fair negotiation of the claim can be accomplished.

In a recent case, the plaintiff suffered dramatic injuries after running head on into the defendant who was making a left-hand turn on a busy street. The plaintiff was in a coma for six weeks and wasn't able to testify about what happened. The 80-year-old defendant told her insurer that the plaintiff was speeding. As a result, he caused the accident. No one on the defense side really checked to see if their client was lying. However, the plaintiff's counsel was conscious and did investigate the defendant. What he found was that she was not permitted to drive a motor vehicle because she had been diagnosed by a leading medical facility as being legally blind before the accident occurred. The plaintiff was holding onto this evidence for court, but disclosed it to me during the mediation. I was instructed not to share this information with the defendant.

The defense hired experts to testify about the speed of the plaintiff being the sole and proximate cause of the accident. Their testimony was based exclusively on the purported observations of the 80-year-old defendant. Since there was no one to controvert her, the defense did not think they had much exposure if the case went to court. One thing the defense didn't consider was that the client concealed the fact that she was legally blind.

Fortunately, plaintiff's counsel allowed me to share the information about the defendant with her counsel on the condition that if counsel agreed that the information was relevant, the case would settle for a specific amount of money. Defense counsel was honorable and agreed to abide by the request. Almost immediately after the information was disclosed, the case settled.

In another case, involving sexual harassment, a long-term employee quit her teaching job on the premise that the principal had sexually harassed her. A critical moment was when a parent of one of the students called the principal to complain about the teacher using sexual innuendo and providing the students with graphic sexual photographs during class. The principal called the teacher into the office to inform her of the complaint and request that she cease and desist from such conduct without permission from the parents and principal. The teacher bolted out of the principal's office and wrote a threatening letter to the board of education, complaining about the sexual behavior of the principal! In short, in self-defense, she tried to wound the principal by claiming that he was the culprit, not her.

During the mediation, the forensic psychiatrist for the school was able to demonstrate a 20-year history of sexual assault, violence, and other problems that were in the extensive records of the plaintiff. Needless to say, her lawyer wasn't aware of any of these records until they were disclosed in the mediation. He just believed his client. It was quite a wake-up call to learn that his client had severe psychological problems. The case went away after the disclosure of this information.

There are factors common to both of these examples. The new information provided by the mediation process enabled the recipient of that information to make a decision based upon greater intelligence—and to do so earlier rather than later.

3. A Safe Environment

To establish a safe environment is to create a process within which parties are encouraged to communicate productively. It is an environment in which they are comfortable enough to send and receive clear messages. This environment is generally created with a simple ground rule prohibiting comment, criticism, or any other form of behavior that might in any way distract a party while he or she is speaking. The mediator acts as a sort of filter through which the discussion will be allowed to drain.

The result of using this procedure may include any of the following:

- When meeting together as a group, the parties may express their entire view of the dispute without fear of interruption, criticism, or even comment.
- When meeting privately, the parties are open to brainstorming openly because they are not obliged to make commitments at that time. At the same time, the discussion of the case is realistic, as opposed to simply posturing about positions.
- In private, parties may explore settlement scenarios with the aid of mediator, i.e., use the mediator's "sense" of where the other side is at, and hence more effectively explore options for resolution.
- Throughout, the safety of the process permits the parties to achieve a sense of having reached their optimum resolution.

In other words, the safe environment of mediation is for lawyers who want to get their point across to the other side with the client in attendance; who want to be sure all alternatives have been fully explored; and who want to get a greater sense of what caused the other side to take its position before disclosing fully its own position. For example, if the defense wants to deliver the message that it thinks elements of the plaintiff's case are suspect, it can do so without fear of retribution or retaliation because the mediator may do the talking. This allows each side the ability to explore the full potential of each other's case before committing oneself to a position that might be both embarrassing and financially challenging.

4. Confidentiality

The idea of confidentiality is the foundation upon which mediation is built, and the reason mediators are able to resolve cases. What does that mean to the consumer? It means that they are encouraged to tell the mediator their secrets without fear of having this information used against them at any time in the future. This is a powerful asset to an injured victim who might have sensitive issues surrounding his claim, such as pre-existing injuries, questions concerning the medical treatment, and so on. Using this asset as a sword to get a case settled is precisely what drives the successful settlement.

To confirm the availability of confidentiality, the mediator usually promises not to divulge any information without the permission of the parties. This allows the mediator to build trust and openness, and encourages an honest disclosure of information and cooperation. Without it, parties are hesitant to reveal too much, fearing delicate information might be used in a later court proceeding. Confidentiality, therefore, encourages candor, a full exploration of the issues, and the possibilities of settlement.

Many states, such as California, have statutes which provide limited protection against the release of confidential information in civil proceedings. For example, Evidence Code §1115-1128 protects disclosure of settlement discussions in a court or administrative proceeding. Skilled mediators will make certain that any information is not transmitted across the table without the permission of all parties involved.

5. *The Probability of Settlement*

There are at least three reasons why the mediation process enhances the probability of settlement:

- The information is coming through a neutral, increasing the chances that it will be heard objectively, and not defensively. As such, it is more likely to be analyzed effectively.
- Because the parties are present, participate actively in the exchange of old and new information, and understand the process in which new directions are explored, they are more likely to understand recommendations of others.
- The mediator has created a safe environment by developing ground rules that preclude interruption and unwelcome cross-examination and assure a respectful and polite atmosphere. In this environment, the parties feel empowered and are in a frame of mind to resolve their dispute.

The safe environment of mediation and the confidential sessions with the mediator offer an opportunity to explore alternative outcomes. This joint effort of parties to produce, with the aid of a mediator, an outcome based on both old and new information leads to a greater likelihood of achieving an expedited result that reduces or eliminates drawn-out litigation.

6. Eliminating Wasteful Litigation

The idea of abolishing litigation that is going nowhere fast is the goal of mediating suspicious cases. This goal can be achieved in every case with the determination of counsel who is willing to look at his case with candor and openness. At a minimum, counsel learns why the case is dragging on for so long and might find an exit strategy for a case that is going nowhere fast. At best, the case gets settled and a settlement check is received within a few days of the mediation conference.

Litigation is wasteful if it is either initiated inappropriately or maintained beyond a point where resolution appears reasonably feasible. Inappropriately initiated litigation is litigation that does not require the intervention of the judicial process, but that could be resolved through more meaningful communication among the parties to the litigation.

In the area of fraud, the elimination of wasteful litigation often results when a mediation session provides an opportunity to review scenarios likely to occur outside the courthouse as well as inside. These scenarios may include: pending or likely agency actions; the value of ongoing relationships with either the plaintiff or the defendant; and the desirability of controlling the outcome of a matter, as opposed to "rolling the dice" where ethics, morality, and perhaps even criminal conduct have been brought into question.

While it would generally appear to be in the best interests of attorneys and their clients to prevail in court, the existence of other, and potentially larger, interests may dictate that the legal positions be abandoned. Frequently, the mediation session produces an awareness of broader interests and an assessment of their importance relative to the legal action, which is the subject of the mediation. This assessment, coupled with a reasoned evaluation available in a safe environment, often leads to the termination of actions otherwise labeled as fraudulent.

Convening the Parties to the Mediation

How would a lawyer respond to a telephone call from a mediation provider who has been requested by a party to mediate a case? Is there a downside in investing in a private, confidential conversation with an opposing party about the case? If you are the defendant, how would you respond if the plaintiff made the same request of you?

There is a perception on the part of both defendant corporations and trial lawyers that he who recommends mediation first is viewed as weak. They wince at the idea of agreeing to come to the bargaining table, particularly when fraud is suspected. A simple strategy works—allow the neutral to act as the go between or "convener," i.e., the person that makes the call. This allows for face-saving in the event the other side says no, and might even provide you with some clues as to why the case is dragging on for so long.

Another strategy is to encourage parties to participate in a "pledge" or agreement to mediate any cases with a particular insurer. Here is an example of how some trial lawyers and insurers addressed the issue of convening a mediation without looking weak: The insurance carriers entered into an agreement in which they pledged to mediate certain types of disputes submitted by plaintiff's counsel. The pledge enabled either party to serve upon the other a Request to Mediate, followed by the selection of a mediator and scheduling within 90 days. Given the widespread acceptance of mediation, it is not surprising that the program has received broad support from both the insurance industry and the plaintiffs' bars. Furthermore, the existence of the pledge alone makes it simpler to convene the mediation. For those still clinging to the fear that a request to mediate may be a sign of weakness, the pledge is helpful because it applies to all cases and, as such, does not imply a "message" as to any single case.

Litigants in other areas of law have expressed interest in entering into a pledge similar to the one above. Given the potential savings of time, effort, and cost, and given the fact that mediation is entirely voluntary and can terminate at any time, the implications of the pledge remain primarily positive. For counsel involved in large-volume personal injury cases, the potential, through the pledge, for productive discussions and early resolution of cases through mediation is enormous.

The insurance industry has already evidenced its broad acceptance of the mediation concept. This acceptance is an opportunity for the plaintiffs' bar to assess the potential for broader-based, more productive settlement discussions available through the simplified access to mediation offered by a pledge to mediate. Before dismissing mediation as just one more "hoop" to jump through, skeptics should remind themselves of the potential benefits of this hoop, which has a settlement rate in excess of 85%.

Conclusion

The ability to find out the reasons why a claim is bottlenecked in the system is a smart investment that yields high returns. Using the mediation process as an affirmative business strategy will either unlock the door to settlement of the case or, at minimum, understanding why things have stalled. With that understanding, an intelligent, financially responsible strategy can be designed for the case.

IV. Evaluative Mediation Is Not Practicing Law

The Case Against Treating Evaluative Mediation As the Practice of Law

by Bruce E. Meyerson[*]

An addition to the American Bar Association (ABA) Model Rules of Professional Conduct (Model Rules) on the role of a lawyer as a neutral,[1] and a resolution adopted by the ABA Section of Dispute Resolution on mediation and the unauthorized practice of law,[2] should bring to a close the debate[3] on whether certain conduct by mediators constitutes law practice that could violate statutes on the unauthorized practice of law (UPL). The outcome of the debate affects lawyers and non-lawyers alike.

The ABA Model Rule and the resolution adopted by the Section of Dispute Resolution are based on the correct premise that the practice of law must involve an attorney-client relationship or its equivalent in order for a person to be considered rendering legal services. Because the parties to mediation do not have such a relationship with the mediator, and they do not rely upon the mediator to protect their respective

---

[*] Bruce Meyerson is a mediator and arbitrator in Phoenix, Arizona. He serves on the roster of neutrals of the American Arbitration Association and is a member of the editorial board of ADR Currents. Mr. Meyerson is also the Chair of the American Bar Association eCommerce and ADR Task Force.

[1] ABA Model Rule 2.4, approved by the ABA House of Delegates, Feb. 5, 2002.

[2] Adopted Feb. 2, 2002, by the Section of Dispute Resolution Council.

[3] *Compare* B. Meyerson, *Lawyers Who Mediate Are Not Practicing Law*, 14 ALTERNATIVES TO HIGH COST OF LITIG. 74 (1996) *with* C. Menkel-Meadow, *Is Mediation the Practice of Law?*, 14 ALTERNATIVES TO HIGH COST OF LITIG. 57 (1996); *see generally* G. Glass & K. Jackson, *The Unauthorized Practice of Law: The Internet, Alternative Dispute Resolution and Multidisciplinary Practices*, 14 GEO. J. LEGAL ETHICS 1195 (2001); M. Laflin, *Preserving the Integrity of Mediation Through the Adoption of Ethical Rules for Lawyer-Mediators*, 14 N.D. J.L. ETHICS & PUB POL'Y 479 (2000); G. SATO, Comment, *The Mediator-Lawyer: Implications for the Practice of Law and One Argument for Professional Responsibility Guidance—A Proposal for Some Ethical Considerations*, 34 U.C.L.A. L. REV. 507 (1986); D. Hoffman & N. Affolder, *Mediation and UPL: Do Mediators have a Well-Founded Fear of Prosecution?*, DISP. RESOL. MAG. 20 (Winter 2000); A. Morrison, *Is Divorce Mediation the Practice of Law? A Matter of Perspective*, 75 CAL. L. REV. 1093 (1987).

individual interests, what the mediator does in mediation does not constitute the practice of law and cannot violate UPL statutes.[4]

Those who have argued that mediation is the practice of law tend to single out "evaluative" mediators. So-called evaluative mediators assist the parties in assessing the strengths and weaknesses of their case, helping them reach a mutually acceptable resolution through a clearer understanding of their alternatives to a negotiated agreement, which includes discussions of the probable results of litigation, and its attendant costs, delays and disruptions. Those who believe that evaluative mediation constitutes the practice of law reason that because lawyers assist clients in assessing the strengths and weaknesses of the case and predict the probable outcome of litigation, mediators who help the parties evaluate their respective cases and assess possible litigation outcomes also must be practicing law.[5]

The critics of evaluative mediation[6] have a view of what occurs during the evaluative phase of a mediation that is different from my practice and what I believe good evaluative mediators do. I submit that most good evaluative mediators do not tell the parties what their case is worth and what the outcome will be.

Mediation is not black or white. Any successful mediator must bring a variety of skills to the process, including the ability to be facilitative and evaluative. The evaluative portion of the process is subtle and much more sophisticated than simply saying who is right and who is wrong. During the evaluative phase, good mediators enable the parties to carefully analyze their positions, fully understand the legal aspects of their problem, consider how the case could play out before a judge or jury, and look into the future to understand all possible outcomes, including appeals.

It is the feedback, analysis and impressions of the mediator that provides the parties with important new information about their problem. This information is critical because it enables the parties to examine the problem from another perspective and see the other side's point of view.

---

[4] Others also have advanced this view. *See, e.g.*, J. Cooley, *Shifting Paradigms: The Unauthorized Practice of Law or the Authorized Practice of ADR,* DISP. RESOL. J. (2000); S. Purnell, Cmt. *The Attorney as Mediator—Inherent Conflict of Interest?*, 32 U.C.L.A. L. REV. 986 (1985).

[5] *Laymen Cannot Lawyer, But is Mediation the Practice of Law?,* 20 CARDOZO L. REV. 1715 (1999).

[6] *E.g.*, K. Kovach & L. Love, *'Evaluative' Mediation is an Oxymoron*, 14 ALTERNATIVES TO HIGH. COST OF LITIG. 31 (March 1996); L. Love, *The Top Ten Reasons Why Mediators Should Not Evaluate*, 24 FLA. ST. U. L. REV. 937 (1997).

Once that happens, they can move toward a common understanding of what might constitute a fair settlement.[7] My experience as a mediator convinces me that the parties and their attorneys are looking for precisely the type of feedback that evaluative mediators provide.[8]

The view that evaluative mediation is the practice of law has been expressed most strongly by the State Bar of Virginia's Guidelines on Mediation and the Unauthorized Practice of Law (Virginia Guidelines).[9] The Virginia Guidelines advise that Virginia law and ethics rules prohibit mediators from giving "legal advice."[10] The Virginia Guidelines go on to say that applying legal principles and making recommendations constitutes giving legal advice in mediation:

> [A]t a minimum, a mediator provides legal advice whenever, in the mediation context, he or she applies legal principles that (1) in effect predicts a specific resolution of a legal issue or (2) directs, counsels, urges, or recommends a course of action by a disputant or disputants as a means of resolving a legal issue.[11]

The Virginia Guidelines indicate that the rule against giving legal advice applies to lawyer and non-lawyer mediators. Non-lawyer mediators who give legal advice "engage in unethical mediation practice, which may lead to decertification" and "criminal prosecution or civil action for UPL." Lawyer-mediators "have likewise engaged in unethical mediation practice which may lead to decertification" and "discipline."[12] In addition, the Virginia Guidelines acknowledge that a lawyer-mediator who gives legal advice during mediation likely will have engaged in dual representation, an ethical violation. In addition to these consequences of giving legal advice, a settlement agreement could be challenged and set aside by a court.

---

[7] *See generally* D. Golann & M. Aaron, *Using Evaluations in Mediation*, 52 DISP. RESOL. J. 26 (1997).

[8] R. Wissler, *Court-Connected Mediation in General Civil Cases: What We Know from Empirical Research,* 17 OHIO ST. J. DISP. RES. 641, 684 (2002).

[9] Available at www.courts.state.va.us/ drs/upl/preface.html. *See also* the N.C. Guidelines for Ethical Practice of Mediation and to Prevent the Unauthorized Practice of Law.

[10] Va. Guidelines, § 2, Legal and Ethical Prohibitions on Giving Legal Advice, *citing* Va. Sup. Ct. Rule Pt. 6, § I(B)(1), and Va. Rule of Prof. Conduct 2.11. Other conduct by a mediator also may constitute giving legal advice under the Virginia Guidelines.

[11] Va. Guidelines, § 2, *supra* n. 10.

[12] *Id.*

The Virginia Guidelines are based on the rationale that an important aspect of a lawyer's role in assisting a client is to apply law to specific facts and predict how a court might rule on a particular issue. But those who take this view fail to consider that in order to be engaged in the practice of law there must be a client—a person who has placed her trust and confidence in the alleged provider of legal services to provide advice and assistance solely on her behalf. In mediation, however, the parties are not the mediator's clients in this sense of the word. Moreover, the parties do not rely on the mediator to protect their individual interests and cannot reasonably do so. This is clear from cases defining activities that constitute the practice of law.

In my view, the position that evaluative mediators give legal advice and thereby engage in the unauthorized practice of law is incorrect. The ABA Model Rules and the recently adopted resolution of the Section of Dispute Resolution, discussed below, "got it right," as did the many bar associations and courts that have articulated the view that mediation does not involve the practice of law.

Judicial Definitions

Court rulings on activities that constitute the practice of law vary in their approach. The practice of law, as courts and court rules have defined it, all have at their center the principle that the client places her trust and confidence in, and relies upon, the provider of legal services to protect her personal interests with respect to a particular matter. This principle is absent in the relationship between the mediator and the parties.

Surprisingly, courts have struggled with developing a single comprehensive definition of the "practice of law." The Supreme Court of Arizona, in *State Bar of Arizona v. Arizona Land Title & Trust Co.*, acknowledged this difficulty when it stated: "[I]t is impossible to lay down an exhaustive definition of the 'practice of law' by attempting to enumerate every conceivable act performed by lawyers in the normal course of their work."[13]

Courts have held that the following activities constitute the practice of law: representing another in court; holding oneself out as a lawyer; preparing, filing or signing documents in legal proceedings; threatening to file suit on behalf of clients; negotiating a settlement of legal claims or

[13] State Bar of Ariz. v. Arizona Land Title & Trust Co.,. 366 P.2d 1, 8-9 (Ariz. 1961).

a plea agreement; taking depositions; recording deeds; and interviewing clients.[14]

Courts have applied a number of different "tests" to determine whether an activity constitutes the practice of law. The "professional judgment" test considers whether the activity in question requires specialized legal training or skills not ordinarily possessed by the average person. *In Oregon State Bar v. Smith*,[15] the court held that the practice of law involved the utilization of "professional judgment" in applying legal principles in the giving of assistance or advice to address an individual's needs. Professional judgment also has been defined as the lawyer's "educated ability to relate the general body and philosophy of law to a specific legal problem of a client."[16]

The "client reliance" test examines whether or not the client believes he is receiving legal services. The Arizona Supreme Court concluded that "[r]eliance by the client on advice or services rendered...is more pertinent in determining whether certain conduct is the purported or actual practice of law."[17]

The Florida Supreme Court applied the "client reliance" test in *Florida Bar v. Brumbaugh*.[18] In that case, the respondent ran a secretarial service that prepared legal forms for individuals in various legal proceedings. Although she did not hold herself out as an attorney to the individuals for whom she provided this service, the court found that respondent engaged in the unauthorized practice of law. The court based its decision on the fact that the respondent's customers trusted her to advise them as to which forms to use and relied on her to prepare the appropriate forms. The court explained: "Although Marilyn Brumbaugh never held herself out as an attorney, it is clear that her clients placed some reliance upon her to properly prepare the necessary legal forms for their dissolution proceedings (emphasis added)."[19] The court observed that the rationale for regulating the attorney-client relationship is the trust clients place in the alleged providers of legal services to help them with their problem:

---

[14] *See generally* G. Hazard, Jr. & W. Hodes, 2 The Law of Lawyering § 46.4 (3d ed. 2002 Supp.); R. Rotunda, Legal Ethics § 39-1 (2000).

[15] 942 P.2d 793, 799 (Or. App. 1997).

[16] Committee on Prof. Ethics & Conduct of Iowa State Bar Ass'n v. Baker, 492 N.W.2d 695, 701 (Iowa 1992).

[17] Arizona Land Title, *supra* n. 13, 366 P.2d at 9.

[18] 355 So. 2d 1186, 1189 (Fla. 1978).

[19] *Id.* at 1193-94.

> [The] tendency of persons seeking legal assistance to place their trust in the individual purporting to have expertise in the area necessitates this Court's regulation of such attorney-client relationships, so as to require that persons giving such advice have at least a minimal amount of legal training and experience.[20]

Another test courts have used is the "attorney-client relationship" test. Under this test, an activity constitutes the practice of law if a personal relationship is formed that is tantamount to that of attorney and client.[21]

Some courts look to see whether an activity that is alleged to be the practice of law affects important legal rights. Thus, courts have found that preparing instruments and contracts by which legal rights are secured indicates the practice of law.[22] For example, in *Palmer v. Unauthorized Practice Committee of the State Bar of Texas*,[23] the court found that the sale of will forms constituted the practice of law, because "confidential communications regarding family relations are often necessary." Thus, untrained non-attorneys who sold these will forms were violating the law.

All of the tests for the practice of law assume that there is a client who has placed trust and confidence in the alleged provider of legal services and is relying upon the provider to protect her individual interests in the matter at hand. When such a relationship exists between the two parties, a reasonable person could believe that the provider is functioning as the client's attorney. The Arizona Supreme Court reached this conclusion in a bar disciplinary matter:

> [W]here a person holds an objectively reasonable belief that a lawyer is acting as his attorney, relies on that belief and relationship, and the lawyer does not refute that belief, we will treat the relationship as one between attorney and client....[24]

In another context, the Arizona Court of Appeals held that the existence of the attorney-client privilege "hinges upon a client's belief

---

[20] *Id.* at 1193.

[21] State Bar of Mich. v. Cramer, 249 N.W.2d 1 (Mich. 1976).

[22] State Bar of N.M. v. Guardian Abstract & Title Co., Inc., 575 P.2d 943, 948 (N.M. 1978).

[23] 438 S.W.2d 374 (Tex. App. 1969).

[24] *In re* Pappas, 768 P.2d 1161, 1167-68 (Ariz. 1988).

that he is consulting a lawyer in that capacity and upon his manifested intention to seek professional legal advice."[25]

The premise that the client must have a reasonable belief that the alleged provider of legal services is acting as her attorney also is illustrated *in Dietrich Corp. v. King Resources Co.*[26] In this case, two law firms employed a law professor as a consultant on legal accounting issues who was not admitted to practice law in the jurisdiction. A dispute later arose over his fee application to the court, which was challenged on the ground that his services constituted the unauthorized practice of law.

The Tenth Circuit held that, although the law professor provided services in the field of his legal expertise, his actions did not constitute the unauthorized practice of law because the "licensed attorneys alone remain[ed] responsible to the client." Because the client was represented, it was not reasonable to think that the law professor was acting as a legal representative. The court observed that the party's own attorneys acted as a "filter" between the unlicensed consultant and the client.[27]

The judicial decisions on the practice of law do not support finding that mediation is an activity that constitutes law practice. There is no attorney-client relationship, no trust and confidence placed in the mediator to represent each party's interests, and no reasonable belief that the mediator is acting as an attorney. This is especially so in the case of represented parties, whose counsel act as a "filter" between the parties and the mediator.

Court Rules

A number of court rules address directly or in comments the question of whether a mediator is engaged in the practice of law.[28] The majority of these hold the view that mediators are not practicing law.

Rules promulgated by the District of Columbia Court of Appeals on the unauthorized practice of law define the practice of law as the "provision of professional legal advice or services where there is a client relationship of trust or reliance."[29] The Comments to this rule directly address alternative dispute resolution and they indicate that the practice of law does not include the provision of ADR services:

---

[25] G & S Inv. v. Belman, 700 P.2d 1358, 1365 (Ariz. App. 1984).

[26] 596 F.2d 422 (10th Cir. 1979).

[27] *Id.* at 426.

[28] *See generally* S. Cole et al., Mediation: Law, Policy & Practice, § 10:5 (2d ed. 2001).

[29] D.C. Court Rule 49(a)(2).

> The Rule is not intended to cover the provision of mediation or alternative dispute resolution (ADR) services. This intent is expressed in the first sentence of the definition of the "practice of law" which requires the presence of two essential factors, the provision of legal advice or services and a client relationship of trust or reliance. ADR services are not given in circumstances where there is a client relationship of trust or reliance; and it is common practice for providers of ADR services explicitly to advise participants that they are not providing the services of legal counsel.

Rule 901(d) of the Rules of the Supreme Court of Kansas similarly take the view that "[a]n attorney acting as a mediator is not the legal representative of the parties and there is no attorney-client relationship between the parties and the attorney-mediator."

Maine Bar Rule 3.4(h)(2) explains that "[t]he role of mediator does not create a lawyer-client relationship with any of the parties and does not constitute representation of any of them."

Ethics Opinions

The majority of bar ethics opinions I have examined have reached the conclusion that mediation is not the practice of law.[30] For example, a

---

[30] *E.g.*, Ky. Bar Ass'n Ethics Op. 377 (1995) ("Mediation is not the practice of law...."); Mich. State Bar Standing Comm. on Prof, and Judicial Ethics, Op. No. RI-256 (1996) ("By definition, a neutral arbitrator or mediator has no client with respect to the matter being arbitrated); Miss. Bar Op. No. 241 (1997) ("At the present time mediation...services are not considered the practice of law per se."): N.Y.S. Bar Ass'n, Comm. on Prof. Ethics, Op. 736 (2001) ("As we have recognized in the past, a lawyer who serves as a mediator to assist in the resolution of a possible dispute does not 'represent' either party as a client for purposes of the conflict-of-interest rules and other rules governing the lawyer-client relationship."); Pa. Bar Ass'n Comm. on Legal Ethics and Prof. Responsibility, Informal Op. No. 96-167 (Dec. 30, 1996) (mediation is not considered to be a "legal" service when provided by a non-lawyer): S.C. Bar Ethics Advisory Comm., Ethics Advisory Op. No. 97-03 (Mar. 1997) ("A lawyer serving in the role of an intermediary is not engaged in the practice of law while acting as the intermediary. Moreover, the ethical obligations of an arbitrator may be more nearly analogous to those of a judge, than of a member of the Bar."); Utah State Bar Ethics Advisory Op. Comm., Formal Op. 97-03 (Apr. 25, 1997) ("ADR services are not considered by the Utah Legislature to be legal services or the practice of law."); Wash. State Bar Ass'n, Comm. to Define the Practice of Law, Final Rpt. (July 1999), adopted by Wash. State Bar Ass'n Bd. of Governors, Sept. 1999 ("[P]ersons acting in [the] capacity of [mediator, arbitrator, conciliator or facilitator] are not engaged in the practice of law."); *contra* Iowa Sup. Ct. Bd. of Prof. Ethics and Conduct, Op. No. 96-30 (June 5, 1997) ("Alternate dispute resolution done by others than lawyers has not been held to be the

Connecticut Bar Association ethics opinion concluded that "[a]t all times in the process, the lawyer acts as mediator between the parties, not as an advocate for either one."[31] An Indiana Ethics Opinion concluded that "because the Supreme Court permits non-attorneys to act as mediators and because the nature of...mediation is substantially different from the practice of law, mediation service is not the practice of law."[32]

ABA Model Rules

The ABA Model Rule on the role of the lawyer as neutral supports the view that serving as a mediator does not constitute the practice of law. The new rule acknowledges, for the first time, that a lawyer may serve in a nonrepresentational capacity. Model Rule 2.4 provides that a lawyer may serve as a "third-party neutral when the lawyer assists two or more persons who are not clients of the lawyer to reach a resolution of the dispute or other matter that has arisen between them." A "third-party neutral" is defined in the Comments as a person such as a "mediator, arbitrator, conciliator or evaluator who assists the parties...in the resolution of a dispute or in the arrangement of a transaction."

Rule 2.4 implicitly recognizes that a neutral role does not constitute the practice of law because it does not create an attorney-client relationship. Rule 2.4 states that the neutral "shall inform unrepresented parties that the lawyer is not representing them." The Comments explain that when the parties are not represented, it is conceivable that there could be confusion over the role of a lawyer who is serving as a neutral. Thus, the Comments instruct the lawyer neutral to inform pro se parties of the "important differences between the lawyer's role as a third-party neutral and a lawyer's role as a client representative, including the inapplicability of the attorney-client privilege."

Rule 2.4 does not require the neutral to inform parties who are represented by counsel that the neutral is not representing them. Presumably, the drafters believed that when parties are represented by their own counsel, the parties could not reasonably believe that the neutral was serving as their attorney.

---

practice of law....But when done by a lawyer it becomes the practice of law."); N.J. Sup. Ct. Advisory Comm. Prof. Ethics, Op. No. 676 (Apr. 4, 1994) (holding that when a lawyer serves as a third-party neutral, he or she "is acting as a lawyer").

[31] Conn. Bar Ass'n, Comm. on Prof. Ethics, Informal Op. No. 97-12 (June 4, 1997).

[32] Ind. Ethics Op. No. 5 (1992).

Section of Dispute Resolution

The resolution recently adopted by the Section of Dispute Resolution declares that the practice of mediation is not the practice of law:

> Mediation is a process in which an impartial individual assists the parties in reaching a voluntary settlement. Such assistance does not constitute the practice of law. The parties to the mediation are not represented by the mediator.
>
> The resolution acknowledges that the mediator's discussions with the parties may involve legal issues, but concludes that these discussions do not involve law practice.
>
> Such discussions do not create an attorney-client relationship, and do not constitute legal advice, whether or not the mediator is an attorney.

The resolution also states the principle that the mediator has the responsibility to inform the parties about the mediator's role and that this role does not involve giving them legal representation. Unlike ABA Model Rule 2.4, however, it does not distinguish between pro se and represented parties in this regard.

The resolution recognizes that the attorney-client relationship must be present to be engaged in providing legal advice. The Comments following the resolution point out that "many parties, and their counsel, hire mediators precisely to obtain feedback about their case." The Comments further explain why this is not the practice of law:

> Even though mediators who engage in these discussions do sometimes aid the parties by discussing possible outcomes of the dispute if a settlement is not reached and [by] providing evaluative feedback about the parties' positions, this conduct is not the practice of law because the parties have no reasonable basis for believing that the mediator will provide advice solely on behalf of any individual party. This is the important distinction between the mediator's role and the role of an attorney. Parties expect their attorney to represent solely their interests and to provide advice and counsel only for them. On the other hand, a mediator is a neutral, with no duty of loyalty to the individual parties.

Perhaps the clearest example of this distinction is when a judge serves in a settlement capacity. The stereotypical view of a settlement judge is one who is engaged in a highly evaluative process. Is the judge who conducts an evaluative settlement conference engaged in the practice of law? I don't think so. Why not? Because no one in the room reasonably believes that the judge—a neutral third party—is acting on behalf of the individual, personal interests of either party.

Indeed, the mediator's obligation of impartiality to the mediating parties is fundamentally incompatible with an attorney's obligations to her client.[33]

Conclusion

Mediation has become a hot topic in state legislatures and courts. The practice and utility of mediation could be seriously damaged by the type of regulation that Virginia has adopted. The ABA House of Delegates and the Section of Dispute Resolution have provided a thoughtful framework from which it can be clearly concluded that evaluative mediation is not the practice of law.

---

[33] Model Standards of Conduct for Mediators, II. Impartiality: A Mediator Shall Conduct the Mediation in an Impartial Manner. These standards were prepared from 1992-1994 by a joint committee of representatives of the ABA, the American Arbitration Association and the Society of Professionals in Dispute Resolution.

INDEX